Language Development and Age

Julia Herschensohn

CAMBRIDGE
UNIVERSITY PRESS

CAMBRIDGE UNIVERSITY PRESS
Cambridge, New York, Melbourne, Madrid, Cape Town,
Singapore, São Paulo, Delhi, Mexico City

Cambridge University Press
The Edinburgh Building, Cambridge CB2 8RU, UK

Published in the United States of America by Cambridge University Press, New York

www.cambridge.org
Information on this title: www.cambridge.org/9781107404885

First published 2007
First paperback edition 2011

A catalogue record for this publication is available from the British Library

ISBN 978-0-521-87297-3 Hardback
ISBN 978-1-107-40488-5 Paperback

Cambridge University Press has no responsibility for the persistence or
accuracy of URLs for external or third-party internet websites referred to in
this publication, and does not guarantee that any content on such websites is,
or will remain, accurate or appropriate.

To the memory of my mother, Jean Gallivan Rogers, and my surrogate mothers, Mary Gallivan, Eleanor Gallivan Lent and Sylvia Rosenbaum Herschensohn

Contents

Figures

Tables

Preface

The notion of a critical period for acquisition of first and subsequent languages is the topic of this book, which investigates the following questions:

(i) What is the evidence for a critical period for language acquisition?

(ii) Is there a critical period for first language acquisition?

(iii) Is there a critical period for subsequent language acquisition?

These questions raise corollary issues concerning the nature of language acquisition, variables that drive and constrain it, and the role of biological maturation. The book demonstrates that first language (L1) is in large part susceptible to age constraints, whereas second language (L2) – a term conventionally referring to any language learned after the first – is only indirectly so affected. Evidence from L1 shows a clear effect of age on acquisition, for language is not thoroughly acquired if age of onset passes seven years, and it is acquired with major deficits if age of onset passes twelve. Evidence from L2 acquisition also shows effects of age of onset, but the range of variation due to individual and socio-motivational differences prohibits a strict definition of a sensitive period for L2. Indeed, the L2 competence of expert adult learners, the unequal achievements of child L2 learners, variation of L2 endstate for learners with different L1 and the lack of consistent empirical evidence for a maturational cutoff, all cast doubt on a critical period for second language acquisition (L2A). Furthermore, the reasons for the deterioration of acquisition potential are only partly maturational, since experience with the native tongue shapes the neural networks of the brain dedicated to language.

This book investigates the question of a critical period for both L1 and L2A, reporting on the extensive empirical research done in the past decade (and earlier) that has mainly been published in articles. It reviews very recent literature on non-typical development in L1 and L2 (e.g. Williams Syndrome, Specific Language Impairment), evaluates relevant psycholinguistic and neurolinguistic studies, and considers recent debates of the critical period question.

The first chapter traces the history of the notion critical/sensitive period from the nineteenth century, giving examples from other species' development as well as non-linguistic aspects of human behavior. It reviews Lenneberg's seminal work on the biological foundations of language and subsequent research based on his premises. The chapter concludes with a discussion of two theory families, domain-specific nativism and domain-general associationism. While favoring an innatist approach, the book nevertheless subscribes to the necessity of taking both innate predisposition and environmental experience into account.

Chapter 2 describes first language acquisition (L1A) using a framework that includes the importance of both innate predisposition/linguistic universals and environmental experience. The third chapter considers whether there is a critical period for L1A, using evidence from a range of empirical data on atypical acquisition, by deprivation of environment or deprivation of organismic system. The former is exemplified by late L1 learners of sign language, the latter by cognitively impaired individuals. Despite major language deficits of late L1 learners, even the biological data does not indicate a threshold of offset after which L1A is totally impossible.

Chapters 4 and 5 describe patterns and stages of L2A and then examine the evidence adduced for a critical period for this phenomenon. Studies of child/adult L2A, age-linked deterioration in grammar acquisition and expert adult learners show that there is questionable substantiation for L2 age sensitivity. The sixth chapter pursues the question further by examining non-biological L2 influences and biological studies of L2 neural processing. The final chapter reexamines the facts presented in the previous six to arrive at conclusions for L1A and L2A.

This book has profited from a great deal of input and help from colleagues and friends. I wish to thank Michael Herschensohn, Marc Jampole and fifteen graduate seminar students for reading the entire manuscript and making very helpful comments throughout. For reading and commenting on an entire chapter or more, I thank Susanne Carroll (who actually read two), Joe Emonds, George M. Martin (who also read two and encouraged me to look into olidodendrocytes), Fritz Newmeyer and Martha Young-Scholten. For more general discussion and support I acknowledge John Archibald, Debbie Arteaga, Dalila Ayoun, Barbara Bullock, David Birdsong, Robert DeKeyser, Laurent Dekydtspotter, Cheryl Frenck-Mestre, Randall Gess, Judy McLaughlin, Silvina Montrul, Florence Myles, Toshi Ogihara, Lee Osterhout, Joyce Parvi, Philippe Prévost, Bonnie Schwartz, Mike Sharwood-Smith, Roumyana Slabakova, Kathryn Speranza, Rex Sprouse, Jeff Stevenson, Jacqueline Toribio, Jonathan Washington, Lydia White and Richard Wright. Thanks also to my family and friends for all their encouragement.

Acknowledgments

The author and publisher acknowledge with thanks permission granted to reproduce in this book the following material previously published elsewhere or in the public domain.

Figures 1.1, 6.1 and 6.2 are furnished by the National Institute of Neurological Disorders and Stroke of the National Institutes of Health which offers this material in the public domain to be freely copied. We greatly appreciate this NINDS-prepared information, thanking the NINDS and the NIH.

Figure 3.1 is reprinted with permission of the American Speech-Language-Hearing Association from p. 1266 of Rachel I. Mayberry (1993), First-language acquisition after childhood differs from second-language acquisition: the case of American Sign Language, *Journal of Speech and Hearing Research* 36, 1258–1270.

Figures 5.1, 5.3 and 6.3 are reprinted with permission from Elsevier Ltd. from (respectively) p. 79 of Jacqueline Johnson and Elissa Newport (1989), Critical Period effects in second language learning: The influence of maturational state on the acquisition of English as a second language, *Cognitive Psychology* 21, 60–99; p. 240 of David Birdsong and Michelle Molis (2001), On the evidence for maturational constraints in second language acquisition, *Journal of Memory and Language* 44, 235–249; and p. 204 of Lee Osterhout, Judith McLaughlin and Michael Bersick (1997), Event-related brain potentials and human language, *Trends in Cognitive Sciences* 1, 203–209.

Figure 5.2 is reprinted with permission from The Perseus Books Group from p. 68 of Ellen Bialystok and Kenji Hakuta (1994), *In Other Words* (New York: Basic Books).

Abbreviations

2L1A	bilingual first language acquisition
ABSL	Al-Sayyid Bedouin Sign Language
CPH	Critical Period Hypothesis
DS	Down Syndrome
EOI	Extended Optional Infinitive [period]
FFFH	Failed Functional Features Hypothesis
FTFA	Full Transfer/Full Access
HAS	High Amplitude Sucking
ISN	Idioma de Señas Nicaragüense ("Nicaraguan Sign Language")
L1A	first language acquisition
L2A	second language acquisition
LAD	Language Acquisition Device
LSN	Lenguaje de Señas Nicaragüense ("Nicaraguan sign pidgin")
MLU	Mean Length of Utterance
OI	Optional Infinitive [period]
PDP	Parallel Distributed Processing
PLD	Primary Linguistic Data
PPVT	Peabody Picture Vocabulary Test
RI	Root Infinitive
SLI	Specific Language Impairment
SLM	Speech Learning Model
TD	Typically Developing
UG	Universal Grammar
V2	verb second
VOT	Voice Onset Time
WS	Williams Syndrome

1   Just in time: is there a critical period for language acquisition?

1.0   Introduction

David Sedaris (2000, 160–161), in describing his initial experiences in French language immersion in a Normandy village, points out an age disadvantage for adults learning language: "I'd hoped that language might come on its own, the way it comes to babies, but people don't talk to foreigners the way they talk to babies. They don't hypnotize you with bright objects and repeat the same words over and over, handing out little treats when you finally say 'potty' or 'wawa.' . . . I wanted to lie in a French crib and start from scratch, learning the language from the ground floor up. I wanted to be a baby, but instead, I was an adult who talked like one, a spooky man-child demanding more than his fair share of attention." Sedaris presents an anecdotal view of language acquisition reflecting the folk wisdom that infants learn language with apparent ease, no instruction and in very little time. Adults, on the other hand, find learning a new language to be cognitively challenging, labor-intensive and time-consuming. While Sedaris ostensibly puts forth the view of infant language acquisition as a result of positive reinforcement, he makes the reader wonder why Burgundy wine, camembert cheese and Limoges dessert plates do not constitute the "little treats" that might entice *him* to learn French. He also admits the social dimension of adult language learning in pointing out that the learner feels reduced to child-like behavior, while the interlocutor finds him overly demanding. Sedaris implies that there is a limited time span, a critical or sensitive period, for language acquisition – it's something that infants do with ease and adults with difficulty.

On the one hand, it seems obvious that there is a difference between children and adults with respect to language learning since the former do accomplish the task much more efficiently than the latter. But on the other hand, there is abundant evidence that adults can learn foreign languages to a sophisticated degree of fluency, as for example Joseph Conrad learned English or Samuel Beckett, French. Certainly, the difference between learning a first language as a child and a second language as an adult is

1

dramatic enough to warrant the idea that there is a crucial chronological threshold which, when crossed, marks an irreversible deterioration of language learning ability. The familiar example of immigrant families dealing with a new language seems to suggest that children can learn a second language to the same extent as their first, whereas their parents speak the new tongue with foreign accents and grammatical mistakes. It appears that our brains are designed to learn our native idiom effortlessly, but that subsequently our neural aptitude fades with increasing age, a reduction in ability that seems to indicate age sensitivity for second language learning. For native language there is little empirical evidence to disprove a critical cutoff, since nearly all infants are exposed to language and acquire it normally.

A definitive view of maturational restriction to acquisition has been questioned in recent research, as cognitive scientists examine the finer points of adult/child similarities and differences in acquisition (Bailey et al. 2001; Birdsong 1999a; Doughty and Long 2003). Proponents of a critical period for language acquisition have proposed several ages as the threshold of the sensitive age for second language learning: six years (Long 1990) or younger, puberty (Lenneberg 1967; Scovel 1988), fifteen years (Patkowski 1990) and beyond. The diagnostics of foreign accent and grammatical deficit do not, however, apply unproblematically, for "no study has as yet provided convincing evidence for the claim that second language speech will automatically be accent-free if it is learned before the age of about six years and that it will definitely be foreign-accented if learned after puberty" (Piske et al. 2001). There is likewise no agreed-upon threshold for grammatical deficits in second language learning (Birdsong 1999b, 2005a, b; Birdsong and Molis 2001). Recent research has elucidated the importance of early exposure to first language, but has not definitively indicated a cutoff point after which acquisition of some language skills is totally impossible. In addition to the variety of age limits that scholars have proposed for a critical period, they have also put forward an equally diverse range of reasons for such a temporal limit, from biological necessity to sociocultural bias.

The notion of a critical period for acquisition of first and subsequent languages raises the following questions to be addressed in subsequent chapters:
• What is the evidence for a critical period for language acquisition?
• Is there a critical period for first language acquisition?
• Is there a critical period for subsequent language acquisition?
These central questions raise corollary issues about the nature of language acquisition, variables that drive and constrain it, and the role of biological maturation. The book will demonstrate that first language (L1) is

susceptible to age constraints for complete acquisition, whereas second language (L2, a term conventionally referring to any language learned after the first) is only indirectly so affected. For first language, evidence shows a clear effect of age on acquisition, for L1 phonology (sound system), grammar and stylistic mastery are not thoroughly acquired if age of onset passes five to seven years, and L1 is acquired with major deficits if age of onset passes twelve years (Newport 1994). L2 evidence also shows effects of age of onset, even for very early L2 learners of three or four years. But for L2A, the range of variation related to individual and socio-motivational differences is so wide that it prohibits a strict definition of a sensitive period for L2 (Hyltenstam and Abrahamsson 2003; Moyer 2004). Indeed, the L2 competence of expert adult learners, the unequal achievements of child L2 learners, variation of L2 endstate for learners from different native languages, and the lack of consistent empirical evidence for a maturational cutoff all cast doubt on a critical period for second language acquisition.

1.1   Central themes

1.1.1   Age and language acquisition

First language and subsequent or second language acquisition (L2A) are two distinct processes that share a number of patterns, but which also differ in crucial respects. L1A is, except in unusual circumstances, broadly successful, while L2A shows wide variations because of motivational, cultural and social influences that lead to marked dissimilarities among individuals in their proficiency. Age at onset of acquisition (AoA) is irrelevant for normal L1A since it is universally the moment of birth (or before); for L2A, however, age at onset seems to make a difference, as Sedaris suggests. In considering age of onset though, one must tease apart the influence of maturation – the physiological changes induced by growth of an organism – as compared to experience with the native language. Is it age of onset that is the crucial factor or the amount of exposure to the first language that the L2 learner has already experienced? While L1 learners thoroughly acquire all aspects of the native language, for L2A there are differential age effects in different domains – for example L2 learners notoriously have more difficulty getting correct pronunciation than they do fluent syntax.

In the case of first language acquisition, it is virtually impossible to create an empirical test of a critical period with a normal population since all hearing infants are exposed to language and acquire the ambient language as a developmental milestone. Dispossessing a child of language would be the "forbidden experiment" (Shattuck 1980), and the rare instances of children who mature without human contact, and whose asocial environment deprived them of most human attributes, are questionable as test cases. What can provide insight for L1A is evidence from children whose deprivation is mainly restricted to language, deaf children of speaking parents whose exposure to signed language is delayed, and from children with language pathologies resulting from brain damage or genetic characteristics. These atypical cases can be compared to normal language development to afford investigation of the sensitive period question for L1A (Mayberry 1993).

Acquisition of a single language is the norm in monolingual areas, but the ability to speak more than one language is the standard in most of the world (Cook 1993; Saville-Troike 2006). *Bilingualism* (often used to stand for multilingualism) can be defined generally as the practice of alternately using two languages (Weinreich 1953), although a stricter definition considers bilingualism to be native-like control of two languages. Such truly balanced bilingualism (resulting from "double" first language acquisition) is rare, since knowledge of the languages is usually unequal (Cook 1995). A more realistic view of bilingualism is that it includes the ability to produce complete meaningful utterances in two languages, a definition to be adopted in this book. *Early bilinguals* are individuals who learn a second language during childhood, whereas *late bilinguals* do so as adults. Two other bilingual factors relating to age and acquisition are the intermingling of languages in bilinguals and the possibility of L1 attrition. Bilinguals often mix their languages in conversational *code switching* (Myers-Scotton 1993) or adapt the phonology of one language to another (Singleton and Ryan 2004). Bilinguals for whom the second language becomes dominant lose ability in their first language to varying degrees (Isurin 2000; Schmid 2002), in a process of *attrition*.

In contrast to monolingual L1A, the case of second language acquisition provides perhaps too many means of testing the sensitive period question – longitudinal investigations, cross-sectional studies, controlled experiments on various aspects of the L2, native-like behavior as evaluated by native speakers, and even neurolinguistic testing. Nevertheless, the confounding factors of individual variation and socio-motivational differences interfere with an examination of the age factor for L2A. For example, identical twins raised in the same environment may have nearly indistinguishable native language performance in L1, yet differ substantially in L2 behavior. This book investigates the notion of a critical period for language acquisition by examining the evidence from first language acquisition, second language acquisition and studies of early and late bilingualism.

1.1.2   Summary of chapters

This first chapter introduces the central issues and summarizes the book by first examining the notion of sensitive periods in other species and definitions of a critical period for language acquisition. Chapter 1 introduces the neurological basis of human language to discuss the theoretical foundation of the Critical Period Hypothesis (CPH) attributed to Lenneberg (1967) for first language acquisition and extensions of the Hypothesis for subsequent language acquisition. Chapter 1 also presents the dialogue in cognitive science between domain-general associationism and domain-specific nativism to elucidate the theoretical frameworks in which current research is grounded.

Chapter 2 examines the schedule, manner and end result of first language acquisition. It describes the infant's development of native ability in *phonology* (sound system), *lexicon* (vocabulary), *morphology* (grammatical endings and words), *syntax* (word order of sentences) and *pragmatics* (the discourse appropriateness of speech), from birth through age of fluency. Recent research has shown that newborn infants are sensitive to both phonological and lexical characteristics of the ambient language that they perceive in utero (de Boysson-Bardies 1999), and that the young learner acquires substantial vocabulary through the teen years (Bloom 2002). Nevertheless, the core of the L1A process occurs between eighteen months and four years, at which time the normal child is in command of basic vocabulary, phonology and syntax (Guasti 2002).

Chapter 3 revisits Lenneberg's hypothesis in examining the empirical substantiation for a critical period for L1A. The chapter explores the genetic predisposition for language manifested in cross-linguistic uniformity of L1A, dissociation of language and cognition (Smith and Tsimpli 1995), and spontaneous development of creoles (Bickerton 1995; Kegl, Senghas and Coppola 1999; Padden et al. 2006). While little evidence exists from the forbidden experiment of depriving a child of L1 exposure, there is documentation for a few individuals who underwent such a deprivation (Curtiss 1977; Shattuck 1980). More relevant perhaps to the question, and more prevalent in terms of available data, are the studies of deaf individuals whose first exposure to language – often in this case signed language – may vary (Mayberry 1993; Newport 1994).

Chapter 4 examines the timing, manner and end result of second language acquisition. Unlike the strictly circumscribed schedule of L1A, L2 learning varies significantly in a number of ways. The development of ability in phonology, lexicon, morphology, syntax and pragmatics does not follow the pattern of L1A and does not result in equal achievement in all areas (Robinson 2002). Phonetic accuracy in L2 may be quite elusive, whereas mastery of word order is gained early; acquisition of lexical items surpasses that of morphology, especially when nonnative features (e.g. gender) are characteristic of the L2, but not the native language (White 2003).

Chapter 5 examines the evidence for a sensitive period for L2A, looking at experimental studies on apparent deterioration of L2 phonology (Scovel 1988) and morphosyntax (Johnson & Newport 1989) that measure effect of age of first exposure to the L2. A critical examination of these studies does not confirm a precipitous loss of ability, but rather a fading into adulthood. A lifelong weakening in language learning ability does not support a monolithic critical period cutoff, but rather a gradual decline (Bialystok 2002a). In contrast, several studies of ultimate achievement verify that adult L2 learners can be near-native in their mastery of syntax, morphology and the lexicon (Birdsong 1992; Ioup et al. 1994; White and Genesee 1996), achievements that also argue against a critical period threshold for L2A.

Chapter 6 looks at biological and non-biological causes for linguistic deficits in recent studies of bilinguals that examine processing and memory of various language functions, complex socio-economic and educational factors (Bialystok 2001). There has been substantial new research on neurological processing, particularly of fMRI and Event Related Potentials (ERPs) measuring brain activity (Dehaene et al. 1997). Processing reactions to native language anomalies of both lexico-semantic (N400) and syntactic (P600) types have been documented for some time (Osterhout and Holcomb 1993). Processing reactions of L2 learners have demonstrated qualitatively parallel reactions, especially of near-native speakers, but some studies indicate distinct profiles of L2 learners that seem to relate to AoA (McLaughlin et al. 2004). In an area of research that is just getting underway (Schlaggar et al. 2002), use of neural imaging has produced a rich array of data on language processing of mono- and bilinguals. Finally, there are external factors such as environment, education and culture that affect the acquisition and final state achievement of second language (Bialystok 2001).

The final chapter summarizes the arguments presented throughout the book and draws conclusions concerning a critical period for L1A and L2A. Substantial evidence exists that favors Lenneberg's notion of a critical period for L1A: late L1 acquisition (Curtiss, 1977), neural development (Lenneberg 1967), signed language acquisition (Mayberry 1993; Newport 1994), creoles (Bickerton 1995). Although apparent longitudinal deterioration of L2 ability in syntax and phonology seems to suggest a biological basis to L2A as well, a number of factors render the critical period only indirectly applicable to nonnative language learning. For child L2A, it appears that age five to ten is a period of diminishing ability in language acquisition, but not a sudden loss, and that there is, in fact, no precipitous end of acquisition capacity. Furthermore, other evidence argues against a critical period for L2A: adults learning an L2 may be capable of near-native acquisition (Sorace 2003), and deterioration of language learning ability varies substantially from individual to individual (Long 2003).

1.2   Background research on critical periods

1.2.1   Biology, maturation and behavior

The idea of a *critical or sensitive period* in biological development first emerged in the late nineteenth and early twentieth centuries through the study of experimental embryology (Scott 1978), and was developed substantially in the twentieth century, especially with respect to language (Bailey et al. 2001; Birdsong 1999a, b; Bornstein 1987a; Bruer 2001; Krashen et al. 1982; Rauschecker and Marler 1987; Scott 1978; Scovel 1988; Singleton 1989; Strozer 1994). Stockard (1978 [1921], 25) demonstrated a "critical moment" of embryonic development of minnow eggs by interrupting growth (with temperature change) during a sensitive period of rapid cell proliferation, an intervention that inhibited normal development and resulted in "a great variety of monsters." His original hypothesis had been that the cause of abnormality was the interfering agent (e.g. a noxious chemical), but he later realized that the abnormality was a function of the timing of the interference. His experiments demonstrated that timing is crucial to the development of an organism, and that intervention at different moments in the sequence results in predictable abnormalities. The notion was extended throughout the twentieth century to apply to animal imprinting (Lorenz 1978 [1937]), human behavior (Gray 1978 [1958]), neurological development (Hubel and Wiesel 1962), birdsong learning (Nottebohm 1978 [1969]) and human language (Lenneberg 1967).

Scott (1978, 82) notes that bonding in domestic chicks had been observed even in the nineteenth century, but that it was Lorenz (1978 [1937]) who first recognized its importance for animal behavior and established the term *"imprinting."* Lorenz, who was aware of the attachment pattern of birds (which bond to the first moving object they perceive, usually the mother or another member of the species), demonstrated this connection in an experiment with a greylag gosling. He kept the gosling isolated from other birds for a week after hatching so that it attached to humans, and then he transferred it to a turkey hen. The baby goose followed the turkey and used it for warmth, but would abandon the hen whenever a human came into the environment, the hen being a poor substitute for the original imprint-target of the gosling, the human. Lorenz (ibid., 87) compares this imprinting to embryological development, laying out two significant points relating to the notion of critical periods. "(1) The process is confined to a very definite period of individual life, a period which in many cases is of extremely short duration . . . (2) The process, once accomplished, is totally irreversible, so that from then on, the reaction behaves exactly like an 'unconditioned' or purely instinctive response." The extrapolation of the notion of critical period to behavior led to the observation of sensitive periods for bonding in a wide range of animals and humans as, for example, Gray's (1978 [1958]) discussion of critical periods for human socialization parallel to those of animal attachments. However, the wide range and unpredictability of human behavior, including language, render the critical period question much more complex, as subsequent discussion will show.

Timing is a clearly critical element in the physiological development of vision, a phenomenon first observed by Hubel and Wiesel (1962). These scientists induced irreversible loss of *binocularity* by depriving kittens of input to one eye during a critical moment of their infancy. Numerous experiments of this type – in which kittens were deprived of input to one eye that was sewn shut – followed, to confirm the importance of adequate input to both eyes during the critical period to insure binocular mature eyesight. The onset and termination of the critical period were determined by systematically varying the onset moment and duration of the deprivation with different subjects. Timney (1987), in discussing monocular deprivation, points out that there is not a single sensitive period, but rather that different physiological functions develop during different sensitive periods; furthermore, the intervention does not result in irreversible damage if corrective measures are taken to restore adequate input during the sensitive period. Deprived kittens whose previously sewn eye is reopened may reverse the loss of binocularity if the opening is done within a certain time frame.

The area of critical period research that is perhaps most informative on the question of human language is the learning of *birdsong*, a phenomenon that displays several complexities of timing, triggering models and adaptability. Research substantiates the restriction of song learning to a specific period of life for many species (e.g. the white crowned sparrow) labeled *closed-ended*, although there are other species that continue to be able to learn new song later in their lives (e.g. canaries), known as *open-ended*. Young birds (usually male) learn their song through exposure to the melodies of adult members of their kind, most often as a result of hormonal stimulation, and they "subsequently convert this memory to a motor pattern of song production in the sensorimotor phase of development"

(Brenowitz 2004, 561). Sex hormones are essential at the learning phase, but also for production and for continued availability of song throughout life, particularly during the reproductive cycle when song is deployed to protect territory and attract females. Thus, the elements that enter into play for development of song during a sensitive period – sex hormones, relevant areas of the brain, species-specific song, seasonal changes – are also crucial to the adult bird's annual cycle. In both open and closed-class species, areas of the brain related to song increase up to 200 percent during breeding season, as, for example, in song sparrows whose neuron number increases from 150,000 in the fall to 250,000 during the breeding season (ibid., 564). The annual metabolic changes are influenced by day length, social cues from females and seasonal hormonal variations. "Rather than representing two distinct adaptations, juvenile and adult song learning may represent a continuum of [brain] plasticity," Brenowitz (2004, 578) concludes.

In a classic experiment demonstrating a sensitive period for a closed-ended species, Nottebohm (1978 [1969]) performed an experiment with a chaffinch to tease out the elements of the learning process. Male chaffinches (the singers) learn their repertoire when exposed to the spring song at around nine months of age (the onset of "puberty" when testosterone turns their beaks blue). By one year they have established stereotyped song themes that they cannot alter for the rest of their lives, and they cannot learn new songs after this point. In Nottebohm's experiment, he deferred puberty by castrating a male chaffinch and depriving him of song during the age of nine to twelve months. A year later the bird was given testosterone and exposed to two songs, A and B, both of which the chaffinch learned. This same experiment was conducted the following year with the same bird, but at that point the chaffinch had established his inalterable repertoire, demonstrating that the critical period could be deferred, but that it was inalterable once completed.

Marler (1987), who has used both live models and taped models to train sparrows, finds that the birds trained with taped models are subsequently able to learn new songs presented by live models even after they have solidified their knowledge of the tape-induced songs. He also observes that the input required for learning is distinct for different stages of development, especially in the species that could have extended periods of song acquisition. He concludes that the sensitive period for birdsong learning is flexible since sparrows are able to extend their learning period when exposed to live models, but that this period is susceptible to several variables.

Orca whales also develop communication systems during maturation, with specific dialects and unique name calls. "Each dialect is an acoustic badge of identity; youngsters learn their pod's dialect from their mothers and older siblings. They also learn to recognize the dialects of other pods"

(Chadwick 2005, 94), since they need to pick mates among distantly related pods. Gould and Marler (2004 [1987], 207) – after discussing the preprogramming and time-sensitive nature of instinctive learning in a variety of species, including language learning in humans – conclude "that human learning evolved from a few processes, which are well illustrated in other animals, to fit species-specific human needs." Indeed, Doupe and Kuhl (1997) elaborate similarities between human language and birdsong: innate predisposition, production after perception, specialized forebrain, sensitive period learning, necessity of modeling and feedback, and sustained plasticity.

1.2.2   Definitions of critical period

What are the defining characteristics of a critical period? Scott (1978, 11) points out the biological basis of a sensitive period, "the idea that critical stages occur at times when rapid cell proliferation and rapid developmental changes are occurring." He also observes the irreversibility of the developmental change. In principle, a critical period "implies a sharply defined phase of susceptibility preceded and followed by lack of susceptibility" (Bateson 1987, 153). In fact, though, there are many variables for behaviorial phenomena found in animals: nature of the input (e.g. taped or live models), schedule of onset (e.g. delayed start of input), length of time (e.g. shortened or lengthened exposure), and traits of the individual subject. The studies of birdsong learning have shown a good deal of flexibility in the many variables and indicate an adaptability that enables the songbird to stretch the sensitive period in different ways.

Looking more specifically at language, Eubank and Gregg (1999, 67) define critical period as "a physiological phenomenon that implicates some aspect of the central nervous system," interacting with input from the environment during the course of development. Bruer (1999, 110) postulates that critical periods make evolutionary sense "because they rely on stimuli that are ubiquitous within normal human environments – patterned visual input, the ability to move and manipulate objects, the presence of speech sounds. These kinds of stimuli are available in any child's environment, unless that child is abused to the point of being raised in a sensory deprivation chamber." Bornstein (1987b, 5) identifies five parameters for describing sensitive periods:

- onset
- terminus
- intrinsic maturation event
- extrinsic trigger
- organismic system affected

By way of example, for birdsong learning the onset is marked by the convergence of puberty and seasonal changes, while the terminus coincides with the completion of the learned repertoire. The intrinsic maturation event is the hormonal change triggered by the ambient birdsong and the daylight hours. The system affected includes the neural architecture and the sensorimotor circuits linked to the brain's memory of the song. Biologists have studied a range of species in considering critically timed development, often carefully manipulating the variables concerned. Bruer (2001, 12–13) lays out criteria for designing experiments to test the existence of a sensitive period: a well-defined experimental manipulation, explicit outcome measures and systematic variation of duration.

Although Scott's discussion emphasizes the biological dimension of the notion of critical period, a good deal of research has focused on behavioral aspects of such a temporal limit. More recent work returns to Scott's emphasis in detailing the exact cellular changes that constitute the development of the phenomenon in question, as Knudsen's (2004) clear definitions of "sensitive" and "critical" periods demonstrate. "The term 'sensitive period' is a broad term that applies whenever the effects of experience on the brain are unusually strong during a limited period in development ... Critical periods are a special class of sensitive periods that result in irreversible changes in brain function ... Imprinting causes neurons in a particular nucleus in the forebrain (the intermediate and medial hyperstriatum ventrale) to undergo changes in architecture and biochemistry and to become functionally selective for the imprinted stimulus" (ibid., 1412–1413). Knudsen points out that sensitive periods are properties of predisposed neural circuits that are exposed to reliable and precise input at the correct time in their development. The input experience is not only a trigger to development, but actually reshapes the neural circuit to lead to the mature behavior that is eventually evident.

What is key, then, is the necessary interaction at a sensitive time of two crucial components, the *organismic system* and the *environmental input*. The *onset* is defined by the genetic endowment of the organism since the biological system has to reach a threshold of maturational readiness at which it must be exposed to the triggering stimuli. The *terminus* is defined by the endpoint of the necessary duration, after which the stimulus has no further effect and the developmental change is irreversible (for critical, but not sensitive periods, in Knudsen's terminology). The terminus is crucial, especially for a strict definition, for in principle it marks a threshold of irreversible development that is fixed in the organism for life. Given the variables presented, the criteria for defining a critical period are:

- What is the organismic system?
- What is the environmental input?

- What maturational threshold marks the onset?
- What is the duration of the developmental period?
- Does the terminus mark an irreversible change after which the input no longer has effect?

These criteria will allow us to test the evidence for L1A and L2A in subsequent chapters.

1.3   Language and brain

1.3.1   Physiological studies

For more than a century before Lenneberg discussed in detail the biology of language, scholars had been determining the physiological components of speech, particularly the brain mechanisms involved (Bouillaud 1825; Broca 1861; Calvin and Bickerton 2001; Corballis 1991; Dax 1865 [1836]; Head 1926; Penfield and Roberts 1959; Wernicke 1874). Mainly through observations of different kinds of *aphasia* (language loss), and with the corroboration of brain autopsies after the subjects' deaths, several nineteenth-century physicians began mapping language functions in the brain (Eling 1994; Jakobson 1980). The two most recognized are Pierre Broca and Carl Wernicke who, in 1861 and 1874 respectively, identified the special importance of two regions on the left side of the brain that now carry their names. Each had observed a clustering of aphasic properties in individuals who had suffered brain damage. Later, in performing autopsies, Broca and Wernicke independently noted that the cluster of observed defects corresponded to cerebral damage in a particular area of the left hemisphere.

The language functions of interest are located in the cerebral cortex, the wrinkled covering that is the outermost region of the brain, and whose surface is 2,400 square centimeters (Byrnes 2001). This extraordinary surface area fits into the cranial cavity because the cortex creases and crumples into fissures and folds. The cortex hosts the major cognitive functions such as language, vision, memory and reasoning. The "topography" of the cortex is described directionally (anterior-posterior, or forward-backward; superior-inferior, or upper-lower); in terms of two hemispheres, left and right; and four lobes (in each hemisphere), frontal, temporal, parietal and occipital. Language functions are mainly located in the left hemisphere, and this is mostly true for both right- and left-handed individuals, as right-handers are 95 percent left hemisphere dominant and left-handers are 70 percent left hemisphere dominant (McManus 2003, 213–220).

Broca's region is in the frontal area, while Wernicke's is in the temporal region, more posterior and lower than Broca's. Broca observed his subjects having problems in using the grammatical function words, although they had relatively good comprehension. Wernicke in contrast noted comprehension problems, along with fluent yet meaningless grammatical speech. The differing results of damage to the two distinct areas indicate a separation of language functions, with many language production tasks localized to Broca's area and comprehension tasks localized to Wernicke's area. Broca's aphasics show serious problems with use of grammatical elements of language – their understanding of the meanings of words (semantics) is intact, but their ability to put words together (syntax) is impaired, so that they have words but cannot combine them. Their production consists of individual words articulated with great difficulty. In contrast, Wernicke's aphasics are capable of putting words together into phrases and clauses, but the words put together do not make sense, since these aphasics have substantial difficulties with semantics. Saffran (2003, 277) gives examples of utterances of a Wernicke and a Broca aphasic respectively:

Wernicke's aphasia: I like meats, I have liked beef, the Germans, you know, and what, well the French you koot the whole, I can't recall the word that I can't thay. It was the where you make all the food, you make it all up today and keep it till the next day. With the French, you know, uh, what is the name of the word, God, public serpinz they talk about, uh, but I have had that, it was ryediss, just before the storage you know, seven weeks, I had personal friends that, that I would cook an food the food and serve fer four or six mean for an evening.

Broca's aphasia: Long ago Cinderella. One time many years ago two sisters and one stepmother. Cinderella is washing clothes and mop floor. One day big party in the castle. Two girls dresses is beautiful. Cinderella is poor. Two sisters left. In the castle Cinderella is . . . Godmother. Oh, what's wrong? No money. A little mouse. Cinderella hurry. Queen. Magic wand. Mouses. Oh big men now. Magic wand pumpkin then chariot. Cinderella dresses no good. Cinderella. Oh my god beautiful now.

The distinction between the two components of language, grammar and vocabulary, is also documented by Ostrin and Tyler (1995) in their examination of aphasic "JG" who has "asyntactic comprehension." Through seven experiments on vocabulary, morphology and syntax, they find that he has intact semantic representations but shows "impairments in the use of lexical syntactic information and morphological structure" (ibid., 383).

Over the past two hundred years, studies of recovery from aphasia and of aphasics' autopsies have furnished a rich body of knowledge on the location of linguistic functions in the brain (Fabbro 2002; Safran 2003). Bilingual aphasics, who may show selective debilities in different languages, provide equivocal substantiation of neural separation of functions for different languages and differential recovery from cerebral lesions. For example, Fabbro (2002) describes the case of EM, a bilingual Veronese (L1)-Italian (L2) speaker who lost all ability in her first language but retained command of her L2; after a certain amount of time, she re-learned Veronese, but with an Italian accent. EM's pattern of losing her first language contradicts the pattern that was originally put forth (Jakobson 1968 [1941]), that languages of polyglot aphasics are lost in reverse order of acquisition. In fact, Fabbro points out that evidence of recuperating bilingual aphasics demonstrates that no "tenable explanations" of recovery can be attributed to the many variables examined: nativeness, age of acquisition, length of usage; language most familiar to the patient, most socially useful, most affectively loaded; language of environmental recovery; strongest language; or even type of injury. Not one of these characteristics applies in a majority of cases of bilingual aphasia. On average for recovering bilingual aphasics, about two thirds show parallel recovery of the two languages, and the remaining third shows a recovery of either the first or the second language. More recent studies using neuroimaging and other non-invasive techniques confirm that the distribution of language functions in the monolingual and bilingual brain is complex, a topic addressed in Chapter 6.

These two cerebral areas crucial to language processing are complemented by numerous regions on the left and right hemispheres that relate to physiological motor activities, conceptual knowledge and other cognitive features that affect language ability (Calvin and Ojemann 1994; Hellige 1993). Networks of *neurons* (brain cells) that enable electrical impulses to connect crucial areas in language processing link the brain areas involved in a speech act. In the twentieth century, neurologists such as Wilder Penfield and Lamar Roberts probed the living brain while doing brain surgery to alleviate epileptic seizures and thereby gained further information about the localization of speech. "Local anaesthesia was used during the operations...Since the patients were talking and fully conscious during the procedures, it was possible to discover what parts of the cortex were devoted to the speech function" (Penfield and Roberts 1959, 5). The authors use their own studies and others to map in much more detail the brain areas devoted to speech functions, and they also point out the central left hemisphere location of anatomical motor control related to speech, the Rolandic motor area 4 seen in Figure 1.1.

In the final chapter of their book (written by Penfield), "The learning of languages," Penfield muses on the signficance of neurological findings for second language instruction. He recalls an address to a secondary school audience in which he said that the human brain becomes rigid after the age of nine, and that the adult's brain is inferior to the child's for language. He advocates exposure to more than one language at an early age to engender natural bilingualism in the child. "Language, when it is learned by the normal physiological process, is not taught at all. It is learned as a

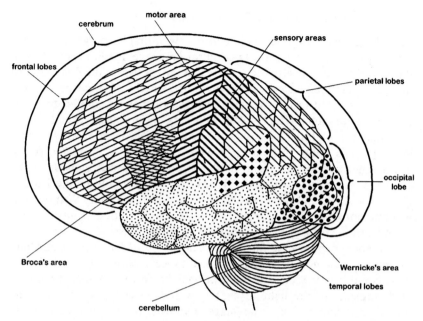

Figure 1.1 Left hemisphere of brain showing areas important for language functions ("Know your brain," National Institute of Neurological Disorders and Stroke, NIH).

by-product of other pursuits" (ibid., 257). Penfield practiced what he preached, plunging "his four children into a German-speaking and then a French-speaking milieu for several years of their early life to give them a chance to develop increased second language fluency" (Scovel 1988, 54).

The brain does show age effects through a reduction of *plasticity* in advanced years (Burke and Barnes 2006), effects not related to cell loss (as previously believed), but to a lessening of neural network branching. Penfield's presumption of "rigidity" has been a standard assumption that is being challenged by recent research showing persistent plasticity in adult brains, with the creation of new neurons (*neurogenesis*) often the result of increased brain stimulation. For example, William Greenough and colleagues have found that the neurons of rats reared in an enriched environment have more complex neural networks than those of control animals (Briones et al. 2004). In one experiment, they exposed a group of adult rats to a complex living environment with objects and mazes replaced daily, while the controls lived in normal cages. The complex exposure group showed significantly more neurons and neural links (*synapses*) in the visual cortex, suggesting that increased brain exercise correlated with increased cortical structure.

1.3.2   Lenneberg's Critical Period Hypothesis

Lenneberg (1967) proposed a biological view of first language acquisition, claiming that there is a critical period for language development between the ages of two and twelve. Lenneberg was not, however, the first to notice that young children have a special propensity to acquire language, nor was the idea restricted to the twentieth century. In the sixteenth century, for example, Montaigne (1962 [1580], 172–173), in advising a friend on the upbringing of children, describes his own acquisition of Latin as a first language. His father hired a tutor who spoke only Latin to the young Montaigne, and all members of the household learned enough of the language to converse with him. "I was over six years old before I heard French or the local dialect any more than I heard Arabic. Without art, without book, without grammar or instruction, without whip or tears I had learned Latin, as pure as that of my school master."

Lenneberg explores the *Biological Foundations of Language*, describing its physiological correlates, neurological aspects, pathologies, relation to other cognitive functions and maturational dimensions. After a discussion of "Language in the light of evolution and genetics" (Chapter 6), he concludes (Chapter 9) that language is species specific, environmentally determined and maturationally delimited. "This basic capacity develops ontogenetically in the course of physical maturation; however, certain environmental conditions also must be present ... language-readiness begins around two and declines with cerebral maturation in the early teens. At this time, apparently a steady state is reached and the cognitive processes are firmly structured, the capacity for primary language synthesis is lost, and cerebral reorganization of functions is no longer possible" (Lenneberg 1967, 375–377). He assumes that the species-specific genetic capacity requires an underlying identity of type in all languages to account both for the uniformity of L1A and the universal properties found cross-linguistically.

Using a range of evidence to argue for his proposal, Lenneberg relates a "critical period" to cerebral lateralization, which he assumes takes place between infancy and puberty. First, among his arguments, there is the regularity of onset and universal pattern of language development between the second and third year of life, with important milestones reached in a relatively constant fashion in both normal and abnormal environments. He cites cases of hearing children born to deaf parents who learn language on a normal schedule. Second, in addition to normal language development, he notes that corroborating evidence can be found in abnormal development, which demonstrates a *dissociation* of language and other cognitive attributes. Language eventually develops even in the absence of normal cognitive development in other domains, as in the case of Down syndrome children. Although motor development and speech may be synchronous, they are not mutually dependent, as evidenced by selective impairment of either. He cites a case of a child with comprehension abilities intact but incapable of producing speech.

A third piece of evidence cited by Lenneberg is recovery from aphasia. Brain damage to the left hemisphere causes aphasia, the loss of language ability. Adults rarely recover their capacity for language after such trauma, but young children are often able to regain language. For two- or three-year-olds, cerebral trauma incapacitates the patient for a while, "but soon he will start again on the road toward language acquisition, traversing all stages of infant vocalization, perhaps at a slightly faster pace, beginning with babbling, single words, primitive two-word phrases, etc., until perfect speech is achieved" (ibid., 150). Claiming that the infant begins life with equipotential hemispheres, Lenneberg attributes the capacity to recuperate from left hemisphere damage to the plasticity of the still lateralizing brain of the young child and claims that lateralization is completed by puberty. He notes that concomitants of physical maturation also include structural, chemical and electrophysiological changes to the brain. A final category of evidence he notes is the existence of critical periods for other species: "many animal forms traverse periods of peculiar sensitivities, response-propensities, or learning potentials" (ibid., 175; cf. Lenneberg and Lenneberg 1975).

Lenneberg's discussion relates mainly to L1A, although he notes that L2A becomes increasingly difficult with increasing age. His comments appear to be anecdotal, and he equivocates on the notion of sensitive period for L2A.

Our ability to learn foreign languages tends to confuse the picture. Most individuals of average intelligence are able to learn a second language after the beginning of their second decade, although the incidence of "language-learning-blocks" rapidly increases after puberty. Also, automatic acquisition from mere exposure to a given language seems to disappear after this age, and foreign languages have to be taught and learned through a conscious and labored effort. Foreign accents cannot be overcome easily after puberty. However, a person can learn to communicate in a foreign language at the age of forty. This does not trouble our basic hypothesis on age limitations because we may assume that the cerebral organization for language learning as such has taken place during childhood, and since natural languages tend to resemble one another in many fundamental aspects, the matrix for language skills is present (ibid., 176).

Lenneberg's delineation of a biological basis for human language ability provides a physiological justification for Chomsky's (1965) proposal of an innate template of properties common to all languages, Universal

Grammar. Both authors argue that this innate ability – and not behavioral training of infants by their parents – guides children through L1A, so it is no surprise that Chomsky (1959, 43) cites Lenneberg, or that the latter includes a 45-page appendix by Chomsky ("The formal nature of language") in his 1967 book.

1.3.3   Follow-up to Lenneberg

Although Lenneberg never directly put forth a "*Critical Period Hypothesis*," he gained attribution of the term, a standard nomenclature in many publications (Birdsong 1999a; Singleton 1989; Singleton and Ryan 2004; Scott 1978; Scovel 1988; Strozer 1994). During the period following publication of Lenneberg's book, various strands of research both disproved and extrapolated different points of the Critical Period Hypothesis. As Chapter 2 will demonstrate, he was correct in noting the universal schedule and sequencing of first language acquisition, although subsequent research has shown that the acquisition process begins even before birth, not at two years as Lenneberg thought. The first two years – which Lenneberg treated as rather insignificant – are a crucial period for the establishment of phonological and syntactic categories in the infant's language development.

Individuals who are cognitively impaired yet linguistically competent bear witness to Lenneberg's claim that language is dissociated from other cognitive functions. For example, Smith and Tsimpli (1995) study in detail a congenitally brain-damaged 30-year-old, Christopher, whose native English is without flaw, and who is also knowledgeable about several other languages. Although he cannot perform cognitive tasks that would be accessible to a young child, he is able to learn new languages to a remarkable degree of mastery. Likewise, Laura, a cognitively challenged individual studied by Yamada (1990), shows fluency in her spoken English, but is incapable of solving simple problems. Another class of individuals who have been studied for this same sort of linguistic facility, is those with Williams Syndrome, a disorder that affects language somewhat less than other cognitive abilities (Bellugi et al. 1993; Karmiloff-Smith et al. 1997).

The case of Alex, a speechless child who underwent a left hemispherectomy at age eight and subsequently acquired language, attests to Lenneberg's claims of hemisphere plasticity and dissociation (Vargha-Khadem et al. 1997). Before his operation, Alex had suffered Sturge-Weber Syndrome, a congenital disorder that caused multiple daily seizures and atrophy of his left hemisphere. Before and just after the operation, and for the following ten months, Alex showed no linguistic abilities. At this point seizure medicine was withdrawn completely, and Alex began to develop speech. By age ten he could "converse with copious and appropriate speech" and "progressed within a few months from articulating consonants for the first time to uttering single intelligible words and then to producing full-length sentences" (ibid., 174). By age fifteen his language abilities were those of an eight-year-old, although he showed some weakness in morphology and phonology. His development of language was not matched by other cognitive development, corroborating other examples of dissociation of linguistic ability and general intelligence.

Lenneberg's central proposal that lateralization of the brain determines the critical period has, however, proven to be wrong, since subsequent studies (Krashen 1973, 1975; Witelson 1987) show that lateralization is completed much earlier than puberty. Corballis (1991), who devotes a book to the asymmetry of the human brain, points out that the brain is already lateralized at birth and simply specializes its neural networks in the ensuing years, retaining the lateralization that is essential to language acquisition and use. Yet in support of Lenneberg's puberty cutoff, Neville (1995) notes that adult-like lateralization of cerebral language functions occurs between eleven and fifteen years of age. Generally, however, Lenneberg's proposal of lateralization beginning at two and ending at twelve is not accurate.

A broader view of neural development can adapt Lenneberg's hypothesis though, since other aspects of physical maturation complement the lateralization arguments. Scovel (1988, 151), who discusses the weaknesses in Lenneberg's lateralization arguments, develops parallel maturational arguments based on other aspects of brain development such as structural, chemical, electrophysiological changes and myelination. Scovel argues for a puberty cutoff point for the development of native phonology, which he claims has a "physiological" basis related to neural development. The brain develops in the infant by first proliferating neural branching and increasing the number of synaptic connections, and then by pruning superfluous branches and creating dedicated connections to achieve mature linguistic, visual, auditory and other cognitive specializations. Bruer (1999) claims that critical period developmental phenomena are *experience expectant* – organismic systems in search of targeted environmental input, plasticity that operates by synapse pruning – whereas other developmental occurrences are *experience dependent* – growing new or strengthening existing synapses to learn from personal experiences (e.g. culture-specific knowledge such as appreciation of Mozart or sushi making). Experience-expectant developments inevitably take place, given the proper input; experience-dependent phenomena also depend on the input, but are not necessary ontogenetic developments.

Corballis (1991) also relates the growth of language to neural development, but he proposes a different timeline. He suggests that the asymmetry of the brain derives from differential growth rates of the two hemispheres and the long period of human cerebral development compared to other primates. "The acquisition of language may therefore be orchestrated by genes controlling the rate of development, so that different neural circuits involved in language mature at different times and are modified by appropriate inputs from the linguistic environment" (ibid., 292). Corballis says that the crucial period for this development is from age two to four, during which the bulk of morphosyntax is acquired and the left hemisphere takes over the language function.

As for evidence of child recuperation from cerebral injury, Corballis points out that the recuperation of language functions is not as complete as Lenneberg suggests. Children who sustain left hemispheric damage during the first two years have difficulty with complex grammar such as passive negative sentences, but are otherwise fluent in the language functions that have been reassigned to the right hemisphere. A more recent case of a child undergoing a left hemispherectomy and regaining basic language abilities is that of Alex, whose speech development did not begin until age nine (Vargha-Khardem et al. 1997). Lenneberg was thus incorrect in claiming that infants have equipotential hemispheres, but correct in noting the stark contrast in recuperation from left hemisphere damage between very young children and adults, even if the children do experience some residual linguistic problems. Lenneberg's argument about critical periods of other species is certainly as solid today as in 1967. There are indeed sensitive periods in the biological growth of many organisms, but the fact that more complex behavioral learning entails a number of variables that impact the maturational process renders the notion of critical period less precise in the area of language acquisition.

Research since 1967 has on the one hand disproved all of Lenneberg's claims (Snow 1987), and on the other presented evidence to bolster the spirit of his biological timetable for L1A. There appears to be substantial evidence – universality of L1A, dissociation of intact language from other impaired cognitive functions, recovery from left hemisphere trauma in children but not adults – for the existence of a period of heightened sensitivity for first language acquisition. The onset is at birth, but it is unclear when the period ends and whether there is a prolonged offset. For L1A, we might initially establish two benchmarks for offset of terminus, Lenneberg's date (twelve years of age) and a younger age at which normal L1A is mostly complete (five years of age) to evaluate the "precipitous" threshold version of the CPH.

1.4　Theoretical frameworks

Two complementary theoretical approaches of the early twenty-first century can trace their lineage back several centuries to Locke's empiricism on the one hand and Descartes' rationalism on the other. The rationalist approach attributes cognition to the very nature of the species – humans acquire certain kinds of knowledge such as language because they are destined to do so through innate abilities. In contrast, empiricism emphasizes the importance of input to the maturation of the human mind; it is the environment that nurtures and triggers development. Contemporary cognitive theory opposes nurture to nature in terms of two general approaches characterized here as *associationism* and *modularity*, to be discussed in this section.

1.4.1　Associationism

In the first half of the twentieth century the theory of *behaviorism* dominated American psychology and linguistics. A leading proponent of behaviorism, B. F. Skinner, authored *Verbal Behavior*. As the empiricists of the eighteenth century, the behaviorists believed that human (and animal) learning was accomplished through an external trigger, in this case reinforcement, the repetition of certain associations that eventually were ingrained, resulting in the mature construct. Positive reinforcement – repetition and "handing out of little treats" – recalls Sedaris' opinion of why French babies learn French. Skinner (1957) proposed such a model of language learning, assuming that parents taught their toddlers to speak through positive reinforcement. Chomsky's (1959) review of Skinner's book, in which he argued that the child's knowledge of language far surpassed anything that parents could teach, was instrumental in diminishing the influence of behaviorism.

In the past twenty years *associationism* – a kind of neo-behaviorism modeled on computer networks – has developed. Associationism proposes that all learning is triggered by environmental input creating specialized associations based on frequency (Elman et al. 1996; MacWhinney 1999; MacWhinney and Bates 1989), thus diminishing the role of innate mechanisms. This approach posits a unitary all-purpose learning theory: feedback mechanisms permit modifications to the learning process and result in differentiation among distinct areas of specialization. For example, a single computational system gradually learns the structure of all aspects of a language by adjusting weights of connections based on statistical contingencies (Ullman 2001b). So learning language and developing visual acuity – that is, creating specialized areas of the brain for different functions – are at origin prompted by the same learning mechanisms. Feedback may change the nature of the learning and processing mechanism by creating networks of associations relevant to each domain.

Connectionism or *PDP* (parallel distributed processsing) has been quite influential in providing an application of computational models to human knowledge and behavior. Plaut (2003, 143) explains that "cognitive processes take the form of cooperative and competitive interactions among large numbers of simple, neuronlike processing units. Unit interactions are governed by weighted connections that encode the long-term knowledge of the system and are learned gradually through experience." The PDP model has been applied to various areas of cognitive processing by adapting associationism to neural networks and assuming that frequency of input coupled with interactionism results in inference of correct cognitive structure (Elman et al. 1996). A seminal paper on the development of connectionism is Rumelhart and McClelland's (1986) work on the acquisition of English past tense morphology. The authors create a computer program that parses the input of regular and irregular verbs to infer past tense forms. The program creates networks of similarities, with regular -*ed* forms constituting one category, while irregular forms are linked in subcategories that may vary according to a vowel change (e.g. *ring*/*rang, sing*/*sang*). It is trained on the correct present and past forms, and a feedback loop adjusts networks as a function of the correctness of the response. The authors discover that the program is able to reach a high degree of accuracy, nearly total for the training verbs and about 75 percent for new verbs.

The three strongest points of associationist approaches are the *unitary learning mechanism*, the importance of *frequency and saliency of input*, and the role of *cross-domain interaction*. The model, which is crucially dependent on external input, is an *instructive* one which sees the mind starting as a tabula rasa that is shaped by the input and feedback interactions. While connectionism has attracted a great deal of interest in its clarification of the role of frequency of input, it is, as one of its proponents notes, limited in its applications. "The reality of connectionist modeling is more sober and modest. In fact, much of the work to date has focused on the learning of narrow aspects of inflectional morphology in languages like English and German" (MacWhinney 2000, 125).

A related approach, *emergentism*, attempts to account for interactions between biological and environmental processes and the influence of this interaction in the child's development, but it is not strictly anti-nativist. For language acquisition, an emergentist account (MacWhinney 1999; Weismer and Thordardottir 2002) sees L1A as a process that is informed by the interactional feedback it receives in a range of domains, not simply the linguistic ones. In his preface, MacWhinney (1999, xi) notes "emergentism views nativist and empiricist formulations as partial components of a more complete account." Newmeyer (1998) is an avowed nativist-modularist who nevertheless recognizes the role of performance considerations and frequency in the shaping of grammars and the implementation of language usage. He notes (2003, 688) that not all cognitive scientists see modularity and associationism as incompatible, quoting Steedman (1999, 615). "The emphasis in the connectionist sentence-processing literature on distributed representation and emergence of grammar from such systems can easily obscure the often close relations between connections and symbolic systems . . . Connectionism is no more intrinsically non-modular than any other approach, and many connectionists . . . have explicitly endorsed modular architectures of various kinds." Associationism, with its unitary learning mechanism and self-regulating differentiation, sees individual development (ontogenesis) as a function of input and feedback, not a function of maturation. The notion of a critical period has little meaning, since according to this model age deficits are side effects of neural network establishment, not results of maturational sensitivity or decline.

1.4.2   Modularity

Associationism – which is often set in opposition to nativist *modularity* – is not, however, without its detractors. The decline of behaviorism following Chomsky's review of Skinner led to the development of disciplines that attribute human cognitive properties more to genetic predisposition than to external influence. This more rationalist model envisages the mind as an organ predisposed to develop in particular ways given the proper triggers. Rather than being instructive, it is *selective* in that the developing child comes equipped with a predisposition and a set of options. Guasti (2002, 23) describes this selective process of L1 acquisition as one "in which experience narrows perceptual sensitivity and thus enables learners to choose the phonological system instantiated in the input from among those that characterize human languages as a whole and that are encoded in Universal Grammar."

According to this view, cognition starts out pre-programmed, with dedicated subparts or modules, each with a unique pattern of development. Some nativists, such as Lenneberg or Pinker, see the early emergence of language in the young child as indicative of a critical period. "Lenneberg relates his species-specific, nativist perspective both to the age-related sequence of speech milestones and to his conception of the critical period of language readiness" (Singleton and Ryan 2004, 188). A nativist perspective does not necessarily entail a strict interpretation of a critical period for language acquisition, because the language learning capacity is available to adults and children (Epstein et al. 1996; Herschensohn 2000; White 2003). The modular approach is "based on the hypothesis that not just formal grammar, but *all* human systems (or at least all those at work in language) are autonomous 'modules,' each governed by its particular set of general principles" (Newmeyer 1983, 3). Modularity has been used to describe the interaction of various cognitive modules such as principles of learning and concept formation with conversational principles, but also to describe the subcomponents (e.g. phonology, syntax) of the formal grammar itself.

Fodor (1983) puts forth a view of the mind in which six modules (the five senses and language) handle in a rote manner the enormous quantities of sensorial data received, while the central cognitive system houses conscious faculties such as memory and reason. Modularist accounts usually subscribe to nativism, but do not agree on all theoretical issues (Fodor 2001; Sperber 2001). Fodor notes that the six modules possess nine typical characteristics including domain specificity, mandatoriness, speed, fixed neural architecture and sequence of development. For example, vision is mandatory (one must close one's eyes to avoid seeing), immediate, located in the occipital lobes of the brain, and subject to developmental constraints (as the kitten experiments have shown). Modular accounts assume that linguistic knowledge is largely independent of other cognitive domains, resulting in dissociations of language and other cognition as in the case of Christopher, the language savant. This stance is rejected by associationists who see the interdependence of different cognitive domains as crucial to learning procedures that are not domain-specific. A difference in perspective between the two approaches is that modularity admits the possible interaction of different domains while focusing on a particular one, whereas associationism relies on interactions while denying the independence of the particular domain.

Disapproval of associationism ranges from specific rebuttals of the Rumelhart and McClelland study (Pinker 1999) to more general criticism of the theory (Marcus 2001). As the description of the brain earlier in this chapter suggests, the cerebrum is already at birth specialized to have dedicated functions develop in selected areas, areas whose function has been observed at least for the past two hundred years. Gazzaniga (1998, 15) contrasts the associationists' idea of a common mechanism to the reality of the brain. "When the common mechanism confronts language issues, it winds up building the brain one way; when it confronts the problem of detecting faces, it builds it another way – and so on. This sort of assertion leaves us breathless because if we know anything, it is that any old part of the brain can't learn any old thing." Likewise, Corballis (1991) adduces evidence from L1A that the indubitable "hard-wiring" of several aspects of language in the infant brain permits the child to achieve developmental milestones in a timely fashion. He asserts that a connectionist network would need to have some built-in structure to mimic the complexities of a complete grammar of a human language.

Pinker (1999), reprising Pinker and Prince (1988), presents several arguments against the Rumelhart and McClelland model. He notes that the model can only produce past-tense forms, not recognize them, as humans do, and that it cannot distinguish homonyms. Relying only on the sounds (phonemes) of a verb, without having a means of representing it as a word, also speaks against the usefulness of this model. Phoneme order is irrelevant for its design, yet is the very basis of word formation in human language. A related problem is that words that might constitute a morphological "family" may not line up in a left-to-right array.

While Pinker makes very clear arguments for the necessity of linguistic categories and information (hierarchical, sequential, phonological and morphological) for the representation of English past tense (and presumably other morphological phenomena), he adopts the associationist treatment of irregular verbs. He maintains that regular morphology is determined by rules, while irregular morphology is learned as individual items, words, which may show associationist links to other words or bits of words. Unlike the unitary Rumelhart and McClelland model, his proposal uses linguistic units such as stems, onsets, vowels and features – a rich array of linguistic building blocks. His hybrid model combines Chomskyan rules with connectionist networking and recalls the coalition approach of Hollich et al. (2000).

Just as some connectionists are open to aspects of modularity, some modularists are open to aspects of associationism. Marcus (2001, 171) thinks that cognition must include mechanisms that are capable of symbol manipulation, but also ones that are sensitive to frequency. "It seems likely, in fact, that an adequate account of cognition will have a place for both memory mechanisms that are sensitive to frequency and similarity and for operations over variables that apply equally to all members of a class." Using evidence from language and other cognitive systems, he attempts to integrate the modularist idea that the mind manipulates symbols with the connectionist idea that the mind constitutes large networks of neurons.

1.5   Conclusion

For millennia, humans have been fascinated by language acquisition, often believing that some universal language is at the base of infants' ability to learn the native tongue. For example, the Greek historian Herodotus

(1954, 102–103) recounts the Egyptian king Psammetichos' experiment of raising two infants deprived of speech. As the story goes, at the age of about two they spoke the word *bekos* which means "bread" in Phrygian, the language that Psammetichos determined to be the mother tongue, and "in consideration of this the Egyptians yielded their claims and admitted the superior antiquity of the Phrygians" (ibid., 103). We know now that children completely deprived of language do not spontaneously develop Phrygian, or any other full-blown tongue. Input is essential, but cannot of itself explain language acquisition. A genetic predisposition characterized by cross-linguistic similarity in L1A patterns and resulting in consistent dedication of neural architecture is also a necessary component of acquisition. Both nature and nurture must be present. Subsequent chapters will bear out the necessity of both the human language predisposition and environmental input to L1 and L2 acquisition. We will see that factors such as frequency and saliency, considered quite important by associationists, are indeed important, but not exclusively so. We will also see that experience alters the brain as it is developing, as for example the slightly differing cerebral specializations for language that distinguish spoken and signed languages (Sacks 1990).

This chapter has given a brief history of critical period research, from embryonic development of minnow eggs to seasonal hormonal changes relating to birdsong learning. In terms of biological maturation, it delineated components of a critical period – Bornstein's (1987b) onset, terminus, intrinsic maturation event, extrinsic trigger, and organismic system – and furnished Knudsen's (2004) clear definitions. A sensitive period is an interval during which the effects of experience on the brain are unusually strong, while a critical period is a sub-class that results in irreversible changes in brain function.

The next chapters will evaluate the Critical Period Hypothesis to answer several questions:

- whether first and second language are limited in their acquisition by a critical period
- how they compare in process and endstate
- whether they correspond or diverge in behavior and neural representation
- which innate and environmental factors determine their development.

The range of evidence brought to these questions will include studies in both modularist and associationist veins which will show that while there are undeniable deficits in both L1A and L2A as age of onset increases, there is no absolute threshold of a critical period terminus. Rather, unlike many species of birds, whose song learning is clearly restricted to a critical period, humans are able to learn aspects of language at any age.

2   Right on time: process and schedule of first language acquisition

2.0   Introduction

In the chapter "Baby born talking – describes heaven," Pinker (1995, 269–270) quotes Adam, the toddler whose corpus of evolving speech has furnished data to generations of scholars (the first number after Adam's name refers to the year and the second to the month of his age).

Play checkers. Big drum. I got horn. A bunny-rabbit walk. (Adam 2;3)

That birdie hopping by Missouri in bag. Do want some pie on your face? Why you mixing baby chocolate? I finish drinking all up down my throat. I said why not you coming in? We going turn light on so you can't see. (Adam 2;11)

So it can't be cleaned? I broke my racing car. Do you know the light wents off? What happened to the bridge? When it's got a flat tire it's need a go to the station. Can I put my head in the mailbox so the mailman can know where I are and put me in the mailbox? Can I keep the screwdriver just like a carpenter keep the screw-driver? (Adam 3;2)

Adam, like all children, was not born talking, but by two years three months he was combining words in a toddler-like fashion; a year later his language was nearly that of the adults and children he had been listening to for the first three years of his life. To be able to consider whether there is a critical period for L1A, we must first understand the process and schedule of typical development of native tongue.

Language is clearly a species-specific attribute of humans, who are born with dedicated neural architecture for developing linguistic abilities and learn the language that they encounter in their environment, not a generic human communication system that is identical world-wide. Clearly, both *nature* – the genetic predisposition to learn and use language – and *nurture* – the linguistic, social, cultural and emotional input that feeds acquisition – are crucial to learning a first language. Nevertheless, scholars of L1A have for decades debated the importance of two contrasting factors, a debate that Hirsh-Pasek and Golinkoff (1996) characterize as interactionist *outside-in* (nurture) theories as opposed to nativistic *inside-out* (nature) theories, two approaches that frame our examination of L1A.

Interactionist theories emphasize the importance of social and cognitive factors to the acquisition process and subscribe to domain-general learning procedures. For example, Tomasello and Akhtar (1995) highlight the consequence of pragmatic cues to differentiate nouns and verbs, while Carpenter, Nagell and Tomasello (1998) attribute acquisition procedures to motivation to communicate and inseparability of language from social interaction. For them, the acquisition process is an instructive one in that children "work very hard in the process of comprehending and producing utterances" (Snow and Tomasello 1989, 358), and a constellation of non-linguistic factors contribute to learning. Another outsider vein is that of associationists such as Plunkett (1997) and Smith (1999), who subscribe to the importance of frequency and saliency, presenting evidence that generalized learning theories can account for acquisitional processes. Generally, these approaches see language acquisition emerging from an interaction of the "instructional input" (social, distributional) and the developing cognitive-linguistic abilities (MacWhinney 1999).

Nativist theories presuppose the idea of *Universal Grammar* (UG), the innate linguistic template that determines both language acquisition and the universal properties of human languages around the world. The availability of a universal language capacity responds to the "logical problem of language acquisition," that is, how children come to have such a rich body of linguistic knowledge (in so short a time), with "impoverished input" (Baker and McCarthy 1981; Wexler and Culicover 1980; Pinker 1989). Guasti (2002) argues that language acquisition is a selective process that allows the young child unconsciously to develop the correct linguistic settings for the language that he hears, without instruction or correction, thanks to guidance of inborn UG. She points out that while connectionist models may be useful to describe some aspects of language learning, they cannot account for developmental sequencing or for the eventual surplus linguistic knowledge such as ability to discern ambiguity or ungrammaticality.

Hirsh-Pasek and Golinkoff point out several criticisms of both theories before proposing their own coalition model that uses aspects of each. Outside-in theories often treat linguistic knowledge as non-linguistic, whereas inside-out theories subscribe to an idealized "instantaneous" view of L1A, and see the environment only as a trigger. Their *coalition model* draws from both theories. "Children are sensitive to information in the input...and at some point to the syntactic configurations in which words appear...In short, children try to use all the pieces of information at their disposal, although not necessarily at the same time, in abstracting the units and relations of grammar" (Hirsh-Pasek and Golinkoff 1996, 51). Using research deriving from the theoretical perspectives just outlined, this chapter explores the path of L1A to elucidate what might be stages of a critical period. The survey, representative rather than exhaustive, will begin with sounds (phonology), track sounds to words (lexicon), then words to sentences (syntax), and finally look at grammatical inflection (morphology).

2.1   Phonology

Before a child can begin to learn words, she must deconstruct the sound system of the ambient language by first discerning the sounds and their significance, and then learning to approximate them in production. Research in the past forty years has revealed the astounding abilities that newborns start with, and how they shift their perceptual skills to language production later in the first year of life. Children do not perfect their native pronunciation for several years, but they establish crucial phonological patterns in the early months that serve them for life.

2.1.1   Phonemic discrimination

In 1971, Peter Eimas and his colleagues published an article that provided remarkable insight into the innate predisposition for human language that young babies bring to the acquisition task. It led to dozens of subsequent studies contributing further information about infant perception of human speech. Eimas et al. showed that babies have the same perceptual abilities to distinguish sounds (*phones*) of their native language as do adult speakers of that language. Subsequent studies of infant perception have further shown that even younger babies, newborns, have crucial perceptual abilities not just for the ambient language, but for any human language, an ability that declines, however, with age to the point that a one-year-old only discriminates the native language. In fact, children already have the ability to recognize speech sounds, particularly those of their mother, even while still in utero (de Boysson-Bardies 1999).

   Eimas et al. (2004 [1971]), who used the technique of *high amplitude sucking* (*HAS*) to follow infant attention, revealed that one- and four-month-old infants show the same ability as adults to distinguish sounds such as the *phonemes* /p/ and /b/. These phonemes differ only with respect to *voice onset time* (*VOT*), the lag between the production of the consonant and vibration of the vocal folds (voicing), with /b/ showing sooner voicing than /p/. The difference is relative rather than absolute because actual realization of the phonemes covers a broad range of VOTs, a range that can be reproduced by systematically varying the VOT of synthesized sound incrementally. Adults, when presented with mechanically incremental shifts in VOT, do not randomly perceive some tokens as /p/ and some as /b/, but rather hear the voicing distinction as *categorical*, with all tokens to one side of a VOT threshold (mainly less than 25 milliseconds) as /b/ and to the other (mainly more than 25 milliseconds) as /p/.

Capitalizing on the nonnutritive sucking of young infants, many studies of early perception use the HAS technique in which children suck on a pacifier wired to a device registering the amplitude of sucking. After a baseline level of sucking is determined, "the presentation and intensity of an auditory stimulus [is] made contingent upon the infant's rate of high-amplitude sucking" (Eimas et al. 2004, 281). Habituation leads to a fall-off of sucking, while introduction of something novel (in this case, a new sound) leads to an increase, so a control group given no novel sound can be compared with an experimental group which undergoes a change in stimulus. In the Eimas et al. experiment, the researchers exposed infants to the incremental VOT changes that have been described for the adult experiments. The babies continued with the habituation sucking when the tokens were close, but not perceived as categorically different; how-ever, they perceived as novel (with increased sucking) a token that had passed the VOT threshold. The authors found that their subjects behaved like adults in distinguishing consonants on the basis of voicing, and in doing so in a categorical manner, responses that they interpreted to mean that the infant's biological makeup included perception in a linguistic mode, "operative at an unexpectedly early age." The biological predispo-sition for categorical discrimination has been verified with various conso-nants (differing in place of articulation) and with vowels in numerous languages to which the infants – some only three days old – had never been exposed. Jusczyk (1997, 58) points out that some other species (e.g. chinchillas) appear to have categorical discrimination, but that such behavior "does not rule out the possibility that species-specific mechan-isms are involved in human speech perception."

Young infants are primed to perceive the distinctive sounds in any lan-guage of the world, but this remarkable ability is lost by twelve months of age, as Werker and Tees (1984) demonstrate in a study of three groups of infants six to twelve months of age. The authors, who investigate the perceptual discrimination by English learning infants of non-English con-sonants such as Hindi dental stops, find that six- to eight-month-olds are still able to distinguish the Hindi consonants, that fewer eight- to ten-month-olds are capable of doing so, and that the group of ten- to twelve-month-olds almost completely loses the ability. In contrast, Hindi-exposed infants are perfectly capable of distinguishing the sounds in their native language. These results have been interpreted to mean that infants during the first year gradually lose their ability to perceive all distinctive sounds of the world's languages, and by the age of one year are focused on the distinctive sounds of the language that they are learning. Clearly, the flexibility to learn new sounds can be reactivated in early childhood L2A, and bilingual L1A exposes the young child to two phonological systems. Jusczyk (1997, 81) emphasizes that the decline is not – unlike the deprivation of kitten binocularity – irreversible. Since children are beginning to learn words at this period, the restriction of phonemic inventory to the native language can be seen as a means of perfecting native perception and restricting the search space for new vocabulary. Werker and Tees (1999) describe a first year "transactional" development of perception, which evolves in concert with other abilities, as a series of cerebral reorganizations.

One factor that contributes to children's narrowing down of the hypothesis space for determining the native language inventory is the reliance on prototypes of speech categories (Kuhl 1991a, b). Just as consonants naturally differ in their realization, vowels also are produced with a range of acoustic realizations, stemming from the variation of individual speakers, to the much broader disparities arising from the tonality of different speakers (e.g. a man's voice compared to a woman's), and to the phonetic properties of the language itself (French and English /a/ are not identical). Nevertheless, adults are able to compensate for such variation, an ability that Kuhl partially attributes to a *perceptual magnet effect* of native phoneme prototypes which develops around six months of age. "The *prototype* of the category thus serves as a powerful anchor for the category, and the prototype's functional role as a perceptual magnet for the category serves to strengthen category cohesiveness" (Kuhl 1991a, 99). When presented with a range of vowel tokens after habituation to a vowel prototype, adults and children do not perceive the variations as novel. If the subjects are presented outlier tokens without habituation, they perceive the outliers as novel. Kuhl and her colleagues (1992) demonstrate that children as young as six months are sensitive to the vowel space of their native language when habituated with a prototype: American children respond to the magnetic effect of native /i/, whereas Swedish children do so with their native /y/, a front rounded vowel. The children do not respond to the nonnative vowels as prototypes, but rather as novel tokens, indicating that they have at this young age already established native vowel space categories broad enough to accommodate a range of variation within, but not outside, their native range.

2.1.2   *Suprasegmentals*

Phonemes constitute the segments, the building blocks of words of a language, but it is *prosodic* or *suprasegmental* factors – stress, intonation, rhythm, syllable structure – that provide the means of combining phonemes into words and words into sentences. Segui and Ferrand (2002) show that for adults structural properties of the word are stored and retrieved independent of phonemic content of the word, a pattern that can be observed in infant learning. Following a pioneering investigation by Mehler et al. (1988), a number of studies have demonstrated that newborn infants are able to distinguish their native language from other languages. In the original experiment the researchers, using the HAS technique, exposed French language newborns to the speech of a bilingual (French and Russian) adult, finding that the babies sucked at a higher rate when listening to French than Russian. The babies seemed to prefer the ambient language they had already been exposed to in utero. Later studies have shown identical results for Spanish, English, Catalan, Italian and Dutch, and have also shown that newborns are capable of distinguishing two nonnative languages (Guasti 2002). Variations on the experiment that cut out the segmental information (*low-pass filtering*) show that the infants are paying attention to prosodic patterns, not to phonemic information, to distinguish native language. Since the babies would have received low-pass filtered ambient language during their last trimester in utero (at a time when their hearing was developed enough to register such sounds), their reliance on suprasegmental over segmental information antedates their birth.

Investigations of newborn perception of nonnative languages have revealed that infants achieve their perceptual abilities through their sensitivity to *rhythmic features* of the languages (Kehoe and Stoel-Gammon 1997; Mehler et al. 1996), a sensitivity that is apparently shared by other species (Bakalar 2005). The languages of the world can be categorized as *stress-timed* ones (e.g. English, Dutch) that show major distinctions between stressed and unstressed vowels; *syllable-timed* ones (e.g. French, Spanish) that show a more homogeneous syllable type; or *mora-timed* (e.g. Japanese) ones that have short and long vowels. In stress-timed languages the rhythmic unit is stress, so the number of syllables between stressed vowels may vary (compare the number of syllables in limericks such as "there was a young boy named Tom" vs. "there was a young boy from Nebraska"). In syllable-timed languages all syllables have equal length, stressed or not, while in mora-timed languages morae (subunits of the syllable) are of equal length. In mora-timed languages long vowels and long consonants are "heavy" and double the number of morae. For example, Japanese *obaasan* "grandmother" has a two-mora second syllable in contrast to *obasan* "aunt" whose second syllable has one mora (Major 2001, 18). Mehler et al. (1996) propose that infants initially discriminate beween languages on the basis of rhythmic properties, but by about two months of age start to lose the ability to discern differences between two nonnative languages. They note that the mechanism used cannot be based on "statistical computations over large samples of speech" (p. 112), but rather supports the assumption of a biological endowment permitting newborns to discriminate all languages.

2.1.3   Babbling

Despite their acuity in perception, during the first half year of life infants don't make linguistically signficant sounds; around six months of age, they begin to produce consonant-vowel sequences such as *bababa*, termed reduplicated or *canonical babbling*. Canonical babbling is followed by a stage of *variegated babbling* in which consonants are varied. By 12–14 months of age "the child begins to produce a variety of consonants overlaid on a sentencelike intonation pattern" (Jusczyk 1997, 175). Hearing-impaired children exposed to signed languages go through a period of gesture babbling that corresponds to the oral variety of hearing children (Petitto and Marentette 1991; Iverson and Goldin-Meadow 1998), suggesting that the emergence of babbling is related more to development of linguistic areas of the brain than to maturation of the vocal tract. While physiologically capable of oral babbling, deaf infants do not produce the same range of vocal babbling that hearing children do (Stoel-Gammon and Otomo 1986), pointing to the interaction of biological development with the input of the ambient language.

Although earlier descriptions of babbling based on Jakobson's (1968 [1941], 1990 [1971]) evaluations assumed that babbling was prelinguistic articulatory practice unrelated to the subsequent production of words, that view has been revised on the basis of numerous studies (Menn and Stoel-Gammon 1995). De Boysson-Bardies (1999, 55), reporting on her own extensive research in babbling and that of others, emphasizes that babbling definitely involves a "mutual adjustment between the genetic and physiological equipment of children, on the one hand, and the effects of experience with the language spoken by their parents, on the other." Early babbling includes the low vowels /a/ and /æ/ preceded by /p/, /b/, /t/, /d/, /m/, especially, but also /k/, /g/, /n/, /ŋ/, the stops and nasals that constitute over 80 percent of the early consonants. Later babbling includes a wider variety of consonants and vowels, and syllable structure that includes final consonants by children exposed to languages that have them. Petitto (2000) points out the importance of the "rhythmic timing bundle" characteristic of babbling, because it is a common point between both spoken and signed babbling.

While children favor low vowels and stops cross-linguistically, they put their native language stamp on the production of the vowels and consonants, as the construction of phoneme prototypes and inventory is influenced by native tongue. De Boysson-Bardies et al. (1989) measure the vowel space of French, English, Chinese and Algerian ten-month-olds recorded in their home countries. They find that the realization of vowels is quite distinct for each language group. "This parallelism shows that children already have a representation of the vowel space of the language that allows them to realize vowels as a function of the perceived character-istics of vowels they have heard" (de Boysson-Bardies 1999, 60). It appears that the native character of the vowel space is related to the establishment of vowel prototypes through the earlier perceptual magnet effect; Kuhl points out that their biological endowment allows children to test hypoth-eses and to make selections – of, for example phonemes, phonetic detail or prosodic patterns – to narrow down the options in constructing their native language. She also notes the importance of timing: "an absence of early exposure to the patterns that are inherent in natural language – whether spoken or signed – produces life long changes in the ability to learn language" (2004, 831).

2.1.4   Finalizing phonology

The transition from babbling to the use of first words – first words being relatively unanalyzed phonologically and often overgeneralized semanti-cally – essentially is seamless, with the two kinds of production overlap-ping around 12–14 months of age. "In all likelihood [first words] are recorded only with reference to prosody, syllabic structure, and a few articulatory features. When the number of memorized words increases, this method of representation is no longer sufficient. Such undefined representations do not allow the items of a large vocabulary to be distin-guished, stored or produced" (de Boysson-Bardies 1999, 190). The devel-opment of words – that is systematic and repeatable combinations of the sounds that children have been mastering – leads ironically to an apparent reduction in the baby's phonological repertoire. For example, children who have shown articulatory command of certain phonemes may either substitute another one (e.g. *guck* for *duck*, even though they pronounce /d/ in other words), or show variability in pronunciation. These difficulties may arise from the increased processing load of producing a systematic sequence of sounds.

A study by Pater et al. (2004) sheds light on the interaction of children's representation of phonological knowledge with processing constraints in word learning. It has been shown that young infants are capable of perceiving subtle distinctions in phonological features such as VOT, that by twelve months of age they are quite adept at recognizing sounds of their native language, and that at fourteen months they can enlist their ability to perceive a minimal pair distinction in words that they already know, such as *ball/doll* (Fennell and Werker 2003). Furthermore, Stager and Werker (1997) observe that fourteen-month-old children respond with increased looking time (the novel, not habituated response) to a switch between nonsense [lɪf] and [nim] in a word-learning task. In this experiment the nonsense lexical items are paired in a video with two brightly colored objects (e.g. crown or ball) that move across the screen; the switch changes the audio sequence associated with the video image ([lɪf] + crown → [nim] + crown), while the habituation control continues with the same pairing. This procedure is used in subsequent experiments.

To determine how much sensitivity fourteen-month-olds show to more closely matched phonological features, Pater et al. (2004) test the same age group on three different types of minimal pairs, [bɪn]/[dɪn], [bɪn]/[pʰɪn], [dɪn]/[pʰɪn], the first segment of which differs by place of articulation and/ or voicing. What they find in all three tests is that the children fail to notice the distinction; that is, the toddlers give the habituated response even with a switch that should be comparable to [lɪf] and [nim]. The authors blame processing demands for these confusions, since children do use phonological contrast information in words that they have already acquired. "Before being fully acquired, contrasts are partially integrated into the phonological system, during which time their maintenance is affected by processing demands such as the establishment of sound and meaning pairings" (ibid., 399).

The word learning process is one which requires children to marshal additional cognitive resources beyond those of normal processing. They must balance several tasks as they learn vocabulary and perfect phonology during the second year of life. The result is a stage of language production that is not adult-like. As in the babbling stage, children favor vowels, glides, stops and nasals, which they substitute in simplifying fricatives, affricates and consonant clusters: *fis* for *fish*, *tap* for *chap* or *tuck* for *truck*. Clark (1995, 85) observes that children who mispronounce consonants are aware of the correct adult pronunciation, as evidenced by their displeasure at adult mimicry of their mistake. As they mature, they eventually add these consonants, liquids ([r,l]) and more unusual vowels, while extending their syllable structure in languages with complex syllables (English permits up to six consonants for a syllable, CCCVCCC as in *strands*). For example, in a study of Spanish and German children's acquisition of affricates and consonant clusters, Lleó and Prinz (1997) document the production of affricates (as initial [ts] in *Zug* "train") from about the middle of the second year. Consonant clusters, on the other hand, are not produced until the children establish their syllable onset structure at age 1;10 for German and 2;1 for Spanish.

The evidence from phonology development quite compellingly illustrates that babies are born with the ability to acquire the sound system of any language of the world, that they are prepared to do so even in utero, and that they use an inborn sensitivity to linguistic rhythm to begin discerning the maternal language. Their bias to look for certain phonological information is aided by the limited types of prosodic systems that typify the world's languages – stress-timed, syllable-timed and mora-timed. As babies mature, their experience with the ambient language(s) shapes their linguistic attention: at birth they can distinguish two non-native languages; by two months they no longer distinguish between non-native languages; and by six months they have established prototypical vowel systems for their native language. Their babbling of the second half of the first year also exploits their ambient phonology and prepares them to make use of the sounds to create a phonemic system that serves as the vehicle for the words that they begin to gain around one year of age.

2.2   Lexicon

The first year of life sees children move from the language-general ability of neonates to a language-specific focus, once they have narrowed down native phonology both perceptually and productively. The prosodic features of the language, such as rhythm, syllable structure and stress, help sorting input into words and larger syntactic units. The acquisition of words is not as simple as it might seem. This section discusses what is involved in learning the lexicon and then describes the scaffolding devices, both linguistic and non-linguistic, that children use.

2.2.1   The signifier and the signified

Ferdinand de Saussure described the linguistic "sign" as consisting of the *signifier* (*signifiant*), the word that a given language arbitrarily agrees on, and the *signified* (*signifié*), the abstract referent indicated by the signifier. Thus, the word *tree/arbre* represents a concept of tree-ness that speakers of English or French have as part of their linguistic knowledge; given the context, it may refer to a specific tree, a class of trees, a fictional tree or any tree that the human imagination could devise. The concept of tree-ness must be associated with the acoustic symbol representing it, an association of sound and meaning that is unmotivated in any predictable way. Saussure called this link the arbitrariness of the sign (*l'arbitraire du signe*), the lack of any systematic relationship between the signifier and the signified. The exclusiveness of vocabulary to a particular language – extracting away from language borrowings, language family shared roots, etc. – indicates how words are quintessentially language-specific, and must be learned one by one.

A simple associationist approach – whereby seeing a tree and hearing the word *tree* repeated – might account for word learning in the case of simple nouns, but the task becomes much more complex when we consider words like *see, would, over* or *him*. For example, *see* and *would* are verbs whose meaning must include the complements that they can take and their extended interpretations. Landau and Gleitman (1985) show that blind children acquire the same semantic and syntactic features for verbs of visual perception as do sighted children, even though they have had no physical experience to establish the verbs' meaning. The meaning of *over* might be physically obvious in *over the fireplace*, but becomes less straightforward in *jump over* (directionality) or *do over* ("repeat"). And why should *him* be used instead of *he, me* or *you* since all can be used to refer to the same individual? A final task that children must accomplish in gaining vocabulary is to learn contentful *lexical* categories such as *see* and *dog* and grammatical *functional* categories such as *the* and *-ing*. Word meaning is not self-evident, as the examples above indicate, and caregivers do not define new words, they simply provide imperfect examples to children.

Learning a word entails learning its possible meaning/reference, but also its phonological representation and its syntactic function. On the one hand, the learner is faced with a speech stream that does not segment words into individual units, but embeds them in utterances that concatenate words in an uninterrupted flow. Witness the ambiguous Jimi Hendrix lyrics "excuse me while I kiss the sky," which can also be interpreted as "excuse me while I kiss this guy." On the other hand, young children are equipped linguistically, cognitively and socially to pay attention to relevant aspects of the environment and the language they hear, while their interlocutors (often adoring parents) facilitate the task through child directed speech and social devices such as eye gaze or pointing (de Boysson-Bardies 1999; Bloom 2002). Children use prosodic cues to help segment the speech stream, semantic cues to help infer the syntax, and syntactic cues to help discern the meaning of words, strategies that are grouped under the rubric of *bootstrapping*. They are also able to make inferences on the basis of frequency and of social intentions, as they become more and more aware of the behavior of others in their environment.

2.2.2   *Bootstrapping*

The term bootstrapping refers to the exploitation of the learner's knowledge of one area of linguistic competence to facilitate acquisition of another area. *Prosodic* or *phonological bootstrapping*, which helps children to discern words, word order, syntactic constituents and subsequently syntactic category, is operative from birth in that infants process input in terms of the rhythmic structure of the ambient language. Adults segment the speech stream with the help of their knowledge of syntax, semantics and the real world, but rely quite a bit on language-specific rhythmic information (stress for English, syllables for French). Cutler and colleagues (1994, 1996, Cutler et al. 1992) have shown that adults persist in using their native rhythmic sensitivity for processing, even if the language in question does not conform to that rhythmic pattern; for example, French speakers use syllables for determining word boundaries in both English and French. They claim that this tendency is corroborated by studies of balanced bilinguals – with two first languages such as French and English from infancy – who use a single rhythmic strategy, rather than accessing two. A French–English bilingual uses either a stress-based or a syllable-based approach to processing both French and English, but does not develop a dual strategy for the two languages. While English speakers primarily use stress to segment, they do not ignore syllable structure entirely; rather, they make use of syllabic information later in the processing than do francophones (Segui and Ferrand 2002).

Given that rhythm sensitivity is set once and for all for a single language type during the first year, Cutler suggests that it is the early establishment of language-specific rhythm sensitivity that is key to helping infants learn to segment their ambient language in the second half of the first year. She points out (1996) that a connectionist approach predicting word boundaries on the basis of segment sequence probability cannot account for infant segmentation, whereas her explicit approach to segmentation accounts for both adults and infants.

During the second six months of life, babies use pauses, syllable length, distributional regularities and *phonotactic* patterns – the constraints determining which phonemes can be used sequentially, and what types of syllable structure are allowed in a given language – to parse words, phrases and clauses. The sensitivity of infants to native language pauses is demonstrated by Hirsh-Pasek et al. (1987) in an experiment with seven- to ten-month-olds. They observe head-turning to determine if the babies notice the difference between a narrative with normal pauses at syntactic boundaries (1) and a narrative whose pauses have been displaced to implausible locations (2), as these examples from the Cinderella story show.

(1) she had two stepsisters / that were so ugly
(2) she / had two stepsisters that were so / ugly

The children do indeed notice the difference, and they prefer the version where the pauses appear in the syntactic boundaries over the random placement of pauses. Similarly, experiments have shown that eight-month-olds are sensitive to distributional regularities, typical word shapes and phonotactic constraints (de Boysson-Bardies 1999; Guasti 2002; Hirsh-Pasek et al. 1996; Jusczyk 1997). Infants learn quickly to discern word stress patterns of the ambient language (French has final syllable stress, English prefers initial stress), and by the end of the first year they choose native language stress in listening preference experiments.

Infants are also able to distinguish between identical sequences of segments which differ in being word internal or external. For example, the sequence /kn/ is not a possible consonant cluster in English words, although it does exist in other languages such as Dutch, and it is licit in English at word boundaries as in *tack near the edge*. Experiments with nine-month-old Dutch and English learners listening to words with the same phonemes in the two languages show that each language group distinguishes the native language on the basis of phonotactic constraints since those differ in English and Dutch. English babies recognize that /kn/ could only correspond to a word boundary in English /k#n/, not a word initial cluster /#kn/. It appears then that infants make use of their implicit knowledge of phonotactic constraints to infer word boundaries; if they are unconsciously aware that /kn/ is not a licit sequence in English, then /tæknir/ cannot be a single word, but must have a word boundary between /k/ and /n/, /tæk/nir/. Frequency clearly plays a role since infants are sensitive to distributional regularities and become progressively more adept at recognizing native language over the course of the first year. Nevertheless, "the perceptual representation of words in children's early repertoire does not specify a sequence of phonemes but rather a sequence of more global, less analyzed units. These units no doubt depend on the structure of the language" (de Boysson-Bardies 1999, 118).

The babbling of one-year-olds overlaps with their first word productions, but their first words are but approximations of the adult versions. Demuth (1996) observes that the early productions may be ill formed segmentally (mispronunciation, consonant cluster simplification), syllabically (omission of weak syllables) and morphologically (lack of inflection), but that these words are prosodically well formed "minimal words," consisting of one binary foot (CVCV, CVV, or CVC). She argues convincingly that "children learning languages as different as English, Dutch, Sesotho, and K'iche' all have early sensitivity to the prosodic structure of words [...that] comes in part from Universal Grammar" (ibid., 181). The innate language program that children are born with helps them first to discern the prosodic pattern of their native language, then to attune their perception to its rhythm, and finally to allow them to translate their perceptual sensitivities to productive ones. Hirsh-Pasek et al. (1996)

conclude a volume on phonological bootstrapping with the observation that prosodic information furnishes important cues to children's lexical and syntactic development. Future studies, however, need "to examine how children use prosody in conjunction with syntactic, semantic, social and morphological cues" (ibid., 449).

The idea of bootstrapping was first suggested by Gleitman and Wanner (1982), who pointed out the advantages to the infant "innately biased" to treat prosodic segments as syntactic segments, and whose article led to studies of other varieties of bootstrapping that could help children once they had a phonological handle on the word. Pinker (1984, 1989, 1994a) advances the idea of *semantic bootstrapping*, the use of semantic properties such as the concept of "thing" or "action" to determine syntax. He suggests (1984, 39) that notions such as physical object, physical action, agent, "are available to the child perceptually and are elements of the semantic representation" to which language acquisition mechanisms are sensitive. Children infer syntax by first generalizing agent (semantic notion) to subject (syntactic role), then generalizing the canonical subjects (agents) to non-canonical subjects. They gain a handle on action verbs with agents (*Mary hits the ball*), and later extend the subject verb relationship to non-agentive verbs (*Mary receives a gift*). Pinker's bootstrapping proposal is not a monolithic engine driving lexical acquisition, but is a resource that integrates other kinds of bootstrapping and distributional inferences on the part of children. *Syntactic bootstrapping* (Gleitman 1990; Grimshaw 1994; Fisher et al. 1994) complements semantic bootstrapping in that information about the argument structure of verbs – the kinds of complements that they take – furnish the learner with certain aspects of the verb's meaning. The authors show that children are better at intuiting the meaning of unknown verbs when they have information on co-occurring nouns. Although advocating the importance of syntactic information, Gleitman (1990) emphasizes that children come to the acquisition of vocabulary with a smart perceptual system, sophisticated mental models and intuitive semantic notions, all of which work together to help them learn.

2.2.3   The path of word learning

The refinement of perceptual abilities of the first year is brought to bear by eleven-month-olds in their babbling, which is interspersed with what Vihman (1996, 130) calls protowords, "relatively stable child forms with relatively consistent use which *lack* any clear connection with the form + meaning unit of a conventional adult model." These protowords appear to serve the same function as consistent gestures used by children at this age. For example, her subject Deborah from nine to eleven months used the protoword [pwi] to indicate focused attention as a response to unfamiliar visitor, salient sound pattern (*baa baa*), or mother's return to room. From twelve to fifteen months it was replaced by [aha], [haha] with show/give gestures (p. 242). These "practice" words are phonetically consistent and partially correlated with recurring conditions, but they lack characteristics of true words, which must resemble adult forms in interpretation and distribution, and have consistent phonetic shape. Vihman (1996, 149–150) gives ten criteria for identifying true words, including determinative context, repeated use, match to adult form, consistency, and appropriateness. The developmental shift to true words represents a major cognitive leap. Suddenly, children are using symbols, starting with context-bound lexical items (and sometimes undergeneralizing to a particular item), but quickly moving to a more general reference to things or events that are displaced in time or space. The earliest instances of true words are often overgeneralized, for example using the term "dog" to refer to all domestic pets (Singleton 2000). Vihman (1996, 138) gives the example of an insightful moment for her young daughter fetching a toy monkey to compare it to a monkey picture in a book while repeating the Estonian word for monkey *ahv*. Similarly, relational words such as *allgone* and *more* often imply a comparison between two times, clearly a precursor to the semantics of verb tense.

One view of the course of word learning sees the early period as a virtually nonlinguistic stage of building a vocabulary of around fifty words, followed by a sudden acceleration at sixteen months, the "word spurt," during which children acquire ten to twenty words per day. Bloom (2002, 35) calls this view a myth, for he sees children's acquisition of words as a continuous process that builds on its own success. Ten-month-olds have a receptive vocabulary of thirty-five words, and one-year-olds begin using protowords which, albeit not adult-like in every way, still share many properties of true words. The increase in word learning after the fifty-word threshold is not, however, a spurt that characterizes a stage in L1A during the second and third years of life. Rough approximations of vocabulary acquisition (Table 2.1) indicate that "word learning typically reaches its peak not at 18 months but somewhere between 10 and 17 years" (ibid., 44).[1] Bloom suggests that initial word learning is influenced by the emergence of phonology, the development of conceptual abilities and increased

---

[1] Inferring the vocabulary numbers from various studies, Bloom gives these rather conservative approximations in various places in his book. Other scholars furnish different numbers; for example, Clark (1995, 21) says that 18-month-olds have 50–200 words and two-year-olds have 500–600, while de Boysson-Bardies (1999, 190) claims that 24-month-olds gain four to ten new words a day.

Table 2.1 *Rate of acquisition and median vocabulary (cf. Bloom 2002)*

Age	Rate of acquisition	Median vocabulary
12–16 months	0.3 words/day	6 words (12 months)
16–23 months	0.8 words/day	40 words (16 months)
23–30 months	1.6 words/day	311 words (24 months)
30 months-6 years	3.6 words/day	574 words (30 months)
6–8 years	6.6 words/day	10,000 words (6 years)
8–10 years	12.1 words/day	40,000 words (10 years)
10–17 years	7.8 words/day	60,000 words (17 years)

Table 2.2 *Relative production of nouns, verbs and other categories (age 10–18 months)*

	Nouns	Percentage	Verbs and others	Percentage
French	76	68.5	35	31.5
American	91	74.6	31	25.7
Swedish	74	67.9	35	32.1
Japanese	56	50.9	54	49.1

memory, while later learning is influenced by syntax, semantics and literacy.

Even at an early stage, children sort words into syntactic categories, with lexical categories dominating initially and functional ones being added much later. In English, children with fewer than fifty words first acquire nouns, a lexical category that constitutes a greater percentage of vocabulary items for most languages. There are nevertheless differences in proportional distribution that derive from both linguistic and cultural biases, as de Boysson-Bardies' data (1999, 185) in Table 2.2 indicates (the children are ten to eighteen months old). She attributes some of the differences to cultural traits such as French "hedonism," American "pragmatism and sociability," Swedish "activeness" and Japanese "aesthetic sense."

The predominance of nouns for American children is undoubtedly related to both linguistic and cultural aspects of the input. On the linguistic side, nouns tend to be more heavily stressed and often occupy final (more prominent) position in the sentence; on the cultural side, caregivers handle and talk about concrete objects in the immediate environment. For example, de Boysson-Bardies quotes Mary, mother of a fourteen-month-old: "Look at the cat. It's a cat. Look at the cat. Cat." Her daughter responds "[a]," to which Mary says "Good girl. You say 'cat, a cat.' Good girl." The author describes this as "the highly didactic tendency of American middle class mothers" (ibid., 180).

Bloom points out that the ability to learn words – which improves over the childhood years – is facilitated by *fast mapping* (Carey 1978), the process of learning a new word on the basis of minimal exposure. Bloom and his colleagues have done a number of experiments with children and adults to test retention (immediate, one week and one month) and trigger (linguistic or visual) for the learning of novel words for novel objects. Markson and Bloom (1997) found that 69 percent of adults and 65 percent of children taught a new word *koba* for a novel object were able to identify the object after one month. They also were able to identify the object given linguistic information ("the one my uncle gave me"). "In contrast, in the 'visually presented fact' task [applying a sticker to the object], adult performance was considerably diminished after a week and a month, and the three-year-olds and four-year-olds, taken together, showed a significant decline over time and did significantly worse than in the koba and uncle conditions" (ibid., 29). In other words, the linguistic triggers were far more effective than visual triggers for vocabulary acquisition. Bloom concludes that fast mapping applies to object names, that there is no critical period for this process, and that it applies not just to word learning, but to other linguistic information as well. While Bloom's studies investigate the relatively simple naming procedure of assigning a signifier to a novel object, they suggest that the fast mapping process can be adapted to the acquisition of the tens of thousands of words that the individual will eventually master.

2.2.4   Theories of word learning

Vihman's monkey anecdote highlights the role of caregivers in the emergence of communicative language, a role whose importance has been proven in a range of observational and experimental studies (de Boysson-Bardies 1999, Vihman 1996). Beginning with birth and continuing through childhood, parents engage their offspring in numerous social interactions that prepare them for society while teaching them about language. The mutual gaze, perhaps the first interactive milestone between parent and child, constitutes a basis for future joint attentional endeavors such as imitation (reciprocal behavior), turn-taking, pointing (the demonstrative gesture that indicates the here and now, in linguistic terms *deixis*) and parentese (infant directed speech or motherese). The expanded pitch range, rising intonation, exaggerated modulations, frequency of repetition, shorter utterances and longer pauses of *parentese* appeal equally to newborns and one-year-olds, and demonstrably aid the children in perceiving prosodic traits of their native language. While higher pitched speech may help infants in western European language situations, de Boysson-Bardies reminds us that not all cultures use special infant-directed language, and that after all, parents do not teach children language but simply furnish models; children learn language with or without parentese.

Social-pragmatic approaches to L1A emphasize the interrelationship of social-cognitive development and communicative skills, and the importance of joint attentional focus between child and adult. Carpenter et al. (1998) describe the infants' progression from sharing, to following, to directing others' attention and behavior; they see this as crucial to infant development and pivotal in the emergence of the *theory of mind*, the capacity of humans to attribute intentions to others that may differ from their own. In a number of studies focused on 19 to 24-month-olds' learning of novel words, Tomasello and colleagues have shown experimentally the importance of joint attentional focus. For example, in a study of two-year-olds that elicited the difference between noun (novel object) and verb (novel action), Tomasello and Akhtar (1995), after presenting repetitions of a novel word (*modi*) either with a novel object or with a novel action (applied to several different exemplars), asked the children "Show me modi." The children had been primed with familiar objects and actions – "Show me spoon, show me eat" – morphologically cueless sentences that are distinctly ungrammatical but were apparently comprehensible to the youngsters. With no morphological or syntactic cues the children responded with a verb (9/12) to novel action, or with a noun (7/12) to a novel object. In a second experiment it was the experimenter's intentions (as indicated by gaze and dialogue) that were manipulated. The authors conclude on the basis of these and other past experiments that pragmatic cues "are sufficient to enable young children to determine when an adult is intending to indicate a novel action versus a novel object" (ibid., 220).

Plunkett (1997) disagrees with the importance of joint attention, arguing instead that it is the interaction of general learning mechanisms that are sensitive to statistical regularities with a "richly structured environment" that drives linguistic development. This *associationist/connectionist approach* points out the importance of distributional information in the input for children's acquisition of perceptual distinctions in the first year, word learning in the second, and morphology development in the third. Associationists emphasizing the importance of "dumb attentional mechanisms" such as frequency and perceptual saliency, have done experiments that replicate social-pragmatic results using frequency or saliency of input (e.g. a glittery context) for novel object naming (Plunkett 1997; Hollich et al. 2000).

A compromise, the *emergentist coalition model* (Hollich et al. 2000), maintains that children need a combination of social interaction, distributional information and innate lexical constraints to implement vocabulary acquisition. The authors extend Markman's (1994) proposal of three word-learning principles guiding children's hypotheses – *whole object*, *taxonomic* and *mutual exclusivity* – to a two-tiered model with domain-general and domain-specific constraints. The whole object constraint biases children to assume a name goes with a whole object rather than a part of it; the taxonomic constraint leads them to infer a member of a set reading (grouping apples with oranges as members of the set "fruit") rather than an associative interpretation (apples with trees); mutual exclusivity means one object–one name. Although all three easily find contradictions in language – there are names of parts and wholes, associative words (*appletree*) and more than one name for an object – they have been shown to have a certain validity in experiments.

For the emergentist model, Tier 1 is operative in the first year to help children sort roughly through the input data in establishing the early vocabulary which is, as we have seen, both semantically and phonologically incomplete and unstable. The three domain-general principles are *Reference* (words map to objects), *Extendability* (word labels extend to a class of objects) and *Object scope* (words map to whole objects, not to parts of objects), biases that guide children to establish rudimentary vocabulary and to build the scaffold upon which the subsequent principles can be established. Tier 2 becomes operative as word learning accelerates for "children form ever more refined hypotheses about the way words work … as children learn more words, their word learning strategies change" (Hollich et al., 7–8). The three domain-specific principles are *Conventionality* (speech community agrees on terms), *Categorical Scope* (objects are categorized taxonomically) and *Novel name–nameless* (novel names map to unnamed categories), biases that build directly on Tier 1.

To evaluate these points, the researchers develop a new experimental model, the interactive intermodal preferential looking paradigm (*interactive IPLP*) through which they quantify child attention (looking at one of two objects) in response to manipulation of object saliency, social cues (eye gaze, object handling) and linguistic labels. In a series of experiments with novel word-objects, the authors test three age groups, 12-, 19- and 24-month-olds, manipulating the variables mentioned. Saliency, as exemplified by "interesting" (colorful, noisy) objects, is important to all age groups, but is the preferred factor for labeling only with the youngest group. Twenty-four-month-olds preferentially follow eye gaze when presented with a novel word applied to an uninteresting object. Twelve-month-olds are sensitive to social cues, but they only use them in conjunction with other factors such as salience. The authors suggest that twelve-month-olds begin to develop the Reference principle by associating words and objects, and that this principle evolves during the next year to become the abstract symbolic relationship at the basis of subsequent word learning. It is not, however, any signifier that can serve as an associative label for one-year-olds, as one experiment demonstrates: toddlers do not accept digitized noises as equivalent to words, even when trained with mechanical [boink, boink] in the same manner as with human lexical production. This discrepancy implies that children are primed to develop language and are sensitive to linguistic units; they are not simply associating repeated sounds of any sort with target objects.

The hybrid coalition approach brings together innate principles, social-pragmatics and associationism as follows (ibid., 18):

- Children are sensitive to multiple attentional, social and linguistic cues
- The weighting of cues changes over the course of development
- New principles progressively emerge as each earlier principle matures.

The empirical data presented thus far demonstrate these principles: children are sensitive to multiple cues and the weighting changes over time. The emergentist coalition approach provides an attractive model to account for the evolution of lexical learning from young infants' attention to prosody, through toddlers' attempts to master phonological shape and conceptual meaning of words, to children's ability to fast map new words to objects, actions, abstract concepts and grammatical morphemes, and finally to teenagers' ability to achieve more sophisticated vocabulary through literacy.

2.3   Syntax

Once children begin combining words, they embark on the production of syntax, the linguistic component allowing them to create sentences and longer discourse that can describe objects and events displaced in time and space. But before they reach the syntax production stage, they prepare their syntactic pathway in the second year of life – much as they prepared for phonological mastery during the first year – by setting the native language parameters for word order directionality and morphosyntactic structure. After this initial presyntactic period, the early syntactic period sees verb inflection being solidified; the final period involves setting of the major parametric differences that distinguish languages one from the other. Language is not isolated from other cognitive developments. For example, children have available, from about age two, linguistic markers of new information such as indefinite articles, but they make mistakes. The errors are caused by "difficulties for the children in evaluating the difference between their addressee's perception from their own in certain situations" (De Cat 2004, 124). There is an interaction of universal linguistic factors with cognitive maturation such as development of theory of mind.

2.3.1 Protosyntax

Children begin producing their first words around one year of age and spend the next twelve months adding to their lexical repertoire, sometimes using *unanalyzed chunks* such as *bye-bye* or *allgone* in the period known as the *holophrastic* or one-word stage. Around the age of two, children begin combining words into two or three word utterances that are *telegraphic* in style, very short and non-adultlike in not containing function words or grammatical endings. The length of children's sentences is measured in *mean length of utterance* or *MLU*. We have already seen that processing limitations restrict the young child, who balances phonology, semantics, articulatory gestures and sequencing of linguistic units by keeping utterances to a minimum. The telegraphic aspect of early syntax recalls the phonological simplifications of the first word period.

Before children begin putting words together, they must sort out the morphosyntactic properties that characterize their language as opposed to others, and how to sequence words. To investigate the comprehension abilities of pre-syntactic children, Hirsh-Pasek and Golinkoff (1996) develop the *intermodal preferential looking paradigm* (*IPLP*), the predecessor to the interactive IPLP described above. Rather than having a human facilitator, this design uses two television screens that the child turns his head to view. The youngster, who sits on a blindfolded caregiver's lap, is presented two video images on the two screens, one image that matches a linguistic stimulus (from a speaker between the screens) and one that doesn't match. Numerous trials show that the child spends more time looking at the matching screen, thus indicating that he understands the linguistic stimulus. A major advantage of this methodology for testing young children is that it requires very little effort on the part of the child, simply a head turn and gaze.

What do toddlers know about the syntactic constituents that make up a sentence – the noun phrase (NP) subject or the verb phrase (VP) predicate consisting of a verb plus direct object NP? Infants are sensitive to the prosodic characteristics that often correlate with constituent boundaries, even during their first year of life (Hirsh-Pasek et al. 1987). In an experiment testing children's ability to discern syntactic constituent structure, Hirsh-Pasek and Golinkoff (1996) explore the comprehension of varied direct objects with a single verb by thirteen- to fifteen-month-olds. One scenario involves a linguistic stimulus of a woman kissing some keys or kissing a ball, two unlikely events in the real world. The participants presumably hadn't encountered these sorts of events, so would be responding to the linguistic prompt that distinguishes the two direct object complements of the verb phrase, *keys* or *ball*. The video images contain keys and a ball in both versions, with the unkissed item saliently moving across the screen, to insure that children are not simply relying on saliency or presence of object on screen. The video images that match the linguistic stimuli average 2.72 seconds to the nonmatch 2.23 seconds, indicating that the infants are "predisposed to organize their input into packages of words that represent relationships" (ibid., 86). At this very young age the toddlers package VPs and match sentences to the correct image in their gazing.

To ascertain whether the children can understand English word order before they produce it, Hirsch-Pasek and Golinkoff conduct an investigation of comprehension abilities testing sixteen- to nineteen-month-olds (at the one- to two-word production stage) on sentences with a reversible subject and object. Using the same paradigm, the researchers test sentences such as "Look! Cookie Monster is tickling Big Bird!" with images of Cookie Monster either tickling or being tickled by Big Bird; these were balanced with Big Bird tickling Cookie Monster stimulus sentences (also *hug, feed* and *wash*). For all images both the muppets performed actions, so that if Big Bird tickled Cookie Monster, Cookie bounced up and down, and vice versa (to control for the saliency of action versus non-action). If the children were simply looking at their favorite Sesame Street characters, a random response would be expected. The researchers find that 75 percent of the children show more visual fixation on the linguistic match than on the nonmatch, indicating that the toddlers are using word order in the reversible sentences to match the audio prompt to the meaning.

These experiments show that pre-syntactic children are already aware of word order and constituent structure in the language they are learning, but push back to yet an earlier stage the problem of how toddlers come to this knowledge. Mazuka (1996) addresses the issue of how children infer the directionality of the language they are learning before they combine words, noting that once children produce two word sequences, they use the correct order. Children must then infer directionality before they begin producing telegraphic speech. For verb phrase directionality (and most other categories as well), English is head initial and right branching, while Japanese is head final and left branching (Figure 2.1).

Mazuka (1996, 327) suggests that infants learn to recognize the branching directionality of their native language by relying on prosodic cues during the first year. "If one assumes that young infants are predisposed to pay attention to particular acoustic cues (e.g. those that mark clause boundaries and branching direction), the difficulty [of setting syntactic parameters] will be significantly reduced."

Another prosodic property that can contribute to the infant's acclimation to the native syntactic categories and directionality is the difference

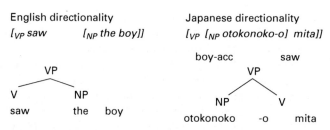

Figure 2.1 English and Japanese directionality

between lexical and functional categories (Selkirk 1996). While lexical category words are always stressed and unreduced in English, functional category words can appear in many guises – either a stressless weak form or a strong form. So, for example, the functional modal *can* (as in *can go*) is realized as stressed [kæn] or as unstressed [kən], but the lexical noun *can* (as in *tin can*) is always realized as [kæn], never as [kən]. The variability of phonological realization of functional categories is true cross-linguistically, with variants ranging from morphological form (French) to loss of high tone accent (Japanese), and often including the option of clitic realization (e.g. *n't* for *not* as in *didn't*). *Clitics* are unstressed function words like pronouns or negations that attach to fully stressed words. Selkirk suggests that children might exploit these differences to infer which words are lexical (always stressed) and which are functional (variable), differences that would focus them early onto the more prominent lexical words and give them a syntactic template in the alternation of lexical with functional in the speech stream.

While children predominantly acquire lexical words before function words, they show evidence of knowing about functional categories before regularly producing them. Gerken and colleagues (Gerken et al. 1990; Gerken 1996) have shown that two-year-olds, who do not consistently produce functional category determiners such as *the*, are impeded in a repetition task when *the* is missing. Thus, the children seem to have a representation of the determiner, even though they usually produce bare nouns, and they use the determiner in comprehension to help them parse the incoming sentence. The presence of unrealized functional categories is demonstrated in Romance languages (Italian, Spanish, Catalan) as well, for children in their second year produce prenominal vowels as kinds of proto-articles with their early one-word utterances (Bottari et al. 1993/94; Hawayek 1995; Lleó 2001). In these languages the obligatory article is a prenominal clitic that agrees in gender and number with the noun (e.g. Spanish *el-m libro* "the book," *la-f mesa* "the table"). The children's use of a proto-article indicates not only that they have a place holder for the functional category determiner, but also that they are learning the gender as part of the lexical information about the noun. Another study that corroborates the existence of functional categories in the proto-grammar of two-year-olds is by Demuth (1994), who notes cross-linguistic variability as a consistent characteristic of functional category realization in English and Sesotho. She argues that infants' sensitivity to prosodic factors such as stress and syllable structure lead them to infer functional categories (whose realization is vulnerable to destressing and reduction). "I demonstrate that the omission of auxiliaries, determiners, agreement morphemes, tense markers, and even pronominal subjects is part of a much larger phenomenon that characterizes unstressed, extrametrical syllables in general" (ibid., 131).

The non-adultlike telegraphic style of two-year-olds appears indeterminate, much as the first protowords of the previous year, but, just as the protowords have their predecessors in babbling, the bare nouns and missing auxiliaries of two-word utterances reveal an underlying comprehension of emerging language. By twenty-four months children have worked out the syntactic structure and morphosyntactic patterns of their native language and they are trying to break through the difficulties of producing it. All this while they are learning new vocabulary, perfecting their phonological production and developing language-boosting strategies that will permit them to gain the whole grammar perfectly within a few more years.

2.3.2   Optional infinitives and null subjects

Researchers responded to Chomsky's (1959) challenge to investigate first language acquisition in the following decades (Bloom 1970; Bowerman 1973; Braine 1971; Dale 1976; deVilliers and deVilliers 1979). Roger Brown (1973) made a major contribution to L1A, when he followed the progress of three young subjects, Adam, Eve and Sarah. His research group tape recorded two hours of mother–child speech every two weeks for up to two years (Klima and Bellugi Klima 2004 [1966]), resulting in transcriptions that are still a rich source of data. The earliest word combinations include adult-like phrases such as *all dressed, more toast, dry pants*; sentential sequences such as *look at this, mama come* and *see baby*; and inappropriate generalizations of "pivot" words such as *more* or *allgone* in *more sing* or *allgone outside* (once the door is shut) (examples from Goodluck 1991, 76). Although the productions are minimalist, word order is essentially correct – "children have a grammar that is incomplete, but already adapted to their language, on which later grammatical development is founded" (de Boysson-Bardies 1999, 201).

During the third year of life, when children are consolidating their ability to create sentences by using an inflected verb and a nominative subject, they show systematic acquisition patterns cross-linguistically. Let us consider English and French, whose mature grammars have a functional category Inflection that provides the verb with an anchor in time and space. A verb such as *eat* or *speak* is non-finite unless it has a finite tense (present, past) and a person (*I*, *you*) to ground it in a particular context. The sentence *She spoke* conveys the information that the speaking event took place in some past time and was performed by a single female. Both French and English mark tense and person Inflection on verbal elements, but they do so in slightly different ways. A sentence is represented graphically by a *tree*, which consists of projections of *lexical* heads (the "content words") – Noun Phrase (NP) and Verb Phrase (VP) – and *functional* heads (the "grammatical words") – Determiner Phrase (DP) and Inflectional Phrase (IP) – that contextualize the lexical nouns and verbs respectively. The descending lines of the trees are called *branches*, and the left branch of a projection contains its *specifier*. IP, the projection of the category I, must contain a correctly inflected verb (one that has inflection for tense and person), and it must match the verb with a nominative subject which is located in the left branch specifier of IP. The subject, selected by the main verb, is not initially in that position, however, but raises to the IP position from the specifier of VP position. For example, the verb *buy* requires a human subject and purchasable object, arguments that originate in the VP. The IP and subject DP in its specifier require the correct morphology of tense and nominative case to provide the grammatical context.

The trees depicted in Figures 2.2 and 2.3 demonstrate the implementation of relatively simple sentences in English and French, showing the differences between the two languages in their syntax. The necessity of positing the hierarchy in English is dictated by the position of negative *not*,

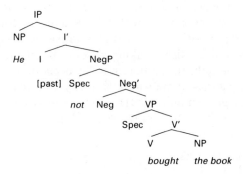

Figure 2.2 Phrase structure, English

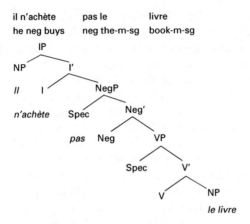

il n'achète   pas le   livre
he neg buys   neg the-m-sg book-m-sg

Figure 2.3 Phrase structure, French

which precedes main verbs, but follows auxiliaries (Emonds 1978; Pollock 1989) in English as in *he did not buy the book*, the negative version of *he bought the book*. The requirement of realizing the tense/agreement features of I necessitates a dummy auxiliary *do* to carry the features (*do*-support).

In English the main verb remains in the VP, while the I node carries tense inflection and checks the subject's nominative case; I may be filled by an auxiliary (*he has bought the book*). The placement of *not* shows that *bought/ buy* remain in VP since one can say *has not bought* or *did not buy*, but **bought not/*buy not* are ungrammatical. The verb *to be*, on the other hand, does raise to I as in *is not here*. In the Romance languages, in contrast, all inflected verbs and auxiliaries raise to I, as is demonstrated in Figure 2.3 *il n'achète pas le livre* for the French equivalent of *he doesn't buy the book*.

Pas is the main negator with *ne* often being deleted in the spoken language. In French the subject raises to the specifier of IP position as in English, but French does not use dummy auxiliaries such as *do*; instead, the verb itself is able to carry the tense/agreement features necessary for I, and the main verb raises to that position to the left of negative *pas*.

Once young French- and English-speaking children begin producing combinations of subject + verb, their utterances for a period of several months fall into two categories, those with a correctly inflected verb (3) and those with a root (English) or infinitival (French) form (4), termed *root infinitives* (Guasti 2002, Pierce 1992, Wexler 1994, 1996).

(3)   Inflected verbs
      a. we goed to the beach (Eve 2;2)
      b. didn't come out (Peter 2;1)
      c. moi, je tousse encore (Philippe 2;2) "me, I cough again"

   d. écris pas, moi (Philippe 2;2) "I don't write."
      write not me

(4)   Root infinitives
      a. no ride a bike (Peter 2;1)
      b. not Fraser read it (Eve 1;9)
      c. chercher   les crayons (Philippe 2;2)
         to look for   the pencils
      d. pas la poupée dormir (Nathalie 1;9) "the doll doesn't sleep"
         not the doll   to sleep

Root infinitives are characteristic of overt subject languages and have been documented in German, Dutch, Swedish, Danish and Norwegian (Rasetti 2000). In German, for example, children use the infinitival form -*en* as *Hubsauber putzen* "helicopter to clean" (Hamann 2002, 152) with the intention of saying that someone is cleaning the helicopter. In null subject languages, children acquire verbal inflection in a very early period and do not manifest the optional infinitive stage. For overt subject languages, this stage is known as the *Optional Infinitive* period since children use both sentence types optionally until they solidify use of verb inflection and nominative subject, usually by the age of three. Post-verbal negation always appears with inflected verbs in French and auxiliaries in English; preverbal negation accompanies root infinitives. Nominative subject clitics are mainly (96 percent) found with finite verbs in French (Pierce 1992), indicating the implementation of agreement between subject and inflected verb. Root infinitives have, in addition to null subjects, default pronoun (*me, moi*) or lexical NP subjects which often appear in the specifier of VP position (e.g. 4d). Root infinitives occur in declarative sentences, usually indicate present tense, do not appear in questions and are incompatible with auxiliaries (Déprez 1994; Guasti 2002; Wexler and Harris 1996). Root infinitives are then minimal syntactic predicates that show no functional morphosyntax of IP or the higher functional projection Complementizer Phrase CP; rather, root infinitives represent VP structures.

   Another characteristic of the period after the second birthday is the lack of an overt subject, a phenomenon that Rasetti (2000, 246) observes in her six French subjects at 88.7 percent for root infinitives and at 26.4 percent for finite verbs. The preponderance of null subjects with infinitival forms conforms to adult grammar, which prohibits overt subjects with infinitives (Wexler 1994), but the existence of null subjects with finite verbs cannot be explained by adult grammar.

   Various ways have been proposed to account for the null subjects, unraised verbs and infinitival morphology of the optional infinitive stage (e.g. Boser et al. 1992; Clahsen et al. 1993/1994; Hyams 1996; Radford 1990; Wexler 1994). Radford, for example, proposes a *discontinuity or weak continuity approach* that posits an early stage which has no functional categories (determiner, tense, complementizer); later, children's grammars mature to develop these categories. A more recent and perhaps the most comprehensive *continuity approach* is Rizzi's (1994, 2000) *truncation* hypothesis. Rizzi proposes that adult grammars contain the principle that the root clause of the sentence is CP (5), that is, that CP is the highest node projected to assure that the sentence contains a tensed verb, nominative subject in IP and discourse features in CP.

(5) Root = CP

The principle derives from Rizzi's idea of *categorial uniformity* requiring that all clauses have the same syntactic structure. The appearance of complementizers in embedded clauses (10) and interrogative/exclamatives in matrix (root) clauses (6) illustrate the elements that may fill the CP node.

(6) He asked [CP *if* / *whether* / *when* [IP Mary had seen Bill.

(7) a. [CP *When did* [IP Mary see Bill?
     b. [CP *Never have* [IP I seen such a sight!

Adult speech may sometimes contain elliptical syntax, a fact that Rizzi accounts for by a *principle of structural economy* ("use the minimum of structure consistent with well-formedness constraints," Rizzi 2000, 288). Rizzi's ideas mesh with Weissenborn's (1994, 216) idea of local well-formedness requiring that "the representation of any utterance of the child is locally well formed with respect to a representation of the adult grammar." In overt subject languages a style such as diary prose (8a) – which permits null subjects – may allow the root to be IP rather than CP (Haegeman 2000), as can be seen by the ungrammaticality of null subjects embedded under a CP root (8b).

(8) a. Cried yesterday morning.
     b. *I said [CP that [IP cried yesterday morning.

   According to Rizzi, "the issue of categorial uniformity does not arise in the initial period ... in that phase, structural economy is not countered by any problem of categorial uniformity" (ibid., 289). The infinitival VP (with null or VP internal subject) or the null subject IP are options. The principles underlying the truncation proposal reasonably account for child and adult data and developmental trajectory.

2.3.3   *Parametric variation*

Babies are born with the ability to begin learning any language in which they are immersed and by one year have focused on its rhythmic structure, morphophonological features and syntactic directionality. During the second year they first build up a lexicon and then begin minimally combining words in keeping with the constraints of the native syntax. While they are working to flesh out the morphology of the language and to put together sentences that are longer than two or three words, they have already determined the major parametric settings that distinguish the syntax of their language from other tongues. All languages embrace similar syntactic categories – lexical noun, verb, adjective and preposition; functional complementizer, tense, inflection, determiner – and use the clause as the core syntactic structure. Languages vary in morphosyntactic detail (e.g. whether nouns have gender and agreement) and in the way that words can combine, but the variations or parameters are systematic and simple, often binary (Atkinson 1992).

Three major parameters of subject–verb placement, studied extensively in western European languages and illustrative of these points, are the null subject (9), verb raising (10), and verb second (11) parameters.[2]

(9) null subject
   a. [Yo] quiero una manzana. "I want an apple." (Spanish)
   b. *(I) want an apple. (English)
   c. Quiero yo una manzana. "Want I an apple."

(10) verb raising
   a. Je (ne) veux (pas) la pomme. "I (do not) want the apple." (French)
   b. I want (*not) the apple. I do not want the apple. (English)
   c. Ils veulent tous/absolument la pomme.
   d. They all/definitely want the apple.

(11) verb second
   a. Ein Buch kaufte Johann. "John bought a book." (German)
   b. Johann kaufte ein Buch. "John bought a book."
   c. *A book bought John. (English)
   d. John bought a book.

Null subject languages such as Spanish or Italian allow the subject to be unexpressed and inferred from the verb morphology or other features that can identify the null constituent (9a). A clustered characteristic is the possibility of a VP internal subject (9c). Overt subject languages such as English, French or German require an explicit subject in every sentence (9b). Verb raising is characteristic of the Romance languages, which

---

[2] Other parameters that have been examined in the L1A context are pronominal binding (Chien and Wexler 1990, Avrutin and Wexler 1992, McKee 1992, Avrutin and Thornton 1994) and WH movement (Penner 1994, Thornton and Crain 1994, Guasti 2000, Hamann 2000).

require all verbs to raise to an inflection node above negation (10a), adverbs and quantifiers (10c), whereas English prohibits raising of lexical verbs (10b, d). The placement of negation, adverbs and quantifiers is seen as a clustering property of verb raising. Germanic languages such as Dutch, German, Norwegian and Swedish require the verb to raise in matrix clauses to the second position in the CP, the first one being occupied by some other constituent (*ein Buch* in (11a) and *Johann* in (11b)). The verb second structure exists in English only in questions and exclamations, while declarative sentences are subject-verb-object (S-V-O, 11d).

Infants are sensitive to the setting of their native language for these parameters from their first word combinations. For example, Valian (1991) in a study of American and Italian children aged 20–24 months found that even at the two-word stage, the English-speaking children used lexical and pronominal subjects twice as often as Italian children who were already sensitive to the optionality of subjects in their language. The richness of verbal person marking – often linked to the possibility of null subjects whose identity is licenced by verb inflection – is early acquired in null subject languages such as Spanish, Catalan and Italian (Grinstead 2000, 2004; Guasti 1993/1994; Hyams 1986; Pizzuto and Caselli 1992). Children learning these languages do not go through an optional infinitive stage, but rather, from the age of twenty months on, they acquire conjugational marking that permits them to create minimal subjectless sentences with a more fully articulated functional structure than root infinitives. They begin by mastering singular morphology and later gain plural persons (Guasti 2002; Mueller Gathercole et al. 1999), but are generally quite accurate in their choice of person ending.

As we have seen, children are sensitive to the word order of verb raising, consistently using only inflected verbs and auxiliaries in the inflectional position, while allowing truncated VP syntax with infinitival forms (Déprez and Pierce 1993, 1994; Hyams and Wexler 1993). They use explicitly nominative forms (e.g. clitic subjects in French, *I*, *he* in English) only with inflected raised verbs or auxiliaries, and they use root infinitives only in the VP environments, not IP (e.g. never with auxiliaries) or CP (e.g. not with questions). Infinitives are found consistently with preverbal negation, while inflected verbs are found with postverbal negation in French and English. Although youngsters learning overt subject languages do not acquire correct verbal morphology in as short a time as those learning null subject languages, they nevertheless are sensitive to the syntactic structure of the sentence, the necessity of raising verbs or auxiliaries and the agreement of subject with inflected verb.

Germanic languages require that the inflected verb be located in the second structural position in the sentence (V2), just as the inflected

Table 2.3 *Finiteness versus verb placement in German data from Andreas (2;1)*

	+Finite	Percentage	−Finite	Percentage
V2	197	97	6	3
Verb final	11	23	37	77

auxiliary or modal is placed in English questions. These two positions are located in the highest functional projection in the sentence, Complementizer Phrase or CP. In the question *How many apples did he eat?* the WH phrase *how many apples* occupies first position (the specifier of CP) while the auxiliary *did* occupies second position. In German, nonfinite verbs and subordinate clause verbs are in sentence final position. Children learning Germanic languages in the optional infinitive stage produce clauses with root infinitives (12) in final position and clauses with inflected verbs (13) in second position (Ingram and Thompson 1996; Weissenborn 1994; Whitman 1994), as these examples in German show (Poeppel and Wexler 1993).

(12) S[ch]okolade   holen (Andreas 2;1) "I/you get [the] chocolate"
     chocolate   get-INF

(13) a. Da is[t] er (Andreas 2;1) "He is here"
        here is he
     b. Das macht der Maxe nicht (Simone 2;1) "This, Max does not make"
        this makes the Maxe not

Poeppel and Wexler calculate the distribution of two-year-old Andreas' verb forms (Table 2.3), noting a strong correlation between position and finiteness of the verb.

Clahsen's (1988) discussion of L1A of German V2 and inflectional morphology demonstrates well the linked development of the two phenomena. In two early stages children show some variability in word order and in inflectional mastery of the verb, particularly of the second person singular ending *-st*, which does not appear in the earliest stages. His longitudinal data demonstrate that subsequently "the acquisition of the verb-fronting rule for main clauses developmentally co-varies with the attainment of the (subject–verb) agreement system of German. The adult agreement system may be said to be finally attained in Stage III ... The characteristic feature of Stage III is the emergence of the inflectional formative *-st*" (Clahsen 1988, 55).

Children learning V2 languages are sensitive to the contingency between finiteness and verb raising to C and already conform to the syntactic patterns of the matrix clauses of their language, just as children learning null subject languages are sensitive to the importance of verb inflection and the optionality of subjects. English learning children discover the necessity of *do*-support while French learning children raise the main verb to I with correct tense/person inflection. At an early age (eighteen months) toddlers who have but a few words to produce are able to comprehend accurate word order and lexical/functional category distinctions, thanks in large part to their acuity of parsing the incoming speech for prosodic qualities. Once they begin combining words at two years they have established correct directionality and systematically and accurately distinguish VP morphosyntax from IP and CP morphosyntax.

2.4   Morphology

Brown (1973, 270ff.) observed that Adam, Eve and Sarah showed a good deal of overlap in the order of their acquisition of the basic grammatical morphemes of English. Although their consistent (90 percent for three sessions) use of a given morpheme varied slightly from child to child, they generally gained present progressive -*ing* before past irregular (e.g. *went*), before third person regular -*s*, before past regular -*ed*. Uncontractible copula and auxiliary (*is, has*) were acquired before contractible ones, although the latter were probably more frequent in the input. Brown (ibid., 272) observes "the developmental order of the fourteen morphemes is quite amazingly constant across these three unaquainted American children."

Children appear to gain morphological competence in tandem with syntactic competence, although the match is not inextricably linked. In overt subject languages children persist in using nonfinite verbs alongside finite verbs for a period of several months, indicating that the mature syntax is not achieved overnight. In null subject languages, verbal morphology and adult-like use of null subjects are acquired very early, but a causal relationship between null subjects and inflection can't be established because in overt subject languages children also use null subjects. In the nominal domain, gender–number agreement of determiners and adjectives in Romance is often linked to the licencing of null nouns as *el rojo [pro]* "the red one" in Spanish *noun-drop*. Snyder et al. (2001) note the potential link between Spanish rich nominal marking and noun-drop developmentally. This section looks at two examples of L1 morphology acquisition in languages with explicit inflection – gender in the determiner phrase and tense-person agreement in the verbal domain – and then discusses a theoretical framework for explaining morphology development.

2.4.1   Nominal gender and verbal inflection

Two developmental areas that are representative of young children's acquisition of inflectional syntax are the Noun Phrase and Verb Phrase. Even in the second year, toddlers learning Romance languages – which have masculine–feminine noun class gender distinctions and require agreement of the determiner and adjective with the noun – use prenominal vowels as proto-articles, indicating the presence of a functional category whose gender is part of the lexical information about the noun (Bottari et al. 1993/94; Hawayek 1995; Lleó 2001). In mature Spanish, articles and adjectives agree in gender and number with the noun (e.g. *el-m libro-m rojo-m* "the red book," *la-f mesa-f blanca-f* "the white table"), so even in their earliest productions Spanish-speaking children begin to distinguish masculine from feminine. López-Ornat (1997) and Snyder et al. (2001) describe the earliest period of noun phrase (NP or Determiner Phrase, DP) development, and Pérez-Pereira (1991) investigates gender acquisition by children four to eleven years of age. These examples of Spanish gender are language-specific, since gender may be realized quite differently (or not at all) in different languages.

The earliest productions, which are limited to one or two words, do not include adjectives and often omit determiners as well. López-Ornat's study of a single child María covers age 1;7 to 2;1, during which time she observes a marked decrease in null determiners (43 percent to 8 percent) and increase in overt determiner (2 percent to 71 percent) with the remainder comprising nouns with prenominal vowels. Snyder et al., who examine María's later productions and those of Koki (1;7–2;2), find "clear evidence for knowledge of the gender and number marking on Spanish determiners" (ibid., 164) with statistically significant accuracy by 2;1 for María and 2;2 for Koki. At this age both girls are using correctly agreeing adjectives, illustrated in (18)–(19).

(14) María
    a. co[n] el pepe male, sabes "with the-m-sg bad joe-m-sg, you know" (2;1)
    b. ahora viene ot[r]a chiquitita "now comes another-f-sg tiny one-f-sg" (2;3)
    c. mira, a unos pequeños "look, some-m-pl small-m-pl ones-m-pl" (2;3)

(15) Koki
    a. [l]as medias coloradas "the-f-pl red-f-pl stockings-f-pl" (2;1)
    b. el oso chiquitito "the-m-sg little-m-sg bear-m-sg" (2;5)
    c. el pelito ve[r]de "the-m-sg green-m-sg hair-m-sg" (2;5)

The masculine is correctly used in (14a, c) and (15b, c) and the feminine in (14b), (15a), with singular and plural (14c), (15a) also accurately marked. The children learn the nouns with the determiners and learn gender as a morphophonological trait. The examples cited show phonological reduction, but not of the crucial inflectional markers.

Spanish speakers continue to acquire vocabulary throughout their lives and must learn the gender of each new noun as they encounter it. Psycholinguistic studies indicate that gender (as opposed to number) is treated as intrinsic to the noun, and that gender concord is accessed to facilitate processing (Friederici et al. 1999; Grosjean et al. 1994; Schrieffers and Jescheniak 1999). To determine what clues are used in acquiring the gender of new vocabulary items, Pérez-Pereira (1991) conducts an experiment with 160 Spanish children (four to eleven years of age) to whom he presents twenty-two nonsense nouns with varying clues to gender, *extralinguistic* (male/female), *morphophonological* (masculine -*o*, feminine -*a* suffixes) and *syntactic* (determiner and adjective agreement). The children perform most accurately when there is a convergence of cues, but pay more attention to morphophonological form than to natural gender in cases of conflicting clues. The older children note that syntax can override phonology (e.g. *el programa* "the program" which is masculine but has -*a* ending) and then learn to rely more on agreement as a clue. Pérez-Pereira concludes that "it is mainly intralinguistic information that Spanish children use to establish the gender of nouns and hence, the agreement of adjectives with nouns." (ibid., 584) His findings also support the idea that children use a coalition of cues to help them acquire language.

A second example that demonstrates acquisition of morphology is tense/agreement (person) inflection which is gained by children from the second to third year. Children learning a null subject language master singular persons earlier than plural, and learn person inflection much earlier than children learning overt subject languages, although evidence from several languages indicates that two-year-olds already use inflection to some degree (Legendre et al. 2002). Brown (1973, 271) observes that Adam, Eve and Sarah master present progressive and past tense before third person present (90 percent accuracy over three speech samples), a dichotomy between tense and agreement confirmed by more recent studies (Ingham 1998; Legendre et al. 2002). In both French and English, children acquire tense morphology before accurate person agreement, a sequence that is also true for children with specific language impairment (Paradis and Crago 2001).

2.4.2   Words and rules

How do children acquire morphology? Investigating this question in English, Berko [Gleason] (2004 [1958]) tests 80 four- to seven-year-olds on their ability to add plural, past tense and progressive to nonsense words such as *wug, gutch, loodge*. Using the responses of twelve adult controls as comparison, Berko [Gleason] finds that the first grade children match the adult answers at better than 90 percent for simple final consonants (*wug, lun, tor, zib*), indicating that the children have developed unconscious rules for regular plural, past or progressive in dealing with new words. Overall the first graders (six- to seven-year-olds) perform significantly better than the younger children, but both groups have difficulty in forming the plural of sibilant final words such as *niz, kazh* and *gutch*. Although 99 percent of the first graders could form the plural of *glass, glasses*, only 39 percent created the parallel *tasses* for *tass*, indicating that "they do not as yet have the ability to extend the /-əz/ allomorph to new words, even though it has been demonstrated that they have words of this type in their vocabulary" (ibid., 263). The example also indicates the importance of lexical exemplar learning as a preliminary stage to rule governed morphology. Just as two-year-olds first acquire individual lexical items before generalizing a syntactic pattern, six-year-olds acquire a lexical plural before generalizing the morphophonological plural rule for words ending in a sibilant. Another child–adult difference is the treatment of irregular verbs as evidenced by the nonsense *gling*: over 80 percent of the first graders provided the regular *glinged*, whereas 75 percent of the adults provided *glang* or *glung*. Berko [Gleason] notes that the children "could not be expected to use this pattern since we could not demonstrate that they had the real form *rang* in their repertory" (ibid., 272).

Subsequent work in morphology has supported the idea of children acquiring rule governed inflections alongside irregular forms that are either rote memorized (*go, went*) or members of a mini class of irregulars (*ring-rang*). Brown (1973, 274) uses this framework to describe the mean order in which grammatical morphemes are learned by his young subjects: present progressive, *in/on*, plural, past irregular, possessive, uncontractible copula, articles, past regular, third person regular, third person irregular, uncontractible auxiliary, contractible copula, contractible auxiliary. The early acquisition of the past tense of irregular verbs precedes the establishment of a regular past rule using *–ed*, which may then be generalized to irregular verbs in *goed, falled* or *holded*, a pattern of development known as a *U curve* (the children eventually regain the correct irregular past). Although plural, possessive and third person verb marking all use the same suffix realized the same way /-z/-/-s/-/-əz/, children clearly perceive them as syntactically and semantically distinct since they are acquired at differing rates. The mastery of uncontractible copula (*is*) and auxiliary (*have*) before contractible (-*'s*, -*'ve*) reminds us that young children learn to parse the rapid (contracted) input, extract the crucial information and then reconstruct the morphosyntax. The production lag between uncontractible and contractible may be attributed to the limited processing powers of the young child.

Rumelhart and McClelland (1994 [1986]) propose an alternative to the notion of implicit morphological rules in a parallel distributed processing (*PDP*) model making use of a pattern associator network which learns the relationship between a base verb form (input) and the target past-tense form compared to its output. When the output is correct, nothing changes, but if the output is incorrect the model changes the weighting of its connection strengths. "Our simple learning model shows, to a remarkable degree, the characteristics of young children learning the morphology of the past tense in English. We have shown how our model generates the so-called U-shaped learning curve for irregular verbs and that it exhibits a tendency to overgeneralize that is quite similar to the pattern exhibited by young children" (ibid., 465–466). Their influential study – which has inspired a range of responses (e.g. Orsolini et al. 1998; Pinker 1994b; Pinker & Prince 1988) – shows that a frequency based connectionist model can reproduce both the end result (the implicit rule-like behavior) and the pattern of acquisition, although – often by their own admission – the model is not similar to human language or its acquisition in several respects. The input received by the model is always correct, consistent and carefully structured (first training on the ten high frequency irregulars, then on the 410 medium frequency mostly regular, and finally on the 86 low frequency), whereas children never receive input so carefully packaged. The model produces a number of guesses that are distinctly non-human, such as past form *membled* for *mail*, and mini regularizations such as past *crang/crung* for novel *cring*. Citing Berko [Gleason], the authors see their model's deficiencies as no greater than those of "native speakers of comparable experience" (ibid., 465); however, contrary to their citation, the *cring* response is not characteristic of "comparable" children learning morphology, but rather of the adult controls that Berko [Gleason] tested. Finally, the term "simple learning model" is questionable given the elaborate programming, adjustment and idealized input that are required to make it work.

Pinker (1999) combines the notion of rule-like learning, rote learning and probabilistic learning in his words and rules model that posits a dual mechanism for storage and processing of morphology. Although he rejects the PDP model as a unitary device, he incorporates some of the ideas put forth by Rumelhart and McClelland in creating a hybrid model. Noting that response time reactions to regular and irregular verbs in English differ according to frequency, he proposes that regular verbs are handled by rules that apply across the board while irregular verbs are "listed" separately and accessed in relation to their frequency. His experiments have shown that subjects respond in the same amount of time to high and low frequency regular verbs such as *walk* or *balk*, but that they respond more quickly to high frequency (*go-went*) irregulars than to low frequency ones (*smite-smote*). Taking into account mini-series of irregulars such as vowel alternations in *swing-swang*, the model can account for storage, processing and acquisition. The dual mechanism model has been applied to other languages (Clahsen et al. 2002), and has been substantiated by neuro-imaging studies showing distinct neural responses to regular as opposed to irregular morphology (Jaeger et al. 1996).

2.5 Conclusion

Native language acquisition, whose core schedule lies in the period from birth to four years, requires input from the ambient language; draws on innate predispositions at every stage; exploits linguistic, pragmatic, social and environmental scaffolds; uses prosodic, semantic, syntactic and lexical bootstrapping; calculates frequency and saliency of input; and completes the process by creating native competence in grammar. Once the phonology and morphosyntax are adult-like and processing has become more automatic – that is, once they have achieved ceiling competence in their native tongue – older children continue to gain vocabulary, a capacity that continues to adulthood.

An anecdotal observation of a toddler speaking to his mother serves to illustrate the language acquisition process of young children. This 2½-year-old asked his mother for a snack, a simple request that reveals much of the complex nature of the process described in this chapter:

Boy: *Me want dat, me want dat.*
Mother puts pieces of fruit and crackers on plate
Boy: *No, I don't want cwackers.*

A casual observer would probably find nothing unusual about the exchange, but these few words demonstrate a remarkable window into a child's acquisition of English. Within less than a minute he produces both a sentence with adult-like syntax, using auxiliary *do*, correctly placed negation *n't* (in contracted form, no less) and nominative subject pronoun *I*; and a double repetition of a root infinitive uninflected verb *want* with default pronoun *me*. The child has a good handle on the phonology of English, but is still working on fricative *th* /θ/ and liquid /r/ in initial consonant clusters.

During his first year of life, we know he narrowed down his phonemic inventory from all the world's languages to only the sounds used in English, and he began practicing those sounds in babbling. Tuning in to the rhythmic structure of English (as opposed to the other languages he heard occasionally), he began to deduce the morphosyntax that he would need to be able to speak. In his second year, he began acquiring single words – at first not quite accurate and poorly articulated – and when he had a critical mass he began combining them. Having already figured out the word order of English long before he could say much, his early combinations conformed to most syntactic patterns of his language, and he was also sensitive to the functional words that constitute the grammar. Now in his third year, he persisted in using the root infinitival truncated VP syntax alongside fully inflected and correctly ordered sentences. The burden of online processing – automatic and incredibly rapid for the adult – is still a challenge for two-year-olds who must search their limited vocabulary, refine correct pronunciation, create morphosyntactically accurate combinations and try to assemble more than two or three words. It's little wonder that they resort to minimalist *me want dat* in the optional infinitive stage!

What can typical development tell us about critical periods? In the next chapter we see variations of organismic system and environmental input that shed light on onset, duration and terminus of L1A.

3 All in good time: a window of opportunity for first language acquisition

3.0 Introduction

A satirical piece in the *New Yorker*, "Talking chimp gives his first press conference," parodies trained primates, the media, the scientific community and a number of other institutions. "Hello? Can everyone hear me? Anyone? Check, check. Check, one two. Is this thing on? Not the microphone – I mean my Electronic Larynx Implant device . . . The development of the ELI was a long and arduous process, and there were more than a few times – usually after being shot with a tranquillizer dart and then waking up hours later with excruciatingly painful bleeding stitch holes in my neck and chest regions – when I wasn't sure if it was worth it. But I guess it was, because here we are today, in this beautiful conference room at the Sheraton" (Simms 2005, 44). The humor of this monologue derives not so much from the reportorial scientific discourse or the monkey-business of the speaker (whose preoccupations are kibbles, orange wedges and bodily functions), but rather from the irony of our closest relative's inability to produce fluent language. Trained primates have learned vocabulary such as *red toy* or *orange*, and might be able to communicate (with signs) "hello" or "check, check," but they could never articulate the complex syntax, temporal displacement and sophisticated vocabulary of the first full sentence. Our human physical needs for water and food are quite similar to those of chimps, but our mental capacities are worlds apart, mainly because other primates are incapable of learning a first language under any circumstances.

Unlike chimps, under normal circumstances children by the age of four years have mastered their native morphosyntax, phonology and core vocabulary (Paradis 2004), even if born prematurely (Menyuk et al. 1995) or if acquiring two first languages (Paradis and Genesee 1996, 1997). Chapter 2 has demonstrated the universal sequencing of first language acquisition that begins before birth and drives the infant to gather language information from the environment through all means possible. The baby's sensitivity to prosodic characteristics of her language leads her to fix settings for phonology and morphosyntax before even starting to produce words, while the toddler's use of linguistic, social, and cognitive bootstrapping allows her to enrich vocabulary and to select the correct grammar for the native tongue. Research in L1A has certainly supported Lenneberg's first argument for a critical period, the regularity of onset and universal pattern of language development.

This chapter further explores the question of whether there is a sensitive period for first language acquisition, looking at Lenneberg's arguments and additional empirical cases that test the Critical Period Hypothesis, for which the criteria are:

- What is the organismic system?
- What is the environmental input?
- What maturational threshold marks the onset?
- What is the duration of the developmental period?
- Does the terminus mark an irreversible change after which the input no longer has effect?

In the case of normal L1A the organismic system is the human infant's brain, which undergoes exponential growth in the first years of life and which at birth has had only limited auditory input of language, rendering its innate genetic endowment obviously crucial. The environmental input is simply the ambient language that is perceived by the child during the first years of life, essentially beginning at birth (the maturational threshold marking the onset). Some scholars such as Bortfeld and Whitehurst (2001, 175–176) emphasize the role of maturation in language development, noting "to the extent that language develops in a lockstep maturational progression that requires little or no interaction with the environment, an inquiry into periods of special sensitivity to environmental stimulation is pointless." Their perspective is indeed perplexing given the crucial role of the environment acknowledged by scholars of all persuasions, but it highlights the importance of the genetic endowment. The core period for the development of grammar is principally birth to five years; vocabulary continues to be added throughout life. The notion of irreversible change – if it applies at all – could only hold of selected aspects of language such as phonology or morphosyntax.

This chapter looks at cases in which the organismic system or the environmental input is altered, thus modifying the onset, maturation period and terminus. The initial section looks at L1A in exceptional circumstances, individuals who have Down Syndrome, Williams Syndrome and specific language impairment (SLI, Rice 1996). The evidence supports Lenneberg's dissociation of language from other cognitive attributes and points to an innate predisposition to learn grammar even with impoverished cognitive ability or input. The second section documents the forbidden experiment, deprivation of children isolated from human linguistic input during several years of their young lives (Curtiss 1977; Itard 1801; Skuse 1993). The third section explores the development of language of deaf children who, if exposed early to signed language, acquire manual signing with the same pattern and rate as hearing children do spoken language (Emmorey 2002). Deaf individuals also provide examples of delayed exposure to language and hence test the notion of a sensitive period through a systematic variation of age of onset (Newport 1994). The last section examines language "creation" by children developing creole languages (Bickerton 1981, 1990; 1995, DeGraff 1999).

Generally, there are two theoretical camps that reject the notion of maturational dimensions to L1A, the associationists who see all learning (including L1A and L2A) as a function of connectionist network establishment, and the social interactionists who see interaction with the environment as the main driver of learning (L1 and L2). These scholars subscribing to unitary learning believe "direct evidence in support of the critical period for L1 acquisition is thin and based on theoretical arguments and analogy to other well-explored developmental processes, such as visual development in the cat" (Hakuta 2001, 194). They attribute deficits of late L1 learning more to sociocultural and input factors than to maturational causes. The previous chapter has borne out the value of input frequency and social interaction (among other external influences) to the acquisition of L1, but it has also underlined the importance of innate genetic predispositions and maturational patterns, advocating a partnership of factors in L1A. This chapter confirms a biological dimension for complete L1A since late acquisition results in deficient native grammar. Optimal onset of L1A is birth, but it may extend to six years of age for relatively normal acquisition. The apparent maturational factor underlines de Boysson-Bardies' (1999, 91) observation that "the evidence suggests, then, that there are critical periods for certain linguistic aptitudes. These critical periods are not a property of growth as such, but they do reveal the loss of plasticity that occurs when neuronal connections become specialized."

3.1 L1A in exceptional circumstances

Lenneberg used the example of *Down Syndrome (DS)* children's eventual acquisition of language to highlight the non-dependence of L1A on cognition, given the impaired cognitive but normal language abilities of these individuals. Subsequent research has partially borne out Lenneberg's contention, but has also shown that DS children do not show a uniform path of acquisition or complete mastery of their language's morphosyntax

(Chapman 1995). Another group of cognitively deficient individuals, those with *Williams Syndrome (WS)*, more clearly manifest the dissociation of language and cognition and thus support selective preservation of language as opposed to other higher cognitive functions (Bellugi et al. 1993). Bates et al. (1995, 145), who do not subscribe to a modular approach, point out that "these contrasts between Down Syndrome and Williams Syndrome provide an important challenge to interactive theories of language and cognition and appear at first glance to provide considerable support for the autonomy of language from other cognitive systems." Another area of exceptional L1A, *specific language impairment (SLI)*, supports a dissociation of grammar from cognition. SLI is a heterogeneous disorder characterized by delayed language acquisition by otherwise cognitively normal children who show particular difficulty with the grammatical elements of language such as inflectional morphology and function words (Oetting and Rice 1993; Rice 1996). This section explores each of these populations of language acquirers.

3.1.1 Down Syndrome and Williams Syndrome

Lenneberg (1967, 155) adduced evidence from L1A by Down Syndrome children to support his claim that puberty marked the terminus of the critical period, for his subjects' "progress in language development was only recorded in children younger than fourteen . . . The observation seems to indicate that even in the absence of gross structural brain lesions, progress in language learning comes to a standstill after maturity." Although his conclusion implies that the acquisition process cannot be delayed beyond puberty and then follow a normal course, subsequent studies have shown that language development does continue through the teenage years in DS sixteen- to twenty-year-olds (Chapman 1995, 651–652; Rondal 1993, 169).

Down Syndrome is a condition caused by an extra copy of a segment of chromosome 21, characterized by cognitive delay and specific physical features, some of which contribute to a high mortality rate (20 percent in the first two years of life) and may impede speech. Marveling that DS children succeed in L1A, Rondal (1993, 166–168) underlines the "number and severity" of factors that hinder acquisition: mechanical problems in articulation with abnormal mouth cavity, tongue size, soft palate and respiratory apparatus; sensory deficiencies (60 percent show some hearing impairment); and reduced cognitive capacities (attention span, reaction time, short-term memory, ability to abstract). Although DS children show a range of abilities, they often acquire a mental age equivalent to a *typically developing* (TD) four-year-old at DS age 12–15 years; they pass through an early stage (comparable to a TD 18-month-old) at DS age 4–6 years, and a second stage (comparable to a TD 30-month-old) at DS age 8–11 years. Variation from one individual with DS to the next is quite broad, so that the same developmental milestone may be achieved at ranges that vary up to nearly three chronological years.

Generally, language development is delayed, but similar in sequence to TD L1A: DS children go through a babbling stage, then a phonological acquisition stage including phoneme simplification seen in normal development, then a one-word utterance step and eventually a period of syntactic combinations. Unlike typically developing children, DS learners often persist in difficulties with phonological realization (linked in part to their physiological differences), and most continue to omit obligatory morphemes even when they have achieved an endstate grammar. While it appears that DS L1A is a delayed version of TD acquisition, there are qualitative differences between the developmental trajectories. The normal correlation seen in L1A between extent of vocabulary and onset of word combination is not true for DS children, who – when matched against TD children for *MLU (mean length of utterance)* – score "significantly below the grammatical levels," indicating that lexical size is a "necessary but not sufficient condition for the acquisition of grammatical function words" (Bates et al. 1995, 147). Summarizing, Lenneberg's observation of dissociation between language and cognition in DS is supported, although ultimate achievement – usually less than perfect – is not determined exclusively by age (i.e. termination of L1A at puberty) or by cognitive development.

If Down Syndrome does not present the neat picture of delayed but near perfect L1A described by Lenneberg, Williams Syndrome – a pathology associated with mental retardation, characteristic facial appearance, and heart defect (Bellugi et al. 1993, 2000, 2001) – better exemplifies impaired cognition with spared language (cf. Smith and Tsimpli 1995). The WS impairment, attributed to a defective site on chromosome 7, was first documented by J. C. P. Williams in 1961 and affects one in 20,000 live births (Lenhoff et al. 1997). WS children show cognitive development comparable to that of DS children (e.g. difficulties understanding shape to volume and sequencing relationships, IQ around 60), with delayed acquisition of language that is also comparable. When grammar emerges, WS children "improve dramatically," much like TD children, whereas DS children fall further and further behind (Bellugi and St. George 2000). WS adolescents and adults are able to comprehend and produce complex syntactic structures such as compound tenses, multiple embedding of relative clauses, conditional sentences and passives, but they nevertheless omit obligatory morphology on occasion, unlike typically developing

(TD) counterparts. They are also very adept at using unusual vocabulary – for example *zebra, hippopotamus, chihuahua, ibex, koala* when asked to name animals – and engaging narrative techniques to involve their audience. They do not, however, always understand the sophisticated lexical items they use and may have unusual semantic processing (Bellugi et al. 2000; Karmiloff-Smith et al. 1997).

Losh et al. (2000), who compare the narratives of WS children with those of TD matched children on morphology, syntax and narrative technique, find that the former make signficantly more morphosyntactic errors, but use far more engaging narration than their TD counterparts. Compared to TD children who match in chronological age (4;9–10;8) and in mental age (TD 3;5–WS 8;1), the WS children use morphosyntax that is comparable to their mental age TD peers, but far more flawed than older TD children. Their ability to narrate, though, seems to surpass that of TD peers, "dramatizing their narratives through the use of character voice, sound effects and audience hookers" (Losh et al. 2000, 281). The examples in (1) demonstrate the sorts of sentences they use in recounting the story – given to them in a series of uncaptioned drawings – of a pet frog who goes missing.

(1)   Sample sentences by WS children
    a. Here's the boy and the dog. And the frog's gone. The frog went away. I don't see any frog anywhere. Do you see the frog? (10;3)
    b. "I'm looking for . . . a frog," said the little boy. "Oh, here froggie, froggie, he said." (6;8)

WS adolescents and adults show far superior language skills than DS counterparts (with equal cognitive abilities), but they do not achieve the level of morphosyntactic competence of the general population.

3.1.2   Specific language impairment

In contrast to Williams Syndrome, which exemplifies reduced cognitive abilities with mainly intact linguistic ones, specific language impairment (SLI) describes normal cognitive abilities with reduced grammatical capabilities (Eyer and Leonard 1995; Gopnik 1990, 1997; Levy and Schaeffer 2003; Newmeyer 1997; Rice 1996; Tromblin 1996, 1997). Unlike Down and Williams Syndromes, SLI's genetic base is only weakly established, for it is a heterogeneous disorder rather defined by exclusionary criteria and affecting 2–3 percent of the preschool population. "SLI exists when the child has poor language achievement despite normal non-verbal IQ (above an IQ of 85), normal hearing, normal social development, normal emotional status and normal motor skills"

(Tromblin 1997, 92). The children with SLI exhibit normal hearing in tests of non-language perception, although they may show processing difficulties in linguistic comprehension. The poor language achievement is selective in that the deficits affect morphosyntax but not vocabulary. While two language-external variables, mother's education and IQ, affect rate of vocabulary growth of TD children, the two variables have no effect on the development of verb finiteness in SLI children (Wexler 2003, 43). Although not all cases of SLI are necessarily familial, there have been detailed studies of families with a heightened rate of SLI, suggesting a genetic origin to the disorder (Gopnik et al. 1997; Tromblin 1996, 1997).

Children with SLI show a grammatical morphology deficit, with their language acquisition lagging particularly with respect to functional categories such as determiner, complementizer, tense and verb agreement (Eyer and Leonard 1995; Fletcher and Ingham 1995; Hamann 2004). They especially have trouble marking verbs for tense and person agreement, and in languages with gender, they have difficulty with gender marking (Paradis and Crago 2004). In 20–50 percent of the children the language disorder "fully resolves as they get older" (Gopnik et al. 1997, 113). There are three possible sources of their deficiencies: phonology, morphology and syntax. It is true that SLI speakers have phonological problems which may contribute to their inability to realize functional morphemes, but Gopnik et al. argue that phonological processing constraints alone cannot account for the morphological omissions, since speakers disproportionately omit morphological consonants such as past *-ed* or plural *-s*. The authors propose that SLI speakers have difficulty with morphology because they are unable to create implicit inflectional rules in the Pinkerian sense (for example, "add *-ed* to make a verb past tense") and rather learn all morphological forms of a word by rote, thus storing *walk-walked* in the same manner as *go-went*. The authors test SLI and unimpaired subjects in English, Greek and Japanese, finding that in all three languages the SLI impaired subjects are unable to change the tense of a verb ("Everyday he walks eight miles. Yesterday he ___") or pluralize nonsense words ("This is a wug. Here are two ___"). "In sum, we see the impaired subjects failing to apply grammatical rules to words that could not have been learned lexically, regardless of the category to which they belong (verb, noun, adjective, compound), which implies that the impairment affects their ability to construct morphological rules" (ibid., 133). They also have problems accurately judging grammatically accurate versus inaccurate sentences. The SLI subjects clearly have processing difficulties, morphological deficits and syntactic production problems.

Table 3.1 *Group means for chronological age, PPVT and Block Design (WISC-R)*

	N	Age	PPVT	Block D
SLI	28	6–14 (8.96)	84.96	10.4
WS	23	9–25 (15.2)	63.69	2.5
DS	14	9–21 (15.0)	42.33	3.0
FL	14	6–15 (7.8)	104.38	9.9
TD	29	6–15 (9.5)	111.93	11.1

The SLI inability to use tense and verb agreement indicates a significant shortfall in the verbal domain that has been described by Rice and Wexler (1996) as characteristic of an *extended optional infinitive* period. The authors use the metaphor of language acquisition as a train to demonstrate that the SLI children are on the same track and follow the same route as TD learners; however, the SLI train leaves late and the cars are not coupled tightly, resulting in differential development of different aspects of language. The optional infinitive stage begins later for SLI children and lasts longer. "What is not known is whether or not the language train of the individuals with SLI ever comes to fully align in the same way as the train of nonaffected individuals" (ibid., 226).

Two recent studies (Nichols et al. 2004; Reilly et al. 2004) compare verbal learning by the three groups described above – DS, WS and SLI – with that of TD controls and of children who experienced focal brain lesion (FL) before six months of age. The early brain lesion children are similar to the subjects described by Lenneberg whose hemispheric damage is early enough to allow reassignment of linguistic functions from the left to the right hemisphere. To level the field of comparison TD controls are matched with non-TD groups of the same cognitive developmental level or mental age. Nichols et al. examine five groups (Table 3.1) matched for mental age (8.0 for WS and 7.9 for DS) on a task that requires them to learn fifteen words (fruit, clothing and toys) on a "shopping list" that they are later asked to recall under varying conditions (e.g. after hearing a different list of fifteen items).

Table 3.1's scores on the *Peabody Picture Vocabulary Test (PPVT)* and on the Wechsler intelligence scale (WISC-R) Block Design test illustrate comparable scores of SLI, lesion (FL) and TD groups on general intelligence measures (while WS and DS have much lower scores). This result is expected since SLI, lesion and TD are deemed to have TD cognitive ability while WS and DS do not. However, all groups show a graduated range on the PPVT vocabulary test, with SLI children performing well below lesion and TD, WS below them, and DS with the lowest score. Infants with cerebral damage (focal lesion) appear to restructure linguistic functions and to acquire language normally, as long as the damage occurs when the child is very young. They nevertheless show residual difficulties compared to TD children.

The results of the test battery confirm the range of linguistic abilities indicated by the PPVT scores and earlier studies of the five populations. The focal lesion group performs below but very close to the TD group, except for the longest delay recall task, which elicits a significantly lower response. Their deficits are minimal by the time they are eight or nine years old. SLI children, on the other hand, experience substantial difficulty even though the task is lexical, not grammatical, and the WS children – despite their linguistic fluency – perform even more poorly on the tasks, showing weakness in verbal learning and memory. DS children are the weakest group, as would be expected.

Reilly et al. use the frog narrative to make two comparisons, one of SLI and focal lesion children with controls, and another of SLI and WS with controls. The first comparison looks at morphological errors and complex syntax in three age groups, four to six, seven to nine and ten to twelve. Although the youngest SLI and FL groups score far below the TD group (with SLI scoring lower than FL), the seven- to nine-year-olds make steady improvement, and by ten to twelve the SLI and FL groups almost match the TD children in morphological accuracy and complex syntax. The authors conclude that for the FL group, the unaffected tissue has sufficient plasticity to reassign core language functions of syntax and morphology so that by the age of twelve the FL child is as linguistically adept as the TD peers.

The second comparison contrasts children with SLI and those with WS to TD counterparts on morphological errors, complex syntax, narrative performance (how well the key elements of the narrative were included) and evaluative techniques. As in the case of the first comparison, SLI and WS children at the younger stage made substantial morphological errors and used little complex syntax, but in the older groups the errors decreased (nearly to the level of the TD group) and syntax became more complex. The oldest WS children matched the typical group in story length, while the SLI group remained below both. Narrative cohesion – which is more related to cognition than affective engagement – was a weak point for WS children who treated each frame as a separate description rather than tying together the whole narrative, whereas the oldest SLI group achieved a level that was comparable to the TD peers. Finally, the WS group surpassed the other groups in its use of colorful and engaging evaluative language, as the examples in (2) illustrate.

(2)   Examples of frog narration, SLI, WS, TD
    a. The dog is trying for the bees and the boy's looking for the frog. (SLI, 9;6)
    b. So many bees! The boy said "Ow! Somebody stung me!" (WS, 9;10)
    c. The boy stuck his head in a hole, looking for the frog, while the dog was barking at some bees. (TD, 9;10)
    d. And the boy and the dog are happy and the boy gots a frog. (SLI, 10;4)
    e. Here's the frog and he's in love! And he says "Hooray! Hooray! Hooray! I found my froggie!" And then he says "Byeee!" (WS, 10;0)
    f. I guess the one frog is his so he gets one of the frogs, and that's it. (TD, 9;8)

The authors emphasize the dissociation of cognition from linguistic ability so clearly demonstrated by the SLI and WS populations and the uniformity of morphological error types in all populations. "The children in these groups come to the language learning task with very different brain structures and organizations, nonetheless, the acquisition of the morphology and syntax of English appears to follow a similar path . . . Language learning can be mediated by a variety of neural substrates and different factors underlie the linguistic abilities of each group" (ibid., 14). The authors emphasize the similarity of developmental trajectory and error patterns of all the groups of learners, despite the differences that they undoubtedly have in cerebral organization. Differences in cognitive ability are seemingly irrelevant, pointing to the common linguistic propensity of the individuals with SLI, DS, WS or cerebral lesions, a commonality that some linguists could attribute to Universal Grammar.

3.2   L1A in extreme deprivation

Stories of abandoned children adopted by animals have existed for millennia, beginning with the story of Rome's founders, Romulus and Remus, who were, according to legend, suckled by a wolf. The eighteenth-century taxonomist Linnaeus documented nine cases of what he called *homo ferus*, "wild or feral man," and the following centuries recorded an additional forty cases (Armen 1971; Gesell 1941; Maclean 1977; Singh and Zingg 1966; Skuse 1993), most of which were poorly authenticated. Children isolated from society during their formative years constitute the forbidden experiment envisaged by eighteenth-century philosophers such as Montesquieu (1949 [1777]), who even suggested raising a group of children as animals, cared for by goats or deaf nurses, to see if they created a language that could be examined, freed from culture or instruction and thus a window on human thought. The actual results of depriving children in this manner are far from the idealization of pure language and human thought proposed by Montesquieu, as a few selected examples will show.

3.2.1   Victor

Victor, discovered in the southwest of France (Saint-Sernin, Aveyron) and subject of Truffaut's film "The Wild Child," has fascinated scholars and the public for 200 years (Itard 1801; Lane 1976; Shattuck 1980). Captured January 9, 1800 at the age of "eleven or twelve," Victor (a name given him by his tutor) was taken eight months later to the Institute for Deaf-Mutes (*Institution Nationale des Sourds-Muets*) in Paris, where he would remain for several years under the tutelage of Jean-Marc-Gaspard Itard. Victor's story, well documented by his protector, exemplifies both the eighteenth-century interest in the individual in society and the nineteenth-century belief in the human capacity to implement change through scientific intervention. Victor, however, never mastered human language.

Victor's case is of particular interest because it is so well substantiated, from the time of his discovery by the cleric Bonnaterre who had studied zoology in Paris, to newspaper accounts as the boy made his way to Paris, and finally to the careful records of Itard. Victor's behavior betrayed his isolation from society, for – in addition to not speaking – he conducted himself unusually, rocking back and forth, staring blankly in corners for long periods of time, sniffing his food, eating only potatoes (which he threw in a fire for a short time and then extracted with his bare hands), and "relieving himself wherever and whenever he felt like it" (Shattuck 1980, 7). He was initially impervious to heat and cold, refusing clothing, was quite adept at running and climbing trees and bore the scars of survival in the wild (with one on his neck even suggesting he might have been cut by a knife). Later, his caregivers acclimated him to the manners of society so that he learned to wear clothes, be sensitive to heat, eat prepared food and bend to the scholastic expectations of Dr. Itard.

After the boy's arrival in Paris in August 1800, he underwent a battery of physiological and psychological exams, leading Dr. Pinel, head of the main insane asylum of Paris, to classify him as an "idiot," incapable of rehabilitation. Itard, who assumed his post at the end of the year, did not share this opinion and set out to show that the wild child could be reintegrated into society. Itard established five goals for Victor, each more ambitious than the prior:
- to attach him to social life
- to awaken his "nervous sensibility" (emotional well-being)
- to extend the sphere of his ideas
- to lead him to speak
- to have him perform simple mental operations.

The tutor implemented a systematic method of instruction based in large part on the work of the eighteenth-century empiricist Condillac, whereby he used physical techniques to lead to mental, emotional and social changes. For example, by having Victor repeatedly bathe in hot water, Itard made the child aware of heat and cold; by playing a shell game with an edible chestnut beneath, the tutor developed visual dexterity in his pupil. Victor became emotionally attached to Itard and to his "foster mother" Mme. Guérin, showing sensitivity when the latter was widowed, and crying on various occasions to show his dismay.

Itard tried to train Victor to speak, first by modeling speech sounds and teaching him words, but the boy only managed to make the sounds "O Diie" (which Itard attributed to Mme. Guérin's exclamation "Oh heavens!"), [li] and [la]. Itard's attempts to teach the word for water, *eau* [o], with a glass of water did not succeed, although at one point he "heard Victor pronounce distinctly ... the word *lait* ('milk') that he immediately repeated" (ibid., 62). Later – as Itard published in his report to the Society of Observers of Man in summer of 1801 – he trained Victor to recognize geometric figures and tried unsuccessfully to get him to associate the written word with the correct object. While Victor showed a basic level of cognitive functioning, he never learned language, prompting Itard to say of his fourth aim: "If I had wished to produce only happy results, I would have suppressed from this publication this fourth aim, the means that I put in use for completing it, and the scarcity of success that I achieved" (ibid., 50). For four more years, Itard continued his training of Victor with little progress until the onset of puberty in 1805 created such crises that the scholar was obliged to abandon his project. Mme. Guérin continued to care for Victor in a house near the Institute until his death in 1828. Itard, after writing a second more sober report in 1806 that assessed the last four years of Victor's training, returned to his work with deaf-mutes while practicing as a physician in Paris.

What can we conclude about a sensitive period from Victor's case? It seems that he was pre-pubescent upon discovery, although over ten years of age, and that he had had limited encounters with humans in the years preceding his capture, since there were reports of his being fed at farm houses or foraging root vegetables in gardens. If we consider – in the light of research on infant perception of language – Victor's abilities, we are drawn to the conclusion that he was not cognitively average, but rather retarded or autistic. Indeed, some accounts suggest that Victor was probably autistic (Skuse 1993, 44) or cognitively deficient, for even at his discovery, observers thought he might have been abandoned by parents dismayed by his slow wit. Such ideas are corroborated by his inability to perceive phonemic distinctions, to imitate words, to recognize symbolic reference (that *eau* signifies water) or to perform simple cognitive tasks. In any case, his story does not disprove the idea of a critical period for language acquisition, but cannot be taken as strong evidence for it either, since his mental capacities were so limited that he displayed lacunae in all areas of development.

3.2.2   Genie

Like her nineteenth-century counterpart Victor, Genie – a 13½-year-old discovered in the Los Angeles area in 1970 after a lifetime of isolation and deprivation – never mastered language (Curtiss 1977, 1988; Curtiss et al. 1974; Rymer 1993). Genie's biological family had lived in fear of a psychologically unstable and abusive father who confined her to a potty chair and a caged crib in an isolated bedroom, beating her if she made any noise. She consequently learned to suppress all sound production and acquired no language during her childhood. After her discovery, Genie was hospitalized for seven months, during which time she recuperated from malnutrition and made progress in cognitive and linguistic skills. Much like other such deprived children, she was oblivious to heat and cold and had trouble eating. Her lack of vocalization led her initially to express emotion by silently "flailing about, scratching, spitting, blowing her nose and frantically rubbing her face and hair with her own mucus" (Curtiss 1977, 10). A research team – consisting of psychologists, psychiatrists, and linguists primarily at UCLA – observed Genie's behavior during her hospital stay, and then followed her very closely with cognitive and linguistic tests for the following four years.

One of the first reports on Genie's linguistic development during the first two years echoed the enthusiasm of Itard's first 1801 publication. "Her language acquisition so far shows that, despite the tragic isolation which she suffered, despite the lack of linguistic input, despite the fact that she had no language for almost the first fourteen years of her life, Genie is equipped to learn language and she is learning it. No one can predict how far she will develop linguistically or cognitively" (Curtiss et al. 2004 [1974], 142). The initial diagnostics indicated that on standard cognition tests (Vineland and Leiter) she scored at the four- to seven-year-old level (ibid., 127), but had very little language, especially in terms of grammar. By the time Curtiss began following her in June of 1971 (about seven months after her discovery), Genie had already acquired a receptive vocabulary of several hundred words and a productive one of several dozen. Curtiss and the linguistic team undertook the instruction of first language to Genie and were, over a couple of years, able to facilitate her comprehension of plural marking, negation, modification, possession and several relations marked by prepositions and adjectives. Other tests indicated that she had not mastered the comprehension of more complex syntax such as passive and WH questions, and her production did not match her comprehension. For the first two years she remained at the one-word stage, and in the next two years created two-word and longer utterances, with some formulaic phrases such as "May I have X."

A major impediment for her oral language was the fact that her phonation was so repressed that she never was able to acquire accurate spontaneous production of English phonemes, although her receptive skills for phonemes and for rhymes were nearly perfect. It was not her phonetic articulation which was inaccurate because she often imitated perfectly the sounds that she had just heard; rather, it was her abstract phonology, the ability to use a phonemic inventory, phonotactics and phonological rules to realize combined phonemes spontaneously in a real context. Her vowels were laxed and centralized and her speech generally breathy, imprecise and quite variable. She frequently omitted consonants, especially in final position and simplified syllable structure by inserting extra neutral vowels as in [bəlu] for *blue*. While babies learning first language perceptually master the phonology of their native tongue by 10–12 months (essentially ignoring phonological distinctions in nonnative languages), Genie got only a rudimentary version of English phonology. She learned words, but did not have a handle on their exact pronunciation.

Her early productions were single words, but after July 1971 she began to combine words as noun phrases (3a), possessives (3b), predicate nominatives (3c), negatives (3d), locatives (3e) and verb phrases (3f).

(3)   Genie's productions (Curtiss 1977, 146–156)
      a. little white clear box (7/17/72)
      b. Sheila mother coat (2/20/72)
      c. Curtiss car big car (1/24/72)
      d. No stay hospital (1/22/73)
      e. Stay bathtub long time (2/13/72)
      f. Mike paint. (10/27/71)

She became capable of creating complex sentences with embedded clauses or infinitivals as (4) indicates.

(4)   Embedded clauses (ibid., 158–159)
      a. Ask go shopping (1/29/73)
      b. I want think about Mama riding bus (11/20/74)
      c. Teacher said Genie have temper tantrum outside (5/2/75)

While the lack of inflectional morphology is evident in the preceding examples, its omission was probably prompted in part by Genie's inability to pronounce final consonants. In comprehension exercises and in instructional activities with written words she demonstrated recognition of plural and possessive -*s*. She sporadically used some irregular past tenses such as *gave*, but did not acquire the past regular and did not comprehend past tense even though she eventually was able to recount events from the past (5).

(5) Genie's description of past events (ibid, 159–160)
   a. Father hit Genie cry longtime ago (5/2/75)
   b. Dentist say drink water (3/12/75)
   c. Mr. W say, put face in swimming pool (6/10/74)

The examples in (3)–(5) manifest many of the characteristics of the optional infinitive stage of L1A, a parallel that shouldn't be too surprising. Like those of two-year-olds, the utterances in (3)–(5) show correct word order (NP and VP directionality), command of lexical categories as opposed to functional ones (hence bare NPs, lack of functional determiners and prepositions), null subjects, omitted auxiliaries and copula, lack of tense/agreement on all verbs (root infinitives) and VP internal syntax consistently shown by negation placement to the left of the main verb. Genie's understanding of constituent type and order is shown in responses to questions such as *What did you do? Play. What kind of car? Red car.* First person *I* and *my* are used correctly, but Genie never mastered the other pronominal persons, confusing *you/me* and resisting third person even when taught. In fact, she never got beyond this stage that resembles the optional infinitive period for TD children, and – in addition to producing sentences that were representative of toddler speech – created utterances whose syntax was not that of the optional infinitive stage (6).

(6) Genie's highly ungrammatical utterances (ibid, 163–164)
   a. Fred have feel good (6/12/73)
   b. I supermarket surprise Roy (4/22/74)
   c. Where is stop spitting? (6/5/74)

(6c) and similar WH non-sentences resulted from an attempt to teach Genie to ask questions, an endeavor that was abandoned after several months. In terms of current views of L1A, Genie's grammar appears to be frozen at the optional infinitive VP stage, with only occasional functional category realization, preverbal negation, bare NPs and lack of IP and CP syntax.

Despite her limited syntax, Genie acquired a relatively extensive vocabulary, especially focusing on visual aspects of her environment such as color and shape. By 1976 she scored at the six-year-old level on the PPVT (ibid, 212). Dichotic listening tests revealed that she was a right hemisphere language learner, a fact that Curtiss (ibid., 216) attributes to maturation; she suggests that "after the 'critical period,' the left hemisphere can no longer assume control in language acquision, and the right hemisphere will function and predominate in the acquisition and representation of language." The UCLA team also administered tachistoscopic tests (related to visual field) and evoked potential EEG tests, both of which indicated right hemisphere activity for Genie's language and visual processing. Evidence from young children's recovery from left hemisphere brain damage has confirmed that they can relocate language to the right if the recovery is early enough. Whether the left hemisphere atrophies and transfers language learning to the right in older children unexposed to language has not been tested in anyone besides Genie.

Despite intensive efforts to teach Genie language, she was successful only in her vocabulary acquisition, but remained at an agrammatical stage of word combination. Whether the extreme degree of deprivation and abuse that she had suffered hindered her further development (language is, after all, acquired in a sociocultural context of interpersonal exchange), or whether she was actually incapable of language acquisition from the start because of reduced intelligence or left hemisphere damage are questions that remain unanswered. Nevertheless, Genie, much more so than Victor, demonstrates substantial acquisition of language, with a vocabulary of several hundred words and syntax that resembles that of the optional infinitive stage. The fact that her relatively good cognitive skills and vocabulary are disproportionately matched by her very poor phonology-morphosyntax strongly suggests a dissociation of the grammatical phenomena from other cognitive and linguistic (e.g. vocabulary, pragmatic skills) functions. Genie's inability to use language in a socially acceptable way (she couldn't use a name to attract someone's attention) certainly seems related to her lack of socialization over the years. Her inability to use WH questions or plural marking hardly seem attributable to lack of socialization or lack of input since she had ample relevant input. Her case suggests a sensitive period threshold in late childhood for acquisition of correct morphosyntax (but not vocabulary and basic lexical category directionality).

3.2.3   Sociolinguistic integration of isolates and adoptees

The well-documented cases of Victor and Genie suggest that children isolated in abusive situations may make gains in non-verbal behavior after rehabilitation, but that their linguistic abilities are destined to remain at a very primitive level. An overwhelming number of the cases of deprived children cited in the literature of past centuries describe youngsters who fail to thrive after isolation and abuse, and who particularly fail to learn language, unsurprising results given the primitive level of medical and socio-psychological care in the past. The twentieth century has, on the other hand, furnished more detailed accounts (and more systematic intervention and rehabilitation), with several instances of children who do recuperate language and socialized behavior.

Skuse (1993) describes ten children discovered between 1938 and 1978 who had experienced extreme isolation and deprivation and were incapable of speech upon discovery. Three (including Genie) never learned language, while the other seven – whose age at discovery ranged from sixteen months to seven years – developed normally. "Following removal from deprivation the evidence suggests that, if recovery of normal language ability is going to occur, rapid progress is the rule with substantial achievements being made within a few months" (ibid., 44). Genie's two language impaired peers – who were discovered at age 5;11 and 2;4 – appeared to have additional problems such as autism. Aside from Genie, there are no well documented twentieth-century cases of pubescent social isolates. The fact that the successful cases described by Skuse are age seven and below is probably not insignificant and seems to indicate a sensitivity for L1A linked to early acquisition. The case of Alex (Vargha-Khadem et al. 1997), a left hemispherectomy patient who begins language acquisition at age nine, pushes the limit for L1A above age seven for AoA. Unlike the children described by Skuse, however, Alex is raised in a loving and caring environment. An aspect of Skuse's descriptions (and Alex's development) characteristic of critical periods in other species is the rapid progress made when deprivation is replaced by appropriate input. Such rapidity is reminiscent of Nottebohm's (1978 [1969]) delayed puberty experiment with songbirds, in which puberty was delayed for a year and input was withheld for the same period. The previously deprived chaffinch learned the appropriate songs in the same way as the control population.

In addition to Tarzancito, discovered at age five and fluent in Spanish within a year or so (Singh and Zingg 1966, 259–268), Marie-Angélique Leblanc, a nine- or ten-year-old girl discovered in Champagne, France in 1731, presents an L1A success story documented by a number of eighteenth-century French writers. This case, almost unmentioned in recent literature on socially deprived children, is a classic example of the Enlightenment preoccupation with the human condition and the place of the individual in nature. It poses a dilemma for the Critical Period Hypothesis in that Leblanc achieved fluency in French, unlike most other documented cases of such deprived learners. In contrast to Victor and Genie who never integrated into society, Marie-Angélique did assimilate to society, and more importantly, learn language. At her discovery in 1731 she manifested impoverished social and expressive skills and the heightened physical power and agility characteristic of other socially isolated children. Unlike the others, however, she became "tamed," gaining the French language and a religious education. Leblanc's case is documented by newspaper articles, baptismal records, a lengthy report by Condamine written in 1755, and several other contemporary accounts (Racine 1808 [1747]; Tinland 1971). Although the various sources give different versions of some aspects of her story (an important point being her age at time of discovery), they describe her initially as knowing no language. Her language acquisition progressed gradually and was clearly effective because she is later described as using complex French quite fluently (Douthwaite 2002). Caspar Hauser (Singh and Zingg 1966, 277–365) is another case of an isolate who became a language acquirer; however, the authenticity of his isolation has been questioned.

Marie-Angélique's story raises the question of whether she escaped sensitive age constraints or actually already had a first language. Her case thus poses a greater dilemma than that of Victor whose behavior resembles that of numerous children who failed to learn language and assimilate to society. Recent treatments point out the thin line between fiction and reported fact in the eighteenth century. "Looking for authoritative, documentary proof of the wild girl's foreign identity, they borrowed legends recounted in voyage literature and invented fictions rivalling the most extravagant novels of the day" (Douthwaite 1994–95, 15). Nevertheless, it is clear that Marie-Angélique was a real person who lived in the wild and acquired many asocial characteristics. The very few hints to her linguistic development suggest that she did have a language, and that her eventual acquisition of French was that of a second language, not a first. Although she suffered attrition of her first language since she appeared not to speak a full-fledged language (she was reported to converse in selected words only) when discovered, she gradually acquired French, and by the time she entered a convent – where she spent the remainder of her life devoted to religion – she was quite fluent, producing complex sentences with subordinate clauses, even in subjunctive mood (a feat undoubtedly admired by students of French grammar). It appears then that the key conditions permitting Leblanc to become a fluent speaker were her possession of a human language to begin with, coupled with her relatively young age at discovery.

A final group that is less deprived yet shows similar characteristics to the children reintegrated after social isolation is that of young children adopted into a new linguistic environment. International adoptions by North American and European families have increased in recent decades, particularly for *adoptees* from Eastern Europe and China. For example, within the past fifteen years over 50,000 Chinese children have been adopted in the United States (Pollock and Price 2005). These adoptees of recent years have usually spent time in an orphanage in the birth country where – despite documented nurturing on the part of the staff – they have inevitably experienced medical and developmental risks that children born in more developed countries do not encounter (Glennen 2005; Krakow et al. 2005). The children frequently show delayed or impaired native language development at the time that they are adopted into an environment that has an ambient language that is quite distinct from their own. How do they fare?

A recent issue of *Seminars in Speech and Language* (26, 1) on international adoptees provides evidence that these young learners of a "new first language" show very similar patterns to infants acquiring L1. They are usually able to overcome their initial handicap of disadvantaged environment to gain linguistic skills in English during their preschool years, although a third of them show some linguistic difficulties (Glennen 2005). Krakow et al. (2005), who compare the development of infants (7–9 months at adoption) and toddlers (24–32 months at adoption) from China, find that after one year the toddlers have quickly learned more English vocabulary and irregular morphology (what they are tested on) than the infants. When the two groups are later compared at the age of 2;6, the infant group outperforms the group that arrived as toddlers, indicating that the younger group learned more by the same age. Pollock (2005) also finds a disadvantage for older arrivals from China, "with delays in expressive syntax and grammar larger than those in vocabulary" (ibid., 23). Eventually the older adoptees overcome developmental differences to gain the same abilities in English. Geren et al. (2005) look at an older group of preschoolers (2;7–5;1 at adoption) from China, who also steadily gain vocabulary and grammar as a function of their length of residence. Age at arrival seems to be less of a factor for these older children who would have established a firmer native language base. Noting that the preschoolers do not go through slow early lexical development, the authors point out that "these children went through many of the stages that we see in first language acquisition, albeit at a faster pace" (ibid., 53). Their accelerated learning recalls the quickened pace noted by Skuse for his socially deprived L1 subjects.

3.3   Deafness

Most of the children deprived of language input during formative years present cases of ultimate language failure. Their social deprivation and abusive environment so profoundly alter normal circumstances that it is difficult to isolate their linguistic development from social and emotional variables. Another group that often experiences delay in language input comprises deaf infants whose deafness is not diagnosed early or who are not exposed to *signed language* as early as possible. Children who learn sign language as natives follow a pattern of acquisition similar to those learning spoken language (Chamberlain et al. 2000). Deaf individuals whose initial exposure to sign, such as *American Sign Language (ASL)*, varies from infancy to adulthood demonstrate a progressive decline in linguistic competence with increasing age of inception of language acquisition. This section considers normal and delayed acquisition of ASL, while the next looks at the evolution of a new creole, Nicaraguan Sign Language.

3.3.1   Normal L1A of sign language

American Sign Language (ASL) – like all sign languages of the world – is a system of human communication with all the properties of spoken languages (Aronoff et al. 2005). It has a phonology whose distinctive features are based on hand shape, place of articulation and hand movement (Chamberlain et al. 2000; Emmorey 2002), just as oral phonology segments are based on place and manner of articulation. These "meaningless" segments are combined to create words (morphology) that subsequently form sentences (Padden 1988). Unlike spoken languages which rely on concatenation (a function of the linearity of speech and writing), sign languages create complex words and phrases through "processes in which a sign stem is nested within various movement contours and planes in space" (Emmorey 2002, 14). Sign languages are capable of expressing ideas available in any human language and have the capacity to create sentences that are in principle infinite, the creative aspect of language shown by the potential addition of another phrase or clause to any given sentence. Furthermore, despite the markedly different physical realization of signed and spoken languages, both are controlled by the same areas of the brain, mainly on the left hemisphere. Poizner et al. (1987) describe six cases of native ASL signers who experienced brain lesions: those with left hemisphere damage showed symptoms resembling Broca's and Wernicke's aphasia, whereas those with right hemisphere damage retained their linguistic abilities despite weakened muscle control on the left side of their bodies.

It is not surprising that infants exposed to sign language – both deaf and hearing children of signing parents – acquire it in the same manner as those exposed to a spoken language acquire theirs (Schiff-Myers 1993). At 10–14 months babies go through a stage of babbling (Petitto 2000; Petitto and Marentette 1991) that manifests reduplicated movements resembling the syllable structure of the language being acquired. First words follow quickly upon babbling, if not emerging simultaneously, at the end of the first year. Gestures are not the sole domain of the child exposed to sign language, but are part of the speaking child's repertoire as well (Caprici, Montanari and Volterra 1998; Goldin-Meadow 1998; Iverson and Goldin-Meadow 1998). All infants, who have more control over manual gestures than vocal articulators at the end of the first year, create prelinguistic communicative gestures, a fact that has recently led to the encouragement of "teaching" ASL to babies to facilitate their communication. The early emergence of gestures with and without spoken language, the persistent use of gestures to accompany adult spoken language, and the rich linguistic evidence of sign languages have led some researchers to propose that these manual languages were actually the prototype for spoken language (Corballis 2002). Iverson (1998) points out that all children gesture, even blind children who have no visual model yet make gestures that resemble those of sighted children.

Children learning manual language produce baby words that are sign combinations simplified from the adult versions, retaining place of articulation but with abbreviated hand configuration. The kinds of phonological errors they make – comparable to speaking children's substitution of *dere* for *there* – are systematic substitutions based on phonological similarity of signs. Deaf parents facilitate their children's acquisition of ASL by using child-directed "longer and larger signs" (Emmorey 2002, 179) that help babies segment the visual input. Furthermore, deaf parents displace signs so that the sign and the targeted object is in the infant's view, thus promoting the shared gaze that is so beneficial to word learning.

Once signing toddlers have mastered a number of words, they begin combining them in simplified sentences, while at the same time acquiring the additional morphology required for the mature language as, for example, the raised or furrowed eyebrows that signal questions in ASL. In learning question formation, children at first make superficially correct visual gestures, but "these signs are produced as unanalyzed gestalts or amalgams" (Emmorey 2002, 185). As a typical case of *U pattern learning* (correct-incorrect-correct), they next retreat to making no facial marking for questions before arriving at the final correct target stage. The complex morphology of classifier constructions and the ability to finger spell are aspects of sign language acquired later and may not be mastered until age eight or nine.

The role of the environment is crucial to the child acquiring language, for infants are already developing phonological systems and words from the ambient input before the age of one year. Nature and nurture are quite evident in early acquisition, as the natural predisposition that infants bring to the learning task is shown in their ability to use both gesture and vocalization for proto-communication demonstrates. This predisposition is further elucidated by deaf children who do not receive optimal language input, but who "develop gestural communication systems which share many – but not all – of the structural properties of the early linguistic systems of children exposed to established language models" (Goldin-Meadow and Mylander 1994 [1990], 509), the topic of the next section.

3.3.2   Delay in L1A, signed language

The "gestural communication systems" that have been documented cross-linguistically in profoundly deaf children born to hearing parents (90 percent of the deaf children) are known as *homesign*, a conventionalized gesturing that remarkably shares many properties, even though the children have no contact with each other. Goldin-Meadow and Mylander (ibid., 514–519) describe three classes of gestures:

- *deictic* (pointing to something in the immediate environment; deictic linguistic elements refer to the here and now, often pointing to objects or participants in the immediate environment)
- *characterizing* (e.g. flapping the hands to indicate a pet bird)
- *marker* (conventionalized signals to mean, for example, "wait" or "no").

The children establish a set of signs with a signifier (form) linked to a signified (meaning) that they then use to create sentential strings organized like early language utterances such as agent-action. For example, one child commented on a toy train circling a track by first pointing to the train (agent) and then making a circular motion to indicate the action. The children studied use a fairly restricted ordering of gestures and seem to adapt their gestures in a kind of morphological inflection through variation in place of articulation.

There are few documented cases of L1A in adulthood, but one is that of Ildefonso (Schaller 1995), a prelinguistic 28-year-old Mexican immigrant taught the rudiments of ASL by Schaller. Initially he "had no verbs, no tense, and never signed more than two signs in a row" (ibid., 66), but he continued to learn ASL and within a year his "grammar and vocabulary were still simple, like a young child's" (ibid., 131). Although when Schaller finds Ildefonso again after several years he is able to sign with ease and communicate his thoughts, she does not describe in any detail his linguistic abilities, and he claims that he is "still learning," an indication that he has not totally mastered ASL morphosyntax and processing. Without detailed observations of his capabilities, it's impossible to infer too much about his acquisition of grammar.

Other cases of prelinguistic deaf adults Schaller describes communicate in what might be described as proto-pidgin, a communication system that uses homesign (varying among individuals) in place of substrate words (varying among the native languages). "They used only about a dozen common signs. Every other gesture was either a spontaneous invention or used by only one individual. Any sign that became adopted by the entire group had to be repeated and tested in many different stories and tried by everyone. If they could not achieve total consensus, the sign was dropped or remained the property of one person. I saw no common grammar or structure, but individuals developed their own systems for communicating ideas" (ibid., 181–182). Since Ildefonso actually participated in these proto-pidgin communications before learning ASL, his experience may have helped him to do as well as he did in acquiring sign, and in distinguishing his apparently higher success rate than Chelsea, a deaf adult learner discussed in section 3.3.3.

The evidence from deaf adults indicates that it is very difficult to learn L1 sign language as an adult, although language is not totally unlearnable (Johnson and Newport 1989). The cases of prelinguistic deaf adults Schaller documents represent far more frequently languageless individuals than late L1 learners. Although there are few well-documented studies, those that have been done show impaired grammar opposed to good vocabulary and discourse skill acquisition (Curtiss 1988). The dramatic difference between vocabulary acquisition – available to all humans throughout their lifetimes – and that of grammatical morphosyntax points to a sensitive window of opportunity for L1A of grammar. "Age 13 or 31 is too late by far. There appears to be a critical or sensitive period for language acquisition, a consequence of maturational changes in the developing human brain" (Gleitman and Newport 1995, 12).

While total linguistic deprivation is not well documented, there are recorded cases of deaf individuals exposed to sign language input at a range of ages that permits testing of Gleitman and Newport's claim. The evidence indicates that there is a diminution of grammar learning ability with increasing age of exposure to robust language input. In a study of ASL learners whose age of first exposure varied from birth to after age 12, Newport (1994 [1990]) characterizes her thirty subjects as *Native* (birth), *Early* (age 4–6), and *Late* (after age 12) acquirers. All subjects have a minimum of thirty years of exposure, so age of first exposure is the crucial variable. She tests her subjects on a variety of ASL morphosyntactic structures such as verbs of motion, word order, verbal agreement, use of classifiers and derivational morphemes. The tests include a spontaneous production section based on the subjects' description of short videotaped events, and a comprehension section during which the subjects carry out the task described in an ASL video. The results of the tests show no difference in basic word order for the three groups, but clear differences in morphology. Natives are uniformly accurate and consistent in their use of grammatical morphemes such as verb agreement or motion verb morphology, whereas Late Learners are inconsistent individually and as a group, use unanalyzed lexical items ("frozen" without internal morphology), and even omit obligatory morphemes. "These results provide strong evidence for an effect of age of acquisition on control over a primary language: The later the language is learned, the less its use is native (with crisp and grammatically consistent forms) in character" (ibid., 549).

Newport proposes a *Less is More* account of the age difference in acquisition ability, whereby the limitations of the child's processing powers furnish the basis for language acquisition. She observes that the errors older learners make are predominantly inconsistent morphology and unanalyzed wholes, pointing to an inability of these acquirers to perceive and store component parts. Children, on the other hand, have an advantage in their limited cognitive abilities, being able to perceive and store only component parts, and not complex wholes (the forte of older learners). "If children perceive and store only component parts of the complex linguistic stimuli to which they are exposed, while adults more readily perceive and remember the whole complex stimulus, children may be in a better position to locate the components" (ibid., 554). She concludes that such an explanation does not dispense with the need for an innate linguistic propensity, but that it may help to explain the younger/older differences and the gradual decrease in language acquisition capacity.

Besides weaknesses in morphology, other aspects of ASL inferior in late learners include processing ability, comprehension, prosodic structuring and stylistic variation (Emmorey 2002 213–215; Lillo-Martin and Berk 2003). Processing in late learners is far slower than in native signers, an inability that results in diminished comprehension in experimental tasks testing recognition of specific semantic information or morphosyntactic errors. It appears that the extra cognitive energy that late learners expend to process less than automatically, removes their attention from the utterance stream, distracting them, so to speak, from the message. Late learners also lack mature prosodic features such as rhythm, leading Emmorey (2002, 215) to conclude "these findings indicate that childhood language acquisition is critical for automatic and effortless phonological processing. Because phonological structure requires additional effort and attention for late learners, lexical, sentential and discourse structures are harder to construct and maintain." The crucial grounding of a phonological base – best if done during the first year of life – is essential not only for phonology, but for all the other language domains built upon it, syntax, morphology, semantics and discourse. Similarly, Lillo-Martin and Berk (2003) find that a delay of a few years hinders acquisition of stylistic variation in syntax production. While native signers from age two on begin using a variety of word orders proportionate to adult ASL usage, the two subjects whose age of acquisition (AoA) was beyond six years "use the canonical SVO order most of the time," proving knowledge of basic word order, but "they have not yet mastered the conditions for use of variations in word order" comparable to adult usage (ibid., 493).

A final study of ASL that sheds light on the sensitive period question is Mayberry (1993), who compares late L1 learners of ASL (congenitally deaf) with age-matched learners of ASL who lost hearing after learning English as an L1. The thirty-six subjects (controlled for amount of ASL experience, 20+ years and designated by age of ASL acquisition, AoA) comprise four groups of nine, Late-second (AoA 8–15), Late-first (AoA 9–13), Childhood (AoA 5–8) and Native (AoA 0–3), and are tested on processing recall and production (imitation of long and complex ASL sentences). As expected, the age of acquisition correlates inversely with grammatical accuracy for the L1 learners of ASL, and, as expected, the native signers outperform all other groups (Figure 3.1). However, the Late-second group perform as well if not better than the Childhood group, and substantially better than the Late L1 group.

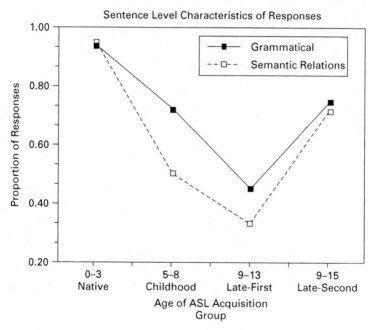

Figure 3.1 Early vs late ASL LIA: The mean proportion of the subject's total responses that were grammatically acceptable and semantically parallel to the stimuli for subjects grouped by age of ASL acquisition and first versus second lanuage acquisition (Mayberry 1993, 1266).

The evidence shows that late L1A is much more susceptible to age effects than is L2A at the same age of acquisition, even though L2 learners do not acquire the language with native-like automaticity of processing, morphological crispness, and subtlety of lexico-semantic knowledge. The chronological decline in L1 acquisition of grammar may stem from changes in cognitive maturation *à la* Newport (whose strict view of a critical period is based on maturational decline in a child's sensitivity to linguistic detail, her "less is more" thesis), decline in neural plasticity à la Lenneberg, cerebral development of non-linguistic specialization in the areas that should be linguistic (because of lack of appropriate input) or a combination of several factors. The decline probably does not result from the overriding influence of first language experience, since this is absent, but rather seems to relate more to cerebral maturation. However, the non-experience of spoken or signed language does not mean that the neural networks that are programmed to develop from infancy through childhood do not change at all (proliferating syntactic connections and then pruning). Rather, it appears that on the one hand they might procrastinate, much as the delayed chaffinch does in pubescent learning of songs; and on the other they might develop alternative networks that are not linguistically significant and can only partially be exploited for later learning of a first language. The paucity of evidence of L1A after twelve years of age leaves this question open to further research.

An exemplary documentation of language regained by a deaf-blind person is Helen Keller's (1954 [1902]) autobiography in which she describes her early abilities in English before a devastating illness struck when she was just beginning to talk. Before learning a manual language beginning at age seven, she developed a system of homesign with which to communicate with her family, a system that resembles those described by Goldin-Meadow and Mylander (1994 [1990]). Keller recounts her ability to remember words, an ability that is rekindled when she learns to associate the manual spelling of "water" to the flowing liquid, thanks to Annie Sullivan. Given the importance of early exposure to language, and its crucial role in later L2 development, there seems little doubt that Keller's early formation in spoken English helped her to reacquire language, even in a different modality. It is also important to note that her acquisition process seemed to be accelerated, much as the cases of language deprivation described by Skuse.

3.3.3   Delay in L1A, spoken language

Deaf children deprived of language entirely during childhood are unable to gain thorough linguistic competence as adults. Curtiss (1988) documents the case of Chelsea, a deaf individual incorrectly diagnosed as retarded and thus never sent to school. She lived with her supportive family, but received no language input until her deafness was discovered when she was thirty-one years old. Given hearing aids that brought her perception to audible levels, she began L1A of spoken language in a rehabilitation program. She quickly gained vocabulary and social formulas (e.g. "How are you?") that she used quite appropriately, but she failed to gain competence in morphosyntax, as the examples in (7) illustrate.

(7) Chelsea's ungrammatical utterances (ibid., 85–86)
     a. the small a the hat
     b. banana the eat
     c. the woman is bus the going
     d. Peter sandwich bread turkey

The last sentence was produced in 1987, seven years after she began her L1A process, at a time when she was being followed by Curtiss, whose tests indicated that Chelsea's non-grammatical knowledge was "quite good (e.g. 80 percent correct)." Curtiss (1988, 86) points out that Chelsea's mastery of social conventions of discourse distinguishes her from Genie, who was unable to be socially adept. "While in both Chelsea and Genie's cases the integrity of lexical semantic acquisition was dissociated from grammar acquisition, we see from the differences in the two cases the additional separability of social and communicative linguistic abilities from each of these other areas."

On the other end of the age spectrum, children receiving *cochlear implants* also provide evidence of age effects for acquisition of spoken language by congenitally deaf individuals, according to Sharma and colleagues. A *cochlear implant* is an electronic device that mimics the functioning of the inner ear (cochlea), by transmitting external sounds through a microphone to electrodes implanted in the damaged cochlea. As in the case of vision, hearing is a phenomenon that is as much based in the brain's processing of the sensory data as in the physiological transmission. The establishment of proper neural pathways to perceive language has been shown to be age-sensitive. Sharma et al. (2002a), in an investigation of three-year-old children, find age-appropriate cortical responses by eight months after implantation and conclude that there is "a high degree of plasticity in the central auditory pathways of congenitally deaf children who were fitted with a cochlear implant early in childhood" (ibid., 1368). In a companion study, Sharma et al. (2002b) compare early (<3.5 years) and late (>7 years) implanted children with normal hearing peers. The early group matches the normal group, while the late group shows delayed cortical responses; the authors conclude that the brain's plasticity to develop oral language within normal parameters is limited to the first four years of life. More recently, Sharma et al. (2005) offer a more complex analysis of the age sensitivity, noting that late-implanted children are not simply slower in response, but show a different pattern of auditory development than early implanted ones.

Diminishing language ability with increased age of first exposure is also shown in research by Yoshinaga-Itano (2002) who studies 150 deaf and hard-of-hearing infants and toddlers, half of whom were early identified with hearing loss and the other half who were later identified. She finds "significantly higher language development among children identified with hearing loss and placed into intervention by six months of age. The first six months appear to represent a particularly sensitive period in early language development" (ibid., 60). One is drawn to conclude that exposure to language input from birth on is crucial, and that any delay in exposure can be detrimental. These findings complement the Newport study, which doesn't address the very early period of acquisition, but rather indicates that delay in onset of exposure results in progressively weaker acquisition of grammar, with significantly inferior morphology in learners whose age of onset is past 12 years.

3.4   Language creation

A last area of exceptional L1A explored in this chapter, creole languages, displays the innate human propensity for language creation even given incomplete input. *Creoles* are languages that seem to develop *de novo* usually from the input of pidgins, verbal communication systems spoken in environments where bilingualism is not possible (e.g. when there are too many mutually incomprehensible languages). The following section describes spoken and signed creoles.

3.4.1   *Spoken creoles and pidgins*

If children with SLI, WS or DS approach normal language input with very different brain structures, children exposed to pidgins have normal brain structures but receive unusual input. Nevertheless, children may "create" from multilingual input a fully functional and systematic language, a creole. *Pidgins* are communication systems that arise when commercial trade or interethnic exchanges result in population shifts bringing together linguistic groups that speak mutually incomprehensible languages. Prime examples are the languages that developed in the Caribbean during the slave trade of the seventeenth to nineteenth centuries (DeGraff 1999) or those of the plantation workers who moved to Hawaii in the nineteenth and twentieth centuries (Bickerton 1981, 1990, 1995). Pidgins – which have no native speakers – display reduced propositions (usually four words long), no functional categories (e.g. articles, tense or agreement inflection, complementizers or grammatical prepositions), variable syntactic order (often related to the native language of the speaker), random vocabulary borrowing and very little embedding. The contributing languages that form the base of pidgins and creoles are the *substrate* languages of the populations that are displaced (e.g. African languages in the Caribbean, Pacific rim languages in Hawaii) and the *superstrate* language of the socially dominant group/colonial power (English, French, Spanish in the Caribbean, English in Hawaii).

Creoles, on the other hand, are the languages that develop out of the contributing substrate and superstrate input. Quite pertinent to a description of the process of creolization are the observations of creole sign languages emerging in Nicaragua and Israel to be discussed later in this chapter. The children who grow up signing refine and grammaticalize the input they receive so that the linguistic systematicity of the evolving creole increases with succeeding "generations" of learners. A more idealized development is proposed by Bickerton, who describes the rise of plantation creoles in a single generation. Children who are exposed to a pidgin (and undoubtedly the native language of their parents) in the first years of life converge on a communication system that includes all the characteristics of true language, which a pidgin does not. Bickerton's single generation model is appealing as a representation of language creation, but creole development often takes place over several generations, with increasing stabilization over time (DeGraff 1999; Sandler et al. 2005). DeGraff, in sketching the development of Haitian Creole, points out that the eventual stabilized language undergoes "successive nonnative approximations" during the stabilization of the ancestor pidgins. Creoles – generally learned as first languages – display sentences of any length with grammatical embedding (certain words become generalized as complementizers marking subordinate clauses), functional categories (expressing nominal and verbal features such as tense, mood and aspect), fixed syntactic order, and stable vocabulary.

Bickerton (1981, 11–32), who has studied Hawaiian pidgins (8) and creoles (9) extensively, gives the following examples of "grammatically impoverished" pidgin contrasting with fully functional creole.

(8) Hawaiian pidgin
    a. tumach   mani   mi tink kechi do
       too much money I   think catch though
       "I think he earns a lot of money, though"

   b. wok had dis pipl
      "These people work hard"
   c. josafin brada hi laik *hapai* mi
      "Josephine's brother wants to take me (with him)"

(9)   Hawaiian creole
   a. ai no kea hu stei hant insai dea, ai gon hunt
      "I don't care who's hunting in there, I'm going to hunt"
   b. dei wen go up dea erli in da mawning go plaen
      "They went up there early in the morning to plant"
   c. ai gata go haia wan kapinta go fiks da fom
      "I had to hire a carpenter to fix the form"
   d. eni kain lanwij ai no kaen spik gud
      "I can't speak any kind of language well"

The pidgin shows variable word order with (8a) having a null subject (S), object-verb (O-V) order, while (8b) is V-S and (8c) is S-V. It has no consistent articles, verbal marking, possessive marking, complementation or pronouns. The creole, in comparison, has consistent word order S-V-O, with semantically significant options for movement as the fronting of the phrase "any kind of language" (9d) demonstrates. It has consistent articles (*wan* "a" and *da* "the"), verbal inflection (*stei* habitual, *gon* future, *kaen* modal), prepositions (*insai*, *in* which licitly join the adverb *dea* and noun phrase *da mawning* to the rest of the sentence), infinitive markers (*go* in (9b, c) which precede the embedded verbs *plaen, haia, fiks*), relative pronouns (*hu* in (9a)), negation (*no* preceding the verb in (9a, d)), and pronouns (*ai* "I," *dei* "they").

Bickerton adduces evidence from a wide range of creoles to show that they share many syntactic characteristics, such as tense-mood-aspect features, often realized in *serial verb* constructions (complex verbal expressions that concatenate several verbs to create a composite meaning). Cross-linguistic similarities among creoles suggest a parallel genesis that leads Bickerton to propose a *bioprogram* determining the characteristics of human language universally and guiding the acquisition of language by children exposed to even a minimal amount of input (pidgins). "The child will seek to actualize the blueprint for language with which his bioprogram provides him" (Bickerton 1981, 134). His proposal entails a non-gradual shift from protolanguage to true language "without any intermediate stage" (Bickerton 1990, 169), and even suggests a different route of acquisition. "The nature of their origins ought to mean that they are acquired with far fewer mistakes on the part of the children, and in a far shorter period of time" (Bickerton 1981, 210).

Bickerton's idea of a bioprogram has been reevaluated in recent years by scholars such as DeGraff (2003, 2004), who argues that such exceptionalist views of creoles wrongly portray them as abnormal languages, hence inferior. Bickerton (2004, 831), in a reply to DeGraff notes that thirty years ago treating creoles as European dialects was demeaning, but now "some see it as demeaning to Creole speakers if their languages are treated as novel and distinct entities, rather than as dialects of some European language." While Bickerton maintains that DeGraff confuses the idea that creoles are a distinct class with the idea that they are degenerate and inferior, DeGraff's claim that there should not be a dichotomy between language change and creolization is well taken. The development of typologically distinct French or Spanish from Latin may certainly have been similar to the development of Haitian Creole from French – parents who were second language learners undoubtedly used a less than perfect version of the superstrate language and their native language to address their children. Today's immigrants portray a similar family dynamic, with parents poorly speaking the new language and children often ignoring the parental native tongue as the younger generation becomes fluent in the dominant language. What is certain for both language change and creole languages (if a distinction does exist), is that children adopt a consistent version of the new dialect, regularize it, grammaticalize it, and do so in a relatively short time. Whether creoles, diachronically developed from the superstrate in a melting pot with several substrate languages, constitute a different language typology from languages that result from the meeting of only two languages (e.g. Latin and Gallic in Lutetia-Paris) is a question that does not diminish the significance of the creative aspect of creoles. These complete languages are capable – in a single generation or over several – of appropriating the lexicon of the superstrate to render functional categories that resemble those of all other languages in the world, accomplishing this feat without a model for what will become the ultimate output.

3.4.2   Creation of sign language with imperfect input

Studies of homesign indicate that children are innately prepared to learn language and spontaneously furnish certain linguistic structures without input. Studies of the past twenty years have revealed that children exposed to imperfect grammatical models in the form of pidginized input are able to fill in and regularize missing and variable morphology in the ambient language they receive. For example, a case study of Simon (Singleton and Newport 2004) – a congenitally deaf child of two deaf parents who are late learners of ASL – demonstrates that he improves on the input of his parents "to form a cleaner, more rule-governed system than the one to which he was exposed" (Newport 1999, 168). The authors compare a *probabilistic* model of acquisition whereby the learner gains structures in proportion to the input, with a *deterministic* one that would regularize inconsistent data to make it more characteristic of natural languages. Since Simon produces more accurate morphology (88 percent) than his parents (70 percent accuracy) with a far lower rate of error, the deterministic account is favored over the probabilisitic one. The only cases where Simon's morphological errors match those of his parents are when they omit a given morpheme consistently (and he never receives it as input at all). This single case study shows the same pattern of grammar regularization seen in the creole languages discussed above and in a new sign creole on a much larger scale.

A new language being documented in the Negev Desert (Padden et al. 2006; Sandler et al. 2005), the Al-Sayyid Bedouin Sign Language (henceforth ABSL), also shows generational "improvements" (crisper signs, faster expression) by younger learners. ABSL is a third-generation sign language, in use for the past seventy years by hearing and deaf members of a Bedouin community who have a relatively high incidence of congenital deafness. It is quite distinct from the other languages – Arabic (spoken and Classical), Hebrew and Israeli Sign Language – in the regional environment, systematically uses subject-object-verb word order, and has no inflectional morphology. It is unique in not being a creole growing out of a pidgin lingua franca, but rather being a spontaneous creation of deaf and hearing members of a culturally uniform social group. Its systematic syntax and lack of inflectional morphology indicate that new languages do not necessarily blossom with full-blown functional features in a single generation. Sandler et al. (2005, 2665) suggest that case marking and verb agreement – absent in ABSL – are characteristics of language that emerge over time, but that the consistent syntactic order is a conventionalization revealing the "unique proclivity of the human mind for structuring a communication system along grammatical lines."

Another new creole sign language which began in the early 1980s in Nicaragua is providing an evolving example of creole genesis and of universal characteristics of sign language (Kegl, Senghas and Coppola 1999). After the Sandinista government established a school for the deaf in 1980 in Managua, deaf children who had previously been isolated at home suddenly had a community of peers (400 in the mid 1980s) with whom to communicate. They at first used their homesign systems (*mímicas*) to establish a pidgin, *Lenguaje de Señas Nicaragüense* (LSN), but as this highly variable communicative system was taken up by younger deaf children who mostly arrived after 1985, it was transformed into a fully formed sign language, *Idioma de Señas Nicaragüense* (ISN). The genesis of ISN reflects the kind of language creation discussed earlier concerning the development of spoken languages, as fully grammatical creoles develop from highly variable pidgins.

Noting that there is no sign language precedent (substrate) in Nicaragua, Kegl, Senghas and Coppola – who with their colleagues have done extensive studies of ISN – supply ample confirmation of the status of ISN as a robust language with grammatical characteristics such as spatial inflection, size and shape specifiers, object classifiers, and different syntactic verb classes. In 1990 Kegl and Senghas collected narrative samples (based on two nonverbal Czech cartoons that 270 signers were asked to describe) to analyze the accuracy and richness of these grammatical characteristics. Comparing signers of LSN (pidgin) with signers of ISN (creole), they found that the latter made increased use of spatial inflection and object classifiers, and that they were more fluent and efficient in conveying information (their processing was more rapid). While ISN marks a "quantum leap to a full-fledged signed language," it is not static; rather, it continues to evolve, becoming more complex grammatically over the past twenty years, as the authors continue to document.

Researchers are carefully watching the process of this creole development, and the authors determine that the younger children are driving the changes, not the older ones. It is not the date of entry into the school that is the determining factor in what kind of communicative system the newly admitted deaf child adopts, but rather the age of the individual at entry. In examining grammatical richness, the authors compare three groups according to age of entry, young (0;0–6;6), medium (6;7–10;0) and old (10;1–27;5), and year of entry (given that with a later year of entry, ISN would be more grammatically complex and thus furnish better input). They find that young and medium age signers benefit by a later year of entry, but that older signers show no effect of year of entry (ibid., 198). These findings corroborate those that we have already seen for other spoken and sign languages:

- early exposure to language is better than later exposure
- grammatically rich input is far preferable to poor or variable input (although children work to regularize and systematize these "linguistic flaws")
- there is a progressive decline in ability to gain native-like competence with increasing age of first exposure.

The authors argue that ISN arises "abruptly when very young children radically restructured a highly variable, less than optimal signed input by bringing their innate language capacities to bear in acquiring it... the qualitative difference between LSN and ISN appeared quite early but only in children under the age of 10."

In a detailed comparison of three signers who entered the school in the same year, at ages four, seven and nine, the authors find that the older learner not only has more variable signing, but also far fewer serial verb constructions, a characteristic form in ISN, but also in creoles in general. They conclude that the oldest learner is using LSN, and the youngest one ISN (at the time of testing both have become adults active in the deaf community), and that the critical age for native acquisition of input must fall between four and nine years of age. The previous evidence we have looked at correlates with this conclusion: language input at birth is optimal, but children make up for delays and imperfect input up to age five to seven; from six to ten or so there is still a window of opportunity for acquiring native like language with fairly good processing skills and grammatical mastery; but after age ten first language acquirers will show much slower processing, imperfect grammar and lacunae in various other areas, particularly subtle linguistic features. Nevertheless, it appears that late acquirers *can* learn enough of a first language to communicate; certainly they can acquire vocabulary and set expressions and may use these to express grammatical functions as well. Late learners (beyond age 10–12) still offer a rich area of exploration, particularly in terms of their grammatical abilities and cerebral specializations.

In an article describing the recently documented Bedouin sign language (Wade 2005), Senghas is quoted on the evolving grammar of Nicaraguan sign language. She points out that the language has now acquired the signed equivalents of case endings, a feature that the Bedouin language has not yet adopted, instead relying on word order to indicate subject and object roles in the sentence. The Bedouin sign language is used by both deaf and hearing members of the community, which has hitherto been fairly isolated (undoubtedly a factor in preserving the sign language). The documentation of these sign languages attests both to the importance of gesture to language, and to the innateness of the linguistic capacities brought to bear in creating them.

3.5   Conclusion

This chapter has examined cases of exceptional L1A wherein either the learner's brain is atypical (Down Syndrome, Williams Syndrome, Specific Language Impairment), or the environmental input language is altered in quality or quantity (pidgin input, social isolation, deafness). To evaluate the evidence for the existence and nature of a sensitive period for first language acquisition, we consider how much language input is necessary for L1A, the relationship between cognition and language, and the inter-relationship of different components of language.

The cases examined show that "oral language can be learned with considerably less verbal input than is usually available" (Mogford and Bishop 1993, 243). Children exposed to the impoverished stimulus of pidgins create *de novo* a linguistic system with rapid processing and complete morphosyntax, as demonstrated in creoles of both spoken and signed languages. Children isolated from social interaction are able to gain native-like skills in a first language if rehabilitated by age seven; children who are older than ten or twelve (such as Genie) acquire some language, mostly vocabulary, but not a solid grammar. Likewise, deaf learners of sign language are native-like if they acquire ASL early but become significantly weaker in grammar with increasing AoA. Age twelve appears to be the line drawn in the sand, but lack of evidence of L1 learners older than twelve casts doubt on the validity of such a terminus. Indeed, Bortfeld and Whitehurst (2001), Hakuta (2001) and Snow (2002) completely reject a critical period for L1A, dismissing a few of the references cited as inconclusive; however, they do not consider the wide range of evidence adduced in this chapter. The issue does not seem to be black and white, but rather graduated shades of grey.

The relationship between cognition and language that emerges from studies of cognitively atypical individuals confirms Lenneberg's dissociation of language from other cognitive functions including intelligence. The examples of very late acquisition show that lexical-semantic acquisition is a capacity that remains available throughout life, whereas morphosyntax and phonology are susceptible to age deterioration. There is a range of critical moments for development of different linguistic phenomena, and a variety of thresholds within a specific linguistic phenomenon (e.g. within phonology there is perception and production, segmental and suprasegmental information).

Given the evidence of altered organismic system (human brain) and environmental input (ambient language) we conclude that there are periods of heightened sensitivity for the acquisition of first language. However, "rather than thinking of critical periods as windows that slam shut, we might do better to think of them as reservoirs that gradually evaporate during normal development and that can be partly refilled if we know which valves to open and when to open them" (Bruer 1999, 125–126). In examining the onset, duration and terminus of L1A, we see attenuated thresholds, not absolute ones, and an interdependence of three stages. Onset of language acquisition is ideally at birth, but may be postponed up to six years with arguably little visible effect; age of acquisition from six to eleven appears to present diminishing capacity for L1A; and onset after twelve results in substantial grammatical deficits. Age twelve may not represent any terminus, however, since the little evidence we have suggests that adults can acquire some parts of L1, although not an entire grammar. Puberty is not the dramatic cutoff point proposed by Lenneberg, and vocabulary acquisition continues throughout the lifetime.

4   Behind time: process and schedule of second language acquisition

4.0   Introduction

Alice Kaplan (1993, 47) describes the initial phase of her time in a French Swiss boarding school when she hears her roommates speaking German, a language she doesn't know. "Then I started discriminating the vowels from the consonants. The same sounds repeated themselves again and again – those were words – and then I could hear the difference between the verbs and the nouns. I heard the articles that went with the nouns, and then I heard where the nouns and the verbs went in sentences." Kaplan, in this early encounter with German, starts where all language learners must, with the segmentation of the speech stream into phonemes, morphemes, syntactic categories and combinatorial syntax. Her autobiographical account takes her from high school in Switzerland to a position as professor of French literature at Yale University, an odyssey that covers the progressive refinement of her French language skills.

While Kaplan's mastery of French gives her competence comparable to a native speaker, the path to that competence seems to differ from the pattern of L1A. The apparent lack of generalized process and schedule for second language acquisition is at first glance quite different from the tightly choreographed timeline of first language acquisition, to the point that some linguists claim that the two enterprises are not at all similar (Bley-Vroman 1990; Clahsen and Muysken 1996; Meisel 1997a). Indeed, infants – with their exuberant proliferation of synaptic connections – develop language at the same time that they are making tremendous progress in motor skills and cognitive growth as well, and all with no intentional effort. It is true that there is no universal inception point for L2A as birth is for L1A; in L2A there is no guarantee – as for L1A – that after achieving two-word utterances the learner will master morpho-syntax nearly perfectly in just a couple more years; there is likewise no assurance in L2A that the learner will realize perfect pronunciation simply by listening and then producing the ambient sounds, or will gain milli-second processing skills, all of which is a given for children learning L1.

However, the task of L2A is the same as that of L1A in that the learner must master phonology, morphology, syntax, semantics, the lexicon, social usage and the ability to mobilize all in rapid comprehension and production. It should not be surprising to observe a broad range of parallels between the two phenomena. One perspective of this chapter will be to examine the similarities and differences between L1 and adult L2 acquisition; their relationship to child L2A is addressed in Chapter 5.

The cross-linguistically strict timeline and pattern of L1A reflect a biological foundation anchored in age-sensitive thresholds for different linguistic milestones, a foundation that might be characterized as Universal Grammar, the constraints within which language is acquired and operates. UG defines what is possible in human language – a limited range of sounds that exploit a small number of distinctive features such as voicing or place of articulation; relatively restricted means of expanding words morphologically to mark grammatical relationships; universal patterns of syntactic structure such as word order, question formation or coreference; and systematic semantic interpretation of negation and quantification. Infants pick out relevant information from their environment to create anew their mother tongue. The errors they make along the way are explainable in terms of UG, and do not violate universal principles. Likewise – most generative L2 scholars agree – adults learning an L2 conform to UG (Hawkins 2001; Herschensohn 2000; White 2003), making mistakes that often resemble those of infant learners, such as consonant cluster simplification in phonology, overregularization in morphology or infinitival forms in syntax.

In L1A the process of acquisition is spontaneous in the linguistically stable environment, whereas the process of L2A may be affected by a number of external and internal factors such as the environment, socio-economic factors, motivation, and previous language learning. Adults, as children learning the mother tongue, use a partnership of resources to acquire language, but the two processes are not identical. Children are unconsciously expectant in paying attention to the appropriate environmental input at the right time. They first focus on prosody, then the lexicon, then syntax and morphology. Meanwhile they develop other cognitive and social skills that help them to learn language, such as sensitivity to frequency or mutual gaze. Adults on the other hand seem to address all issues at once (and master none for some time), using their already established social and cognitive abilities and additional resources such as instruction, feedback and literacy. This chapter parallels the exposition of Chapter 2 in exploring representative examples of development of L2 phonology, then the lexicon, next syntax, and finally morphology.

4.1 Phonology

Children acquiring L1 initially focus on suprasegmental rhythms of the ambient language before narrowing down phonological features and segments by the end of the first year of life (Jusczyk 1997). They then spend a few more years perfecting pronunciation (sometimes not mastering this task until after they have a solid handle on morphosyntax), although their perceptual abilities are sharp from an early period (Mehler et al. 1988). L2 learners usually do not have the luxury of a year-long pre-vocal period during which they can soak up the phonological features of the target language, but rather must learn perception and production of the sound system as they acquire the lexicon. The difficulty of their undertaking lies not only in their very limited time on task, but also in their cognitive baggage, the native language phonology. The fact that they already speak a language is a hindrance in that native sound categories, patterns and perceptual biases originally interfere with the L2, but it is also a help in that it empowers the learner with phonological principles of UG that serve in the L2 as well (Archibald 1993). The interacting roles of native language and universal principles have been a major focus of L2A work in phonology (Archibald 1998; Archibald and Young-Scholten 2003; Ioup and Weinberger 1987; James and Leather 1987; Leather 1999; Major 2001), a range of which this section examines in studies of L2A of segmental and suprasegmental phonological properties.

4.1.1 Segmentals and phonemic discrimination

Phonology comprises a range of knowledge including phonotactic constraints, phonemic inventory, suprasegmental structure, processes such as assimilation and phonetic realization (Durand and Laks 2002a; Leather 1999). *Phonotactic* constraints indicate the limits on how syllables can be constructed in a given language (e.g. /str/ is acceptable in English *straight*, but /tl/ is not *tlaight*). Distinctive sounds of a language are *phonemes*, segments that may be affected by *suprasegmental* (prosodic) features such as intonation or by interaction with their surrounding environment. The nasal consonant of initial *in-*, for example, *assimilates* the place of articulation feature of the following consonant: *immobile* vs *innumerable*. In a mature native phonology with its idealized set of distinctive features, phonemes and their phonetic variants (*allophones*) may be described in rather abstract terms. For instance, English voiceless stops /p, t, k/ (*speak* = [spik]) have aspirated allophonic variants [p^h, t^h, k^h] in initial position (*peak* = [p^{h}ik]).

Once a cross-linguistic perspective is introduced, as is the case for L2 acquisition studies, phonetic detail may no longer be a simple theoretical

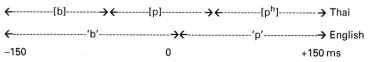

←-----------[b]---------→ ←---------[p]------------ → ←-----------[pʰ]-----------→ Thai

←--------------------'b'---------------------→←-------------------'p'----------------→ English

−150   0   +150 ms

Figure 4.1 Categorization of labial stops along a VOT continuum

construct of what is distinctive (phonemic) versus what isn't (allophonic). Voicing and aspiration are actually a function of *Voice Onset Time* (VOT), the lag between onset of articulation of a consonant and the vibration of the vocal folds. Pater (2003, 210) illustrates the non-congruency of Thai – which shows a three-way phonemic contrast /b, p, pʰ/ in bilabials – and English /b, p/ in terms of VOT (Figure 4.1).

An anglophone learning Thai would need to reconfigure the perceptual and productive thresholds of English bilabials to develop the three-way contrast in Thai, not to mention reconfiguring the allophonic nature of English aspiration to become phonemic in the new system. The learner of an L2 must not only learn what are to her the totally new sounds of the L2, but often she must also modify previously established sounds of the native language to adapt to the L2 phonological system (Flege 1987, 1995; Major 2001).

Although L2 perception and production are not simply two sides of the same coin, there is nevertheless evidence that they are mutually facilitative (Leather 1999; Leather and James 1999), and that a well-formed perceptual target helps to implement the production of L2 phonology (Broselow and Park 1995). Brown (2000) develops a model of speech perception and production that relates the native language feature inventory to the ability to acquire L2 segments that are not present in the L1. She studies phonological perception of L2 English by native Japanese, Korean and Mandarin Chinese speakers on the /l-r/ contrast (non-existent in all three languages). Unlike Japanese and Korean, however, Chinese uses the feature [coronal] – the feature that English uses to distinguish /l/ and /r/ – to distinguish Chinese alveolar and retroflex /s/, so [coronal] is part of the Chinese feature inventory. In her experiment, Brown (2000, 39) does find a difference in perception of /l-r/ by Chinese L2 learners whose performance is not significantly different from the native controls' performance, as opposed to the Japanese and Koreans who are significantly worse than the other groups, and concludes that "the presence of the feature [coronal] in the grammar of Chinese speakers ensures that acoustic stimuli which differ on this dimension will be perceived as distinct, whereas the absence of the feature from the Japanese and Korean grammars causes the acoustic signal for these two sounds to be funneled into a single perceptual category."

The ability of learners to acquire L2 segments has been a topic of research for decades, as it was a prominent area of investigation from *Contrastive Analysis* (CA) in the 1950s to the present. CA scholars such as Lado (1957) sought to explain ease or difficulty of acquisition through similarities or differences between the native and target languages. In the Skinnerian vein, they believed that L2A was based on habit formation. Similarities between native and target language were supposed to facilitate *transfer*, whereas differences would create *interference* (negative transfer). English learners of French should have no trouble with the vowel [a] (*bas* "low") which is in principle similar in the two languages, but would have trouble with [y] (*tu* "you"), non-existent in English. The 1970s saw a theoretical rejection of the psychological and linguistic bases of CA, while acquisition scholars examining *error analysis* (Corder 1967) and interlanguage (Selinker 1972) cast doubt on its empirical validity. Corder noted that L2 errors were not entirely predictable from native language differences, but rather indicated the learner's attempt to systematize the target language, an idea that Selinker popularized in the notion of *inter-language*, the evolving L2 system which was neither the native nor the target language. L2 phonology was in the meantime considered in terms of automatic processes such as L1 transfer or articulatory problems until scholars of the 1990s approached L2 phonology from metrical perspectives (Archibald and Young-Scholten 2003).

An important line of research on acquisition of L2 segments, the *Speech Learning Model* (SLM, Flege 1987, 1995), turns CA on its head by proposing that it is similarity between the native and target languages that causes difficulty of acquisition, not dissimilarity. Flege (1987), who compares the pronunciation of L2 French /u/ (back high rounded vowel as in *tout* "all") and /y/ (front high rounded vowel as in *tu* "you") by anglophone learners, finds that the anglophones pronounce /y/ more accurately than /u/, a trend he attributes to the fact that English has an "equivalent" vowel /u/ (as in *two*) whose native articulation overrides the L2 French specifications. The learner does not create a new category for a segment that he perceives as equivalent to his native segment, whereas he does create a phonemic category for what he perceives as a "new" segment in the L2. The SLM then links L2 production to the perceptual capacities of the learner while incorporating the factors of similarity and dissimilarity, at both the phonological and phonetic levels. Flege and colleagues (Flege *et al.* 1998; Flege and MacKay 2004) have subsequently shown similar patterns in other native and target languages.

Major and Kim (1999, 156) question the concept of (dis)similarity in observing that "what constitutes similar or dissimilar is not always clear," and in a compromise that offers a solution to both the similarity question and the role of markedness, they propose that it is rate of acquisition that is facilitated by similarity, but that markedness considerations impact the acquisition process. In a cross-sectional production study of Korean learners of L2 English /dž/ (as in *judge*, a phoneme present in Korean) and /z/ (as in *zoo*, a phoneme not present in Korean), they find that both more and less experienced learners perform comparably for the L1 similar /dž/ sound. However, the "new" /z/ sound is pronounced far more accurately than the /dž/ sound by the experienced English learners over the inexperienced ones. The authors point out that an important factor to examine is rate of acquisition (here extrapolated from the cross-sectional results), not simply final achievement. Segments that are dissimilar in the native and target language will become target-like at a faster rate than segments that are similar, hence fairly well articulated in an initial stage, but slow to change. They caution that markedness (here measured in terms of frequency and complexity) is a mitigating factor that may slow down the rate of acquisition.

4.1.2   *Syllable structure and stress*

L2 learners must go beyond the segment in acquiring the sounds of the new language. They must gain mastery of L2 syllable structure, stress (lexical and phrasal), intonation and rhythm (Archibald 1993, 1998; Major 2001). Learning these prosodic features of the L2 may involve a change in rhythmic units (e.g. stress-timed to syllable-timed), or the basic characteristics of syllable composition (e.g. the kinds of onsets and codas that are allowed, phonotactics). For syllable composition, a common factor cited in stating co-occurrence restrictions on consonantal sequences is a *sonority hierarchy* (Archibald 1998; Broselow and Finer 1991) that ranks segments in terms of their relative vocality, or the ability to be the nucleus of a syllable (1).

(1)   stops – fricatives – nasals – liquids – glides – vowels
       least sonorous ....most sonorous

The class of consonants comprises everything to the left of vowels, namely
- stops (e.g. [p], [d]) that stop the airflow completely
- fricatives (e.g. [v], [s]) that let some air pass with vibration of the obstructing articulator
- nasals (e.g. [m], [n]) that add nasal resonance
- liquids ([l], [r]) that can constitute a nucleus (e.g. *bridle* [braydl], but not *bridpe* [braydp])
- glides (e.g. [w], [y]) that often alternate with vowels.

Segments that are less sonorous tend to appear at syllable margins, and consonants may be clustered – depending on the exigencies of a given

language – on the basis of sonority distance. The most unmarked consonant cluster would be between a stop and a glide, since they are farthest
from each other in sonority.

Broselow and Finer (1991) examine the acquisition of *syllable structure*
by native Korean and Japanese high intermediate learners of L2 English.
English allows onset consonant combinations with closer sonority distan-
ces (hence more marked, like [str] in *straight*) than many languages; for
example, Japanese permits only stop-glide onsets like [k] + yod in *Kyoto*,
while English allows onsets with stops and fricatives to be followed by
glides or liquids (*piano, play, Sierra, sleigh*). Japanese has one onset cluster
template compared to the four templates of English. The study concludes
that learners develop an interlanguage phonology influenced both by L1
transfer and sonority markedness considerations because they "simplified
only the more marked of the new onset types, rather than simply transferring the onset constraints of the native language" (ibid., 46). The authors
argue that the learners do not transfer only the stop-glide template, but
rather compromise on something intermediate between the L1 and L2.

Isolating a particular variable such as sonority distance may not, however, be an adequate approach to evaluating phonological acquisition.
Archibald (1998, 152) suggests that the sonority hierarchy needs to be
embedded in a framework linking the acquisition of segments and syllable
structure to acquisition of the whole phonological inventory. He points
out that the ability of Japanese and Korean learners to master English
onset consonant clusters including liquids is dependent first on their
acquisition of the English distinction between /r/ and /l/ that is non-
existent in their native language. "The acquisition of English [l], then,
means the acquisition of the contrast between [l] and [r] which means the
acquisition of the representation of [l]; not just the phonetic ability to
produce a lateral" (ibid., 155). He emphasizes that it is the learner's underlying grammar which should be the focus of L2A research, not simply the
superficial production of distinctions.

Broselow and Park (1995), in a discussion of L2A of English *moraic
structure* by native Koreans, argue that the acquisition process goes
through stages that split L1, L2 and universal influences in terms of
perception and production. Mora-timed languages like Japanese (contrasted with syllable-timed French or stress-timed English, Cutler et al.
1992) are sensitive to vowel and consonant length as rhythmic units, not to
stress. Broselow and Park present data showing that when pronouncing
English words that have a tense vowel (phonetically longer than lax
vowels) plus final consonant such as *beat* or *peak*, intermediate Korean
learners add a final (coda) vowel as in [bitV] or [pikV]. The authors argue
that the Korean learners do this to maintain the perceived bimoraic

(double mora) structure of the English tense vowel. Broselow and Park delineate three stages of acquisition of English syllable structure:

I. full transfer of native perception and production
II. learner perceives the L2 moraic structure, but continues to use the native production pattern in using the final vowel
III. learners achieve both perceptual and productive capacity to produce accurate English bimoraic structures with the long/tense vowel and final consonant.

Studies of the acquisition of lexical (word internal) *stress* (Archibald 1993, 1998) indicate that L2 learners are able to restructure the stress patterns from their native language to acquire L2 stress. Archibald (1993, 177) emphasizes the complexity of stress, noting that "correct stress placement results from the proper settings of a number of parameters." In a number of studies on acquisition of L2 English stress by native speakers of Polish, Spanish and Hungarian, he concludes that adults are capable of gaining the English stress patterns and that their interlanguage grammars do not violate metrical universals. He notes influences both of L1 transfer and phonological universals in the correct and incorrect perception and production data that he collects.

Pater (1997) points out that Archibald's subjects might have memorized pronunciation as part of the lexical information of the words in question (and thus not really have inferred phonological generalizations about the stress pattern), and that they could be using phonetic perception for the stress marking task. He conducts an experiment with native French learners of L2 English using nonce words, whose stress could not, of course, be known beforehand. Lexical stress in French is systematically on the final syllable of the word, whereas in English stress is more variable (Chomsky and Halle 1968), as the examples in (2) indicate (stressed syllable bold).

(2) a**ro**ma, **ci**nema, main**tain**, as**ton**ish, **Min**nesota, con**vict**, **con**vict

Pater presents 16 words of three or four syllables as in (3), contextualized as nouns to fifty-seven Quebec French speakers learning English and fifteen English native controls.

(3) ga.di.ma, tu.gum.ster, pa.ri.da.mee, kan.den.ta.la

After practice, the subjects recorded the word alone and in a sentence. The controls' pronunciations mostly conform to linguistic predictions of stress assignment. The learners appear to get some aspects of stress placement right and others wrong, leading Pater to conclude that learners can gain new values of metrical parameters, but that they may also make mistakes on the way.

A study by Eckman et al. (2003) considers L1/L2 differences and derivational considerations in terms of a universal phonological constraint. The authors reexamine the acquisition of the segment – in this case Spanish speaking learners of L2 English /d-ð/ (as in *dare, there*) – in light of native language allophonic variations that obtain at a postlexical (across words) level, not at the level simply of the word. A difficulty for L2 learners (Lado 1957) is the case of two target phonemes that are allophones in the native language. The consonant [d] is an alveolar-dental stop that closes the airflow completely, whereas [ð] is a *spirant* that allows some vibration of the tongue against the teeth. In Spanish [d] and [ð] are allophonically in complementary distribution, with [ð] occurring after continuant segments such as vowels (e.g. *nada* [naða] "nothing") and [d] elsewhere (e.g. *dar* [dar] "to give"), whereas they are distinctive phonemes in English (*there* [ðɛr] and *dare* [dɛr] contrast). Assuming that interlanguage phonology conforms to UG principles, the authors hypothesize that Spanish learners of L2 English will retain their native language allophonic pattern in complex derived words but show target production in simple words that are learned as independent lexical items. In Spanish the spirantization of [d] to [ð] applies in simple and complex words. Examining Spanish learners' pronunciation of English /d/ and /ð/ in basic (monomorphemic) words and derived words, the authors indeed find that learners achieve accuracy earlier in the basic than in the derived words. They conclude that shifting of [d] / [ð] from allophones to phonemes includes three stages: the first stage shows L1 transfer in both simple and derived words; learners spirantize [d] in all contexts of English as [iðɛn] for [idɛn] *Eden* and [əðapšən] for [ədapšən] *adoption*. At the next stage the Spanish rule of [d] and [ð] allophones is restricted to derived contexts; learners produce [idɛn] *Eden*, but [əðapšən] *adoption*. In the final stage the English L2 phonemic contrasts are achieved in all contexts.

The Ontogeny model (Major 1987) and subsequent *Ontogeny Phylogeny Model* (Major 2001) focus on the relative roles of Universal Grammar, L1 transfer and characteristics of the L2. Major assumes that these three components affect the interlanguage differentially over time. L1 transfer decreases linearly, while universal influences – such as markedness considerations – increase at first, and eventually decrease, thus creating a U-pattern. Major also addresses the similarity issue in proposing that for similar phenomena in L1 and L2, transfer will have a greater role than universals, whereas for dissimilar phenomena the role of universals is greater. His model echoes the stages delineated by many other L2 phonologists who see a first stage of transfer of L1 phonological values (e.g. stress assignment, phonemic inventory, phonetic realization), a second stage that draws on all resources to create a systematic and UG constrained intermediate phonology, and a final stage which manifests correct values for the L2 phonology such as correct stress assignment and phonemic inventory. The final stage is not always achieved, and the end state L2 phonology may retain elements of L1 transfer or interlanguage non-target behavior. Major's model provides a framework for viewing the acquisition of L2 phonology both in terms of stages of development and of influences on development.

4.2   Lexicon

Gaining the vocabulary of a second language presents the same challenges as for the native language. People learn to perceive individual words and to understand their meaning, before gaining all the skills – phonological, morphological, syntactic, pragmatic and collocational – necessary to use the words accurately (Coady and Huckin 1997; Singleton 2000; Nation 2001). Just as children acquire their native tongue, L2 learners first must parse the input to discern separate words in an uninterrupted speech stream, a task partially facilitated by their native familiarity with the concept *word* and word learning. They expect the L2 to have words that represent ideas, that are pronounced in a consistent manner, that can be morphologically modified and syntactically arranged according to L2 requirements, and that have patterns of usage that may include levels of formality. Meara and Wilks (2002) show that L2 learners have the same network structure of the mental lexicon as native speakers, with interconnected systems of semantics, phonology, orthography, syntax and encyclopedic knowledge. The L2 network is, however, less dense in that second language vocabulary has fewer associations for each word than the native network.

There are two major thrusts of L2 lexicon building by instructed learners, an initial period during which they memorize a base vocabulary (at the same time they are establishing a base phonology, morphology and syntax), and a later period when additional vocabulary is added much as it is in the native tongue. Vocabulary learning in the classroom is described as *incidental* when learners are focused on comprehending meaning rather than learning new words and *intentional* or *attended* when learning the vocabulary is the purpose of the language-related activity (Wesche and Paribakht 1999). Incidental learning is mainly possible once learners have a critical mass of vocabulary permitting them to guess the meaning of an unknown word. Huckin and Coady (1999, 184–185) indicate that a learner needs between 5,000 and 10,000 words to serve as a base lexicon for incidental learning, and that to guess the meaning of new words in a written text, the reader needs command of more than 95 percent of the text's vocabulary. Naturalistic learners – not focused on intentional learning – gain incidental vocabulary from the start. Klein and Perdue (1992, 1997) note that naturalistic learners from the European Science Foundation project restrict their early productions to lexical categories, excluding functional projections such as determiners, tense and verbal agreement. Another characteristic of these learners is their use of formulas or chunks such as [janapa] "there is none" (Véronique 2005).

4.2.1   Initial stages of word learning

Native and L2 lexicons are similar not only in network structure (Meara and Wilks 2002), but also in knowledge of lexical items (Bogaards 2001) and acquisitional sensitivity to frequency (Abel 2003). Unlike L1 lexical acquisition, which first requires the learner to determine what words themselves are, L2 lexical acquisition proceeds directly to word learning per se, as adults attempt to substitute target language words for the ones they know in their native idiom. Adults, just like young children, have difficulty with longer L2 words, may suffer syllable recall difficulties (resulting in similar patterns of phonological simplifications), and may learn chunked expressions (Myles et al. 1998; Vainnika and Young-Scholten 1994; Véronique 2005). But they usually do not create babble-like protowords with idiosyncratic phonology and imprecise meaning, as children do at an initial stage. Furthermore, whether adults are learning in an instructional or naturalistic environment, they know that they need to memorize the meaning of L2 words and do not rely entirely on joint attentional endeavors, gaze following or saliency to conclude what L2 words refer to. Adults already possess the mature lexical constructs they developed as children to help them to sort out new vocabulary (cf. Chapter 2).

Bloom and colleagues' experiments confirm that both children and adults show similar patterns of learning and retention over time. Markson and Bloom (1997) find that adults taught a new word *koba* for a novel object are able to identify the object at 69 percent after one month, and that linguistic information is retained far better than visually presented identification tasks.

In much the way that children learning L1 vocabulary are negatively affected by extra processing factors (Pater et al. 2004), it appears that adults' learning of new words in an L2 is also inhibited by additional processing demands. L1 word learning requires the child to marshal extra cognitive resources beyond those of normal processing. Similarly, in a study of anglophone learners of L2 Spanish, Barcroft (2005) shows that a sentence writing task impedes recall (in a picture matching protocol) of twenty-four previously unknown Spanish words presented in the experiment (twelve with and twelve without sentence writing). The writing condition negatively affects the subjects' recall of the vocabulary items, with the sentence writing scores averaging about half the accuracy of the non-writing ones. Barcroft (2005, 329) concludes that "different subtasks associated with output, such as grammatical and lexical processing and the motor activities required for writing, can also exhaust processing resources that could otherwise be utilized to encode new word forms during word-level input processing."

Adults seem to have more simultaneous demands during language learning than L1 learning children, since they don't narrow attention to a single domain at a time (e.g. spending six months predominantly on segmentation and native phoneme recognition) but rather develop multiple competencies at once. They are, then, less apt to learn vocabulary incidentally while being preoccupied with processing demands in other linguistic areas, and must make a concerted effort to learn words intentionally. Gass (1999) argues that there is no clear way to separate intentional and incidental learning of vocabulary; both involve a cluster of resources such as cognates, exposure and already familiar L2 words that the learner uses to commit new words to long-term memory. Certainly linguistic and non-linguistic aids such as L2 morphology (e.g. a verb's inflection or a nominal suffix), knowledge of the real world, punctuation, interlocutor feedback or L1 transfer contribute to both intentional and incidental learning, and vocabulary-gaining strategies are both spontaneous and taught (Huckin and Coady 1999). L1 transfer can facilitate learning but is also evident in erroneous semantic mapping (Jiang 2002).

Researchers devote a substantial amount of work on L2 vocabulary learning, both intentional and incidental, to guided acquisition settings in which controlled experiments can measure the influence of various factors on learning rate and retention. Mondria (2003), for example, examines two methods of vocabulary presentation, "meaning-inferred" in which the learner is drawn to infer the meaning of a new word; and "meaning-given" in which the learner is simply told the translation right away. The fourteen- to sixteen-year-old Dutch learners of L2 French were taught vocabulary with the two methods. The first group received a more incidental presentation whereby they encountered the new words in contexts that revealed the meaning; they were then able to verify the meaning by using dictionaries and finally memorized the meaning. The second group was given the translation and also allowed to use verification to help in the memorization process. Mondria finds that the retention rate for both sets of learners is the same, but that the meaning-inferred method is more time-consuming, a finding that suggests early stages of lexical acquisition are perhaps most efficiently served by direct means.

To be sure, the relative importance of naturalistic input versus instruction has been widely discussed (e.g. Doughty 2003; Ellis 1994; Herschensohn 1990, 2000; Klein 1986; Mitchell and Myles 1998; Schachter and Gass 1996), often in terms of the authenticity of the former as opposed to the latter. Guided acquisition differs from spontaneous in its structured presentation of materials, contrived opportunities for practice and systematic intervention; a range of studies supports the importance of guidance. Ellis (1990, 165), in studying structured input in L2A, observes that instructed learners outperform naturalistic ones and that instruction aids learning of useful formulas and linguistic rules. Lexical acquisition is an area that is particularly amenable to guidance, since learners rely on a range of resources, a good example of which is cognates. Arteaga and Herschensohn (1995), in a study of beginning anglophone learners of L2 French, show that explicit instruction in cognate recognition significantly improves inference abilities in the new language. Anglophone subjects in this study were given information on cognate correspondences, but only half received information on the correspondence of L2 French words with a circumflex accent to English words with orthographic -s- as *hôpital* "hospital" or *île* "isle." All benefited from the general cognate instruction (in comparison to an uninstructed control group), but the circumflex group showed a significantly higher score on circumflex vocabulary recognition, thanks to the instructional intervention.

4.2.2   *Extending base vocabulary*

Once L2 learners have a solid vocabulary of several thousand words, they can use methods, especially reading and writing, that more closely resemble their native means of acquiring new vocabulary and extending lexical networks. Nevertheless, their intermediate mental lexicon is not as dense as the native lexical network, and there has been an animated discussion in the literature on the respective roles of form and meaning in the L2 as opposed to native lexicon. This section explores the nature of the L2 lexicon and patterns of later lexical acquisition of individual words, complex words and idioms.

Meara (1983, 1984), who was in charge of the Birkbeck Vocabulary Project, tested anglophone learners' lexical associations of a series of words in L2 French and compared the responses to native French responses. Native speakers typically give semantically based responses such as "hair" as a response to "brush" or "orange" as a response to "fruit." The anglophone learners, on the other hand, gave responses that Meara (1984, 233–234) characterizes as phonological, not semantic, and "quite different from that of the native speaker." Examples of the sorts of

L2 response given are *animal* for *béton* "cement" and *odeur* "odor" for *semelle* "shoe sole." The word for "beast" is *bête*, a source of confusion, as is the English near homonym "smell." The idea that the L2 lexicon is form-biased instead of meaning-biased is often cited as indicating a major distinction between the two sets of vocabulary (e.g. Gass and Selinker 2001, 378).

Singleton (1999), who has participated in another large lexical study, the Modern Languages Research Project, points out a number of problems with Meara's conclusions and gives evidence from his own data to support a semantic basis to the L2 lexicon. Meara's selection of vocabulary included a number of relatively infrequent words that the anglophone subjects could well have not known at all, "a simple state of ignorance which provokes a desperate casting about for lexical straws to clutch at" (Singleton 1999, 132). Furthermore, the responses, even when based on a misunderstanding of the original word (a phonological confusion such as *béton* with *bête*), often indicate a semantic association ("animal") rather than a phonological one. Singleton (1999) attributes the phonological responses to a less developed lexicon characteristic of early stages of L2 development.

Experimental studies reveal the relative importance of different factors that influence vocabulary learning and retention. Ellis and He (1999) and de la Fuente (2002) examine the effects of external factors of negotiated input and forced output in incidental vocabulary acquisition by more advanced learners. In a study of furniture vocabulary using a picture matching test, Ellis and He look at three conditions, "premodified input," additional information about the vocabulary item provided to the learner (e.g. "a cushion is like a pad and you put it on the sofa"); "interactionally modified input," for which the learner could ask further questions of a teacher; and "negotiated output," a procedure that paired two students in a problem-solving task requiring them to produce lexical output. The authors find that the output group significantly outperforms the two input groups, and conclude "producing new words helps learners to process them more deeply, whether for comprehension or for acquis-ition" (ibid., 297). In a similar experiment, de la Fuente tests the same three conditions and also finds benefits in the negotiation plus output condition for acquisition of receptive and productive command of new words, and better word retention. The importance of output and negotiation (Swain 1985, Long 1996), both of which require additional processing resources, appears to be a function of level of L2 ability, since additional processing demands hinder word learning at initial stages (Barcroft 2005).

Other aspects of the lexical network that must be learned at more advanced stages are the formation of complex words in compounds or derivations and the mastery of idioms. Lardiere (1995) and Lardiere and Schwartz (1995), who investigate the acquisition of English -*er* compounds such as *taxi driver*, *dishwasher*, by L1 Spanish and Chinese intermediate learners, find that learners can produce correctly ordered sequences sooner than accurately inflected morphology, and that L1 influence is evident. Both groups of learners make errors in number marking the generic direct object, producing, for example, *dishes-washer* or *flies-eater*, but the error is twice as frequent for the Spanish learners, a fact attributed to the necessity of a plural direct object in Spanish compounds *lava-platos* = wash-3-sg-dishes-m-pl "dishwasher." Lardiere (1995, 51) concludes that "the role of UG is limited to specifying the features visible to syntactic operation. How those features eventually come to be realized phonologically is another matter altogether, and one that is obviously language specific."

Bogaards (2001) and Abel (2003), who examine L2 idiom acquisition, find that neither acquisition nor storage of lexical items is uniform for all classes of vocabulary. Bogaards shows that different types of lexical units (e.g. simple words, complex words, idioms) aren't all acquired in the same way, for learners more easily gain multiword expressions made up of familiar forms than totally new single words. He argues that words have a base meaning that serves as a scaffold to access related lexical items, but that semantically unrelated new meanings have to be learned from scratch. Abel argues for a model of Dual Idiom Representation in which decomposable idioms are stored as the sum of their parts, whereas non-decomposable idioms are stored as distinct lexical entries, a representation recalling the dual mechanism model (Pinker and Prince 1988) for both native and second languages. In a study of native German learners of L2 English, Abel finds that they perceive decomposability in the same way as native English speakers.

4.2.3   *Mastering verbal argument structure*

At early stages learners may commit a word and its translation to memory, yet have an incomplete lexical entry by native standards. Sufficient lexical knowledge at a more advanced state includes knowledge of form, meaning, associations, collocations, grammatical usage, and appropriateness; ability to translate (with multiple meanings), recognize and define; and capacity to retrieve and generate quickly (Henriksen 1999; Joe 1995). Henricksen notes that at advanced levels, vocabulary refinement results in changed systems (much in the spirit of lexical networks) rather than simply item learning. The lexical specification of verbs (hence of related deverbal nominals and adjectives) includes information about the noun

phrases that the verb requires or allows, and how they are marked morphosyntactically. Thus, one aspect of the lexical entry of a word is information about how it can be combined syntactically, that is, its *argument
structure*, the syntactic, morphological and semantic specifications of the
complement phrases that may or must be used with it. While there are
universal semantic and syntactic constraints that determine the composition of verb classes in all languages (Juffs 2000), there is also substantial
cross-linguistic variation in which features are pertinent in determining
argument morphosyntax. The following section examines research in the
L2A of argument structure of verbs (Montrul 2001a).

Intransitive (single argument) verbs fall into two categories, *unergatives*
such as *laugh* that take a nominative external argument as subject of the
sentence (4d), and *unaccusatives* such as *arrive* that also have a single
argument, but one that originates as an internal argument of the verb, as
in (4a, b). Syntactic diagnostics for French and Italian include auxiliary
selection (*be* not *have*) and *ne/en* "of it" cliticization, and inversion (Burzio
1986; Herschensohn 1996).

(4)   a. There arrived three men
      b. Three men arrived
      c. ??There laughed three men
      d. Three men laughed

In a series of articles, Sorace (1993, 1996, 1997; Sorace and Shomura 2001)
investigates the split intransitivity phenomenon in L2 Italian, French and
Japanese, showing that the distinction is "acquired gradually and according to developmental paths which are sensitive to the lexical-semantic
hierarchies that subdivide intransitive verbs" (Sorace 1997, 170). She
notes that even though the two intransitive classes vary cross-linguistically
in composition, L2 learners become sensitive both to class membership in
the new language and to the prototypicality of the verb in question. The
features dynamic/static, telic/atelic, and concrete/abstract contribute to
what Sorace terms the core vs peripheral unaccusative types; learners and
native speakers more easily recognize verbs as unaccusative when they are
dynamic, telic and concrete, the core properties. Her studies indicate that
L1 influence is significant in L2A of argument structure, but that learners
can eventually gain native-like use and intuitions, even if not perfect
mastery of L2 unaccusatives.

Another verb class that shows differing use of semantic primitives in
different languages is that of motion verbs, which may vary in their ability
to accept *goal* (here the destination) arguments. In English, both *directed
motion* (*go*) and *manner of motion* (*walk, run*) verbs allow goal arguments
(5), whereas Japanese motion verbs allow goals only with verbs of directed

motion, not manner (6a); manner + goal can only be indicated by using a directed motion main verb with a gerund (-*te* suffix (6b)) added to the manner verb (Inagaki 2001).

(5)   a. John went to the store
      b. John ran/walked to the store
(6)   a. ?*John-ga gakkoo-ni aruita
          John-NOM school-at walked
          "John walked to school."
      b. John-ga gakkoo-ni aruite   itta
          John-NOM school-at walk-GER   went
          "John went to school walking."

Inagaki adopts a decompositional approach to these verbs (Jackendoff 1990), assuming that argument structure is constrained by syntactic principles (Hale and Keyser 1993b) and that the differences between English and Japanese are determined by different means of incorporation (Baker 1988) of semantic primitives. In English the semantic primitives PLACE and PATH incorporate into the preposition (e.g. *to*), allowing either manner or directed motion verbs, whereas in Japanese PATH is incorporated into the verb, which must be either manner or directed motion (not both). It is the incorporation options – in English to preposition, in Japanese only to verb – that distinguish the argument configurational differences between the two languages. Japanese permits a subset of the argument structures allowed with English motion verbs (prohibiting goals with manner of motion verbs), so Japanese learners need to overgeneralize while English learners need to undergeneralize from their L1 settings. White (1991a) proposes that Japanese learners of L2 English should have an easier task than English learners of L2 Japanese since positive evidence is available for English but not Japanese. L2 English learners hear examples such as (5b) that exemplify manner verbs with goals, but L2 Japanese learners hear no sentences such as ungrammatical (6a), but don't know whether the lack is just a fortuitous gap in the input or a non-existent structure.

In an experiment with Japanese learners of L2 English and English learners of L2 Japanese, Inagaki finds that the Japanese learners acquire the dual options in English, but that anglophones have difficulty recognizing the ungrammaticality of sentences such as (6a) in Japanese. It is, then, easier for the Japanese to overgeneralize their L1 lexical setting than for the anglophones to undergeneralize theirs.

A cross-linguistic study of transitivity in L2 Spanish and L2 English (Montrul 2001b) also finds L1 influence that is more easily overcome in overgeneralization than undergeneralization. Montrul examines the change of state (causative-inchoative) (7)–(8) and manner of motion (9)–(10) alternations in experiments using picture and grammaticality judgements.

(7) Change of state alternation
     a. John broke the mirror
     b. The mirror broke
(8) a. Juan rompió el espejo
     b. El espejo se rompió
(9) Manner of motion alternation
     a. The soldiers marched
     b. *John marched the soldiers
     c. John marched the soldiers to the tents
(10) a. Los soldados marcharon
     b. *El capitán marchó a los soldados
     c. *El capitán marchó a los soldados hasta el campamento

In both directions the L2 learners distinguish between change of state and manner of motion alternations, thus tapping the universal properties of these verb classes. As for the subset difference, anglophones overgeneralize (as in their L1) by not recognizing ungrammatical Spanish sentences such as (10c), and hispanophones undergeneralize the grammaticality of (9c) in English. Montrul concludes that L1 transfer is quite significant at early stages, that universal principles constrain and facilitate lexical acquisition, and that learners' sensitivity to aspectual properties of verbs and phrases may help learners recover from overgeneralization. Her conclusions summarize well the general findings presented in this section on the lexicon, that there is definite L1 and UG influence, that native and L2 lexicon are qualitatively similar, and that process and product (lexical networks) of vocabulary acquisition are similar for L1 and L2.

4.3   Syntax

Just as L2 learners already have a concept of word in their native language, they also have a concept of sentence, expressed in the grammar of questions, commands and declarations, all of which they expect to produce in the new tongue. Eventually, very good adult language learners may attain near-native fluency in L2 syntax (Birdsong 1992; Coppieters 1987; Ioup et al. 1994; White and Genesee 1996). Their initial state of L2 grammar and the stages they pass through are topics of current research, although data collected for the stages is usually not longitudinal. Indeed, Gregg (2003) calls for elaboration of transition theory in addition to property theory. The following section examines theoretical approaches and empirical evidence for three stages of L2 acquisition of syntax, initial, intermediate and endstate, mainly focusing on core morphosyntax, not usage-based discourse phenomena.

4.3.1   Initial state

During the 1980s the European Science Foundation conducted a monumental collection of data on naturalistic L2 acquisition of European languages (English, German, Dutch, French and Swedish) by immigrant workers (speakers of Punjabi, Italian, Turkish, Arabic, Spanish and Finnish). The goal was to analyze the path of L2 acquisition, stages of morphosyntactic proficiency and facilitating factors (Klein and Perdue 1992). The studies produced documentation that continues to be a rich resource for research (e.g. Huebner and Ferguson 1991; Prévost and White 2000b; Schwartz and Sprouse 1996; Vainikka and Young-Scholten 1996; Parodi 2000). The $2\frac{1}{2}$-year longitudinal records show similarities in acquisition path cross-linguistically, variation stemming from learner differences, and influence of the native language. Given the limits of the studies, however, the subjects mainly were at an elementary level of competence in the L2. Klein and Perdue (1997) characterize the earliest stage as the *Basic Variety*, a virtually morphology-free communicative system that is highly variable in word order, displays almost no functional categories such as determiners or verb agreement, uses temporal adverbs to indicate tense, exploits intonation to express questions and necessitates brevity of utterances with its limited vocabulary, all characteristics that are reminiscent of pidgins. In the languages for which data was collected, the authors find parallel pragmatic, as opposed to syntactic, based systems, which don't vary much cross-linguistically. Besides a lack of morphology (seen in the infinitival form of verbs) and variable word order, the early system also makes frequent use of null subjects. The term Basic Variety effects refers generally to these characteristics, although not all scholars agree with the idea of Basic Variety (Meisel 1997b; Schwartz 1997; Vainikka and Young-Scholten 2005).

This rich collection of empirical data on naturalistic L2 learning, in juxtaposition to the less developed theory of the earliest stages, prompts Schwartz and Eubank (1996, 1) to comment "one of the more neglected topics in L2 acquisition research is the precise characterization of the L2 initial state," a lacuna countered by their special issue of *Second Language Research* on that topic. The three proposals in their collection – Minimal Trees, Full Transfer/Full Access, Valueless Features – have proven influential in subsequent debate not only of the initial state, but also of later developmental stages.

The sparse structure of early utterances of L2 learners leads Vainikka and Young-Scholten (1994, 1996, 1998) to propose that the initial state is a reduced grammar without functional categories, only lexical ones, in the spirit of Radford (1990) for L1A. Their *weak continuity approach*, labeled *Minimal Trees* (later *Structure Building* and more recently *organic grammar*, Vainikka and Young-Scholten 2005), holds that the learner's first L2 grammar is pared down to a VP with an uninflected verb, a verbal complement (ordered with the directionality of the native language, which is transferred), and a null or non-nominative subject. Their subjects include Romance and English (head initial), Korean and Turkish (head final) learners of L2 German (a language with matrix V2). Initially then, L2 learners transfer their lexical but not functional categories and feature settings, so at the initial stage Romance and English learners make the verb VP initial, but Korean and Turkish ones make it VP final. Later, learners add a head-initial higher functional projection, a finite phrase FP which shows the beginning of verb raising, some use of verbal inflection and auxiliaries. This stage is similar to that of children learning L1 German (Vainikka and Young-Scholten 1994). At the next stage FP develops into a higher IP, and finally the last stage constitutes the CP level. Vainikka and Young-Scholten use the appearance of overt morphology (60 percent suppliance in obligatory context is taken as the threshold) such as verbal agreement and tense, verb raising and CP-related syntax to determine the stages that they designate. They see a direct link between overt morphology (free morphemes such as auxiliaries) and the development of syntactic competence.

Another linked approach is that of *Valueless Features* (Eubank 1993/94, 1994, 1996), which proposes that functional categories in L2 are initially underspecified and that their activation is directly dependent on the specification of morphology. The initial stage "does not include functional projections at all" (Eubank 1996, 74), but the features of the subsequent state are valueless or inert, leading to an optionality of syntactic movement. His examples of L2 English indicate that native German and French learners optionally allow verb raising alongside non-raising, apparently employing both the native and L2 parameter settings. It is the appearance of inflection that triggers eventual specification of correct L2 functional projections. Other "defective" feature approaches (Eubank and Grace 1998; Beck 1998) also suggest that UG is available to L2 learners and that development of syntax is linked to that of morphology.

A third approach to the L2 initial state proposes full transfer of all lexical and functional category settings from the native language to form the initial interlanguage grammar and gain full access to UG, an approach termed *Full Transfer/Full Access* (FTFA) by Schwartz and Sprouse (1996). The initial L2 grammar starts with all parameter settings from L1, but in later stages restructures the interlanguage grammar as a consequence of "failure to assign a representation to input data" (ibid., 41). This approach assumes a distinct development of L2 morphology and syntax in which morphological incompleteness is attributed to factors other than functional categories, namely difficulties related to morphological spell-out, although it describes neither longitudinal path nor stages of development. Using a case study of an L1 Turkish learner of L2 German, the authors delineate stages in the development of V2 in matrix clauses: initially SOV (with Turkish verb final order transferred), then XSVO, and later XVS. This approach does not link the development of morphology with syntax, nor does it designate universal intermediate stages of interlanguage in restructuring the L1 morphosyntactic settings.

The three approaches share the idea – well documented in subsequent research (overviews in Hawkins 2001; Herschensohn 2000; White 2003) – that UG constrains the grammars of L2 learners, but they differ on a number of points. Minimal Trees and Valueless Features posit universality of acquisition patterns (that all learners start out with the same system) and account for the initial paucity of morphological inflection by positing a lack or deficiency of functional categories at the initial state. While a lack of functional categories may account for such effects, the idea is empirically challenged by learners who do use functional elements at an early stage (Haznedar 2001, 2003; Parodi 2000). The categories acquired do not always progress in the bottom-up fashion described by Vainikka and Young-Scholten (Herschensohn 2004). On the other hand, FTFA favors L1 transfer as the major determinant of that period. L1 transfer has been well documented (Gass and Selinker 2001), and serves as a theoretically transparent primary state encompassing FTFA and Minimal Trees, but empirical data demonstrate that some initial state learners do not show L1 transfer (Yuan 2001; Bruhn de Garavito and White 2002).

Valueless Features' account of optionality, a commonly observed characteristic of L2 interlanguage, as a function of inert features is likewise unsupported by data showing that learners do not treat two parameter values equally (Yuan 2001), a half-and-half proportion that would be expected under Eubank's approach. Yuan's study of anglophone and francophone learners of L2 Chinese, a non-verb raising language, finds that both groups (even at an initial stage) mainly converge on the Chinese parametric value, a contradiction both for Eubank and for FTFA which predicts initial differences for different L1s. Hawkins (2001, 73) compromises by drawing on Minimal Trees and FTFA in his Modulated Structure Building approach. "Learners' initial L2 grammars consist, in principle, of lexical projections like VP, NP, AP, PP and these have the structural properties of their L1 grammars, again in principle (i.e. the position of the head, complement and specifier are initially determined by the L1) ... restructuring towards the L2 may be very rapid, depending on the evidence available to the learner and the nature of the transferred property in question." Hawkins is thus able to account both for Basic Variety effects such as lack of functional projections and for the L1 transfer entailed in the Minimal Trees approach, while hedging his bets with restructuring. An investigation of later stages in terms of these approaches sheds further light on their feasibility.

4.3.2 Intermediate non-finite forms

At a further stage of development, adults learning an L2 still produce utterances with verbs, often using non-finite forms as children do. However, their production is quite distinct from the L1 pattern (Herschensohn 2001; Lardiere 1998a, b; Prévost and White 2000b), for unlike child L1 production, adult L2 non-finite forms do not systematically appear with non-movement syntax. For example in French, negative *pas* precedes L1 root infinitives and follows inflected verbs, but in L2 French non-finites, negative *pas* may follow the infinitive. Prévost and White (2000b, 224) point out that while there is a systematic alternation between finite and non-finite verbs in L1A (during the Optional Infinitive stage), in adult L2A non-finite verbs may appear in finite syntactic contexts (raised or non-raised). Finite forms, however, nearly always appear in the raised position both in L1 and L2 French, indicating an asymmetry of inflected and non-inflected verbs. Prévost and White argue that verb raising begins before morphology is mastered, a development also noted by Vainikka and Young-Scholten (1994) for German. This research supports the idea of *missing inflection* (Haznedar and Schwartz 1997; Lardiere 1998a, b, 2000), holding that adult default morphology does not arise from a syntactic deficit, since word order and other syntactic phenomena may be target-like (Bruhn de Garavito 2003).

Comparisons of L1A and L2A highlight differences between the two processes. Liceras et al. (1999) compare root infinitives in Spanish L1 and L2 acquisition, concluding that the two non-finite uses are quite different. While child L1 root infinitives are preceded by *a*, occur only in matrix clauses, and decrease over time, adult infinitives are not preceded by *a*, are found in embedded and matrix clauses, and persist for a long time in the interlanguage. In another acquisition study, of German, Clahsen (1988) demonstrates that adult learners develop syntactic and morphological mastery independently. Unlike the L1A children, who do not use second person singular -*st* in their earliest stages, adults use all verbal persons (albeit with mistakes) from the earliest stages. The adult learners eventually gain V2 word order for main clauses, but "the agreement paradigm is only gradually attained and its acquisition is independent of the development of verb placement" (Clahsen 1988, 64).

Approaches to the role of functional categories and morphological inflection in the interlanguage grammar – which define differences in analysis of infinitival forms – can be characterized as *linked morphosyntax* (Minimal Trees, Structure Building, Valueless Features) or *separate morphosyntax* (FTFA). For the former, the L2 (as the L1) grammar develops morphology and syntax in parallel, whereas for the latter the two domains develop relatively independently. Another linked morphosyntax approach that has implications for the Critical Period Hypothesis is the *Failed Functional Features* hypothesis (FFFH, Hawkins and Chan, 1997; Franceschina, 2001), which holds that parameterized L2 functional features may fail in post-critical period L2A, leading to surface morphology errors. According to FFFH, native language values of functional features are available throughout life, but after childhood new functional values that differ from native ones cannot be acquired. We return to this hypothesis in section 4.4.

The notion of linked morphosyntax implies a similar pattern of morphology acquisition between L1 and L2, and also suggests a similarity of syntactic development. Researchers such as Eubank and Beck consider the possiblity of an Optional Infinitive stage in L2A, whereby the early L2 grammar has incomplete functional projections correlated with incomplete verbal morphology. In contrast, L2 scholars in the FTFA vein argue that infinitival forms are not examples of root infinitives (such as those of L1 learners), but rather indicators of defective surface inflection (Lardiere 1998a, b, 2000; Prévost and White 2000a, b; Sprouse 1998).

Diagnostics of root infinitives in French are preverbal negation and null or non-nominative subjects. Herschensohn (2001, 2003) finds that two intermediate French L2 learners ("Emma" and "Chloe," teenagers interviewed three times over six months) eventually show around 90 percent accurate use of inflected verbs in finite contexts (and infinitives in nonfinite contexts). As for nominative clitics (indicative of raising), they are used quite extensively with nonfinite verbs by Adbelmalek (33.8 percent), by Emma (44 percent), and by Chloe (71 percent), a characteristic that is quite distinct from the child data. Herschensohn (2001, 304) furnishes examples of raised infinitives (11).

(11)   Raised infinitives
    a. j'aller "I am going" (Chloe) = *je vais*
    b. nous regarder "we watched" (Emma) = *nous avons regardé*
    c. ils arriver "they arrive" (Chloe) = *ils arrivent*
    d. je ne continuer pas "I am not continuing" (Emma) = *je ne continue pas*

Herschensohn concludes that defective inflection better accounts for her data than an optional infinitive analysis, and that syntax and morphology develop independently of each other. It appears that activation of functional categories is not a direct function of acquisition of L2 morphology as demonstrated, for example, by Lardiere's (1998a, b, 2000) subject Patty who shows deficient morphological production but strong evidence of syntactic competence. The L2 grammar does not appear to be limited in the syntactic specification of functional categories, but only in mapping of morphosyntactic features to phonological realization.

4.3.3   Parameter resetting

This section examines L2A of three central parameters determining subject-verb realization and word order, Null Subject (12), Verb Raising (13) and Verb Second (14).[1]

(12)   Null Subject
    a. (Yo) quiero una manzana. "I want an apple." (Spanish)
    b. *(I) want an apple. (English)
    c. Quiero yo una manzana. "Want I an apple."
(13)   Verb Raising
    a. Je (ne) veux (pas) cette pomme. "I (do not) want this apple." (French)
    b. I want (*not) this apple. (English)
    c. Ils veulent tous/absolument cette pomme.
    d. They all/absolutely want this apple.
(14)   Verb Second
    a. Ein Buch kaufte Johann. "John bought a book." (German)
    b. Johann kaufte ein Buch. "John bought a book."
    c. *A book bought John. (English)
    d. John bought a book.

In Chapter 2 we saw that null subject languages such as Spanish allow unexpressed subjects thanks to explicit features that can identify the null constituent (12a). In contrast, overt subject languages require an explicit subject (12b). Romance languages require verbs to raise above negation (13a), whereas English prohibits raising of lexical verbs (13b). In matrix clauses, Dutch, German, Norwegian, and Swedish require further raising of the verb to second position C, the first being occupied by another

---

[1] Some other parameters that have been examined in the L2A context are pronominal binding (Broselow and Finer 1991; Herschensohn 2004; Kanno 1997; Thomas 1993) and WH movement (Bley-Vroman et al. 1988; Hawkins and Chan 1997; Johnson and Newport 1991; Schachter 1996; White 1989). See Herschensohn (2000), Hawkins (2001) and White (2003) for overviews.

constituent (*ein Buch* in (14a) and *Johann* in (14b). In addition to the main effects of these parameters, there are secondary characteristics that cluster with the main effect. L1 researchers (e.g. Clahsen 1988) have argued that children automatically acquire clustering properties with parameter setting.

The Null Subject Parameter seen in (12) has been examined in studies of L2A in both directions (null and overt subject languages as target or native). White (1985, 1989) investigates the acquisition of [+overt subject] for English L2 by native Spanish and French learners, finding that while learners master overt subjects themselves, they may miss parametric features that cluster (non-inverted subjects, obligatory expletive subjects like *it*, *that*-trace effect). In White's study the francophones show slightly higher accuracy in English than the hispanophones on grammaticality judgement and production tasks. The only significant differences between the French and Spanish speakers are on subjectless sentences that the hispanophones are much more likely to accept. As in the case of verb raising, the clustered features of null subjects are not all acquired at the same time.

Hilles (1986), in a longitudinal study of an hispanophone learning English, documents a decline in production of null subjects coinciding with an increasing mastery of *do* support and expletive *it*. Phinney (1987) discusses L2A by both anglophones of Spanish and by hispanophones of English, particularly with respect to verbal morphology and null/overt subjects. Although anecdotal evidence has suggested that morphology is a major error problem for both categories of learners, she finds that the hispanophones "did not omit pronominal subjects as much as might have been expected" (1987, 234).

Liceras (1989), studying the acquisition of Null Subject Parameter effects in anglophone and francophone learners of L2 Spanish, confirms the early acquisition of null subjects and the lack of clustering of parametric properties. Null subjects are "easily incorporated into the interlanguage" (1989, 119) and the two groups also accept (Spanish acceptable) verb-subject word order in their grammaticality judgements. When asked to correct ungrammatical sentences in Spanish (whose English version is acceptable), the anglophone learners substitute an accurate L2 form which differs from the expected L1 transfer.

L2 Verb Raising, particularly by anglophones learning French (or non-raising by francophones studying English) has been examined in a number of articles (Eubank 1994, 1993/94; Hawkins et al. 1993; Herschensohn 2000, 2001; Hulk 1991; Schwartz 1993; Schwartz and Gubala-Ryzak 1992; Trahey and White 1993; White 1990/91, 1992). White (1990/91, 1992) proposes a pivotal analysis of clustering and variability by looking at the interlanguage grammars of francophone learners of L2 English. She finds that the learners adopt an L2 setting for negation, but not for adverbs, a discrepancy also evident in the findings of Hawkins et al. (1993) and Herschensohn (2000) for anglophone learners of French. White argues that learners use two kinds of verb movement, short and long, for adverbs and negation respectively. Short movement, while not correct for L2 and non-existent in L1, is a misanalysis that is nevertheless a UG option. She shows that learners may employ different strategies for dealing with what is a unitary parametric option in the target language.

Hawkins et al. (1993) study intermediate and advanced groups of anglophone learners of L2 French, analyzing the results of a verb raising grammaticality judgment task with adverbs (e.g. *absolument* "absolutely"), negation (*pas* "not") and quantifiers (e.g. *tous* "all"). Negation, adverbs and quantifiers follow the inflected verb in French but precede it in English (13) as a function of verb raising. The authors observe a substantial difference in judgments on adverb-negation compared to quantifiers, discrepancies that lead them to conclude that the three phenomena are not parametrically clustered in L2A. Herschensohn (2000), repeating the Hawkins et al. experiment with a small group of very advanced (expert) subjects, confirms their conclusions regarding parameter setting of advanced language learners.

The German V2 Parameter – requiring raising of the verb to I and then to C, and the raising of a full phrase (e.g. NP) to specifier of CP (14) – has been explored from two perspectives in L2A, first, with respect to the initial state of the L2 grammar (Beck 1998b; Eubank 1996; Schwartz and Sprouse 1996; Vainikka and Young-Scholten 1996), and second, in comparisons between L1 as opposed to L2 (Clahsen and Muysken 1986, 1996; duPlessis et al. 1987; Meisel 1997a; Parodi 2000; Tomaselli and Schwartz 1990). The Initial State studies indicate that learners of L2 German show both L1 transfer and reduced functional categories at an early stage (Eubank 1996; Schwartz and Sprouse 1996; Vainikka and Young-Scholten 1996), that they gradually acquire verbal inflection along with the ability to raise the verb to second position in matrix clauses.

Clahsen and Muysken (1986, 1989) and Clahsen (1988) argue that their data shows distinct paths of acquisition of verb morphology and placement for children in contrast to adults, leading them to conclude that adults rely exclusively on general learning strategies while children rely on UG. Responses to Clahsen's articles by duPlessis et al. (1987) and Tomaselli and Schwartz (1990) argue that adults still have access to UG, that they do not set parameters all at once (and therefore show variability), and that the intermediate grammars are UG constrained. Clahsen and Muysken provide documentation for some distinctions between L1 and L2 acquisition, but they concede that "the outcome of the L2 developmental sequence in some cases mimics that of the L1 sequence" (1989, 24). Their evidence corroborates the view that there are both differences and similarities between L1 and L2 acquisition.

Meisel (1997a) and Parodi (2000) reexamine the German acquisition data, focusing on the relation of verb inflection to raising as diagnosed by negation. Meisel (1997a, 257) reaffirms the L1A/L2A distinction in noting that for both German and French there is in L1A a developmental relationship between "the emergence of the [+/−finite] distinction and verb placement and consequently also target-like placement of the finite verb with respect to the negative element" that does not hold for L2A. Parodi does not find the lack of systematicity of negation in L2A that Meisel does. Her data – from a subset of Meisel's forty-five German learners, namely three Romance speakers followed longitudinally – contain inflected verbs consistently used with correct postverbal negation in L2 German, and "verb raising with nonthematic verbs [auxiliaries and modals] appears to be obligatory from the very beginning" (Parodi 2000, 377). She points out that Eubank's optionality treatment cannot account for the nonthematic/thematic distinction, and she proposes that learners initially use nonthematic verbs to spell out the syntactic features of the functional category Inflection. At this initial stage the learner deals with lexical (thematic verbs) and syntactic (nonthematic ones) information separately, which she connects to observations that early learners rely heavily on lexical means to communicate grammatical information (e.g. adverbs to convey tense, as in Basic Variety).

Studies of parameter setting and acquisition of other syntactic phenomena in L2A indicate that learners initially transfer L1 settings of functional features, but that they are able to gain the new L2 values after an intermediate period of indeterminacy. The interlanguage generally looks like a possible human language, but it may include incorrect L2 syntax in intermediate stages. Learners acquire core constructions before more peripheral ones (Herschensohn 2000), as negation before quantifiers in setting the verb raising parameter in L2 French. Finally, overt morphology and syntax seem to develop independently unlike in L1A, and L2 learners may persistently have difficulties mapping morphosyntactic features to phonological realizations.

4.4   Morphology

Brown's (1973) observations on the order of L1 acquisition of grammatical morphemes in English inspired a spate of L2 studies throughout the next decade which found a remarkably similar order of acquisition regardless of the native language (Bailey et al. 1974; Dulay and Burt 1974a, b; Dulay et al. 1982; Goldschneider and DeKeyser 2001; Kessler and Idar 1979; Krashen et al. 1977; Zobl and Liceras 1994). The order of acquisition for L2 grammatical morphemes correlates signficantly over several populations and differs from the L1A order. For L2 learners, articles, copula (*be*) and auxiliaries are acquired earlier than in L1, while past irregular is acquired later. Goldschneider and DeKeyser (2001) do a meta-analysis of twelve earlier studies involving 924 subjects and conclude that the natural order stems from no single cause, but from five crucial determinants, perceptual salience, semantic complexity, morphophonological regularity, syntactic category and frequency. Their findings support the idea that L2 learners use a coalition of information sources to infer forms and rules of the new language.

It is impossible to discuss morphology without syntax, but we can examine how morphological knowledge is developed, stored and accessed in terms of models of native morphology. The rule-based approach and frequency-based connectionist approach are brought together in the dual mechanism model proposed by Pinker and Prince (1988) and Pinker (1999), who argue that morphological knowledge is stored and accessed in two ways, either as rules that allow formation of novel forms with words not previously familiar (e.g. the plural of *wug* is *wugs*) or as memorized lexical items (e.g. *went* is the past of *go*). To that end, the following section discusses the acquisition of nominal and verbal morphological endings in terms of the Words and Rules model.

4.4.1   *Nominal gender and verb inflection*

Two areas that provide insight into L2 morphology (as contrasted with L1A) are the acquisition of nominal gender and agreement by learners whose native language does not have a gender feature – a topic investigated in several recent articles (Bruhn de Garavito and White 2002; Franceschina 2001, 2002; Gess and Herschensohn 2001; Granfeldt 2005; Hawkins and Franceschina 2004; Parodi et al. 1997; Prodeau 2005; White et al. 2004) – and the acquisition of verb inflection (Herschensohn 2003).

Parodi et al. (1997) look at acquisition of German DP by native speakers of Korean, Turkish, Italian and Spanish, in data that includes use of number agreement (and DP syntactic phenomena). Even though their native languages have inflection for plural, all the learners of L2 German show missing plural inflection at an early stage, preferring lexical means of marking plurality. This last finding indicates that L1 transfer alone is insufficient to describe the developmental errors of L2 learners, and reminds us of the functionally bare VP/NP idea of minimal trees.

The Failed Functional Features hypothesis (FFFH), which considers that inflectional errors result in large part from an underlying syntactic deficit, is adopted by Franceschina (2001) who analyzes in detail the data of Martin, a near-native anglophone L2 learner of Spanish. She maintains that there is a significant difference between his scores and those of a native speaker control, although Martin scores around 90 percent on various nominal categories. His accuracy is 100 percent (the same as the native speaker control's score for all criteria) for noun, adverb and possessive, but his gender concord is defective for other categories, whose accuracy rates are: adjectives, 92 percent; articles, 92 percent; pronouns, 91 percent; demonstratives 85 percent (ibid., 236). There is also a difference between gender and number agreement, with gender accounting for 93 percent of the total agreement errors. Franceschina concludes that anglophone L2 learners show this contrast because they are permanently impaired in acquiring L2 functional features that don't exist in their native language, evidence that she claims supports FFFH.

Franceschina (2002, 2005) provides further evidence for the FFFH in administering a range of gender tasks to a group of sixty-eight subjects whose native languages are [+gender] Romance or [−gender] English and who are near-native learners of Spanish. Although the subjects are generally quite adept in the L2, she finds differences between the Romance and English natives that she attributes to the fixing of the functional feature of [gender] during the Critical Period. Hawkins and Franceschina (2004) likewise argue that L2 learners over nine years of age can only acquire uninterpretable functional feature values available in their native language. They adduce evidence from L2 Spanish and French that indicates anglophone adult learners do not show behavioral responses similar to native and early bilingual speakers of the Romance languages, and never gain 100 percent productive abilities either. They choose the age of nine as a threshold because at that age gendered language children are using syntactic cues of concord – not "lexical" morphophonological cues – to determine the gender of new words. Chapter 6 revisits the question of differential behavioral responses between native speakers and adult L2 learners with respect to gender acquisition.

Bruhn de Garavito and White (BGW, 2002) and White et al. (2004) argue against FFFH in studies of anglophone and francophone students of L2 Spanish. BGW show that learners are neither insured nor prohibited from acquiring a different setting of L2 gender. White et al., who cross-sectionally compare L1 French and English speakers learning L2 Spanish on a variety of tasks, find that advanced and intermediate groups perform similarly to native speakers, suggesting that L2 learners can acquire functional features such as gender whether or not it exists in the L1. Unlike the more advanced learners, lower proficiency anglophone and francophone subjects are more accurate on number than gender, indicating that francophone learners do not transfer gender at initial stages. This difference might also relate to the gender/number discrepancy in Franceschina's findings, for the lack of transfer effects for lower proficiency subjects could be related to intrinsic differences between gender and number, not to native language influence. As in the Parodi et al. study, L1 transfer alone cannot account for the interlanguage data. The investigations of gender acquisition present mixed indications concerning influence from L1 transfer, but despite residual problems for L2 learners achieving mastery of L2 gender, it appears that near-native learners can gain 90 percent accuracy, indicating a fairly solid grasp of this nominal feature which may not be available in the native language.

Granfeldt (2005), who compares Swedish adult learners of L2 French with Swedish-French native bilingual children, finds that the adult learners first gain a default form and then gradually learn the correct gender over a period of time, whereas the children gain gender almost immediately with the learning of the noun. Chapter 2 documents the early learning of gender and concord by children acquiring a gendered language. Since Swedish is a gendered language, it is not clear what his findings mean for the FFFH about which he remains somewhat skeptical but nevertheless undecided. In any case, if native gender does facilitate gender acquisition in the L2, it does not happen immediately, since the Swedish adults do not acquire French gender in early stages.

As in the case of the gender studies in which less proficient learners had difficulty both with gender assignment and with agreement, intermediate learners of an L2 also have difficulty with the realization of verb morphology. Herschensohn (2003) describes morphology accuracy and inflectional errors of the subjects Emma and Chloe whose syntax is outlined in section 4.3.2. These two subjects, followed over six months in three interviews each, use accurate verbal inflection, while continuing to produce some tokens of nonfinite verbal forms through Interview III. Emma's and Chloe's correct suppliance of verbal inflection in obligatory context – at 89 percent and 98 percent respectively by the third interview – is difficult to account for without postulating correct L2 settings for the syntactic categories of Tense and Agreement. As for their morphological realization, an examination of the error rates (Table 4.1) and types of errors reveals a difference between the two subjects. The errors fall into three categories: (1) wrong tense (e.g. present for past); (2) inflection error (e.g. singular for plural form); (3) ellipsis (e.g. missing subject or verb).

Both learners have the ability to use correct verb morphology with a range of regular and irregular verbs in present, past and future uses, and by

Table 4.1 *Errors of verbal morphology, Emma and Chloe*

	Tense	Inflection	Ellipsis	Total errors
Emma I	5	3	2	10
Emma II	7	10	3	20
Emma III	4	6	0	10
Emma total	16	19	5	40
Chloe I	6	10	4	20
Chloe II	1	6	2	9
Chloe III	0	2	0	2
Chloe total	7	18	6	31
Subject total	23	37	11	71

the third interview their knowledge of morphology is fairly comparable (89 percent and 98 percent respectively). Emma and Chloe's experience demonstrates that person agreement is mastered earlier than tense, and their development of verb inflection progresses from person to tense to aspect. Their self-corrections indicate that they have difficulty in morphological realization, not in the presence of the abstract notion of tense (hence the functional category Tense).

In L2A, the development of morphological mastery parallels the acquisition of syntax, but is not linked as it appears to be in L1 acquisition. The data of intermediate speakers who use a preponderance of inflected verbs, yet persist in producing non-finite forms as well, show that L2 learners use infinitival forms, but not in the fashion of L1 learners. In L2 acquisition the mastery of morphology is not directly dependent on the acquisition of syntax or vice versa. We can therefore expect an incomplete mastery of morphological features at an intermediate stage.

4.4.2   Words and rules

The discussion of nominal and verbal inflection raises the question of how morphological knowledge is represented in the L2 grammar and how that knowledge is developed. Clahsen (1997) and Beck (1997) present experimental evidence supporting the *Words and Rules* model of L2 morphology (Pinker 1994b; Pinker 1999; Pinker and Prince 1988), and Herschensohn (2003) uses the model to explain the morphological patterns of Emma and Chloe. Zobl (1998) develops a two-stage developmental model based on dual mechanism that distinguishes rote-learning of irregular morphological forms from rule-governed learning of regular morphology. Regular rule learning is not associated with specific lexical items, but rather generalized to a class. New nouns or verbs, such as *Google*, can be pluralized to *Googles* (noun), or made into past tense *Googled* (verb) by rule. Irregular morphology, on the other hand, is learned as individual items. Native speakers process less frequent irregular morphological items more slowly than frequent ones since they are stored individually, whereas regular morphology shows no frequency effect since it is rule-governed.

Beck (1997) tests (in a timed response experiment) the regular/irregular distinction with near-native English L2 learners, finding in certain circumstances that they do not show a significant difference between more or less frequently used regular verbs. Concluding that L2 learners store regular and irregular morphological information in the same way as native speakers, she adopts the dual mechanism model. In a study of German noun plurals, Clahsen (1997, 124) also finds a regular/irregular distinction in morphology processing indicating similarity rather than difference between native and L2 morphology storage and processing. "The results we have on the acquisition of noun plurals in German, both on L1 acquisition...and on adult L2 development, suggest that even in this case, where learners are confronted with a highly irregular system in the input, qualitative distinctions between regular and irregular plurals are made quite early on." Language learners are, it seems, sensitive to the duality of morphological forms. Regularization, a commonly noted trait of interlanguage morphological forms, is an indication of rule-governed morphology in the L2 and of the fact that inflectional forms are not stored as distinct items. Herschensohn (2003), after an examination of the correct and incorrect L2 verbal inflection in the productions of Emma and Chloe, concludes that the data supports the dual mechanism model. Irregular morphology (e.g. the verb *être* "to be") is quite idiosyncratic and must be learned as individual suppletive items, while regular forms are rule-predictable. Emma and Chloe demonstrate rule-based knowledge in their mostly correct regular verb forms and their regularization of irregular forms.

Zobl (1998) proposes a two-stage developmental model of L2A of morphology based on "listing and computation," the two psychological mechanisms underlying the dual mechanism model. The first stage is the listing one during which the learner masters individual items such as irregular past or suppletive forms; this is then a stage of *lexical learning* (Clahsen et al. 1994) whereby the acquisition of lexical items leads to their later extension to syntactic and morphological generalization. At the second computational stage regular inflection becomes computationally functional. Zobl suggests that at the earlier stage the functional projections that host affixal morphology are either absent or inert. Later, "the productiveness of an inflectional affix is an outward reflex of the ability to separate grammatical features from their lexical hosts, to represent them as a node heading its own projection" (ibid., 349). Zobl's proposal situates dual mechanism in a developmental scheme that takes into account both morphology and syntax.

Birdsong and Flege (2001) provide more definitive evidence for the dual mechanism model in L2 acquisition by comparing L2 English regular and irregular morphology in multiple choice selection of correct form by learners with L1 Spanish and L1 Korean. They find clear evidence of sensitivity to input frequency for irregulars but not regulars (as predicted by dual mechanism), influence of native language, and AoA interaction whereby "computation of irregulars is increasingly deficient over AoA" (ibid., 130). Computation of regular morphology is significantly less affected by increasing AoA, implying that declarative memory (involved in irregular computation) is more susceptible to deterioration with age than procedural memory (involved with regular), say the authors. They suggest that language learning mechanisms are relatively unaffected by increasing age, a topic we return to in Chapter 6.

4.5   Conclusion

L2A shows, as does L1A, a systematicity of acquisition pattern, but they are not the same, and they don't follow the same schedule. Individual variation, L1/L2 pairings and a number of other factors contribute to a wide range of endstate interlanguage grammars among learners. A characteristic L2 narration (of a Florida tornado) by a native Japanese learner of English illustrates several aspects of second language described in this chapter, and highlights differences between L1A and L2A (Gass and Selinker 2001, 35).

(15)   L2 narration
    a. I see somebody throwin a brick onna trailer.
    b. Wind was blowin so hard.
    c. Ana light...outside street light was on.
    d. Oh I was really scared.
    e. So I try to open door.
    f. I could not open.
    g. I say, "Oh, my God. What's happen?"

Unlike the two year-old's simple request for crackers, this speaker – who had lived in the United States for twenty-eight years – is narrating a complex story in the past. Her sentences manifest a number of errors, and she still has difficulty with English phonology (the /ŋ/ of progressive -*ing*, and consonant clusters), but she commands central morphosyntactic features of English. She shows accurate word order (whose directionality is the opposite of her native tongue), uses a nominative subject and verb in every sentence, correctly places negation after the modal verb and is able to create complex sentences. Unlike the L1 learner who is virtually guaranteed perfection in his native grammar, this L2 learner shows several nonnative aspects: her difficulties of pronunciation; her missing verbal inflection (15a, e, g) which could perhaps be caused by her inability to pronounce final consonant clusters; her missing determiners (15b, c, e); and a missing object (15f). While she shows influence from the L1 and non-target interlanguage structures, she has nevertheless acquired a substantial amount of vocabulary and the essentials of English sentential syntax, subject-verb agreement and embedding.

The evidence from L2A of phonology, morphology, syntax and lexicon indicates that learners gain knowledge of the new language that is qualitatively similar to that of native speakers of the same language. Learners use a range of resources including primary linguistic data, native transfer and cognitive strategies to create UG constrained interlanguage grammars which, though incomplete, resemble those of native speakers. Although qualitatively similar to native grammars, L2 endstate grammars, even of expert speakers, never attain the completeness of the native ones. The path followed in L2A is similar in many ways to that of L1A, but usually requires more time to traverse. Certain characteristics – mastery of L1 phonology, clustering in L1 parameter setting, and automatic acquisition of L1 morphological features like gender – distinguish L2A from the native pattern. It is not clear, however, that incompleteness, pace of acquisition or parametric clustering are diagnostics of a critical period. By and large, learners fluent in their L2 have knowledge that is quite similar to that of native speakers, whether they learn the L2 as adults or as children.

5 Pressed for time: age constraints in second language acquisition

5.0   Introduction

Early in the novel *Native Speaker*, Chang-rae Lee's hero Henry Park meets his future wife (a speech therapist, naturally):

"People like me are always thinking about still having an accent," I said . . .
"I can tell," she said.
I asked her how.
"You speak perfectly, of course. I mean if we were talking on the phone I wouldn't think twice."
"You mean it's my face."
"No, it's not that," she answered . . . "Your face is part of the equation, but not in the way you're thinking. You look like someone listening to himself. You pay attention to what you're doing. If I had to guess, you're not a native speaker. Say something."
(ibid., 12)

Henry's perfect pronunciation on the phone seems to confirm the widespread belief that younger learners are more adept than older ones at language acquisition, but his self-consciousness belies the dilemma of immigrants whose nonnative origins surface in subtle ways, both linguistic and social.

Chapter 3 presents evidence that there are biological factors that limit the ability of children to acquire L1 completely under deprived circumstances (with deprivation either of environmental input or of the organismic cognitive system). Normal L1A – most of which takes place in the first four years of life – is quite uniform in schedule and process cross-linguistically. It may be delayed up to age five, but subsequently shows progressive deterioration through childhood. After that stage learners are highly disadvantaged at learning morphosyntax and phonology (Curtiss 1988), although, as all humans, they may continue to learn vocabulary throughout life. Research in L1A has supported Lenneberg's arguments based on regularity of onset and universal pattern of language development. This chapter investigates the notion of a sensitive period for second language acquisition, looking not only at the evidence raised in Chapter 3, but also at patterns of deterioration in L2 learning ability. Let us first recall the properties of biological critical periods (Bornstein 1987b): organismic system, environmental input, onset, duration of the developmental period, and terminus. For L2A the organismic system is the human brain already synaptically connected (unlike the newborn's L1A brain), wired for a native language and a range of other cognitive skills. For L2A, innate genetic endowment is not the central guiding force, and the baggage of cognitive experience may be facilitating or inhibiting. The environmental input is also more complex since it includes primary linguistic data (PLD) and numerous scaffolding devices that mature individuals use to learn. Some are comparable to L1A – learning to parse syntax by segmenting prosody, for example, or using social interactions to infer grammar or vocabulary – but others are quite specific to L2A (e.g. using instruction to learn grammar rules). The maturational threshold marking the onset of acquisition is exceedingly variable, as is the duration of development. There is, however, no terminus which marks an absolute divide after which parts of a second language cannot be learned. Adult humans can learn at least some aspects of a new tongue at any age and may even become quite proficient in a second language well beyond the age of four, fourteen or twenty-four.

Individual achievement in second language is inconsistent, unlike in first language, whose final-state grammar appears uniform across monolingual individuals. Most often, increased age correlates with increasingly incomplete final-state L2 grammars, but there are adult L2 learners who become indistinguishable from natives. Perhaps the first to categorize this "expert" learner was Selinker (1972) who estimated that 5 percent of learners belong to this category. His casual conjecture is often cited as fact (Cook 1993; Strozer 1994; Bruer 1999), although there is no confirmation to support any such number (Herschensohn 2000, 47). Superficial characteristics indicate that L2A does not strictly qualify as a critical period phenomenon, but numerous scholars (Bever 1981; Bruer 1999; Eubank and Gregg 1999; Lenneberg 1967 *inter alia*) simply assume a sensitive period for L2A parallel to that of L1A. For example, Morford and Mayberry (2000, 111) matter of factly note "individuals exposed to language at earlier ages consistently outperform individuals exposed to language at later ages for first and second languages of both signed and spoken languages." This assumption can be questioned, however, so we need to look at a range of evidence that intersects with the substantiation presented for L1A, by manipulating onset and duration of deprivation (organismic system and input) to determine the appropriateness of a sensitive period for L2A. Using paradigms reminiscent of Bruer's (2001) suggestions for designing experiments to test the existence of a sensitive period, many L2A studies address the issue of deterioration in language learning ability with increasing age. Studies of phonology and morphosyntax examined in section 5.3 manipulate onset age (*age of arrival/acquisition* or *AoA*) and duration (*length of residence* or *LoR*), using native-like achievement as the outcome measure. The intial section of this chapter frames the theoretical debate that follows, and the next looks at cases of typical and exceptional L2A of children and adults. The last section examines evidence for and against age limits on L2A in an investigation of endstate grammars as a function of AoA.

5.1   Sensitive periods for L2A

Using the biological criteria outlined, we are first led to conclude that it is fruitless to attempt to scrutinize L2A for a critical period since we cannot provide a reliable and constant answer to Bornstein's five questions (Table 5.1).

The first two points show differences; the last three are totally unpredictable for L2A. The organismic system of the adult, whose brain already has dedicated neural networks for a variety of cognitive functions, is patently different from that of the infant, whose neural *tabula rasa* has few cerebral specializations. For L1A, PLD is "enriched" by social interactions, parentese, co-attention, etc., whereas for L2A the additional enrichments are more explicit and conscious. If we take a more encompassing view of sensitive periods in terms of age constraints rather than thresholds, we can investigate whether and how language acquisition ability declines with age for L2A. A clear formulation of this "quite radical version of the maturational state hypothesis," and a possible refutation are laid out by Long (1990, 255). "There are sensitive periods governing the ultimate level of first or second language attainment possible in different linguistic domains, not just phonology, with cumulative declines in learning capacity, not a catastrophic one-time loss, and beginning as early as age six in many individuals, not at puberty, as is often claimed ... A single

Table 5.1 *Criteria for critical periodhood, L1, L2*

Criterion	L1A	L2A
Organismic system	Synapsible brain	Synapted brain
Environmental input	Enriched PLD	PLD, L1, cognition, study+
Threshold	Birth	??
Duration	0–5 (6–12, 12+)	??
Terminus	5/12	??

learner who began learning after the period(s) closed and yet whose underlying linguistic knowledge (not just performance on a limited production)
was shown to be indistinguishable from that of a monolingual native
speaker would serve to refute the claim." Long's faith in a critical period
is characteristic of research of this period (Krashen 1985; Scovel 1988),
including generative studies that advocate a critical period for accessing
Universal Grammar (e.g. Clahsen 1988; Schachter 1996). Singleton (1989)
presents a comprehensive overview of L1A and L2A in light of the Critical
Period Hypothesis (CPH) and then gives a thorough critique of several
categories of explanation. Fifteen years later, the critical period controversy is as intense as ever, with new studies appearing that favor both sides
of the debate. The following section discusses the influential Fundamental
Difference Hypothesis (Bley-Vroman 1989, 1990) which itemizes the crucial distinctions between the two processes and frames L2 deficits in terms
of Universal Grammar. Subsequent discussions look at more recent
research touching on the pros and cons of a critical period for L2A.

5.1.1   The Fundamental Difference Hypothesis

In a seminal article Bley-Vroman (1990) poses "the logical problem of
foreign language learning," the issue of whether adults' learning of an L2
constitutes a poverty of the stimulus phenomenon involving too little input
to account for the wealth of the final state grammar. In his essay, he
explores and defends "the proposition that child language development
and adult foreign language learning are in fact fundamentally different"
(ibid., 4). His stance counters the idea current in the 1980s (e.g. Dulay et al.
1982) that L1A and L2A show similar universal traits such as order of
acquisition of morphemes. Rather, Bley-Vroman proposes that L1A is
guided by UG and driven by domain-specific acquisition procedures, while
L2A is guided by native transfer and driven by domain-general problem
solving. His proposal defines a critical period for language acquisition in
terms of the availability of UG and unique L1A procedures (a sort of
language acquisition device), both of which become unavailable to the
adult.

Bley-Vroman outlines ten factors that characterize L1/L2 differences in
acquisition (Table 5.2). To use Lenneberg's terms, children succeed in
completely learning their native language with no conscious effort and
mere exposure, while adults fail by incompletely learning L2 with instruction, negative evidence and enforced motivation. The resultant second
language often shows fossilization, indeterminate intuitions and a very
wide range of endstate achievement, all of which constitute a fundamental
difference for Bley-Vroman. *Fossilization* – "permanent plateaus that

Table 5.2 *Characteristics of fundamental difference (Bley-Vroman 1990)*

L1A – children	L2A – adults
1. Complete mastery	Lack of success (incomplete mastery)
2. Complete mastery	General failure
3. Inevitability, systematicity, consistency	Variation in success, course and strategy
4. Lack of goals (unconscious)	Variation in goals (motivation)
5. Uniform inception and result	Correlation of AoA and proficiency
6. Complete final state grammar	Fossilization
7. Sure intuitions of ungrammaticality	Indeterminate intuitions
8. No instruction	Importance of instruction
9. Negative evidence unavailable	Negative evidence useful
10. No role of external factors	Large role of affective factors

learners reach resulting from no change in some or all of their inter-language forms" (Gass and Selinker 2001, 454) – is supported by "little compelling evidence" (Long 2003, 520) and contradicted by substantial indications (Birdsong 2005b, c; Han and Odlin 2005; Han 2004). After spelling out the Fundamental Difference Hypothesis, Bley-Vroman rejects four alternative explanations for the L2A phenomena that have often been invoked to explain critical period effects: L1 interference, inadequate input, adult inhibitions and competing cognitive systems. L1 transfer and adequate input are undeniable influences which have appeared under many guises in Contrastive Analysis (1950s), the Monitor Model (1980s) or recent generative approaches (Full Transfer, Minimal Trees), while inhibitions and cognitive considerations are attested in studies of non-linguistic influences in L2A (e.g. Moyer 2004).

Bley-Vroman concludes that there is "no clear evidence for the continuing operation of a domain-specific acquisition system in adult foreign language learning" (ibid., 44), but concedes that any evidence for adult access to UG "will constitute clear counterevidence to the position argued in this paper" (ibid., 39). Herschensohn (2000) argues that L2 learning by adults is inevitably incomplete and consciously acquired using scaffolding devices. She points out that most of the ten characteristics reduce to the issues of completeness and effort: #1, 2, 3, 6, 7 (failure and variation) indicate incompleteness and #4, 8, 9, 10 (external factors) indicate conscious learning of L2; only one could be considered maturational, #5, "correlation of age and proficiency."

The Fundamental Difference Hypothesis characterizes the major debate of generative studies of L2A during the 1990s (Epstein et al. 1996; Eubank 1991; Eubank et al. 1997; Hoekstra and Schwartz 1994; Ritchie and Bhatia

1996), with critical period proponents (Clahsen and Muysken 1989, 1996; Meisel 1997b; Schachter 1996) espousing UG for children but not adults, and critical period opponents (Felix 1991, 1997; Flynn and Manuel 1991; Martohardjono and Flynn 1995) arguing that UG is available to both children and adults. Meisel (1991, 1997a) clearly shows the differences of acquisition path between adult L2A and L1A, a contrast that he attributes to the loss of UG as a language acquisition device. His logic draws on Lenneberg's characterization of no conscious effort and mere exposure as criteria for evaluating availability of UG. Hilles (1991, 336) likewise rejects UG for adults, giving an unequivocal assessment of her hispanophone learners of L2 English: "One can claim, therefore, that all three [two children, one adolescent] have acquisition guided by UG. In the case of the second adolescent and of the two adults, the answer is also clear: There is no evidence of access to UG."

Differences between L1A and L2A are complex, however, and only partially maturational, not exclusively attributable to UG. In contrast to the no access arguments, another source of evidence responding to Bley-Vroman's UG in L2 challenge is the rich literature arguing *for* the availability of UG to adult L2 learners (cf. Chapter 4), ranging from poverty of the stimulus (Dekydtspotter et al. 1997; Sharwood Smith 1994) or new parameter values (Hulk 1991; White 1989) to acquisition of L2 phonological stress (Archibald 1993, 1995). There is evidence of declining ability to achieve complete morphosyntactic acquisition with increasing age, a possibly biological age effect. A large proportion of the obvious differences between L1A and L2A are, however, non-biological.

Although Bley-Vroman argues a strong and uncompromised case for a fundamental difference, he actually admits of an alternative interpretation on the second page of his article when he notes that the operation of the L1A system might be "partial and imperfect" for the adult. Indeed, this subtler perspective better responds to the arguments he presents and to data amassed on acquisition in the past two decades than the more radical view. On the one hand, data cited in Chapter 3 have shown that there appear to be age effects on L1A morphosyntax with deterioration from age five on, thus supporting a correlation of AoA and proficiency. On the other hand, the review of L1A and L2A in previous chapters has indicated that both processes use a partnership of resources including UG, cognitive strategies, social interaction and scaffolding devices (bootstrapping for infants, conscious techniques for adults), thus including all of the four alternative explanations – L1 influence, input, affective factors, cognition – offered by Bley-Vroman.

In current L2A research L1 interference has not only been admitted as an influence, it is a major focus of investigation, acting as a keystone of theoretical approaches such as Full Transfer/Full Access or Minimal Trees. The role of PLD has also received scholarly attention since 1990 (Schwartz 1993; Schwartz and Gubala-Ryzak 1992), with the notions of adequate and inadequate input being more subtly discussed and deeply analyzed as, for example, *intake* in Carroll's (2001) processing approach. Carroll considers intake to be "literally that which is taken in by the hearer ... it is *input to speech parsers*. Parsers are mechanisms designed to encode the signal in various representational formats" (Carroll 2001, 10). If adult inhibitions *per se* have not been as significant a focus of recent research, motivational, socio-cultural and individual variation are clearly implicated as noteworthy factors in adult L2A (Bialystok 2001; Birdsong 1999a; García Mayo and García Lecumberri 2003; Moyer 2004). Finally, the idea of competing cognitive systems (Felix 1981, 1985) has been reexamined directly (DeKeyser 2000; Harley and Hart 1997) and indirectly in studies of numerous ancillary cognitive factors in L2A (Ellis 1994; Doughty and Long 2003; Gass and Selinker 2001; Ritchie and Bhatia 1996).

5.1.2   Lenneberg's legacy

Several recent overviews (Birdsong 1999b; Hyltenstam and Abrahamsson 2003; Singleton 2001, 2003; Singleton and Ryan 2004) point out that Lenneberg's original claim is based on the idea that during the critical period children learn *native-like language* with *no conscious effort* and with *mere exposure*, three additional factors that have since served as criteria for judging maturational effects. Generally speaking, critical period phenomena such as the development of binocular vision or bipedal mobility, while perhaps neither effortless nor attributable to mere exposure, clearly require no conscious intent. L1A normally conforms to these traits (although it is not obvious that child L2A does as well), but adult L2A clearly doesn't conform since it entails conscious effort, more than just mere exposure and an inevitably incomplete final state (Herschensohn 2000; Schachter 1996; Sorace 1993). It would appear that L2A is out of the running as a strict critical period phenomenon, yet the deterioration of language learning ability so evident to casual observers begs an explanation. Birdsong (2005a, 111) provides a more "sensitive" definition that better accommodates the subtleties and complexities of L2A than the strict definitions for simpler developmental phenomena. "A critical period is considered to be the temporal span during which an organism displays a heightened sensitivity to certain environmental stimuli, the presence of which is required to trigger a developmental event. Typically there is an abrupt onset, or increase in sensitivity, a plateau of peak sensitivity, followed by a gradual offset or decline, with subsequent flattening out of the degree of sensitivity." The term "sensitive" period is a weaker formulation of critical period, indicating progressive inefficiency of the organism to complete the developmental task (Hyltenstam and Abrahamsson 2003). Views of the Critical Period Hypothesis range from the more stringent Lennebergian claim that learners gain native-like ability from mere exposure to the idea that younger learners outperform older ones either in eventual outcome or in learning ability. Scholars on both sides of the debate adduce evidence in these areas to argue their perspectives. Advocates of a critical period limit generally point to either of two offset ages, four to six years of age or puberty, two thresholds we will generalize as five or twelve years of age.

Support *for* a sensitive period for L2A is corroborated by many of the reasons furnished by Lenneberg:
- native-like acquisition by children "within the critical period"
- similarity to TD L2A of L2A by organismically deprived individuals
- deterioration of language acquisition abilities with increasing AoA
Several decades of research supporting maturational deterioration in L2A attest to that point, while the acquisition of language in exceptional circumstances is corroborated not only by L1A, but also by L2A (section 5.2 of this chapter). Changes in the brain related to maturation may not be exactly what Lenneberg proposed, but nevertheless can be summoned as factors (Scovel 1988). Another physiological factor, the development of articulatory finesse in the native (or L2) phonology during the critical period, also fits well with Lenneberg's hypothesis because later acquisition almost inevitably results in nonnative-like phonology (5.3.1). However, Lenneberg's argument for the universality of pattern of acquisition is compromised in L2A since external influences highly impact the acquisition process, thereby reducing the role of maturational factors, even for children. Children and adults do not follow the same path of acquisition, partly because L2A is embedded in non-biological cognitive, educational and social factors.

In a sanguine review of recent research, Scovel (2000) upholds Lenneberg's tradition in commenting that the emerging majority opinion holds belief in some version of the Critical Period Hypothesis, while the minority view is represented by the critical period skeptics. Likewise, Newport et al. (2001) present evidence from late L1A and L2A that learners have deficient phonology and grammar, and that early and late L2 are represented differently in the brain. It is true that most scholars would agree that there are differences between children and adults in L2A final outcome (with adults generally showing greater deficits than children), but the exact nature of the critical period is far from consensus opinion. Even Scovel (2000) – who reconfirms his proposal of the maturational basis of a critical period for mastery of L2 speech (Scovel 1988) – doubts that morphosyntax is vulnerable to critical period effects. His selective sensitive period for phonology derives from the observation that speech is physiological in nature and thus constrained by neuro-muscular developmental limits (whereas morphosyntax is more cerebral than neuromuscular). A more modulated opinion is voiced by Hyltenstam and Abrahamsson (2000, 2003) who conclude that while a strictly Lennebergian view of the CPH has been seriously questioned, there is nevertheless strong support for the existence of constraints in L2A, partic-ularly as elucidated by the studies comparing cross-sectional populations with different age of onset.

Certainly, *maturational effects* are indicated by numerous scholars who demonstrate systematic morphosyntactic deficits as a function of increasing AoA (Bialystok and Miller 1999; Birdsong and Molis 2001; DeKeyser 2000; Jia et al. 2002; Jia and Aaronson 2003; Johnson and Newport 1989; Nikolov 2000). Studies such as these show as a general tendency that early acquis-ition results in native-like proficiency while later acquisition onset results in less native-like L2 grammars under naturalistic ("effortless") learn-ing conditions (technically the only environment permissible under the Lennebergian hypothesis). From another perspective, the "who's a better learner?" (younger or older) version of a critical period ignores nativeness of ultimate attainment and essentially looks at non-biological factors (Hyltenstam and Abrahamsson 2001, 2003; Marinova-Todd et al. 2000).

What are the diagnostics that can be examined to test the critical period hypothesis? One could seek Long's post-critical period learner whose competence is indistinguishable from a native speaker, although a single instance would hardly refute the claim. A more solid refutation might be a substantial percentage of advanced L2 learners with native-like compe-tence, or conversely a substantial group of pre-critical period learners whose competence is *not* native-like. Another criterion to examine would be the nature of the critical period decline, Birdsong's plateau of sensitivity and gradual offset, which should result in differing endstate grammars depending on the AoA. In principle, learners beginning before the offset should attain native-like grammars, whereas learners starting during the gradual offset should show progressively increasing age effects. Learners past the terminus point of the critical period should show no further systematic increase in age effects.

5.1.3   Doubting the critical period

In the face of evidence of decline in acquisition ability, a number of scholars have doubted the critical period in earlier decades, and continue to do so (Marinova-Todd et al. 2000; Snow 1987, 2002; Snow and Hoefnagel-Hoehle 1978), while others seek a more nuanced interpretation of the complexities of age deficits (Birdsong 1999a, 2004, 2005a, b, c, in press; Hyltenstam and Abrahamsson 2003; Singleton 2001, 2003). Snow (2002, 162) argues that Lenneberg's claims have not only been challenged, but "most have been convincingly rejected," and that adult/child differences in acquisition are due entirely to non-biological factors. Her social-interactionist approach sees all language learning in a similar light, with several factors figuring in to create differences between L1A and L2A:

- intensity of exposure (e.g. motherese for L1 children versus complex grammar for adults)
- affective emotional processes (perhaps L1 love versus L2 discipline)
- motivation
- instruction

Another uniformist view of acquisition procedure adduced to doubt a critical period is put forth by the connectionists (Elman et al. 1996), who see all language acquisition as a linear function of quantity and quality of input. In this spirit, MacWhinney's (1997, 115) competition model uses connectionist tenets to interpret critical period data "with the fewest possible theoretical assumptions": communication needs shape acquisition; input drives learning; transfer and emergence create neural networks.

Unlike Scovel (1988, 2000), who remains committed to a sensitive period for phonology, Singleton in recent publications (2001, 2003) becomes even less convinced of a critical period than in earlier work (Singleton 1989), citing four main reasons: although there is general consensus that earlier is better than later for learning an L2, no causal relationship between age and deterioration in language learning ability has been established; there is no sharp terminus; some adult learners gain expert status; non-biological factors are of major importance in L2A. These reasons are briefly outlined here and explored in detail in subsequent sections.

Age at which acquisition begins is fairly reliably the strongest predictor of level of L2 ultimate achievement (Birdsong 2004), yet the relationship between age and deterioration of acquisition capacity is not a necessarily dependent one. If L2 ultimate achievement were exclusively determined by AoA – that is, if there is a clear critical period for L2A – then L2 learners beginning at the same age should have comparable final state grammars, just as L1 learners of any language do. This line of argument has several threads that will be explored in this chapter and the next. First, process of acquisition should be similar for L1 and L2 children (similar kinds of errors, similar asymmetries in subdomain development) but different for adults (section 5.2). L2A during the critical period offset should show progressive deficits parallel to those of late L1A. Second, endstate competence of children learning L2 during the gradual offset should correlate inversely to AoA, whereas adults would show quite variable endstate grammars with no AoA effects (section 5.3). Third, endstate competence of children should be presumably native-like if within the critical period, whereas adult endstate competence should be not at all comparable to that of children and presumably nonnative-like (5.4). Fourth, native language transfer should be irrelevant for children but significant for adults (6.1). Investigations addressing these issues indicate that each point is only partially true, adding fuel to the doubters' opinion, yet not clearly disproving the view of the critical period advocates. A true critical period for acquisition should demarcate by its terminus a clear discontinuity of language learning, with early learners presumably mimicking the L1A pattern and late learners using quite different acquisition strategies.

The evidence in Chapters 5 and 6 will show that L2A before and after the purported critical period thresholds does not profile a clear discontinuity, but rather a continuous negative correlation between AoA and proficiency across a broad range of ages spanning childhood into adulthood (Bialystok 2002a; Birdsong 2004; Singleton and Ryan 2004). Furthermore, although child L2A shares characteristics with L1A and adult L2A, L2 children do not simply replicate L1A, but rather use a range of conscious learning strategies influenced by native language and social, cognitive, and motivational factors (Bialystok and Hakuta 1999). Expert adult L2 learners and early learners with nonnative grammars also challenge an absolute version of the CPH (Marinova-Todd et al. 2000). To untangle the evidence that apparently interweaves confirmation and refutation of the critical period and to understand the scope of differences in adult and child learning, we need to look at both knowledge of the L2 grammar (including phonology, morphosyntax, lexicon and usage) and processing (speed and accuracy of perception and production).

5.2   Child L2A in typical and exceptional circumstances

Although certain social-interactionists and connectionists maintain that L1 and L2 acquisition are essentially equivalent, determined entirely by external factors with neither susceptible to a biological critical period, the correlation of decline in L1 grammatical abilities with increasing age of onset (Chapter 3) argues for some maturational impact on first languages. Given that human language development is biologically constrained to follow a strict timetable and pattern within a limited period (birth to five or six), one is faced with the question of second language acquisition by children. If L2A in the first five years (or twelve, if one accepts puberty as the offset age) is also biologically constrained, then L2A might show a developmental pattern similar to L1A, with similar kinds of errors and developmental patterns overall. For example, one might expect child L2 learners to begin with phonology and perfect subordinate clauses later, or to undergo an Optional Infinitive stage. Under the assumption that child acquisition is uniform in process and limited to a critical period, child L1A and L2A should be similar, while post-critical period acquisition would be distinct. Singleton (2003) questions the idea that after a certain maturational point L2 learning is no longer subserved by the same mechanisms that subserve child language acquisition. "It appears that any decline in L2-learning capacity that occurs at the end of childhood is not of the same magnitude from individual to individual across the human species; this kind of variation is not what one would expect if the underlying cause of the decline were a critical period for language" (ibid., 16). Clearly, there are a number of differences between L1A and adult L2A, not only in age of the acquirer, but also in a wide array of cognitive and social factors (Bley-Vroman 1989, 1990; Moyer 2004). What falls between the two developmental phenomena is TD child L2A, presumably within some definitions of a critical period, but nevertheless built on an L1 foundation that might provide negative or positive transfer.

Another realm of investigation for sensitive period effects is L2A in exceptional circumstances. In addition to the systematic L1A schedule observed cross-linguistically, the evidence of L1 acquisition in exceptional circumstances provides support for a sensitive period for first language. Input may be delayed by five years or so and still allow for fairly normal L1A, but after age five acquisition shows increasing deficits in endstate grammar. Does L2A follow a similar pattern? This section first examines child L2A under typical circumstances and then reconsiders the kinds of deprivation examined in Chapter 3, abnormal deprivation of organismic system (cognition) or input (PLD) in terms of second languages.

5.2.1   Child L2A, typical development

The Fundamental Difference Hypothesis links the critical period directly to the availability of Universal Grammar, a link that formed the basis for a good deal of research in the 1980s and 1990s. According to this view (Bley-Vroman 1990; Clahsen and Muysken 1989; Meisel 1997b), UG is unavailable to adult L2 learners, who are totally restricted to cognitive learning strategies, leading them to create L2 language systems that may resemble language but are actually non-linguistic. Schwartz (1992), in opposing the no-UG in L2 approach, argues that child L2A can provide information on the availability of UG for adult L2A. Assuming that both L1A and child

L2A are UG-guided because children are within the critical period, she reasons that one needs to compare child and adult L2A. "If the same developmental sequence occurs for adult and child L2ers (in their acquisition of X as the [Target Language]) when the L1 is held constant, this suggests instead that a single process, specific to language acquisition, is at work in both – assuming, of course, that UG drives child L2 development" (ibid., 8). She cites evidence on child/adult L2A from two areas, L2 Spanish negation and L2 German word order, both of which show the same developmental sequences for adults and children, to conclude that adult and child developmental sequences support the idea that linguistic-specific mechansims do drive nonnative grammar construction. Her argument is appealing, but not flawless from two perspectives. First, the similarity of the two acquisition paths might be the function of some non-linguistic factor such as frequency or semantic saliency, not the result of UG. Second, dissimilarity in acquisition pattern between adults and children would not definitively prove that UG was unavailable to adults. While Schwartz's formula for determining UG influence versus learning strategies is attractive, the acquisition process is more complicated for both L1A and L2A, with subparts of the grammar being acquired at different rates and with apparently different paths.

Schwartz (2003) revisits the child/adult question by examining ongoing research on L2A of Dutch by children and adults, in which two studies (Unsworth 2002; Weerman 2002) lead to apparently contradictory claims. Unsworth finds that child and adult L2A are similar to each other and different from L1A with respect to the acquisition of scrambling, a stylistically subtle syntactic trait that young children acquire naturally in L1 Dutch, but which L2 learners take time to master. Weerman, in contrast, finds that child L1A and L2A are similar to each other and different from adult L2A with respect to adjectival inflection.[1] Schwartz resolves the dilemma by pointing out that the discrepancy can be explained by the developmental distinction between syntax – where child and adult L2A are similar – and inflectional morphology – where child L2A and L1A are similar. She calls this *Asymmetric Acquisition*, "L2 adults asymmetrically acquire grammar, such that inflectional morphology typically lags behind syntax, sometimes even dramatically" (Schwartz 2003, 46).

Herschensohn, Stevenson and Waltmunson (2005), in a study of six- to seven-year-old children in a Spanish immersion academic setting, come to

---

[1] Dutch has a two-gender system that shows asymmetric inflection between the two in attributive as opposed to predicative uses of adjectives. Gender marking and other nominal inflection are difficult acquisitional milestones in other learning populations as well (Hamann 2004; Paradis and Crago 2004).

a conclusion similar to that of Schwartz. They find that the children's syntax develops (over a period of two years of immersion) to achieve nearly perfect word order in Spanish production, while their verbal morphology (third person present tense inflection) is at less than 50 percent accuracy. Their data suggest that young children follow a pattern of acquisition of morphosyntax that resembles both L1A and adult L2A. The most frequent inflectional error, singular/plural reversal, indicates that the children show a sensitivity to the morphological ending of the verb, a sensitivity to bound morphemes characteristic of L1A. However, they also show an L2A pattern in the quality of the errors themselves and by the accurate syntax compared to the flawed morphology. The errors do not indicate a deficit in syntactic competence, but rather spontaneous performance flaws that vary in form and do not correlate with the essentially target-like word order.

It is instructive to reflect on morpheme acquisition in English (Brown 1973), an area of intense investigation for child and adult L2A in the 1970s (Dulay et al. 1982; Kessler and Idar 1979; Krashen et al. 1977). While some of the studies dealt with child L2A (e.g. Dulay and Burt 1974a, b), and others with adult L2A (e.g. Bailey et al. 1974), the order of acquisition for L2A correlated signficantly over both populations and differed from the L1A order. "Thus, while adults may in general not achieve the level of performance achieved by first language learners or children learning English as a second language ... these results indicate that they process linguistic data in ways similar to younger [L2] learners" (Bailey et al. 1974, 242). Differences between L1A order and child L2A order may stem from the fact that the native language is the starting point: Dulay and Burt (1974b, 256) suggest that seven-year-old children "learning a second language need not struggle with semantic concepts they have already acquired, such as concepts of immediate past, possession or progressive action." The similarity of morpheme acquisition order across populations highlights the importance of universal tendencies, but also the role of non-linguistic influences. Understanding the process of child L2A does not resolve the UG debate, but it does shed some light on general sequencing, and shows that all forms of acquisition share certain characteristics.

5.2.2   Child versus adult L2A

Recent studies of child L2A indicate resemblance to the L1A pattern (Prévost and White 2000b; Prévost 2004; Rohde and Tiefenthal 2000) and comparability to adult L2A in native language transfer (Haznedar 2001, 2003) and path of acquisition (Unsworth 2005). Since balanced bilingual children essentially undergo dual first language acquisition 2L1A (Grosjean 1982; Meisel 1994; Paradis and Genesee 1996), it is reasonable to expect similarities of early L2A to L1A, and intersections of universal properties with native influence in L2A (Lakshmanan 1994, 1995; Schwartz 2003). However, as Belletti and Hamann (2004, 148) note, there is a question "of where to draw the line between very early L2 acquisition and bilingual (L1) acquisition." Some cases of 2L1A involve unequally strong languages. Schlyter (1993), in comparing "weak" and "strong" languages in 2L1 children, finds that the stronger language presents a profile of typical L1 development, while the weaker language shows a great deal of variation, particularly with respect to use of morphosyntax. This sort of omission or developmental lag is remiscent of adult L2 acquisition or SLI children (Paradis and Crago 2004).

An area of particular interest is the developmental pattern of syntax and of morphology, since evidence already presented points to a distinction between adults and children in L2A with regard to these phenomena. Newport's Less is More hypothesis suggests that children are able to focus on detail (such as inflectional endings), whereas adults' comprehensive view of the "big picture" may impede them in acquiring morphological detail (Newport 1991). Vainikka and Young-Scholten (1998, 97) similarly propose that adults use free morphemes as triggers to their acquisition of L2 morphosyntax, whereas children use bound morphemes: "Whereas bound morphemes such as inflectional affixes typically function as triggers in L1 acquisition, it is free morphemes that do so in L2 acquisition."

Unsworth's (2005) significant doctoral thesis specifically targets adult/child and L1/L2 differences in her examination of three learner groups: L1 Dutch by children and L2 Dutch by child and adult anglophones. The focus of acquisition is scrambling, the movement of a direct object leftward, as in (1).

(1) a. Willemijn heeft vandaag [de tuin] omgespit
        Willemijn has today the garden up-dug
     b. Willemijn heeft [de tuin] vandaag omgespit
        Willemijn has the garden today up-dug

The scrambling construction is of interest because it is found in languages as diverse as German and Japanese, because it is a stylistically charged order that is linked to discourse and pragmatic factors, and because it is late acquired in L1. Unsworth uses a range of production and comprehension experiments to document comparisons between the groups with respect to their acquisition path and their final interpretive abilities. Her findings shed light on several developmental questions, particularly one conclusion of relevance to this section: "in production, L2 children and L2 adults were found to pass through the same developmental sequence" (ibid., 378).

Several studies of Prévost deal with the acquisition of tense morphosyntax, comparing adult and child non-finite forms (Prévost 2003, 2004; Prévost and White 2000a, b). Children's use of non-finite forms in L1A is systematic (raised verbs are always finite, unraised ones are non-finite in verb raising languages), whereas L2 adults raise both finite and non-finite verbs, treating the latter as default forms. Prévost and White's (2000b, 224) child L2 learners demonstrate a structurally determined distinction in distribution of finite and non-finite forms similar to L1 learners. "Non-finite verbs are found only in root declaratives and not in CPs; null subjects do not occur in CPs and they disappear when root infinitives do." Likewise, Prévost (2003, 2004) finds that certain aspects of child L2 German and French conform to a Truncation analysis (Rizzi 1993/1994), and that child L2 learners show developmental characteristics similar to L1 use of root infinitives. Myles (2005) also finds that child L2 learners go through a bare infinitive stage as in L1A and corroborates Vainikka and Young-Scholten's suggestion that free morphemes serve as triggers in child L2A. Likewise, Paradis et al. (1998) find that while present tense agreement and verb raising occur early in their child learners of L2 French, past tense does not emerge until later. They see this sequencing as evidence supporting a structure-building approach more than a full transfer one. The OI period in bilingual and child L2A is confirmed elsewhere. Hulk (2004), who follows 2L1A of a Dutch–French child, and Paradis and Crago (2004), who look at four groups of learners – seven-year-old SLI, seven-year-old Typically Developing (TD), seven-year-old L2 and three-year-old TD (MLU matched to the SLI) – find that tense marking is characterized for all groups by an OI period (extended OI in the case of SLI and L2). "Our results support the claim that the OI phenomenon can occur in non-primary acquisition" (ibid., 102).

In contrast to Prévost and White's child L2 findings, Ionin and Wexler (2002) argue that children's L2A resembles that of adults, rather than the L1A of children. Their L1 Russian learners of L2 English do not go through the systematic stage of optional non-finites described above for L1A. Another difference that the authors note is that the children seem to gain the verbal morphology through irregular verbs more than through affixes, and that they overuse *be* in working out the new values for tense in English as opposed to Russian. Belletti and Hamann (2004, 148) also find that their young (3;5–5;5) L2 learners of French are more like adults than L1 children, for they "do not have root infinitives nor child null subjects in their French." Gavruseva (2004) presents data on child L2A of English, showing the influence of verbal aspect in the acquisition process. The question of whether or not there is an Optional Infinitive stage for child L2A is still open to discussion, and it does not look as if the answer will be a simple yes or no.

Another area that has been explored in child research is the nominal domain. Schlyter has done extensive work comparing bilingual children (Swedish–French) with Swedish adults learning L2 French in naturalistic and instructed environments. In recent articles, she has focused on nominal development. In contrast to L2A (Granfeldt and Schlyter 2004; Herschensohn 2004), 2L1A children use clitic pronouns correctly from their first use, a difference that Granfeldt and Schlyter attribute to two possible causes, access to bound morphology and computational principles. They adopt Rizzi's (2000) idea that categorial uniformity doesn't emerge intially in L1A, to argue that cliticization is favored by children since it reduces structure (attaching clitic heads to V-T), whereas adults prefer categorial uniformity in treating DP and pronominal objects in the same way (as DP complements of V).

Granfeldt (2005) documents L1/L2 differences in a comparison of 2L1A French–Swedish children – who learn gender immediately by gaining the article with the noun – and L2 adults, whose acquisition is much more protracted. Granfeldt argues that L2 learners begin with a lexical entry unspecified for gender (indicated by initial default determiners) and later modify the entry to be specified for consistent gender (which is occasionally incorrect). He concludes that children have early access to uninterpretable features such as gender, whose selection is triggered by both morphophonological and semantic properties, and that adults follow a much slower acquisition of gender features and agreement.

Other child L2 studies look at the influence of L1 transfer and the availability of functional categories. Lakshmanan (1998) examines data from L2 English child learners and finds evidence that verb inflection and nominal case are operative from the earliest stages of child L2 acquisition, as do Grondin and White (1996). Haznedar (2001, 2003), in her studies of Erdem, a five-year-old Turkish child learning L2 English, demonstrates that mastery of inflection is not linked to syntactic development as in L1 acquisition. Erdem shows no developmental relation between the use of verb inflection and higher functional categories such as CP, for the use of CP related elements precedes total accuracy in TP related morphology. Haznedar finds no support for a structure-building account of Erdem's development. Furthermore, Haznedar (1997) shows that Erdem manifests L1 transfer in his SOV word order in the earliest transcriptions. After the ninth sample he consistently exhibits the VX word order appropriate to English. Whong-Barr and Schwartz (2002) also report L1 influence in a study of Japanese and Korean child learners of L2 English.

Summarizing, we find evidence of both L1A and L2A patterns of acquisition, native language influence, and no obvious critical period cut-off date either in terms of process or product of child L2A. Indeed, the evidence concerning child L2A does not present a clear picture that resolves the critical period puzzle. Harley (1986, 97), who studies acquisition by children of various ages learning L2 French through academic immersion, sees the process of acquisition to be similar for children and adults. The evidence from empirical studies of the language produced by L2 learners suggests that for children and older learners, the development of the syntax and morphology of the L2 proceeds in fundamentally similar ways, depending on a complex interplay of factors including common language acquisition processes, the nature of the target L2 that serves as input and the learners' L1 background.

5.2.3   L2A in exceptional circumstances

Lenneberg (1967) uses as one of his arguments for a maturational critical period the fact that L1A is a normal development even in cognitively abnormal (deprived) individuals such as those with Down Syndrome. Subsequent research has substantiated and extended his observation of the modularity of language vis à vis other cognitive faculties. In cases of Down and Williams Syndrome and Specific Language Impairment, language emerges more slowly than in typical development, but it is qualitatively the same (as compared to the non-language of Genie or Chelsea); L1A is then possible despite abnormal cognitive architecture. Can second languages be acquired under circumstances of deprivation of organismic system? An obvious a-priori assumption must be that learners with deficient cognitive architecture – who may have an endstate grammar that is quantitatively different from that of a TD peer – could not achieve an L2 grammar that is more developed than that of their first language. The question is whether such an individual could acquire basic aspects of the phonology, morphology, syntax and semantics of the L2, and whether the interlanguage grammar is UG constrained. Two areas of research shed light on these questions: the case study of Christopher, a brain-damaged polyglot, and cases of bilingual individuals who have SLI.

Smith and Tsimpli (1995) document in great detail the non-linguistic disabilities and extraordinary linguistic abilities of a thirty-year-old man institutionalized for much of his life and unable to perform everyday tasks such as tying his shoe. The authors follow Christopher for several years, testing him both on non-linguistic cognition and on his knowledge of native and other languages. Cognitive tests include standardized evaluations (e.g. Raven's Matrices, Columbia Greystone Mental Maturity Scale,

Wechsler Scale test) and theory of mind tasks whereby he is asked to attribute beliefs to others.

On standardized verbal tests Christopher scores in the normal range, twice as well as on the non-language tests, and also shows full competence on an assortment of English language tasks (e.g. grammaticality judgements) that the authors give him. What is perhaps most impressive, though, is Christopher's ability to learn other languages, an ability that the authors attribute to his special *savant* talents. An avid language learner (both spoken and written) and geography buff from an early age, he has some knowledge of sixteen languages as diverse as Greek, Hindi, Finnish, Russian, Turkish and Welsh. During the period of investigation the authors teach him two new languages, Berber (a non-Indo-European language) and Epun, an artificial language that has some rules that would be impossible in a human language. Christopher relishes learning Berber, whose morphosyntax is like no other language he knows, and he does quite well with Epun, except for the non-linguistic rules which he does not master. His achievements, although specific to his personality, clearly demonstrate in the modularity of various cognitive functions that language learning, first or subsequent, is not inextricably dependent on general mental abilities. The logic of Lenneberg's reasoning for L1A does not transfer to L2A since Christopher is well beyond any critical period terminus age; if anything, his ability to learn new languages indicates that L2A is *not* impossible after a certain age.

The opposite kind of dissociation is found in individuals with Specific Language Impairment whose language faculty is hampered, but whose other cognition is spared. These individuals show a grammatical morphology deficit, with their protracted language acquisition slowed, particularly with respect to functional categories such as determiner, complementizer, tense and verb agreement (Eyer and Leonard 1995; Fletcher and Ingham 1995; Levy and Schaeffer 2003; Wexler 2003). For example, in English they have trouble marking verbs for tense and person agreement (Rice and Wexler 1996), and in French they have difficulty with gender assignment and pronoun realization (Paradis and Crago 2004; Paradis et al. 2003). Paradis and colleagues (Paradis and Crago 2004; Paradis et al. 2005) have shown similarities between SLI children and TD L2 learners of French with respect both to tense and to nominal morphosyntax. Both groups show more numerous errors of omitted tense than nominal errors such as missing determiner or wrong nominal gender. The anglophone L2 learners of French have patterns of use for DP morphosyntax close to other L2 learners of French, and they also resemble SLI children and L1A children at the OI stage. It appears that certain error profiles mark intermediate developmental stages of acquisition regardless of the population.

Given the acquisitional handicap of functional category deficit, can those with SLI acquire second languages? A certain amount of research has been done on early bilinguals with SLI who have acquired both languages simultaneously (Jordaan et al. 2001; Paradis et al. 2003), and new studies propose to look at L2A after acquisition of the native language (Paradis et al. 2005). As would be expected, bilinguals with SLI generally have difficulty in acquiring morphological inflection just as SLI monolinguals do (Jordaan et al. 2001), but the difficulties may vary according to the language. Paradis et al.'s (2003) comparison of TD and SLI English–French early bilinguals finds that both populations have more difficulty with French than English pronouns. They conclude that the difficulty lies not with anaphoric binding – which is the same for both languages – but with the more complex morphosyntax of French object clitic pronouns (compared to more straightforward English pronouns). Perhaps surprisingly, though, they also find that "bilingual children with SLI were more accurate than the monolingual children with SLI we have studied" (ibid., 648), a finding that may indicate that the greater experience with language engendered by bilingualism (Bialystok 2001) partially counters the SLI deficits. As for sequential bilinguals (L2 learners), Paradis et al. (2005), who compare TD and SLI children with a variety of native languages learning L2 English, find that tense morphology develops more slowly in the SLI population, but that receptive vocabulary and narrative skills are comparable in the two populations. A special session on "Bilingual/second language children and specific language impairment" at the Xth International Congress for the Study of Child Language (2005) investigates this topic of L2A by SLI children, noting that there are differences between SLI L2 and TD L2, which continue over time in L2 development. The two areas of dissociation that we have looked at support a modular approach to different cognitive abilities and indicate that individuals who have adequately learned a native language (albeit sometimes with some SLI shortcomings in morphology realization) are capable of learning a second language. There is no terminus after which no second language may be acquired, although some individuals (both L2 learners and SLI individuals) will persist in error/omission patterns for an extended developmental period. Lenneberg cites relatively normal development of L1A despite deprivation of organismic system as evidence for the biological inevitability of human language propensities (constrained to a critical period); L2A in the face of such deprivation seems to mimic TD possibilities, but the evidence does not support a maturational terminus for L2A.

Cases of deaf individuals who learn a second language provide insight into the question of partial deprivation and variable age of onset through two kinds of evidence, ASL as L2 and English as L2. Mayberry (1993) compares congenitally deaf late L1 learners of ASL with age-matched L2 learners of ASL (who lost hearing after learning English as an L1), and with two additional congenitally deaf groups. The four groups of nine – Late-second (AoA 8–15), Late-first (AoA 9–13), Childhood (AoA 5–8) and Native (AoA 0–3) – give results similar to Newport (1994) in that the age of acquisition correlates inversely with grammatical accuracy for the L1 learners of ASL. In short, grammatical accuracy decreases as a function of increasing age of acquisition. Also, as expected from Newport's results, the native signers outperform all other groups. What is significant for the question of L2A, though, is that the Late-second group performed as well if not better than the Childhood group, and substantially better than the Late L1 group. This result highlights two physiological factors related to L2A: first, there is a definite decline in L1 grammar acquisition ability with increasing maturation from age five to twelve, with an even steeper decline after age twelve; second, a solid foundation in L1 is necessary to acquire L2, proven in its extreme by Chelsea or Ildefonso, but shown in an incremental way by Mayberry's Childhood and Late L1 groups. The evidence from both deaf children and children deprived of linguistic input (Chapter 3) clearly indicates that the age of five is crucial for near-normal L1A, and that by age twelve L1A of morphosyntax is highly affected. Mayberry's results corroborate these conclusions, indicating that children over five do not attain a complete L1 grammar. While the Late L2 group does not match the native signers, they nevertheless surpass the Childhood-plus learners who have a defective L1 grammar.

A second example of L2A in the ASL population is the acquisition of literate English by deaf signers. In a special issue of *Topics in Language Disorders* (Prinz 1998) several articles discuss the relationship of ASL to English literacy development, and the the most sound pedagogical path to follow. Prinz and Strong (1998) and Strong and Prinz (2000) present evidence that learning ASL enhances the later acquisition of L2 English in its written form. Prinz and Strong compare two populations, one which has a rich signing environment thanks to the use of ASL at home, and a second with less ASL input because the parents are not deaf or native ASL signers. The group that receives more ASL input and uses it in conjunction with English literacy training (essentially a bilingual education environment), performs at a higher level in English literacy than the other group.

Prinz (1998) summarizes the special issue by pointing out that the data presented in its articles support bilingual approaches to teaching literacy to deaf children and underscore the notion that knowledge of sign is key to improved literacy skills and to overall academic performance. These articles also confirm the importance of L1 mastery (and extended use) to the acquisition of an L2. A number of other researchers (several articles in Chamberlain et al. 2000; Woll and Herman 2003) present corroborating evidence for ASL and for British Sign Language.

Summarizing, the studies of L2A under exceptional circumstances – representing deprivation of cognitive system or input – confirm the dissociation of second language from cognition and the importance of early grounding in a first language. For L2A ranging from learners with SLI to ASL signers acquiring written English, the strength of the first language is a gauge to the success of the second language enterprise. A succinct example of this fact is the study by Mayberry in which the Late L2 learners surpass the Late L1 learners in their acquisition of sign at age 8–15; the L2 learners have the advantage of a solid grounding in a first language.

5.3   Grammatical deterioration and age

The principal kind of evidence adduced for a critical period for L2A involves the increased possibility of phonological and grammatical deficits with increased age of acquisition onset or, for immigrants, age of arrival. A number of studies have looked at various aspects of L2 grammars as a function of age of acquisition. These studies all consider that to test for a critical period one needs to hold constant all variables except age of onset and then examine the linguistic competence achieved. Singleton (1989) characterizes these investigations as immigrant studies, since the populations tested are usually immigrants whose AoA varies from early childhood to adulthood, and whose input is mainly naturalistic.

The patterns of L1A and L2A already presented confirm that different components of language – phonology, morphology, syntax, lexicon, pragmatics – are acquired independently of each other and on different timetables. Seliger (1978, 12) describes this developmental dissociation of linguistic functions as a result of dissociated neural maturation (related to brain plasticity), concluding that "there are many different critical periods for different abilities which, in turn, will determine the degree of completeness with which some aspect of language will be acquirable." Long (1990, 1993) also assumes that different abilities develop on different timetables. Other studies have focused on a particular domain, most notably L2 phonology and morphosyntax, selected topics discussed in the following sections (cf. Singleton and Ryan 2004).

5.3.1   Selective deterioration, phonology

To determine degree of foreign accent in L2 pronunciation – deemed by Lenneberg to be impossible to overcome after puberty – a number of studies have measured the degree of "foreign" accent perceived by native speakers who listen to recordings of L2 speakers. In 1969 the first inquiry to look at an immigrant group immersed in English (Asher and García 1982 [1969]) assumed that a panel of American English native speakers could provide adequate judgement of the "nativeness" of the immigrants, an ability that was subsequently confirmed (Major 1987; Piske et al. 2001; Scovel 1988). The format of natives judging nativeness of phonological production by L2 learners is represented in numerous studies all of which show a progressive decline in native-like phonetic detail with increasing age of acquisition onset.

Asher and García, who study seventy-one Cuban (Spanish L1) immigrants to California, look at age of arrival and length of residence. Although not one of the Cubans was considered to have truly native pronunciation, "Cuban children had the greatest probability of achieving a near-native pronunciation of English if they were five or younger and lived in the US more than five years. Children who came to America when they were 13 or older had a small chance of acquiring a near-native pronunciation even if they lived here five years or more" (ibid., 9). In spite of the negative prognosis for older arrivals, however, the authors concede that some older children could achieve excellent pronunciation.

Scovel (1988) brings together twenty years of his research on foreign accent using the native judgement paradigm with theoretical considerations of physiology and critical periods. In his experiments, Scovel records ten native speakers and ten highly proficient nonnative speakers (of ten different L1s) who have lived in an English-speaking country five years or more. The recorded sentences are first judged by thirty adult native English judges whose accuracy in distinguishing nonnatives is at 97 percent (ibid., 107). The same judges achieve 47 percent accuracy in judging nativeness of syntax represented by a written sample from the same ten nonnatives. Scovel uses three other sets of presumably deficient judges, a group of 146 elementary (American English) school children, a group of 24 aphasics (language impaired), and a group of 92 ESL students. The oldest school children (nine- and ten-year-olds) show almost perfect identification while the youngest (five-year-olds) are accurate at 78 percent. The aphasics, chosen for their phonological deficit, perform around 85 percent accuracy, while the ESL students range from 57 percent to 72 percent depending on their level of English. Scovel's results confirm the validity and limits of the native judgement of foreign accent experiment and corroborate the general decline in ability to achieve native-like pronunciation with increasing age of onset of acquisition. Moyer's (1999) similar study of anglophone adult learners of L2 German confirms age deficits in increasing AoA by the nonnative pronunciation of four of the five subjects, despite high motivation and training.

Flege and colleagues have contributed substantial research in the domain of L2 phonology acquisition and progressive age deficits (Flege 1987 a, b, 1991, 1995, 1999; Flege and Liu 2001; Flege and MacKay 2004; Flege et al. 1995; Flege et al. 1999; Piske et al. 2001; Riney and Flege 1998), demonstrating age effects, but "not for the reasons that have been traditionally assumed" (Flege 1991, 252). Flege has emphasized the importance of L1 experience as an influence on the acquisition of L2 phonology, particularly related to length of residence and to quality of input. Flege et al. (1995), who repeat the native judgement experiment with 240 Italian immigrants to Canada (AoA 2–23, LoR 15+ years), find that nativeness ratings decrease as AoA increases. The decline, however, continues steadily for individuals with AoA during teen years. There is no elbow or precipitous decline after a specific age such as twelve or thirteen years. A study of sentence production rate by MacKay and Flege (2004) of early (2–13) and late (15–28) Italian (L1)–English bilinguals in Canada finds that early bilinguals produce shorter sentences in English (than Italian) when asked to speak quickly, whereas late bilinguals do the opposite (shorter sentences in Italian than English). The authors infer that the late bilinguals expend more energy to suppress L1 Italian, and thus take longer to articulate the English sentences. Piske et al. (2001) find that earlier AoA and less use of L1 characterize a more native-like accent in the L2 Canadian English of Italian immigrants.

Little work has been done to elucidate the particular factors that native judges find especially salient in determining how native-like an L2 speaker sounds, but the studies that have been done (Anderson-Hsieh et al. 1992; Magen 1998) point to the importance of prosodic factors. Magen looks at native speaker perception of L2 English spoken by Spanish L1 learners, acoustically manipulating the recordings to isolate different factors such as VOT. She finds that English native listeners are sensitive to syllable structure, final -s deletion, manner of articulation of consonants, and stress, but not voicing variations. Likewise, Anderson-Hsieh et al. find that prosodic variables have stronger effects than segmental variables on raters' judgements. Overall, the native judgement technique produces a fairly reliable measure of phonological production abilities, and the immigrant studies of phonology acquisition document a range of achievement pegged to AoA.

On the perception side, Oyama (1978, 1982) studies sixty Italian immigrants to the United States, whose comprehension of twelve short sentences masked with white noise is examined in terms of age of arrival and length of stay. She finds that subjects who learned English before age eleven have comprehension comparable to native speakers, and that those arriving after age sixteen had comprehension far below natives. She finds no length of stay effect. Her results indicate a dissimilarity in timetable for production compared to comprehension, with the former showing a lower threshold for native-like acquisition.

Experience in the target culture improves L2 learner ability to discriminate phonemes that do not exist in the native tongue, such as /r/ /l/ for Japanese speakers (Yamada 1995); such a distinction can also be induced in L2 perception through phoneme discrimination training (Bradlow et al. 1995). As for the effect of quantity and quality of input on perceptual abilities, Flege and Liu (2001) conduct three experiments with sixty native Chinese learners of L2 English, whose AoA ranges from 16 to 40 years. Half of the subjects have an LoR of less than four years and the other half have 4–15 years' LoR; both long and short LoR groups are further sub-divided into students and non-students under the assumption that students receive more English input than the workers (mostly biomedical researchers) in the other group. The subjects are tested on final stop identification, listening comprehension and on morphosyntactic grammaticality. The results indicate that AoA is not significant, nor is LoR for the two groups of workers; LoR is significant for the students, however, with the longer term LoR group showing higher scores than the short LoR. The authors clearly show the importance of input for learners to overcome native language influence.

In recent, finer-grained studies, Flege and MacKay (2004) and Imai et al. (2005) look at perceptual abilities. Flege and MacKay follow Italian immigrants to North America in analyzing early/late AoA and amount of first language use. They find the standard difference between early and late learners, with early learners who use Italian less frequently able to achieve native-like perception of English vowels. But early learners who use L1 Italian frequently do not achieve native-like English perception, leading the authors to note that early childhood acquisition does not guarantee native-like abilities. Assuming that L2 learners have phonological representations shaped by their native language, Imai et al. (2005) further break down perceptual skills by examining the effect of lexical frequency and "neighborhood density" (how much a word is phonologically unique or similar to other words in the language) on native speakers and on high and low proficiency L1 Spanish speakers of English. The high proficiency learners perceive sparse neighborhood words as well as natives do, but have more trouble distinguishing words from dense neighborhoods; low proficiency learners scored lower for all criteria than the other groups. They suggest that "this may be because bottom-up processing of speech segments in words from dense neighborhoods was more affected by differences in phonological representations as compared to words from sparse neighborhoods" (ibid., 906). The perception and production studies seem to indicate that younger is better for acquiring a native-like accent and perceptual abilities, but they also show that there is no guarantee of success for children learning L2 nor a guarantee of failure for adults, an issue we return to below. Furthermore, the Flege studies demonstrate that AoA is just one of many interacting factors in L2 phonological abilities.

5.3.2   Selective deterioration, morphosyntax

While phonological acquisition has been measured in terms of production with native-like pronunciation, crucial diagnostics of morphosyntax include not only mastery of L2 syntactic production, but also crisp (in Newport's sense) morphology, rapid processing (to which we return in Chapter 6), and the ability to judge subtle ungrammaticality. Following the lead of Patkowski's (1982) study of the syntactic achievement of sixty-seven immigrants with varied AoA, a substantial amount of subsequent research has studied immigrant populations for age effects on L2A. With increasing AoA onset, native-like phonetic detail in the L2 is difficult to gain and is more susceptible to L1 interference than is morphosyntax (Ioup 1984). Yet the latter also shows systematic deficits as a function of increasing AoA.

In what has become a classic critical period text, Johnson and Newport (1989, J&N89) study forty-six native Chinese or Korean speakers whose AoA in the United States was 3–39 years (LoR 3–26 years). Johnson and Newport examine the question of whether there is an age-related effect on learning the grammar of an L2. They postulate two formulations of age effects, the "exercise hypothesis" whereby the language learning capacity must be exercised early in life or else it declines; and the "maturational state hypothesis" whereby the language learning capacity is maturationally restricted to a critical period during childhood. The first hypothesis – a use it or lose it proposition – predicts continuing ability to learn (a second) language throughout the lifetime, whereas the second implies a critical threshold limiting L2A. Given the ample research cited in Chapter 3 and the first part of this chapter, it is clear that the first hypothesis is nearly moot since the language ability must be implemented in the first five years or so of life or the ability to acquire first language skills will decline dramatically. The second option is not, however, the only hypothesis which could be developed to describe a critical period, as we will see.

The J&N89 study asks the subjects to make grammaticality judgements of 276 sentences (140 ungrammatical) presented aurally and containing

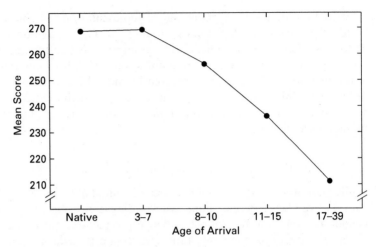

Figure 5.1 AoA and grammar: The relationship between age of arrival in the United States and total score correct on the test of English grammar (Johnson & Newport 1989, 79).

errors such as syntactic order, inflectional marking, and determiner use.[2] "The results show a clear and strong relationship between age of arrival in the United States and performance. Subjects who began acquiring English in the United States at an earlier age obtained higher scores on the test than those that began later, $r = -.77$, $p < .01$" (ibid., 77). The authors find a strong linear relationship in the decline of grammatical ability that correlates with increased age from seven years of age through seventeen (Figure 5.1).

In contrast, the performance of individuals whose AoA is 17–39 shows no significant correlation, a distinction that they interpret to mean that the later arriving group is post-critical period. They claim that adult acquirers cannot become near-native in their grammaticality judgements and also show a wide range of individual variation. J&N89 has been widely cited as strong support for a critical period for L2A, has provoked criticism and has prompted further research using the same paradigm.

Criticisms of J&N89 touch on test methodology, choice of morphosyntax, selection of subjects and analysis of results. The reported post-adolescent (15+ years) elbow that marks the continuing decline in grammatical ability and greater variability in score characterizing the older learners

---

[2] Johnson (1992) repeats the experiment with untimed written materials, obtaining parallel results, but with higher performance. Slavoff and Johnson (1995) examine age effects on rate of acquisition, while Johnson et al. (1996) highlight the indeterminacy of late acquirers' grammars.

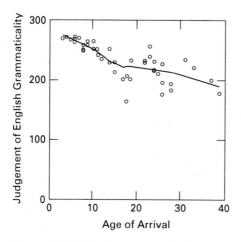

Figure 5.2 AoA and grammar: Performance on English Language Test as a function of Age of Immigration. The disjuncture at age 20 can be seen most dramatically by sliding a blank sheet of paper across the graph from left to right (Bialystok & Hakuta 1994, 68).

should actually be set at 20 years, say Bialystok and Hakuta (1994, 68), as they show in a combined graph (Figure 5.2).

Another factor that may impact performance is the age at time of testing, with older test takers experiencing difficulty with accuracy and response time simply as a function of reduced online general processing skills (as evidenced by the performance of 30+year-olds in native language tasks). Bialystok and Hakuta (1994) note that the younger subjects in J&N89's study (undergraduates) should be better able to respond with "mental vigor" while the older subjects (independent of their linguistic backgrounds) would be slightly handicapped. Indeed, Bialystok (1997) points out that Johnson's (1992) repeat with untimed written material results in higher test scores, indicating that processing demands of the oral task (as opposed to the untimed written one which leaves time for reflection) inhibit performance. She also wonders why the subjects respond differently to different kinds of ungrammaticality: "Why would an age-related effect of learning have differential influence on these structures?" (Bialystok 1997, 124). Kellerman (1995) highlights several methodological problems with the test, such as the nature of nonnative ungrammaticality – a nonnative may mark an ungrammatical sentence as ungrammatical for reasons that are not those of the native speaker – and the inconsistent character of the grammar points tested. For example, he notes that several categories of error are included under the rubric "past," irregular stem vs regular suffix, number vs tense inflection, and aspect vs tense. A more

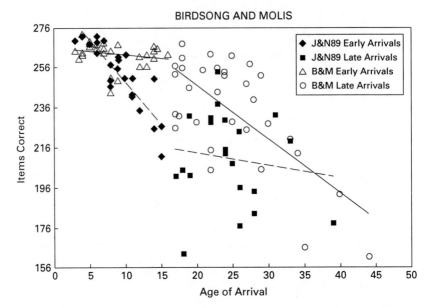

Figure 5.3 AoA and grammar: Number of items correct as a function of Age of Arrival, current study, and J&N89. Regression lines (B&M: solid lines; J&N89: dashed lines) are provided for four data subgroups separated by study and by Early versus Late Arrivals. Cutoff age of AoA = 16 (Birdsong & Molis 2001, 240)

general criticism (not aimed at J&N89) is that grammaticality judgement tasks are methodologically problematic for several reasons (Birdsong 1989; Sorace 1996).

Taking into account these criticisms, several subsequent studies (Bialystok and Miller 1999; Birdsong and Molis 2001; DeKeyser 2000; Flege et al. 1999; Jia et al. 2002; Jia and Aaronson 2003; Nikolov 2000) replicate J&N89 with different L1 populations. All find some age deficits related to AoA, but the deficits may not be related to maturation, since Flege et al. (1999) find that the differences in score are insignificant once variables confounded with AoA are controlled. Birdsong and Molis, who repeat the test with sixty-one native speakers of Spanish (AoA 3–39, LoR 10 years minimum), find no significant correlation between AoA and judgement accuracy for early arrivals (AoA < 16), but do see a strong age effect for late arrivals (Figure 5.3).

The authors suggest (ibid., 242) that the high scores of the Spanish early arrivals reflect a ceiling effect, and clarify differences between their study and J&N89 on several points. Their results indicate that native language influence is quite important, given the dramatic differences between their results with Spanish L1 and J&N89's results with Chinese and Korean L1. A similar disparity is found by McDonald (2000) for Spanish L1 and Vietnamese L1, and by Bialystok and Miller (1999) for Spanish L1 and Chinese L1, with both studies showing higher achievement of Spanish L1 learners of English L2. It is evident that some late learners achieve high levels of accuracy in L2 morphosyntax, clear counterexamples to progressive deterioration, and an indication that L2 grammatical competence cannot solely be predicted by maturational considerations. Hakuta et al. (2003), who statistically analyze 1990 census data from immigrants with different AoA (over two million Spanish L1 and over 300,000 Chinese L1), also find a progressive decline in reported English L2 ability with increasing AoA, but they find no discontinuity in the decline. Stevens (2004) and Wiley et al. (2005) follow up with additional comments and confirmation.

DeKeyser (2000), who tests fifty-seven adult Hungarian-speaking immigrants (AoA 1–40, LoR 10 years minimum) with the J&N89 format, finds confirmation of maturational decline in grammaticality judgement accuracy, and evidence for verbal aptitude as a mitigating factor for late learners. He also observes that the subjects perform differentially on different grammar points, a fact he attributes to perceptual saliency (such as sentence initial or final position) of the grammar point in question. "Learners with high verbal ability can use explicit learning mechanisms to bypass the increasingly inefficient implicit mechanisms, and certain structures, by virtue of their saliency, can be learned explicitly by virtually all learners, regardless of verbal ability" (ibid., 518). DeKeyser concludes that there is a critical period whose terminus occurs between the ages of six and seventeen. Bialystok (2002a) criticizes this logic, pointing out that "evidence for a lifelong decline in language learning ability is not evidence for a critical period but indicates a gradual change in some mechanism responsible for that learning domain" (ibid., 482). She suggests that language learning ability continues to decline throughout life, a suggestion consonant with the results obtained by Birdsong and Molis as well.

Another line of research into L2 syntactic knowledge involves a poverty of the stimulus phenomenon, *subjacency*, a linguistic principle regulating long-distance extraction of WH words (2)–(4).

(2) a. The police said that Bill told them that John saw *the accident*.
   b. The police said that Bill told them that John saw *what*?
   c. *What*$_i$ did the police say that Bill told them that John saw *[e]*$_i$.

(3) a. The police wondered who saw *the accident*.
   b. The police wondered who saw *what*?
   c. **What*$_i$ did the police wonder who saw *[e]*$_i$?

(4)   a. The police are sure of the fact that John saw *the accident*.
      b. The police are sure of the fact that John saw *what*?
      c. *$What_i$ are the police sure of the fact that John saw *[e]$_i$*?

In simplified terms, WH words can be extracted from embedded clauses, even multiply embedded ones (2), but they cannot be extracted from "bounded" categories within the embedded clauses, in these cases an embedded question (3c) or a complex noun phrase (4c). Several studies (Bley-Vroman et al. 1988; Johnson and Newport 1991; Ross et al. 2002; Schachter 1990) investigate the ability of L2 English learners (with native Korean, Chinese, Indonesian, Japanese and Dutch) to make grammaticality judgements about subjacency violations such as those in (3c) and (4c). The logic of the experiments is that an ability of L2 learners to make correct subjacency judgements should indicate access to UG since subjacency is a principle that is never taught and for which there is no negative evidence available. Bley-Vroman et al. find evidence for UG access in that their Korean subjects are able to reject subjacency violations, but Schachter finds quite the opposite. She argues that access to universal principles such as subjacency depends on the availability of the principle in the native language. Her results show that Dutch natives are able to recognize subjacency violations in English because of its availability in both languages, whereas her Korean, Chinese and Indonesian natives cannot tap subjacency because it is not instantiated in the L1. She maintains that the L2 grammar is necessarily incomplete for this reason, essentially a critical period effect (Schachter 1996). Johnson and Newport (1991) also observe inability of the L2 learners to recognize subjacency violations in English, finding age effects as in their earlier study, with the older learners making less accurate judgements.

Ross et al. (2002) look at three teenage populations of L1 Japanese learners of L2 English: a child group that learned English in an anglophone setting during childhood; a teenage group that learned English in an anglophone setting during the teenage years; and a teenage instructed group that studied English in an academic setting in Japan. The authors find that the child learners are slightly better at recognizing ungrammatical subjacency violations than the other two groups, but that all Japanese groups are significantly different from the judgements of the English controls on both grammatical WH-extraction and subjacency violations. There seems to be a mitigated age effect, but early acquisition and authentic PLD provide no guarantee of mastery of subjacency. It should be noted, however, that both the child and teen learners who lived abroad subsequently returned to Japan where they were tested.

Summarizing, the immigrant studies of morphosyntax acquisition document a range of achievement pegged to AoA, but also indicate the importance of additional factors such as native language influence or learner characteristics. The studies point up variability not only among different domains of language (syntax or phonology, for example), but also among different subcategories of a domain such as the range of judgements on different phenomena that DeKeyser attributes to perceptual salience. The immigrant studies indicate that younger is better for acquiring native-like intuitions for grammaticality judgement, but they also show a broad variety of success for L2 learners with a range of AoA.

5.4   Endstate grammars

The studies examined in the previous section investigate specific aspects of the *endstate grammar* of learners whose AoA varies from early childhood through adulthood and whose *ultimate achievement* is proportionately deficient in relation to increasing AoA. Studies of "native-like" L2 achievement presuppose that there is a prototypical "perfect" linguistic competence and performance of native speakers that include diagnostics such as non-accented pronunciation, ability to make subtle grammaticality judgements and error-free morphology production. In fact, this idea of nativeness is characteristic only of monolingual speakers, since bilinguals do not show the same competence in their two languages (Bialystok 2001; Cook 1995; Hyltenstam and Obler 1989) and may show attrition in their first language if it is not actively maintained (Cook 2003; Major 1992; Seliger 1989; Sorace 2003). Presumably, early bilinguals appear to have native grammars, yet demonstrate somewhat variable competence. In addition to attrited L1 speakers and "reduced competence" bilinguals, two other classes of L2 learners demonstrate that early L2A does not always arrive at monolingual competence: early child learners who do not become native-like in the L2 and adult learners who do become native-like.

5.4.1   Deficits in early bilinguals

The numerous studies documenting deficits in phonology and morphosyntax suggest that after five years of age, L2 learners' grammars may display attenuated nativeness in not possessing, for example, native-like pronunciation, accurate perception, flawless morphosyntax or solid grammaticality judgement, not to mention speed of processing. As in L1A, different linguistic subsystems develop at different rates and schedules in L2A. The potential incompleteness of the L2 final state (as opposed to L1) means that L2 learners may show deficits in one area alone, say pronunciation, or in several. While it is generally recognized that "increasing age of onset for second language acquisition is correlated with declining ultimate attainment in pronunciation and morphosyntax" (Harley and Wang 1997, 44) – suggesting a window of L2A opportunity for children – that generalization translates to predict that a certain percentage of early L2 learners do *not* attain native-like competence or performance. The overall picture is that the percentage increases with increasing AoA, quite a different picture from TD L1A where ultimate achievement is uniformly complete and competent. Even the evidence for continuing acquisition ability in childhood actually constitutes counterevidence at the same time, as Ioup (1989, 161) notes for immigrant children: "their English still has quite pronounced nonnative characteristics." Indeed, youth does not guarantee phonological mastery as Pallier et al. (1997) show in their study of very early Spanish–Catalan bilinguals who fail to master a phonemic vowel contrast in Catalan, indicating that even early exposure is sometimes not sufficient, subtle nonnativeness confirmed by Flege and MacKay (2004) as well.

If immigrant children exposed to a new language generally acquire it far more easily and unconsciously than their parents (with greater difficulty as AoA increases), children exposed to a new language in a classroom immersion setting do not show the same acquisition profile. Older children often show stronger acquisition than younger ones (Singleton and Ryan 2004, 75). Harley, who has done a number of studies of Canadian anglophone children in French immersion settings (e.g. Harley 1986, 1993; Harley and Hart 1997), notes that in academic settings, even immersion ones, there is a cognitive advantage for older students, probably attributable to a number of factors. "A reasonable interpretation of the older late immersion students' syntactic and lexical advantage over the early immersion students in the interview setting is that it reflects an interaction of maturational and environmental variables" (Harley 1986, 89). Harley and Hart (1997), in an experiment comparing two groups of eleventh-grade partial (50 percent curriculum) immersion students – one group (n = 36) which had had French since Grade 1 and the second (n = 29) which had begun French immersion in Grade 7 – look at language aptitude (associative memory, text memory and analytic ability) as a factor in L2 achievement (vocabulary recognition, listening comprehension, written production and oral description). They find a correlation between the analytical dimension of language aptitude and higher L2 achievement, a fact that they suggest may corroborate Lenneberg's claim that postpubertal learning is more reliant on analytic ability. They find no correlation between language aptitude and early immersion, however, disproving their hypothesis that early immersion should develop language learning strategies in childhood (ibid., 394).

These immersion results are similar to the rate of acquisition comparisons done by Snow and Hoefnagel-Höhle (1978, 1982a, b) in their studies of acquisition of Dutch by anglophone children and adults. In experiments testing pronunciation, comprehension, morphology, grammaticality judgement and other tasks, the authors find that "youth confers no immediate advantage in learning to pronounce foreign sounds" (1982a, 91) and that the fastest learners were twelve- to fifteen-year-olds, the slowest three- to five-year-olds (1982b). The fast rate of adolescents and adults is a short-term phenomenon, however. In the short run (three months) adults outperform children in acquisition rate, but in the long run (ten months) children gain the most, with more solid achievement (Snow and Hoefnagel-Höhle 1978). Hyltenstam and Abrahamsson (2001) critically examine the methodology used in these experiments and question Snow and Hoefnagel-Höhle's conclusions.

A final study that indicates the nonnative features of final state grammars of early learners is Hyltenstam's (1992) examination of oral and written Swedish by early and late bilinguals (immigrants who learned Swedish at a range of AoA) compared to Swedish monolinguals. Although the learners had no noticeable accent, there were "on measures of lexical/grammatical accuracy ... clear differences between bilinguals and monolinguals" (ibid., 351). Hyltenstam concludes that L2A – even of near-natives who appear to be natives – is incomplete, fossilized, and lacking in correct intuitions. His findings that subtle semantic differences of bilinguals' lexicon compared to that of monolinguals demonstrate that even early learners of an L2 have subtle deficiencies in lexical knowledge, lending support to the idea that monolingual-like attainment in each of a bilingual's languages is a "myth" (Harley and Wang 1997, 44). Although lexico-semantics is presumably an area unaffected by age, the deficiencies can rather be seen as a result of experience (length of time since the word was learned) with the lexical items in question.

5.4.2   Expertise in late bilinguals

In contrast to the small pecentage of young learners who do not achieve native-like mastery in the second language, there is a small group at the other end of the L2A spectrum who undertake language acquisition as adults and achieve native-like abilities. Several individual and group studies document these expert learners through the standard evaluative measures – native speaker opinions of L2 pronunciation, oral and written production tasks and grammaticality judgements.

Neufeld (1979, 1980) examines advanced anglophone L2 French speakers, who began acquisition as adults, on production and perception. Neufeld (1979) presents the nativeness judgements of eighty-five French Canadians who evaluate the pronunciation of seven anglophones who "pass as native" in casual conversations. The judges deem five of the seven to be natives, a finding that Neufeld takes as counterevidence to a strong version of the Critical Period Hypothesis. Neufeld (1980) repeats the perception experiment using fifty-four advanced anglophone L2 French learners with "clear traces of foreign accent" to judge the experts and native francophones. He obtains results virtually identical to those of the native francophone judgements, as the anglophone judges recognize the true native speakers of French and also misidentify the five expert learners as natives. Neufeld concludes that there is "an asymmetry in the adult's receptive and productive performance in L2" (ibid., 295), a conclusion that has been broadly confirmed since his study.

Bongaerts and colleagues, who have conducted a series of investigations on ultimate attainment of phonology by adult learners of L2 English and L2 Dutch, find that a number of expert learners, both instructed and naturalistic, are able to achieve native-like abilities. Bongaerts et al. (1995, 1997) find that a group of native Dutch "carefully screened" and "highly successful" late learners of L2 English "received ratings from inexperienced and experienced English judges that were comparable to the ratings assigned to the native speaker controls" (1997, 462). The authors suggest that the L2 phonological mastery is attributable to numerous factors such as motivation and intensive training, both of which are evident in their learners. Bongaerts (1999) summarizes the earlier research and a similar study of Dutch learners of L2 French confirming the ability of adult learners to achieve native-like command of L2 phonology. Bongaerts et al. (2000) report on a similar look at late learners of L2 Dutch in an immersion setting. Using native Dutch raters, they also find that naturalistic late learners can achieve native-like pronunciation in L2 Dutch, probably because of external factors cited earlier. Birdsong (2007) reports on native-like pronunciation that he attributes in part to phonetic training and high motivation. The work by Neufeld, Bongaerts and Birdsong confirms that it is not impossible for adult L2 learners to achieve native-like pronunciation. Hyltenstam and Abrahamsson (2000) note, however, that expert learners don't really pose a problem for the critical period because they are usually tested on a restricted aspect of the L2 and do not necessarily show an overall ability that is native-like.

In the realm of syntax and morphology, there have been a number of studies of advanced learners showing near-native ability as adult L2 learners. Coppieters (1987), in an influential analysis of expert L2 French learners (from a variety of first languages), finds that his subjects (selected for their near-native level of speech as informally judged by French natives) are very "different in terms of their underlying grammatical system, interpretation and type of intuitions about the language" (ibid., 570) from their native French peers. Although Coppieters' study is often cited as evidence for nonnativeness of L2 learners, the overall picture of his subjects – who perform at better than 90 percent accuracy on grammaticality judgements – is that they are very competent in L2 French. This conclusion is reinforced by Birdsong (1992) whose replication of the Coppieters study with more controlled experimental materials and subject selection criteria finds that some of the expert learners fall within the range of performance of French natives. He concludes that "there are individuals who began L2A as adults and yet demonstrate attainment of native norms" (ibid., 742).

In case studies, individual expert L2 learners demonstrate their skills in a range of linguistic subsystems. Novoa et al. (1988) and Obler (1989) document such successful L2A by an exceptional learner "CJ" who learned French, German and Arabic "perfectly" as an adult. They argue that his unique ability is based on special brain characterisitics related to phonetic coding, grammatical sensitivity, rote memory and inductive language ability, an idea of special neuropsychological talents also explored by Schneiderman and Desmarais (1988). Ioup et al. (1994) and Ioup (1995) report on two judged-as-native learners of L2 Egyptian Arabic, Julie and Laura. Tested on a speech production task, an accent (dialect) identification task and a translation task, both adult L2 learners are rated "as native speakers by eight of the 13 [native] judges (62 Percent)" (Ioup 1995, 106) and perform in native range on dialect identification and translation. They are tested on grammaticality judgement and anaphoric coreference, on which they are comparable to native speakers. The only areas of divergence are subtle interpretations relating to stylistic variations (e.g. a range of scrambled word orders) and discourse semantics, a difficult area also pointed out by Coppieters. Although Julie is a naturalistic learner (while Laura's original entry to Arabic is academic), Ioup concludes that adult learners need input enhancement to achieve native-like command of an L2, enhancement that can be externally (e.g. instruction, negative feedback) or internally (e.g. structural awareness, mnemonic devices) generated.

White and Genesee (1996) examine the rationales for both the immigrant (deterioration) studies and the expert learner studies in a controlled experiment comparing near-natives (similar to the expert learners described in this section), "nonnatives" (very proficient learners who nevertheless were perceived as nonnative by the native judges) and native controls. In this study of L2 English, the learners' L1s vary, as does their

AoA, used to classify four groups, 0–7, 8–11, 12–15, and 16+. To test knowledge of (presumably UG based) subjacency, the subjects complete a grammaticality judgement (monitored for reaction time) and question formation task. On both tasks the near-natives are almost identical to the natives, while the nonnatives score lower than the other two groups and show significantly longer reaction times. The authors find no deficits related to AoA and conclude that "L2 learners can achieve native like competence with respect to constraints of UG, provided care is taken to ensure native like proficiency; this is true even for learners who are first exposed intensively to English as an L2 after the age of 16" (ibid., 251).

It appears that there are adult learners who achieve native-like abilities, but Hyltenstam and Abrahamsson (2000) say that no L2 learner truly achieves native-like ability in L2, regardless of their AoA and perceived nativeness by native speakers. L2 learners always have some imperceptible if not obvious defects. Rather, very good learners may become near-native, if not native-like, and this status is often the level achieved by childhood learners of an L2. Their conclusion obviates the possibility of an absolute terminus point for a critical period.

5.5   Conclusion

To evaluate the evidence for the existence and nature of a sensitive period for second language acquisition, this chapter has considered the perspective of Universal Grammar (Bley-Vroman 1990), AoA deficits (Birdsong 1999a; Hyltenstam and Abrahamsson 2003; Scovel 2000) and cognitive differences. Adults are often incapable of mastering an L2 when presented with an abundance of targeted input and a wealth of scaffolding such as instruction, cognitive strategies, motivation and social pressure. For L2, there is no guarantee of acquisition either for children or adults, even with a wealth of input. The variable attainment achieved by L2 learners indicates that less profuse input and support generally correlates with less complete endstate grammars in L2A, but it seems that age of acquisition may also be a factor in final state L2 grammars.

Studies of child L2A show that, as for adults, different components of L2 (e.g. phonology, lexicon) are acquired at different rates, although the timing of milestones is not the same as for L1A. L2 learners' deficits are most often cited in the areas of phonology and secondarily morphosyntax with AoA after age five, a gradual offset that parallels the incompleteness of L1 learners beyond the age of five. As for cognition and language, cognitively challenged individuals who have selective difficulties with morphosyntax are nonetheless able to acquire second languages, albeit with the same deficits as in their native language (Paradis and Crago 2004).

L2 learners in exceptional circumstances support a modular approach distinguishing language from other cognitive functions.

Empirical findings on age effects in L2A indicate that increasing AoA for L2 correlates with declining ultimate attainment in pronunciation and morphosyntax beginning about age five into adulthood, but does not provide convincing support for a critical period terminus at puberty. Indeed, the studies "do not demonstrate that language completely fails to develop after a given maturational point, which is what one might expect in the case of a critical period for language" (Singleton and Ryan 2004, 44). L2A does not present the profile of a maturational phenomenon susceptible to a critical period for several reasons. First, it is not a universal human developmental milestone like walking, L1A or vision; not all individuals learn a second language. Second, the environmental input – encompassing as it must both PLD and a range of other scaffolding devices – is both unforeseeable and unmeasurable. Third, the threshold, duration and terminus of acquisition are variable, unpredictable and hence cannot be used to define L2A. Furthermore, individual achievement in acquisition is highly inconsistent (even keeping age as a constant), unlike L1A which is overall quite consistent in terms of the "perfection" of the final native grammar. Finally, there exist individuals who, acquiring second languages as adults, become fluent and eloquent speakers and/or writers of that language, indistinguishable from natives. If the evidence for maturational decline for complete acquisition of first language is compelling, the evidence for a sensitive period for L2A is inconclusive at best. The studies documenting L2 achievement (usually endstate grammar) that have been examined in this chapter do not provide a clear understanding of the role of biology in the acquisition of second languages.

6   Biding time: further consideration
of age and acquisition

6.0   Introduction

In Mary Shelley's eponymous novel, Victor Frankenstein, the young scientist who creates a "miserable monster," is frightened in the fourth chapter by the latter's nocturnal visit and his muttered "inarticulate sounds." The reader is led to believe that the monster is unable to speak, an adult faced with the task of first language learning. Evidence from adult learners of L1 such as Chelsea assure us that gaining fluency in a first language is not guaranteed in adulthood. Yet three chapters and just a few months later, the "wretch" is quite fluent in articulating his ideas: "All men hate the wretched; how, then, must I be hated, who am miserable beyond all living things! Yet you, my creator, detest and spurn me, thy creature, to whom thou are bound by ties only indissoluble by the annihilation of one of us. You purpose to kill me. How dare you sport thus with life?" (Shelley 1989 [1818], 58). The monster's prose is quite remarkable for its sophistication – embedded clauses, conditional sentences, careful pronominal agreement, and subtle vocabulary – not to speak of its reasoning. Since late L1A results in defective grammar, the wretch's fluency is implausible unless his mentor merely reanimated the original brain with its language intact. It is impossible that he picked up these sophisticated language skills after reanimation with an infant-like brain, for neurolinguistic studies reveal that the complexity of language knowledge can only develop over several years, mainly during childhood (Kuhl 2004). This knowledge and its implementation in comprehension and production is embedded in neural networks now observable through a number of techniques such as neuroimaging to be explored in this chapter.

The evidence presented in Chapter 3 points to specific maturational effects in L1A related to chronological development: onset takes place at birth and includes a sensitive period for phonetic perception during the first year, a consistent pattern of lexical development during the second, and a perfecting of morphosyntax during the third. Delayed L1A is incomplete when onset is after age four to six, with progressively less complete acquisition as AoA increases; the crucial role of early input is shown by ASL data indicating that late (after twelve years) L1A is less successful than L2A by learners of the same age (Mayberry 1993). The duration of L1A is usually around four years for typical development with the terminus tapering off from about age five, although lexical learning increases in late childhood and continues through adulthood. After age twelve AoA, L1A is quite incomplete, although no study has focused on L1A decline as a function of maturation *after* twelve. L2A is much less clear: beginning at age six and continuing into adulthood, increasing AoA for L2 generally correlates with declining ultimate attainment in pronunciation (especially) and morphosyntax. There is a tremendous amount of individual variation, however, and L2A studies do not provide convincing support for a critical period terminus at puberty. This chapter examines non-biological and biological factors that impact language acquisition to clarify the nature of the so-called maturational or age deficits noted for L2A in Chapter 5. The first section attempts to sort out biological and non-biological causes for L2 achievement and non-achievement; the final sections investigate the brain, its development and its ability to process languages.

6.1   A biological critical period for language acquisition?

Linguistic competence can be traced to double sources, innate genetically transmitted language capacity and socially transmitted language particular knowledge (Klein 1996), the roles of which shift in importance at different stages of development. If L1 learners are destined to accomplish their task unconsciously, even under daunting conditions such as reduced input (creole languages), reduced cognition (Williams Syndrome) or socioeconomic hardship, L2 learners consciously and laboriously undertake a new language, relying on a number of non-biological extra-linguistic factors. These non-biological factors – internal ones such as motivation or aptitude and external ones such as native language influence or instruction – definitely contribute to age-related distinctions of child and adult learners, although it is unclear if they alone can explain perceived maturational deterioration in acquisition ability.

No one denies the existence or importance of extra-linguistic factors, although different theoretical camps view the role of biology differently. According to one view, L2A is affected by non-linguistic factors that vary by age; there is no biological critical period. Both social interactionists such as Marinova-Todd (2003) and generativists such as Martohardjono and Flynn (1995) see acquisition as a similar challenge for all age groups, but think that L2A is determined by a variety of issues (e.g. social, psychological, experiential) whose function could differ greatly for children or adults. On another view, L2A is affected by maturational constraints whereby young children are capable of spontaneous learning but adults are not. Cognitivists such as DeKeyser (2000) and generativists such as Bley-Vroman (1990) attribute child/adult fundamental differences to biological causes. A recent book (Moyer 2004) levels the playing field by considering AoA along with a range of other factors in the acquisition of L2 German phonology by two dozen highly motivated, well-educated individuals with extensive experience in Germany. Moyer's findings provide very pertinent information on the relative importance of the 30 variables she considers in four categories, biological-experiential (e.g. gender, AoA, LoR), social-psychological (e.g. motivation, self-rating), instructional-cognitive (e.g. instructional years, phonological training) and experiential-interactive (e.g. initial exposure, spoken interaction). The following sections explore the areas outlined by Moyer in a survey of non-biological influences – external, internal and experiential – that may impact the search for biological causes of a critical period. The designation of a given variable as internal or external is rather arbitrary, since it is difficult to determine, for example, if a native language is part of one's cognitive baggage, hence internal, or part of the external environment over which one has no control. Nevertheless, here the title *external* refers to native language, socio-economic factors, input and instruction, while *internal* refers to acculturation/affective disposition, motivation, aptitude and cognition.

6.1.1   External factors

The four *external* variables include overall environmental influences that the learner cannot manipulate, native language and sociocultural factors; and other influences amenable to manipulation, input and instruction. Moyer's analysis includes a questionnaire for the subjects on the aforementioned range of 30 topics, recorded speech samples from each subject and native controls, and ratings by native speakers of the subjects and controls. The raters find 36 percent of the subjects to be native-like, and 64 percent nonnative, judging only on the phonological samples. Moyer correlates the background variables with the mean ratings to determine the significance of the factors that the subjects judged to be important to their language proficiency.

Chapter 4 has amply documented the role of *native language* transfer in the acquisition of L2 phonology, morphosyntax and even semantics. Both from the perspective of facilitation and inhibition, interference from the first language affects interlanguage in early differently from later stages. The Full Transfer/Full Access approach takes a definitive stance in characterizing the initial state as one of full transfer, a theoretical construct that explains how later states could only show diminishing proportions of L1 influence (as L2 becomes more fixed in the interlanguage through restructuring). As for ultimate attainment by long-term users of a language, immigrant studies contrasting L1 Spanish learners demonstrate the enduring role of the L1. In these studies their endstate grammar of L2 English is more accurate than their peers with Vietnamese, Chinese and Korean native tongues (Bialystok and Miller 1999; Birdsong and Molis 2001; Johnson and Newport 1989; McDonald 2000). Native language is not a significant feature for Moyer's subjects, undoubtedly because they are ultimately quite fluent in L2 German and have gotten far enough beyond L1 interference.

As in the case of native transfer, the importance of *sociocultural* factors of interpersonal interaction, cultural expectations, contextual variation and discourse conventions for L2A have been extensively studied for decades (Dewaele 2004; Gass and Selinker 2001; Mitchell and Myles 1998). On the interpersonal level, Vygotskian socioculturalism, which sees social mediation as essential for development, has been adopted as a theoretical framework for L2A to furnish a methodology for language learning through classroom interaction and private speech (Ohta 2001). European functionalist approaches growing out of the European Science Foundation's work have emphasized the importance of ethnographic considerations in L2A, exploring the significance of social integration, power relations, self-esteem and cultural integration (Klein 1996; Klein and Perdue 1992; Véronique 2004, 2005). On the macroscopic level, Stevens (1999), in her census-based study of a large national sample of immigrants, points out that the clear AoA effect on ultimate proficiency is not simply a function of age, but also of LoR, family background and education. She notes that immigrants with younger AoA are able to receive education and to engage in beneficial social interactions crucial to language acquisition, whereas later immigrants don't have these opportunities. In Moyer's study, LoR is significant, but it "correlates to numerous other factors"; we return to the intertwined issue of AoA and LoR in 6.1.3.

Input and its complement *output* have also been topics of interest in L2 research for at least the past forty years (Gass 2003), an understandable importance as a sine qua non in language acquisition.

- Corder (1967) distinguishes usable *intake* from simple input;
- Krashen (1985) makes the Input Hypothesis a cornerstone of his Monitor Model;

- Swain (1985) requires comprehensible input *and* output for communicative competence;
- Schwartz (1993) emphasizes the primacy of primary linguistic data;
- Van Patten (1996; Van Patten and Cadierno 1993) founds his instructional paradigm on input processing;
- Carroll (2001) develops a carefully detailed model of input processing on which her analysis of L2A is based;
- Flege and Liu (2001) show that the quality of input is more important than AoA or LoR.

In Moyer's study, input and output, the "frequency of spoken interaction," constitute the only significant experiential-interactive factor, and a factor that eclipses the importance of all other factors in all categories except AoA and LoR.[1]

Input and output are of course crucial to *instruction*, since they constitute at once the raw material that must be processed, the model to be followed and the means of learning (Ellis 1990, 1994). L1A proceeds with whatever primary linguistic data is handy, but L2 learners seek the best input possible, leading pedagogs to devise optimal packaging of PLD. Snow (2002) describes the importance of intensity of exposure, while DeKeyser (2000, 2003) points to salience as a valuable input characteristic, and a broad collection of work espouses the instructional parcelling of L2 material with a *"focus on form"* (Doughty and Williams 1998; Lee and Valdman 2000). Specific training in phonetics is certainly helpful (Bongaerts 1999; Moyer 1999, 2004), as is morphological training (Leow 1998). Among the instructional criteria, Moyer's subjects benefit from "indirect instruction (subjects other than German)" and "instructional years in German language," clear indications of the importance of education in the target language, and confirmation of the pedagogical techniques of content-based instruction (Gohard-Radenkovic 2000; Lee and Valdman 2000; Robinson 2002).

6.1.2   Internal factors

The four *internal* factors include acculturation/affective disposition, motivation, aptitude, and cognitive influences. The idea that cultural assimilation is important to L2A, already suggested in the section on social influences, forms the basis of Schumann's (1978) *acculturation* model maintaining that social and affective variables drive L2A. According to this model, assimilation to the L2 culture entails participation in its

---

[1]   The most significant p value is 0.0009, the probability correlation for AoA, LoR, input and "satisfaction with phonological attainment/self-rating" Moyer (2004, 76).

institutions, contact with native speakers of the language, socialization, etc., all instigated by the learner's attitude which must prompt him or her to want to assimilate. Failure to assimilate results in pidginization, a dead-end version of incomplete L2A. Schumann (1997) has updated his ideas to link affective factors to a neurological cause, the role of the amygdala in providing dopamine to induce positive affective attitudes toward the L2, a proposal that is not without critics (Eubank and Gregg 1995). Acculturation purportedly relates to culture and social assimilation, yet its affective effect is more related to motivation, a topic taken up below.

The importance of *affective attitude* is embodied in the Affective Filter Hypothesis of Krashen's (1985) Monitor Model. The Monitor Model comprises five hypotheses, Acquisition-Learning, Monitor, Natural Order, Input and Affective Filter, broadly influential and controversial ideas (see, for example, Herschensohn 2000, 195–196; Gass and Selinker 2001, 198–206; Mitchell and Myles 1998, 35–39). He maintains that

- adults need to "acquire" languages as children do, not "learn" them
- that input triggers acquisition in a "natural order"
- that the function of "learning" is to monitor the process
- that affective attitudes crucially determine input received.

The "Affective Filter" accounts for the ease with which children acquire first or second languages (their filter is "low," permitting the input to get through), and for the differences among adults in L2 achievement: (anxious, unmotivated) individuals with a high affective filter can't get sufficient input, whereas those (easygoing, highly inspired) individuals with low filters get more input and attain better L2 achievement. Although Krashen does not attribute all adult variation to this device, the Affective Filter has been criticized for its vagueness and the lack of theoretical or empirical support for it.

If affect and acculturation are rather vague, *motivation* is a self-reported factor widely cited as very important for L2 learners (Bongaerts et al. 2000; Ioup et al. 1994; Jia et al. 2002; MacIntyre 2002; Marinova-Todd et al. 2000; Moyer 1999; Snow 2002). It seems obvious that having the desire to learn a second language is important to accomplishing tasks that require not just willing participation, but conscious and laborious effort (attempting to approximate phonetic detail, memorizing vocabulary and morphological inflections, learning grammatical patterns, developing listening comprehension and automatizing processing, to name a few tasks). Nevertheless, motivation alone does not guarantee ease of acquisition or final state superiority. Moyer (1999), for example, finds that of her five graduate student subjects who have advanced proficiency in German and are highly motivated to speak the language well, only one is perceived as a native speaker by native raters listening to tapes of the subjects, while

36 percent of Moyer's (2004) likewise highly motivated twenty-five subjects are perceived as native. Furthermore, motivation is not a unitary phenomenon, but one that has several dimensions, including personal attitudes and socioeducational influences (MacIntyre 2002). The two aspects of motivation that prove significant for the Moyer (2004) subjects are "personal desire to acquire German" (as opposed to professional necessity) and "consistency of motivation." Motivation still places lower as a significant factor in her study (p value 0.03) than the external factors already discussed.

For decades scholars have attempted to delineate the criteria that contribute to a high *aptitude* for language learning (Chee et al. 2004; DeKeyser 2000; Nation and McLaughlin 1986; Obler and Fein 1988; Schmidt 1990, 1992; Schneiderman and Desmarais 1988), noting that general intelligence, multilingualism, capacity to notice pertinent linguistic patterns, inductive ability, phonemic coding, phonological working memory and analytical verbal expertise contribute to the talents of the "good language learner." A simplistic view of the expert learner might characterize such a person as a breed apart, the 5 percent of L2 learners casually mentioned by Selinker (1972, 212) as absolutely successful (contrasted to the 95 percent of failed learners). Such a view, however, is unsupported by research showing that aptitude is not one-dimensional, but must encompass a variety of skills that may operate differently in different individuals. Indeed, Sternberg (2002, 14), who advocates incorporating analytical, creative and practical aspects into aptitude measures, comments "language aptitude is not some single fixed quantity but involves multiple aspects." In this spirit of multidimensionality, Skehan (1998, 2002) proposes that L2 aptitude comprises three modules: *auditory processing* (phonemic coding), *language processing* (grammatical sensitivity and inductive language learning ability) and *memory*. He argues that these abilities are not static, but can be enhanced by fine-tuning the cognitive processing of the L2.

Aptitude might seem inseparable from *cognition*, but the distinction can be drawn to accommodate the difference between innate skills that are presumably stable (aptitude), and those which can be sharpened to improve language learning capacity. As the next section will demonstrate, the brain is not a static organ with fixed capacities, but one that is amenable to change even in adulthood. Piaget (1959, 1971) views the developmental trajectory of language acquisition in terms of cognitive factors. He proposes that through maturation the first language emerges as a result of the sensorimotor stage, as the child's basic motor and cognitive skills appear. He suggests that the onset of formal operations (the ability to carry out more advanced reasoning) at puberty might influence the decline in language acquisition ability during the teenage years. Singleton (1989) points out that while a number of physiological, cognitive and behavioral changes occur at the onset of formal operations, it is not at all clear how these changes (e.g. ability to reason, to create abstract arguments) would have an influence on the ability to learn a second language.

Skehan (2002) mentions several means by which aptitude might be shaped: form and meaning should be noticed in the L2 (VanPatten 1996; Schmidt 1990, 1992). Encouraging learners to focus on form should help them develop useful noticing strategies (Long 1991). Natural orders of development might inform curricular prioritizations (Herschensohn 1990; Pienemann 1998). Finally, procedural sequences such as the progression from *chunking* procedures to *rules* and then to *automatization* should be routinized (Ellis 1996, 2003; Skehan 1998). Robinson (2002, 129) additionally recommends that "patterns of abilities need to be matched to learning tasks and conditions to be effective," taking into account the fact that learners have differentiated abilities. Finally, two general cognitive processes that develop alongside the acquisition of L1 and L2 are *analysis of representation structure* – the building of automatized knowledge out of implicit routines – and *control of attention* – the ability to "direct attention to specific aspects of the environment or a mental representation as problems are solved in real time" (Bialystok 2002b, 153). Analysis contributes to facility in storing and understanding different levels and classes of linguistic knowledge (e.g. how letters combine to form written words, and words make sentences), while control contributes to facility in real-time problem solving (e.g. resolving ambiguities) (Bialystok 2001). Recent L2A work focusing both on classroom learning and on general cognition highlights the myriad variables characterizing cognitive aptitudes and their implementations. Moyer (2004) has no aptitude or cognitive markers strictly speaking on her survey, so those factors are not considered in comparison to the others she looks at.

6.1.3   Age, experience and maturation

The evidence from studies of internal and external factors affecting L2A indicates that it is not simple to draw a line between the biological and non-biological even with respect just to AoA. Dozens of studies have used AoA as a variable whose value (e.g. AoA of eight years) is supposed to represent the same potential for nativeness for L2 learners. Yet native language influence (McDonald 2000), education (Stevens 1999) and quality of input (Flege and Liu 2001) may very directly affect the significance of AoA, which cannot, therefore, be used without qualification in determining age effects. In making a comparison of a group of 100 immigrants of different ages and AoA, one will find a third distinction among them, different LoRs. To reduce variables, one might compare two populations with different AoA, but the same LoR, a comparison that should see AoA as the only variable. However, this comparison is flawed for three reasons: first, because the quality of education and input is far higher for learners with earlier AoA. Second, learners with later AoA have far more experience with their native tongue. Third, the later learners, presumably older on average than the earlier, should be less adept at test taking (even in their native language). All of these factors cast doubt upon the methodology of the immigrant studies of AoA deficits.

Even though maturation alone cannot account for the apparent decline in L2 phonology and morphosyntax manifested by L2 learners with more advanced AoA, the obvious deficits require explanation. Birdsong (2004, 2005a, b, 2007) offers a comprehensive view of this issue, taking into account a broad range of variables, including experience with the native language. Birdsong (2005a) distinguishes between *aging* (a biological process) and *maturation* (a resultant phase of aging). He notes that the geometry of a classic critical period would have an onset incline, a peak-plateau, an offset decline and a terminus-plateau, looking something like a bell. The geometry of the prototypical critical period for L1A would have virtually no onset, a peak-plateau beginning at birth, an offset decline and a terminus-plateau when acquisition is complete. The geometry of a graph based on the maturational deficit studies would correspond to neither of these patterns, since it would have a peak-plateau followed by continuous decline both before and after the purported terminus. The biological notion of critical period includes a plateau after the terminus, not continuing decline. He argues that deficits cannot result from a critical period terminus, since they continue past the purported cutoff (either five or twelve years). They might instead be related to processing constraints, since aging is accompanied by decline in perceptual and productive responses, even in the native language (not to mention other physical abilities).

Another reason for the apparent decline with increasing AoA is the role of experience with the native language, an idea developed from different perspectives by Flege (1991, 1995, 1999, 2002) and Kuhl (1991b, 2000). Flege and colleagues have demonstrated age effects, but "not for the reasons that have been traditionally assumed" (Flege 1991, 252). He has emphasized the importance of L1 experience as an influence on the acquisition of L2 phonology, particularly related to length of residence and to quality of input. In a study that focuses on quantity and quality of input, Flege and Liu (2001) show that AoA and LoR are not significant for two groups of workers, but that for students, who receive higher quality input, longer LoR means higher scores. These results corroborate findings on the importance of aptitude, input and education as mitigating factors to AoA/ LoR (DeKeyser 2000; Moyer 2004; Stevens 1999). Flege and MacKay (2004) also underscore the importance of substantial input and output, even for child bilinguals. If it is not AoA alone or LoR alone that is a cause of age-related deficits, is there a biological reason? Flege proposes that several interactions between the new L2 phonological system and the one already established for L1 contribute to the decline in phonological ability with increasing AoA. The learner has established L1 categories of phonemes and phonetic features (including non-distinctive allophonic ones that are quite language specific, such as VOT) to constitute the L1 perceptual and productive classes. These categories predominate and may be transferred as is to the L2 if they are similar enough (Flege's Speech Learning Model SLM). One type of interference may be perceptual – Portuguese learners of French hear [y] as [i], whereas English learners of French hear [y] as [u] (Rochet 1995) – so the errors in L2 production by Portuguese and English will vary because of perceptual misapprehension. On the other hand, the learner may transfer the native productive values of a given phoneme (e.g. the VOT of [t]), whereas the L2 has different phonetic realization. The SLM holds that phonemes that are similar in the two languages will present more of a problem than phonemes that are quite different from each other. Furthermore, the greater the experience with the native language, the more ensconced it becomes, making it progressively more difficult to overcome the experiential effects to learn new L2 forms. "According to the SLM, the likelihood that L2 learners will establish new categories for L2 vowels and consonants decreases as the age of exposure to an L2 being learned naturalistically increases. It is also hypothesized that the likelihood of category formation for a particular L2 vowel or consonant is related directly to its degree of perceived phonetic dissimilarity to the closest L1 vowel or consonant" (Flege 1999, 126). Flege maintains that adults are physiologically capable of producing the sounds of a new foreign language, but must work at reorganizing their perceptual and productive categories, perhaps with phonetic training that can contribute to overcoming certain effects of the SLM.

Kuhl (2000), summarizing much of her earlier work, provides a developmental rationale for the experiential arguments put forth by Flege, an analysis that rejects maturational deficits as the reason for decline in phonological acuity. Distinguishing between *development* (genetically determined changes in the organism over time) and *learning* (changes that are experience dependent), she argues that it is the latter that characterizes phonological learning in the infant. As we have seen in Chapter 2, babies learn to perceive and begin to produce the phonemes of their native language before one year of age, particularly using the perceptual magnet effect (Kuhl 1991a) to organize the vowels and consonants (Native Language Magnet model, Kuhl and Iverson 1995). The linguistic experience of the ambient language actually "warps" the infant's brain to bias it to the language it will need to learn to process. The language blueprint only strengthens itself further with added experience (establishing neural networks and developing rapid processing procedures), a course of action that with increased age hinders acquisition of a new sound system (cf. Plaut 2003). Kuhl rejects the idea of a sensitive period constrained by time in favor of interference by the native language as the cause of age deficits. The altered brain with its well-fixed phonological prototypes, she suggests, is responsible for foreign accents by late L2 learners. She does not address the issue of early child L2 learners or bilinguals, but in all probability the young child has a sufficiently plastic brain to acquire more than one system at an early age.

Wode (1994), who agrees with Flege and Kuhl that perceptual-productive capacities refined during infancy affect L2A of phonology, puts forward the Universal Theory of Acquisition which holds that the same learning mechanisms are used for L1, L2 and subsequent phonologies. The infant makes use of both the *continuous mode* of perception (minute sound differences in continuum, allophonic) and the *categorical mode* (all or nothing, phonemic) to create the phonological categories for the ambient language. The continuous mode is innate, provided by nature, while the categorical mode is nurtured by interaction of innate propensities with environmental experience. Golato (2002) confirms that late AoA is not a hindrance to acquisition of L2 syllable segmentation strategies (in this case by anglophones learning L2 French). In developing L2 phonemes, identical categories transfer, similar categories are substituted (modified transfer), and new categories are created through recourse to the "original innate sensitivities in response to the external stimulation by the L2 and L3 input" (Wode 1994, 337). Wode, Kuhl and Flege all see the establishment of L1 phonological categories as crucial to the efficient processing of the native language and as a potential inhibitor to gaining L2 phonology. Nevertheless, despite the potentially inhibitory role of dedicated native phonological categories, this dedication of neural networking to phonological categories may also facilitate the activation of novel categories later in life with a different language. Native language experience is unmistakably significant to learning L2 phonology as both an inhibiting and a facililitating factor.

6.2   The brain and language

Since a critical period for language acquisition is necessarily biological, the physiological locus of that phenomenon is the brain, which is not only the storehouse of the lexicon and the facilitator of the grammar, but also the seat of motorsensory control necessary to perceive and articulate rapidly processed language in real time. We have outlined the distribution of language functions in the brain and developmental features of language acquisition in Chapter 1. In this section we examine the architecture of the brain in greater depth, bringing to bear recent neuroimaging studies that contribute to our understanding of linguistically pertinent regions and their interactions. We then look at monolinguals and bilinguals to ascertain the significance of AoA in perception and production.

6.2.1   Neural architecture

Our knowledge of the structure and functioning of the brain comes mainly from indirect sources (Byrnes 2001; Calvin and Ojemann 1994; Obler and Gjerlow 1999; Obler and Hannigan 1996):

- The investigation of behavioral anomalies following brain damage in the examination of affected areas through brain observation or autopsies (the initial studies leading to information on Broca's and Wernicke's areas in the nineteenth century);
- Decline of language skills in degenerative diseases such as Alzheimer's dementia (Hyltenstam and Stroud 1993);
- Anesthetizing one hemisphere (e.g. the left to inhibit language functions temporarily);
- Tachistoscopic presentation whereby visual stimuli are presented to only one hemisphere;
- Dichotic listening whereby auditory stimuli are presented to only one hemisphere;
- Cortical stimulation of patients whose brain is undergoing surgery (e.g. to counter epileptic seizures);
- Imaging techniques such as CAT (Computerized Axial Tomography) scans, PET (Positron Emission Tomography) scans or MRIs (Magnetic Resonance Imaging).

Information gained during the past century has filled in a great amount of detail since the work of Broca and Wernicke, but there still remains a good deal to learn.

The peripheral nervous system is implicated in producing sound in spoken language (jaw, tongue, lips) and gestures in sign and written language. The brain itself has three main parts, the *brain stem* connecting its base to the spinal cord; the *cerebellum*, located above the back of the neck beside the stem; and the *cerebrum*, the third and largest part of the brain located in the upper part of the skull. The brain stem and cerebellum regulate body functions such as breathing and muscle control respectively, while elements of the limbic system embedded in the mid-brain regulate hormones and relate to emotional behavior (e.g. the amygdala is linked to the "fight or flight" response to danger). The cerebrum mainly takes care of higher mental functions such as reasoning, language and vision through the *cortex*, its active exterior layer, and through the subcortical areas, its interior neural wiring. The exterior cortical layer and interior subcortical are termed "gray matter" and "white matter" respectively for their color in a "very dead" brain, while "in the operating room we get to see that the natural, workaday color of the gray matter is really a nice rich reddish brown – rather like color pictures of the Grand Canyon" (Calvin and Ojemann 1994, 32).

The cortex or gray matter is the part of the brain that does the major work of mental functions, as its neurons are connected to millions of networks that run subcortically in matter whose whiteness derives from the fatty *myelin* sheath insulating the long tubular axons. The brain is divided into two *hemispheres*, left and right, each designated as anterior (front) and posterior (back). Being packed into a relatively small volume, the cortex possesses an increased surface area (2,400 square centimeters) by its myriad folds and wrinkles, termed *sulci* (valleys) and *gyri* (hills) that are also used to map the surface. The hemispheres comprise four regions on each side (Figure 6.1) – the *frontal lobe* (behind the forehead, above the sylvian fissure and in front of the rolandic fissure), the *temporal lobe* (below the sylvian fissure, hence below the frontal and parietal lobes), the *parietal lobe* (behind the rolandic fissure and above the sylvian) and the *occipital lobe* (lower back) – and are joined in the middle by the *corpus collosum*.

The regions are also differentiated by diverse types of cells, distinguishable by subtle variations in density noted by Korbinian Brodmann a century ago, and mapped as fifty-two *Brodmann Areas*. Language functions are mainly concentrated in the left hemisphere (in Areas 22, 40, 44 and 45), which also controls the right side of the body, just as the right hemisphere controls the left side.

The main areas concerned with language are *Broca's area* in the frontal lobe, concerned with production and grammar; *Wernicke's area* mainly in the temporal lobe, concerned with comprehension and appropriate lexical choices; and the *arcuate fasciculus* linking the first two, concerned with motor articulation (e.g. the ability to repeat in production a comprehended word). Broca's area is particularly pertinent for grammatical processing and syntactic functions (Caplan et al. 2002; Gaillard et al. 2002; Zurif 2002). Although syntactic functions are not strictly localized, they are mainly restricted to the left hemisphere (Grodzinsky 2000). Grodzinsky, using evidence from Broca's aphasics' performance on comprehension,

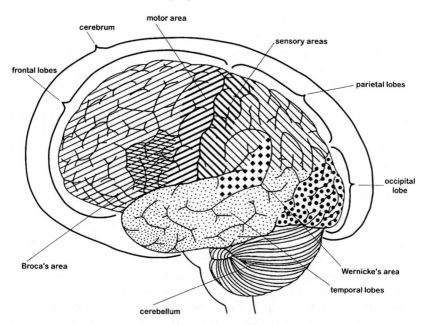

Figure 6.1 Left hemisphere of brain showing areas important for language
functions ("Know your brain," National Institute of Neurological Disorders
and Stroke, NIH).

processing and grammaticality judgement, proposes that Broca's area is
specialized to compute the transformational movement of syntactic
constituents and parts of the syntactic tree higher than tense, but not
syntactic structure building or lexical insertion. Syntactic movement
(which links the pronounced constituent to its site of grammatical origin
necessary for correct interpretation) is a crucially syntactic function of
language which must draw on mental resources to keep track of referen-
tiality, grammatical features and site of origin. His proposal (quite thoroughly discussed and criticized by numerous respondents in the same
issue) reflects the distinction of functional and lexical categories, with the
former playing a more important role in Broca's area. In contrast, Kaan
and Swaab (2002) – who review recent neuroimaging studies of complex
versus simple sentences, sentence versus word lists, jabberwocky and
syntactic prose, and syntactic violations – conclude that syntax is *not*
located in one single area, particularly not Broca's area, that different
syntactic operations engage different neural networks and that the exact
functions of the various networks remain to be explored. They hazard a
few inferences on the location of different linguistic functions (ibid., 355):
"The middle and superior temporal lobes might be involved in lexical

processing and activating the syntactic, semantic and phonological information associated with the incoming words; the anterior temporal lobe
might be involved in combining the activated information or encoding the
information for later use; and Broca's area might be involved in storing
non-integrated material when processing load increases." Other neurological studies that propose yet further variations on these suggestions
(e.g. Vigneau et al. 2005) indicate that the exact location of linguistic
subspecializations is far from obvious. In fact, linguistic subdisciplines
such as syntax and phonology – quite useful constructs for analyzing
languages – may not be the appropriate divisions to seek in understanding
linguistic functioning and topography in the brain. Vigneau et al. (2005)
confirm the importance of "large scale architecture networks rather than
modular organization of language in the left hemisphere."

Broca's and Wernicke's areas are not the exclusive regions involving
language functions, since speech production involves lexical choices,
grammatical combinations and motor realization, while comprehension
involves the decoding of those phenomena using different physiological
mechanisms. Sign languages generally use the same major left hemisphere
language areas of the brain as spoken languages, although they also show
some differences. For example, native ASL signers – both congenitally
deaf and their hearing siblings – recruit the right hemisphere and the left in
processing, whereas late ASL (hearing) L2 learners rely much more on the
left hemisphere, as do natives of spoken languages usually (Neville and
Bruer 2001; Neville et al. 1997). The implementation of language is not
restricted to the left hemisphere. On the one hand reading and writing
engage visual faculties as well. On the other hand, the semantic basis of
language involves cerebral regions that deal with concepts ranging from
spatial relations to concrete objects, among other things. Generally speaking, the location of language functions in bilinguals is similar to that of
monolinguals, with overlap rather than distinct regions for each language –
and both languages are available for processing even if they are not actively
used at a given moment (Grosjean 2004; Paradis 1997). Late bilinguals
show greater involvement of the right hemisphere and a greater reliance on
metalinguistic knowledge (Obler and Gjerlow 1999; Paradis 1994).

For decades, neurologists have monitored the exact location of the
brain's responses while subjects accessed words through picture prompts
(Calvin and Ojemann 1994; Obler 1993). Vocabulary is not stored in a neat
little box in a particular lobe, but is rather networked throughout the
brain. Using cortical stimulus with monolinguals, researchers have found
that *naming sites* for various objects can be disrupted by applying a mild
electrical current (the subject becomes incapable of naming the object
only momentarily). The sites are not usually next to each other, and are

surrounded by "gaps" that induce no naming inhibition if stimulated. Bilingual brains have a similar array, with both languages showing a distribution of naming sites that intersperses the two languages, which are "both tightly interwoven and differentiated to a certain degree" (Obler 1993, 182). Indeed, each individual has a signature distribution of cerebral functions in the brain, so that while there are common patterns in the location of different language components, each person has a "brainprint" that is as unique as a fingerprint.

Vocabulary – which is the lexical basis of syntax and the means of conveying semantics – is not a collection of items stored in one compartment of the brain, but rather a complex system of neural networks that engage not only the left but also the right hemisphere. Antonio and Hanna Damasio and colleagues have contributed substantial research into the location and implementation of different types of vocabulary, particularly in terms of semantic characteristics (Damasio and Damasio 1988, 1992; Damasio et al. 1997; Damasio et al. 2001; Tranel et al. 1997, 2001). They propose that three kinds of neural structures contribute to word form production, "conceptual knowledge" located in both hemispheres, vocal implementation located in left perisylvian language areas (cf. Blumstein 1995; Démonet and Thierry 2002), and intermediary structures that link the first two (i.e. linking sound and meaning). These cerebral structures do not constitute rigid areas or pathways, but rather are supple networks that may even take alternative "routes" under differing conditions. Their framework is not only appealing in its flexibility, but also in its explanatory power with respect to the variation so often observed in linguistic behavior; it is consonant with distributed models of memory that view semantic storage as sets of features rather than as discrete nodes (Frenck-Mestre and Bueno 1999).

Within this context Damasio et al. (2001) use PET scans to study retrieval of concepts relating to actions, spatial relations and concrete objects. They find neuroanatomical separation for word activation that partially involves the conceptual ("real world") component. For example, non-linguistic mental activity related to spatial processing (e.g. activated by visual stimuli depicting spatial relationships), and the naming of spatial relationships both involve the right parietal area. "The retrieval of concepts related to, say, 'inness' or 'onness' or 'betweenness' requires spatial analyses that engage components of the so-called 'where' system" (ibid., 1062). The linking of concepts and word forms is facilitated by neuron ensembles that act as intermediaries in both directions, both perception and production. "These neuron ensembles (convergence-divergence zones) interact dynamically and probabilistically with other regions of cerebral cortex, by means of feedforward and feedback projections" (Tranel et al.

1997, 85). The authors note that the locations of the neuron pathways and endpoints are fairly generalizable in terms of different semantic properties (e.g. actions or concrete objects), but there is still a good deal of individual variation, as each speaker determines unique neural patterns.

The preceding discussion of the location of language areas in a proto-typical monolingual brain is idealized in that first, no two individuals share identical brain topography, and second, the situation of cerebral language regions may be affected by numerous factors. One distinction discussed by Petitto (2000, 148) is the difference between sign and spoken language: "The brain at birth cannot be working under rigid genetic instruction to produce and receive language via the auditory-speech modality, *per se*. If this were the case, then both the maturational time course and the nature of signed and spoken language acquisition should be different, [but acquisition] is fundamentally similar." Neville (1995) finds that congenitally deaf individuals are two to three times more sensitive to peripheral visual stimuli than are hearing controls or those who lost hearing after age four. To explain this example of the influence of experience on the brain's development, she suggests that "in absence of competition from auditory input, visual afferants may become stabilized on what would normally be auditory neurons" (ibid., 220). The recuperation of language abilities in very young children with left hemisphere damage is another source of evidence of the brain's plasticity with respect to localization of linguistic functions, recovery documented by neuroimaging scans (Gaillard et al. 2002).

6.2.2   *Neuroanatomical development of language*

The 100 billion nerves or *neurons* in the brain are the conduits of electrical signals that conduct the brain's business, from guiding motor movements to doing math problems (Lichtman 2001). A speech act is accomplished through networks of neurons allowing electrical impulses to connect crucial areas in language processing. To understand the functioning of language processing and the cerebral architecture prerequisite to language acquisition, we need to look at the cellular structure and function of the cortical constituents. Two types of cells – *pyramidal*, the most numerous (80 percent), and *stellate* (star-shaped) – are situated within the cortex, receiving neurotransmissions through their *dendrites*, branches that reach both vertically and horizontally to make connections with other neurons. Pyramidal cells show a tree-like branching from the cell body into the dendrites, with a single tail-like myelin-insulated *axon* for output from the cell body (Figure 6.2).

While the dendrites serve to capture incoming impulses, the axon, the thin tubular extension (which may extend 0.1 mm or 1000 mm depending on how far it goes in the body) carries outgoing impulses. Calvin describes

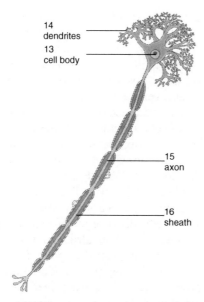

14
dendrites

13
cell body

15
axon

16
sheath

Figure 6.2 Neuron: the cell body (13) contains the nucleus; dendrites (14) extend out from the cell body like the branches of a tree and receive messages from other nerve cells; signals then pass from the dendrites through the cell body down an axon (15). Some types of cells wrap around the axon to form an insulating sheath (16) that can include a fatty molecule called myelin, which provides insulation for the axon and helps nerve signals travel faster and farther ("Know your brain," National Institute of Neurological Disorders and Stroke, NIH).

the dendrites as one-way streets entering into the cell, whereas the cell's axon provides the one-way street for exiting. The transmission of impulses takes place across a gap between neurons, the *synapse*, through the intervention of chemical neurotransmitters. The axon, which transmits impulses away from the cell, also forms synapses with other cells, thus establishing the networks necessary for language processing.

Early development of the neuronal system is a hallmark of the brain's process of maturation. "The brain of a baby in utero develops a massive number of neurons at a rate of around 580,000 per minute, and as cortical neurons form and the fetal brain grows, the neurons migrate from where they are first formed to their final position in the cortex. During this migration, neurons begin to grow axons and dendrites, the structures that will eventually allow them to form synapses and to build neural circuits" (Bruer 1999, 70). Neurogenesis is no longer seen as the exclusive domain of the young child, for recent research demonstrates that adult brains possess "significant numbers of multipotent neural precursors" (stem cells) that may be exploited in cellular replacement (Emsley et al. 2005). Just as birds are able to undergo postnatal neurogenesis, adult mammals too have neurogenesis capabilities in two areas, the hippocampus (important for memory) and the sub-ventricular zone. Although the exact function of hippocampal neurogenesis is unclear (it has perhaps a role in memory), the process may be modulated by behavior (e.g. exercise) and declines with age (ibid., 330). Greenough and associates have demonstrated experience dependent brain development in adult rats exposed to complex environments (Bruer and Greenough 2001) and neurogenesis in the visual cortex of adult rats (Briones et al. 2004). Further research in this area promises clarification of the observed decline in linguistic ability with age combined with the persistent cacpacity to learn new languages.

Prenatal neural development is genetically determined cellular specialization, migration pattern and extension (of dendrites and axon). The eventual specialization of the brain is accomplished through the interplay of a variety of cells that facilitate the development, differentiation and distribution of the central nervous system. Two ways that the specialization takes place are pre-migration dedication – transformation into the dedicated neuron before migration – and post-migration influence – modification of the neuron after relocation through the chemical stimulus of neighboring cells (Byrnes 2001, 28). Axons reach long-distance targets by incrementally increasing their length while adding the myelin sheath (*myelination*) that olidodendrocyte cells specialize in producing. The myelin insulation increases speed of transmission of the electrical impulses constituting the neural path. The growth of dendrites is termed dendritic arborization since the resulting branches resemble a tree.

The newborn child has a lateralized brain with little arborization (branching) and a weight of 335 grams (compared to the adult's 1,300 grams). In infancy and childhood, increased arborization and dendritic density readies the child to undertake more intensive cognitive development including language expansion around age two. In the early growth from birth to three years, neurons make more synaptic contacts than needed to create functional circuits, what Bruer calls a period of "exuberant synapse formation," followed by a synaptic plateau period continuing into puberty. Recent research is providing increasing evidence that astrocytes, the most abundant cell type in the brain, are instrumental in the establishment of synaptic connections, synaptogenesis (Freeman 2005). After the period of synaptic exuberance, two complementary processes work to form the mature brain. On the one hand, necessary synaptic connections, strengthened by environmental input (e.g. language), emerge as networks of cells – *Hebbian patterns*, these neural circuits are called – which "bond together" as they release impulses simultaneously. Hebbian learning may be supplemented by additional cellular and synaptic mechanisms (Feldman and Brecht 2005).

On the other hand, unnecessary synaptic connections are pruned in a process of programmed cell death (apoptosis). Large numbers of neurons that do not reach their targets are eliminated by this mechanism. As the brain reorganizes itself through childhood and adolescence, dendrites atrophy with age (Andersen and Rutledge 1996). In older age, decreased dendritic branching and weaker synaptic connection contribute to a decline in cognitive processes (Burke and Barnes 2006). Two principles thus contribute to the adaptive potential of the brain in early childhood (Byrnes 2001, 44):

Overproduction: Build more brain cells and synaptic connections than most people will need; if proliferation, migration, differentiation, and synaptogenesis are somehow slowed or altered, there may still be enough cells around to create functional circuits.

Flexibility and plasticity: Augment genetic instructions with cellular feedback loops; make use of both experience-expectant and experience-dependent learning processes; make use of alternative brain regions if the typical brain region lacks functional circuits (the latter mostly applies to young children).

The plasticity of the young brain allows reassignment of language functions in very early aphasia, as Lenneberg noted. The maturational process strengthens synaptic formation on the one hand, and reduces "overproduced" cells on the other, to create more dedicated and efficient neural systems. Knudsen (2004, 1415) describes how these mechanisms alter circuit architecture during sensitive periods: "When the activity of a tentative, presynaptic element consistently anticipates (and, therefore, contributes to driving) the activity of a postsynaptic neuron, that synapse is stabilized and strengthend. The distribution of stabilized synapses shapes the growth patterns of axons and dendrites." It is the synaptic connections' networking into circuits that permits the growing brain to function in an increasingly mature manner in terms of language, vision, memory and other cognitive functions. Once the circuits are established, the independent mechanisms suppporting plasticity may continue to operate, Knudsen points out.

Given the evidence of neuron size, dendritic branching, density of synapses, and electrophysiological responses, the human brain is not fully mature until 15–20 years of age, "a long developmental period during which environmental input could shape brain systems," note Neville and Bruer (2001, 152). They point out that different cerebral areas mature at different rates and that environmental influence is crucial in synaptic pruning during later childhood and beyond, but that the notion of a single critical period – even for a unique system such as vision or language – paints "too coarse a picture." Likewise, Abuhamdia (1987), discussing differential maturation of subcomponents of language, observes that phonology production (native accent) – dependent on the early development and myelination of pyramidal cells – is determined at a younger age than syntactic and semantic capacities – a function of later developing stellate cells. Eubank and Gregg (1999) suggest that maturational variations in neural plasticity in different functions might result from differences in neurochemical catalysts at the molecular level. Dendritic N-methyl-D-aspartate receptor molecules that increase synaptic efficiency might be "involved in neural development in response to new information, but not in the subsequent expression or retrieval of that information" (ibid., 69–70).

Pulvermüller and Schumann (1994) provide an account of maturational changes that incorporates observations on cortical development and depicts a role for mechanisms in the subcortical region. They explain critical period variability in L1A and L2A as a function of two learner features, [+/−grammar] and [+/−motivation]. They note that three crucial milestones in L1A are linked to the maturation of left hemisphere language regions in the cortex: babbling leads to the establishment of the phonological system; content word acquisition marks the inception of lexicon building; and acquisition of functors relates to the grounding of the native morphosyntax. Primary sensory and motor areas in the left perisylvian area (where phonological processing is centered) myelinate early, during the first twelve months, whereas the language areas associated with morphosyntax (Broca's and Wernicke's, essentially) myelinate during the second year. Higher order cortical regions such as the prefrontal cortex related to more lexico-semantic properties myelinate later and retain a degree of plasticity into adulthood. "Therefore, loss of plasticity in the language areas during childhood leads to grammatical deficits but to no (or only minor) semantic abnormalities in late learners" (ibid., 713). Their discussion of neural maturation, myelination and differential development of language domains complements and is consonant with other research about grammar.

Their second feature [+/− motivation] is a function of the subcortical causes that they adduce for maturational effects. Pulvermüller and Schumann argue that other brain structures, such as the striatum, the thalamus and the amygdala, are also important for language acquisition. The striatum and thalamus create important subcortical cell assemblies that contribute to selective attention and motor action. The amygdala, responsible for affective states, provides midbrain dopamine input to the striatum, crucially linking cortical and dopamine neurons in the midbrain. The authors infer that it is the amygdala that contributes "affective shading" to vocabulary items and that is key to language acquisition. "Cell assemblies corresponding to language items (e.g. content words and functors) require strengthening of cortico-striatal connections. This strengthening can only take place if dopamine input from the midbrain is present in the striatum. The dopamine input to the striatum can be triggered by the amygdala's evaluation of external stimuli and their corresponding activity in the cortex and the thalamus" (ibid., 709). While subcortical circuits and brain-regulating mechanisms are undoubtedly important to language acquisition and functioning, research has not yet well delineated their precise roles. The complexity of language functions and development are also not well accommodated by the relatively undifferentiated neural mechanisms described by Pulvermüller and Schumann (Eubank and Gregg 1995).

6.3   Processing language

The mature brain possesses networks dedicated to language functions – a lexicon comprising tens of thousands of words and a grammar with phonology, morphology and syntax – that it has itself molded by its simultaneous firing of groups of neurons. This linguistic competence is activated in the performance of language, the comprehension and production effected by its implementation in listening/observing, speaking/signing, reading and writing. These actions, that are effortless and very rapid for the native speaker, constitute *language processing*, the mental activities involved in real-time use. For example, an adult is able to retrieve words in a normal speed conversation 175 times a minute on average (Léwy et al. 2005). *Parsing* refers to the structure decoding processes involved in reading or perceiving words or sentences. The rapid, complex and unconscious nature of language processing has rendered the observation of cognitive and neural functioning difficult in the past, but within the last decade advances in neuro-technology have provided new windows on the operation of the brain.

Studies of processing reveal the location, rate and temporal changes of different language functions and brain reactions to abnormal (e.g. ungrammatical) or unexpected linguistic structures for both L1 and L2 (Felser 2005; Klein 1999; Marinis 2003; Osterhout et al. 1997). Three methods of examining processing are *behavioral* studies that record changes in the subjects' behavior as they process language; *electrophysiological* studies that document the time course of processing; and *neuroimaging* studies that depict areas of activation of the brain during language use. As might be anticipated from the discussion of cerebral architecture, the major grammatical functions, comprehension and production are localized in the left hemisphere, while processing involves a wide variety of mechanisms across both hemispheres (Chiarello 2003). The majority of linguistic investigations have focused on the nature of the L2 grammar, as Chapter 5 indicated, but processing is now receiving more and more attention (Felser 2005; Mueller 2005; Stevenson 2006). For example, White and Genesee (1996), in their study of very advanced near-native (Chinese L1) learners of L2 English, find that a certain percentage of their learners attain native-like competence with respect to subjacency judgements, among other tasks. These advanced subjects, however, have processing problems evidenced by slow reaction times. Likewise, McDonald (2000), in her replication of the Johnson and Newport study, points to processing as a more critical feature than AoA. The psycholinguistic literature is quite extensive, so the research discussed in the following sections will be representative, not exhaustive.

6.3.1   Behavioral studies

Psychologists use standard experimental protocols to observe brain reactions to various cognitive tasks such as processing of visual, auditory or linguistic input, using reaction time, primed decision, and eye movement as well established diagnostics of mental processing. Language studies involve either comprehension or production (or a combination), and focus either on individual lexical items or on complete syntactic units, usually sentences (Costa 2004; Kroll and Dussias 2004). An interactive activation framework for monolingual word recognition posits three levels of representation, the *lexical*, the *conceptual* and the *orthographic/phonological* (Silverberg and Samuel 2004), the signifier, the signified and the sign, to use Saussure's terms. Processing can be viewed from three temporal perspectives, *prelexical access* (the anticipatory stage), *online processing* as the lexical item or sentence is being produced, and *postlexical verification* to ascertain both completion and accuracy of the utterance.

Some common psycholinguistic methodologies use reaction time to primed input to look at the role of facilitating or inhibiting factors, or follow eye tracking in reading activities presented in a "moving window" format. Reaction time is first established for a baseline normal reaction, and then *facilitating* or *inhibiting* factors are introduced to determine what aspects of language, cognition or the environment help or hinder processing. One common technique is to prime the subject by furnishing a token related to a target that will later be elicited (this could be a visual image or a word, for example). Elicited responses that have been primed take a shorter *reaction time (RT)* than those that have not, so priming provides a way of measuring RT differences. Facilitating primes decrease RT, but inhibiting primes – such as non-words in a lexical task or ungrammatical/ unexpected phrases in a syntactic task – do the opposite. *Gating* is a lexical task that provides progressively more and more of a word whose identity the subject is to recognize as quickly as possible, while observers time the RT and accuracy. Often using the format of a moving window which flashes sequential screens of a continuing sentence to be read, eye movement studies – which follow in millisecond detail the steady continuation punctuated by interruptions, pauses and repetitions – provide another means of monitoring the processing of text and thus offer a multifaceted reflection of the reader's perceptual pattern (Frenck-Mestre 2004, 2005).

Psycholinguistic studies of monolinguals have shown that a number of factors affect lexical recognition, including frequency, length, uniqueness, similarity to other words, syntax, semantic and pragmatic constraints, and gender in gender marked languages (Grosjean et al. 1994). The importance of cumulative frequency (Lewis et al. 2001) – the frequency of a word combined with the age at which it was learned – is the topic of several recent articles on lexical acquisition (Ellis and Lambon Ralph 2000; Hirsh et al. 2003; Lewis et al. 2001; Silverberg and Samuel 2004), some of which propose connectionist models to account for lexical acquisition. Frequently used words are understood and produced more quickly than rare words, but the same is true of shorter words compared to longer words (Kutas and Schmitt 2003), indicating that several dimensions enter into a processing act. While probability is undoubtedly important to comprehension and production, the fact that there are multiple factors involved in both lexical learning and syntactic processing necessitates a framework that accommodates a range of influences (Frenck-Mestre 2004; Grosjean 2004), not simply a single mechanism such as frequency. The complexity of word morphology alluded to in Chapter 4 is exemplified in the use of distinct representations and processing mechanisms for monomorphemic, inflectionally affixed, compounded or idiomatically composed words (Allen and Badecker 2000).

Grosjean et al. (1994) use two experiments with French monolinguals, a gating procedure for noun recognition (with and without the gender cue of the determiner) and a lexical decision task (word/non-word). They clearly find a facilitating effect of evident gender marking in decreasing RT and word identification, a gender facilitation that has been reproduced in other languages and with other experiments (Bates et al. 1996; Colé and Ségui 1994). In gendered languages, marking for masculine or feminine facilitates prelexical processing and postlexical verification, while missing or incorrect gender marking inhibits processing. In French, gender agreement plays a role in sentential processing and lexical retrieval (Pynte and Colonna 2001). Investigating L2 gender processing through controlled production tests (gender assignment to words, sentence repetition, gender transformation) and elicited discourse, Prodeau (2005, 148) notes that even when gender is known, for L2 learners "the information is not systematically available, more so when the constraints of the task imply too heavy a cognitive load." The importance of morphological concord is also seen in English, which only shows it in obligatory subject-verb agreement. Using a moving window presentation of sentences with singular and plural agreement in English, Pearlmutter et al. (1999) find that agreement is an integral part of comprehension and is used early in the processing event.

Having established benchmarks for psycholinguistic studies of monolinguals, scholars have turned attention in recent years to processing of bilinguals (Heredia and Steward 2002), both early (AoA in early to mid childhood) and late (AoA in adulthood), with respect to lexical retrieval and syntactic processing. Generally, bilinguals show slower RT in processing than monolinguals, a difference that can be attributed to the added costs of managing more than one linguistic system (Dussias 2003; Frenck-Mestre 2002). Many processes involved in lexical retrieval, parsing, ambiguity resolution and production are similar cross-linguistically, but some are language specific and show contrasting strategies in different languages. As might be expected, L2 learners use the same strategies for native and second language at initial stages. But the native processing strategy is not set for life in that advanced bilinguals adjust to the L2 preference given sufficient proficiency: For example, "English-French [L2] bilinguals will adopt a 'French' strategy of 'high attachment' for the relative clause attachment ambiguity after having been exposed to French for numerous years" (Frenck-Mestre 2002, 230).

As is the case for monolinguals, the age at which the vocabulary item is learned (which means the length of time it has been known) is the most significant predictor of picture naming ability for bilinguals (Hirsh et al. 2003). Since age of learning for any given item determines length of experience with that item, the variable is not maturational, but experiential. Furthermore, there is no correlation of depth of lexical learning with a critical period, as the decline in ability with increasing age continues into adulthood. In a study comparing three types of Spanish-English (L2) bilinguals – early, late proficient and late less proficient – Silverberg and Samuel (2004) test three kinds of cross-linguistic primes in eliciting Spanish target nouns such as *tornillo* "hardware screw." Primed elicited responses require a shorter RT than unprimed ones, so priming provides a way of measuring differences. Although the proficiency of the first two bilingual groups was comparable, the late learners were less able to use semantic primes to activate cross-linguistic semantic networks.

For vocabulary experiments, RTs are slower for later than for earlier learners of an L2, but age is not the only variable to consider. Kim (1997) finds that RT of the late L2 English learners (L1 Korean, AoA 12–14 and

15 +) on syntactic and semantic tasks is significantly slower than that of the younger AoA groups. In English, McDonald (2000) documents faster RT and more accurate grammaticality judgement for monolinguals and early (less than five years AoA) Spanish L1 bilinguals; for later AoA, there is a significant correlation between increasing RT and AoA. For L1 Vietnamese on the other hand, RT and GJ are nonnative-like at all AoAs, with a generally decreasing ability with increasing AoA, leading McDonald to say "the difficulties that come with increased AoA seemed to go beyond that which would be predicted from a simple analysis of L1 and L2 grammatical differences" (ibid., 414). She attributes the difficulties to processing, with the older learners slowed by an increased memory load resulting from decoding problems. Hyltenstam and Stroud (1993) also note processing breakdowns in bilinguals with progressive dementia, which they attribute to the inability of the subjects to inhibit the first language processing strategies. It is plausible to see processing resources as finite, so that for bilinguals, energy devoted to one system makes the second one weaker. Processing cost is also documented by Kroll et al. (2002) who find slower RT in word naming tasks by anglophone learners of L2 French than in more fluent anglophone French bilinguals.

Syntactic processing studies of bilinguals that document eye movement during reading have focused on the resolution of syntactic ambiguities such as the garden path sentences (1)–(4) (examples from Frenck-Mestre 2004).

(1) The student graded <u>by the professor</u> received a degree.

(2) The paper graded <u>by the professor</u> received a high mark.

(3) a. The businessman loaned money at low interest <u>was</u> ready to leave.
     b. Only the businessman loaned money at low interest <u>was</u> ready to leave.

(4) a. Le sous-marin détruit pendant la guerre <u>a coulé</u> en 10 secondes.
        "The submarine destroyed during the war <u>sank</u> in 10 seconds."
     b. Le sous-marin détruit pendant la guerre <u>un navire</u> de la marine royale.
        "The submarine destroys during the war <u>a ship</u> from the royal navy."

Sentences such as these "lead down the garden path" because the "simplest" interpretation (the initial heuristic strategy) makes the first NP the subject and the first verb the predicate of the sentence. In (1)–(4) the first verb is a past participle modifying the subject as an adjectival complement, and the underlined element is the disambiguating cue that is the first indication to the reader that the previously parsed verb is not the predicate. Generally, the initial heuristic strategy is implemented, resulting in syntactic repair to clarify the initial misinterpretation at the moment of the disambiguating cue. This syntax-first strategy, however, is influenced by other factors such as inanimacy (2) and focus quantification (3b) which make the sentences more amenable to the participial interpretation. The sentences in (4) present a similar ambiguity, with *détruit* in (4a) having a participial reading "destroyed," but in (4b) having the expected active (present tense) interpretation "destroys." English-French late bilinguals who are less proficient do not find the second canonical sentence easier to interpret, an unexpected result Frenck-Mestre attributes to the interference of English VP syntax (no verb raising, required adjacency of verb to direct object). Frenck-Mestre and Pynte (1997) in two eye-movement experiments dealing with ambiguity resolution find some influence of the native language (English) on reading by English-French (L2) bilinguals, and they also corroborate the influence of lexical considerations such as selectional features of the verb. They conclude that these two factors are evident but not prominent, and that bilinguals process similarly to monolinguals, relying more on structural considerations than lexical ones.

Another garden path is sentences with relative clauses which can ambiguously be attached to either of two noun phrases, as in *Roxanne read the review of the play that was written by Diane's friend* where the relative *that was written by Diane's friend* may refer to either the play or the review. Monolinguals vary in their preference for "high" (*review*) or "low" (*play*) attachment of the relative clause, with English natives preferring low attachment while Spanish and German natives prefer high attachment. Do learners transfer their L1 strategy to process a new L2 or do they adapt to the L2 strategy? Fernández (1999, 2002), who compares early/late Spanish L1-English L2 bilinguals and English monolinguals in such a task, finds significant differences for all three groups. The English prefer low attachment while the late learners prefer high; the early learners fall in the middle, closer to the late learners than the monolinguals. Other studies (Dussias 2003, 2004, Spanish-English; Papadopoulou and Clahsen 2003, Greek, Spanish, German and Russian) show different relative clause attachment strategies from native controls, and differences from their L1 preferences. They suggest that learners rely more on lexical cues and less on structural ones. Although there are some cases of processing discrepancies between L1 and L2, generally, the behavioral studies show qualitatively similar responses between monolinguals and bilinguals, but slower RT as a function of increasing AoA.

6.3.2   Event related potentials

The electrical currents flowing through the neuronal membranes provide another window onto the timing, sequence and location of cerebral processing of language and other sensory stimuli. Small voltage changes of large groups of neurons (mostly pyramidal) acting in concert can be observed by *electroencephalogram (EEG)* measurements of the "surface" dendritic activity at multiple sites around the scalp. At rest a neuron has a positive or negative *resting potential* that can be subsequently changed by stimulation or inhibition from other neurons with which it is processing sensory input. It is the positive and negative charges traveling through the brain that activate the neural networks. The negative charges can be perceived in the dendritic activity measured through the scalp. To find a point of reference, researchers have sought to isolate stimuli which produce a predictable response to a particular event, such as the presentation of an image or a word, a predictable response called an *evoked potential*. The EEG measurements are gauged with respect to these events to document *event related potentials (ERPs)*.[2] The resulting graph has a horizontal axis related to time (in milliseconds or ms) and a vertical one that records polarity, negative in the upper half and positive in the lower half (Figure 6.3).

To obtain EEG data on ERPs, the reseacher must monitor the subject's electrical brain activity. The subject wears a cap with implanted electrodes that scrutinize the slight electrical activity of the cortex perceptible through the scalp; the signals are amplified and averaged to allow interpretation. "Topographical features of the ERP are referred to as components and can be described in terms of polarity (positive or negative), amplitude, onset, peak latency and scalp distribution. ERPs provide a millisecond-by-millisecond record of the electrical activity that occurs in the brain during the process of interest" (Osterhout et al. 1997, 203). Neurolinguistic studies have especially focused on semantic and syntactic anomalies and have revealed that specific linguistic anomalies evoke characteristic responses in timing and topography (Frenck-Mestre 2004; Friederici et al. 2001; Kutas and Schmitt 2003; Neville and Bruer 2001; Osterhout et al. 1997, 2002; Weber-Fox and Neville 1999). The discussion on brain architecture has already suggested that semantically meaningful lexical words are processed by different regions of the brain from those processing morphosyntactically important grammatical words. It should not be totally surprising then to find differential results for cerebral processing of these two domains.

Studies of monolinguals of the past three decades have shown that in both spoken and written modes subjects exposed to semantic anomalies – either non-words on the lexical level or unexpected words on the syntactic level – show a characteristic ERP response of a negative directional wave

---

[2] Another electrophysiological measure used in neurolinguistic research is the magnetoencephalography (MEG), a procedure that is temporally, but not spatially precise (Beretta et al. 2005; Mueller 2005).

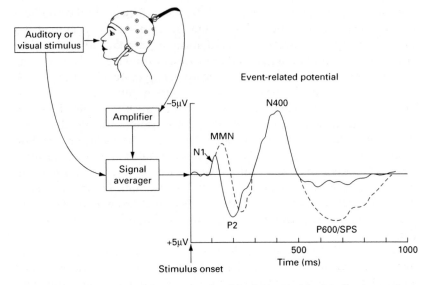

Figure 6.3 Obtaining event-related brain potentials. Idealized waveform of the computer-averaged event-related potential to a visually or auditorally presented word. The ERP is not recognizable in the raw electroencephalogram (EEG) and is extracted from the EEG by averaging over many presentations of phonemes or words from the same stimulus category. ERP components that are observed typically under such conditions include the 'vertex potential' waves (N1 and P2), the mismatch negativity (MMN) and task-related 'endogenous' components (N400 and late positive shift). The mismatch negativity is elicited by auditory stimuli that are physically deviant from preceding stimuli. Endogenous components are influenced primarily by the cognitive, rather than the physical, aspects of the stimulus. The amplitude of the N400 component is affected by the semantic relationship between the target word and the preceding context, with semantically anomalous stimuli eliciting large-amplitude N400s. The P600/syntactic positive shift (SPS) is elicited by syntactically anomalous words (Osterhout et al. 1997, 204).

about 400 milliseconds after the event, an *N400*, while the expected lexical item produces no such negative peak (Kutas and Hillyard 1980). The examples in the b sentences show semantic deviance that elicits N400, while the a sentences don't.

(5)   a. I'd like a <u>bottle</u> of cream.
      b. I'd like a <u>bokker</u> of cream.

(6)   a. I'd like a coffee with <u>cream</u>.
      b. I'd like a coffee with <u>rug</u>.

(7) a. A drill is a <u>tool</u>.
     b. A drill is a <u>fruit</u>.

In the domain of grammar, studies of monolinguals have shown that, in both spoken and written modes, subjects exposed to morphosyntactic anomalies or ambiguities – incorrect phrase structure, agreement morphology errors, reflexive pronoun mismatches, subjacency violations – manifest a characteristic ERP response of a positive going wave 500–800 milliseconds after the event, a *P600*, while the correct grammatical forms produce no positive effect (Osterhout and Holcomb 1992, 1993). The examples in the b sentences illustrate the kinds of anomalies that induce the P600 response, while the correct forms in (8a)–(11a) do not.

(8) a. Karen's <u>proof of</u> the hypothesis.
     b. Karen's <u>of proof</u> the hypothesis.

(9) a. The students <u>walk</u> to the store every weekend.
     b. The students <u>walks</u> to the store every weekend.

(10) a. Fred perjured <u>himself</u> in court.
     b. Fred perjured <u>herself</u> in court.

(11) a. He told me the students were surprised when Doug read <u>that book</u>.
     b. He wonders <u>which book</u> the students were surprised when Doug read.

In gendered languages, gender mistakes in agreement elicit a P600 response. It is assumed that the N400 relates to semantic integration or repair processes while the P600 relates to syntactic integration or repair processes. Looking especially at the N400 and P600, we find a number of recent studies that investigate the ERP responses of early and late bilinguals, partially to consider bilingual processing and partially to test age effects (Frenck-Mestre 2004; Hahne and Friederici 2001; McLaughlin 1999; Osterhout et al. 2004, 2006; Weber-Fox and Neville 1996, 1999).

  In one of the earliest L2 studies, Weber-Fox and Neville (1996) gauge AoA effects in examining behavioral responses (grammaticality judgements) and ERP responses to semantic and syntactic anomalies of Chinese-English bilinguals in five age groups (AoA 1–3, 4–6, 7–10, 11–13, >16). They judged 30 grammatical and 30 ungrammatical written sentences containing either semantic anomalies or syntactic anomalies of the types in (5)–(10), as their GJ and ERP responses were monitored. The behavioral results show that generally the semantic anomaly sentences are more accurately judged (>90 percent accuracy) than the syntactic anomalies, which show marked variation depending on the type of anomaly (e.g. subjacency is less accurate than phrase structure violations). There is a clear deterioration of accuracy with increasing AoA. On the ERPs, all subjects display an N400 response to semantic anomalies, but the late learners (AoA 11–13 and >16) show a delayed N400 peak latency. The P600 response, on the other hand, is similar to that of monolinguals in the early learners (AoA < 11), but is delayed in late learners (AoA > 11) and shows a reduced positivity in the >16 bilinguals. The authors conclude (ibid., 247) "that language proficiency and cerebral organization for language processing are altered by delays in exposure to language, and are consistent with the hypothesis that postnatal maturational processes may underlie critical period phenomena associated with aspects of cognitive development, in this case language learning." The article shows that later learning of an L2 results in slower processing, reduced accuracy and altered neural response to morphosyntax as a function of increasing AoA, with semantic responses less affected by AoA than morphosyntactic ones (Mueller 2005).

Studies of auditory comprehension of L2 German by Russian and Japanese learners (Hahne 2001; Hahne and Friederici 2001 respectively) confirm a semantic anomaly effect in the subjects' clear N400 response (albeit with reduced amplitude and longer peak latency than in the native speaker group). The response to syntactic anomaly differs, however, for the two groups, with the Japanese learners showing no P600 while the Russian learners have a delayed P600. Hahne and Friederici suggest three possible reasons for the Japanese learners' lack of P600: the absence of late syntactic repair, a floor effect and L1 influence. Since slowed processing (particularly at lower levels of proficiency) is well accepted, and since Japanese is quite different from German, the last two factors undoubtedly influence the neural response. Absence of late syntactic repair as a cause for the lack of P600 is countered by evidence from the Russian learners who do show the P600, evidence that not all L2 learners lack late syntactic repair. Hahne (2001) points out that the Russian learners are more proficient in German than the Japanese (error rates 8 percent and 20 percent respectively), leading her to conclude that ERP responses are partially a function of proficiency in the L2. She also notes that semantic integration is the earliest neural response to resemble that of native speakers. Ojima et al. (2005) obtain similar results in their comparison of native English ERP reactions to those of high and intermediate native Japanese learners of L2 English. They find that appropriate semantic processing in L2 is robust from early stages, but that syntactic processing is in part a function of proficiency level (higher level learners have more appropriate processing). In a study of a miniature artificial language, Friederici et al. (2002) demonstrate that "L2 learners" of this language show the same P600 ERP effects for syntactic anomalies that are normally seen in native speakers of real languages.

Anglophones learning L2 French (McLaughlin 1999; McLaughlin et al. 2004; Osterhout et al. 2004, 2006) also show a differential ERP pattern for semantic and syntactic anomalies. In a longitudinal study of first-year college French learners, the N400 effect is observed for word/non-word identification after only fourteen hours of instruction, but the P600 effect is not observable at such an early stage and eludes half of the learners through the entire year they are followed. The "fast learners" do, however, gain the native-like P600 reaction by the end of the year, but first go through a stage of responding to the morphosyntactic anomaly with an N400. Ongoing research by Foucart and Frenck-Mestre (2005) on acquisition of L2 French gender by advanced German learners shows that certain late bilinguals, who have gender concord in their native language (German), show a P600 response for all gender anomalies in French, but that others only manifest the P600 if French gender is the same as German (e.g. French masculine = German masculine). It is unclear if the second group is just not advanced enough to show the P600 for all L2 French gender errors, or if this population is permanently restricted to the native language gender perception. In any case, it appears that a number of factors contribute to the P600 effect and that individual variation is a major one. Overall, the L2 studies show that bilinguals and monolinguals manifest a very similar N400 response, but that bilinguals' P600 is often reduced or later and is influenced by native language and level of proficiency.

6.4 Neuroimaging

Neuroimaging – including *magnetic resonance imaging (MRI), positron emission tomography (PET)* and *computed tomography (CT)* – uses the natural magnetic properties of molecular particles and the electrical pulses which constitute the activity of neural networks to monitor activation of different areas of a brain while it is performing a given mental task.[3] It can thus provide a picture of real-time processing, indicate the regions affected by different kinds of language tasks or measure differences in neural patterns related to chronological changes in knowledge of a language or some other specialization. A recent survey showing the popularity of neuroimaging identified 1058 studies using linguistic and nonlinguistic auditory stimuli to investigate language/speech with neuroimaging (Indefrey and Cutler 2004). The research reported on in this section is mainly limited to functional MRI, currently the favored technique for its non-invasive, non-radioactive nature and fine resolution.

---

[3] Optical Topography (OT) is less intrusive and measures differences in light absorption (Spinney 2005).

6.4.1   Structural and functional MRI

For MRIs, researchers use a strong magnetic field to cause molecules in the brain to align with the field, revealing the location of an area of interest. A structural MRI reveals a static image of the brain, while a functional one (fMRI) takes account of changes as the brain processes something. For fMRIs, the magnetically aligned molecules are subsequently monitored by a radio frequency antenna detecting polarity change and measuring the MR signal (Byrnes 2001; Inoue 2004; Lin 2003). Neural processing requires glucose – metabolized through the flow of oxygenated blood to fuel synaptic activity (Jueptner and Weiller 1995) – so the regions of interest to a cerebral phenomenon under investigation (e.g. a particular aspect of language or a visual function) are presumed to use more oxygen-rich blood than uninvolved regions. The neural change that is easily monitored to detect polarity alteration is the contrast between oxygenated and deoxygenated hemoglobin or the *Blood Oxygenation Level Dependent (BOLD)* contrast. The BOLD contrast is an indirect measure of neural activity since increased blood flow corresponds with oxygen consumption and subsequently with synaptic transmission. Measurements from different angles are taken of a two-dimensional slice of brain, and then the composite 2-D images are put together with neighboring slices to create three-dimensional images. These structural images can be extended by functional imaging which takes time-series images over the course of a cognitive task. The tissue that is scanned is not all uniform, but varies in density depending on the kinds of cells that constitute it. Often the tasks are performed in a block design in which subjects perform a block of trials, rest, and perform another block of trials. One of the two tasks has a single variable of interest which can be isolated in a resulting image by subtracting away the non-relevant activities common to the two trials. The fMRI has become a very prevalent means of investigating cognitive functioning since it is non-invasive, may be repeated, and has excellent spatial resolution.

Nonetheless, there are several shortcomings that need to be taken into account in fMRI studies. They are very expensive (limiting the number of subjects studied to a dozen at most) and require subjects to remain immobile in narrow tubes, potentially inducing claustrophobia. The results also are problematic, since the outcome recorded in a functional image depicts the state of the brain *after* the event in question (a semantic anomaly, for example), given that the BOLD signals are secondary responses to the brain activity. Furthermore, there is a good deal of personal variation in activated areas, for even with a similar task researchers have found quite different results for different individuals (Indefrey and Cutler 2004). Finally, despite the reduction of variables in the tasks of interest, the brains that are scanned may be thinking of many other things as well as whatever they are immediately perceiving, an obvious distraction for the neuroimaging.

Structural MRIs have been used to investigate many areas of cognitive and motor knowledge and reveal pertinent information about the overall structure of the brain and its plasticity in adulthood. Such studies shed light on the question of age sensitivity to learning, particularly in view of claims that crucial neural networks are established early in life and can never be substantially modified later (Kuhl 2004). Maguire et al. (2000) use a structural MRI to compare the brain structure of individuals with expertise in spatial navigation, sixteen London taxi cab drivers, with a control population. They find that the cab drivers have a significantly increased volume of hippocampal gray matter and that there is a correlation of this volume with the amount of time spent driving cabs in London. Mammalian studies have shown the importance of the posterior hippocampus to spatial memory, so finding that the right posterior region is disproportionately large in the cab drivers confirms the importance of this area for spatial memory and navigation. Furthermore, the anterior hippocampus of these same subjects is less developed compared to the controls, leading the researchers to conclude that there is a direct effect of spatial navigation experience (over years in this case) to the overall internal organization of hippocampal circuitry. It is tempting to relate this study to recent findings that relate adult neurogenesis to the hippocampus (Emsley et al. 2005).

In a study of kinesthenic skill, Draganski et al. (2004) use a structural MRI to show transient changes in brain structure induced by a three-month juggling program. The subjects taught to juggle three balls demonstrate significant bilateral expansion in gray matter in the mid-temporal area after the three months' training when compared to the untrained controls. The subjects' expanded gray matter diminishes, however, in the following three months when they no longer use the juggling skills. A more relevant example of how the brain changes structurally in response to environmental influences is a study by Mechelli et al. (2004, 757) of brain differences between monolinguals and bilinguals. They find "an increase in density of gray matter in the left inferior parietal cortex of bilinguals relative to monolinguals, which is more pronounced in early rather than late bilinguals." These studies provide macroscopic information on the overall structure of the brain and how environmental influences can affect it; they do not indicate details on the neuronal developments that cause the structural changes, nor do they describe actual processing operations. Functional images, to be examined below, depict the brain at work.

6.4.2   Neuroimaging of language

Monolingual studies using fMRI have examined perception and production of phonology, morphology, syntax, semantics and discourse. Several recent studies of auditory language processes summarized by Zatorre (2003) find that the left frontal area (most superior and posterior of Brodmann's Area 44) is implicated in phonetic processing for segments and tone, while posterior regions are involved in syllable recognition. The phoneme identification tasks employing Broca's area require pattern extraction across acoustically distinct allophones (a kind of categorization) in a perceptual function. The posterior area, which deals with integrating comprehension, is also involved in production (in the study of meaningless speech syllables). Zatorre (2003, 221) observes that these neuroimaging findings reverse the roles of classical functional models. "The anterior region appears to be consistently active in certain purely perceptual tasks, whereas the posterior region is demonstrated to be involved in a production task in which auditory input was masked." He also notes that while the left hemisphere is specialized for fast processing, the right auditory cortex – the primary area involved with musical stimuli – is better able to process finer-grained frequency differences.

As for word recognition, our earlier discussion of the Damasios' work indicated that the lexicon is not located in a single region. Different lexical categories such as nouns and verbs are not clearly dissociated, but rather activate a scattered collection of areas in the left hemisphere. Shapiro and Caramazza (2004) corroborate Zatorre's classificatory function of Broca's area in observing that grammatical features such as gender are activated in the left frontal lobe, a form of syntactic computation that they attribute to the categorization function of this cerebral region. Friederici (2004) and Kaan and Swaab (2002) find a similar scattering of areas in syntactic processing of various syntactic constructions and violations in numerous studies they review. Friederici, noting that fMRIs do not allow close monitoring of temporal aspects of processing as do ERPs, suggests that the left anterior regions are more involved with word categories and the left posterior ones with syntactic integration. The importance of the language areas of the left hemisphere is evident, but ongoing research continues to inform us of their interconnections to other parts of the brain.

Given the fact that myelination and neural network development take place throughout childhood and adolescence, it is not surprising to find different neuroanatomical patterns in children and adults, an observation made by Schlaggar et al. (2002) in their study of single word processing. A number of other studies have looked at neuroimaging in bilinguals, partially to address the question of whether the dedication of neural networks in infancy and childhood create automaticity of processing which cannot be replicated in an adult language learner. Often taking AoA of the second language as a criterion in distinguishing early (childhood learners) and late (adult learners) bilinguals, studies of word, sentence and discourse processing of bilinguals provide some answers to questions about the cerebral regions and patterns involved in processing two languages.

Word processing studies covering a range of language pairs, auditory and written modalities, various tasks of comprehension and production, early and late learners with different levels of proficiency, all concur that lexical access for both languages of bilinguals involves activation of the left prefrontal cortex, with additional involvement of left temporal and parietal nodes for different tasks (Chee et al. 2001; Hernández et al. 2001; Illes et al. 1999; Marian et al. 2003 and references therein). While these studies agree that both early and late bilinguals access a common semantic system, it appears that late bilinguals activate a greater cortical area (Marian et al. 2003) or involve the right and left hemisphere (Chee et al. 2001). There may also be differences evident in behavioral measures, such as the greater involvement of general executive processing in code switching than in lexical retrieval in a single language by early Spanish-English bilinguals (Hernández et al. 2001). Marian et al. suggest that, during the processing event, early responses (e.g. phonetic) may share cortical structure for the two languages, while later processing (e.g. lexical) may entail separate cortical areas. The studies do not imply that the regions of involvement are completely distinct for the two languages; rather, the second language, particularly if it is less proficient, seems to require additional processing resources in addition to the same region used for L1. Hasegawa et al. (2002) propose that the additional cerebral resources are recruited because of the added difficulties of processing an L2, not unlike the difficulties monolinguals experience in dealing with more complex sentences in their native tongue.

Sentence processing fMRI studies also reveal a complex interplay of various regions of the brain, with the deployment of additional resources for the less proficient language and a differential role of AoA for grammatical versus semantic operations (Hasegawa et al. 2002; Kim et al. 1997; Wartenburger et al. 2003). In an oft-cited article, Kim et al. (1997, 172–173) compare early (AoA infancy) and late (AoA 11 years) bilinguals (several language pairs) in a silent sentence production task and conclude that "activation sites for the two different languages tend to be spatially distinct in Broca's area when the second language was obtained late in life and not when acquired in early childhood [and] that Wernicke's area showed little or no separation of activity regardless of age of acquisition." In contrast, Perani et al. (1998) find no AoA difference in their study of auditory processing of stories by high proficiency Catalan-Spanish early and Italian-English late bilinguals using PET imaging. They find a "strikingly similar" pattern of activation in all the languages and conclude that proficiency is more important than AoA, at least for story comprehension. As for the contrast with the Kim et al. results, they point out that their findings correlate with the evidence for no AoA difference in processing in Wernicke's area, but their investigation of comprehension did not involve Broca's area as did the Kim study. In a study of Japanese-English late bilinguals' sentence processing, Hasegawa et al. (2002, 657) find "considerable overlap in the cortical substrate that supports the processing of auditory English sentences." They also find the additional cortical activity found in bilinguals' L2 processing in many other studies.

Because other studies have shown overlap of processing regions, the question of AoA differences is the focus of Wartenburger et al.'s (2003) careful investigation of German (L2)-Italian (L1) bilinguals. The researchers compare three groups – Early Acquisition (AoA infancy) High Proficiency (EAHP), Late Acquisition (AoA 19 years) High Proficiency (LAHP), and Late Acquisition (AoA 20 years) Low Proficiency (LALP) – on behavioral criteria and neuroimaging, taking into account AoA and proficiency level while the subjects judge acceptability of sentences that are either grammatically or semantically inaccurate. Their results indicate that proficiency is important to semantic processing since both high-proficiency groups show no significant difference in behavioral RT or accuracy and have comparable neural responses, whereas LALP is significantly different on behavioral measures and has more extensive neural responses. For grammatical accuracy, in behavioral terms proficiency is significant for accuracy (EAHP and LAHP are similar), but AoA is significant for RT (both groups of late learners are slower than EAHP). In contrast, neural responses distinguish early and late bilinguals: the two late groups pattern together for the syntactically anomalous sentences which elicit significantly more activation involving Broca's area in their L2 grammatical processing (but not their L1), while early bilinguals exhibit no neural distinction between L1 and L2 processing. The results confirm ERP studies finding a distinction in processing semantic versus syntactic information, with AoA showing some effect on the latter but not the former.

Two recent fMRI studies of phonological processing elucidate another aspect of acquisition capabilities and AoA. Chee et al. (2004) study two groups of Chinese-English early bilinguals (equal and unequal) to investigate the role of *phonological working memory (PWM)* in the auditory recognition of words from unfamiliar French. Both groups are matched for AoA (<5 years), nonverbal intelligence, education and language test scores. The equal bilinguals show greater activation in cortical areas related to PWM than do the unequal bilinguals, leading the authors to conclude that PWM is a crucial feature in L2 acquisition, even for very young children. The finding is quite suggestive concerning individual variability in L2 ability (especially for intransigent phonology) which becomes greater with increasing AoA.

Most of the age-based studies have focused on very young or completely adult AoA (avoiding the gray area of late childhood and adolescence), but a recent master's thesis (Lin 2003) looks at fMRI responses in fourteen-year-olds. Tone in Chinese is phonemically distinctive, so it is a clearly linguistic phenomenon centered in the left hemisphere, as Wang et al. (2004) demonstrate with dichotic listening tests (native Mandarin speakers show a right ear advantage, whereas non-speakers of Mandarin show no advantage). For the Lin study, eight anglophone subjects with no familiarity with Chinese trained to discriminate Mandarin tones; these subjects and eight controls were imaged before and after training. The controls do not recognize or have systematic neural responses to the tones on either occasion, but the eight trainees respond more accurately, have shorter RT and show more constrained and systematic neural responses on post-training evaluations. They display bilateral temporal activation that confirms the added neural effort seen in other studies documenting the difficulties of L2 processing. It appears that despite evidence of English native phonology interference, these fourteen-year-olds still retain the neural plasticity to acquire new phonological contrasts.

On the whole, the neuroimaging studies contribute to our understanding of the complexity of language processing and the intricate interactions of various components in the bilingual brain, although this area of research is still developing criteria for evaluating results. Behavioral, ERP and neuro-imaging provide evidence for similarities and differences in knowledge and processing in native and second languages. Lexico-semantics is fairly similar in L1 and L2, whereas morphosyntax is more susceptible to AoA and proficiency effects. Generally, late bilinguals show delayed RT, lower accuracy and more extensive neural responses than early bilinguals and monolinguals. Yet all bilinguals are different from monolinguals, regardless of AoA and proficiency (Cook 1995, 2002). We concur with Abutalebi et al. (2001, 188), that "the bilingual brain cannot be considered as the sum of two monolingual language systems, but is rather a unique and complex neural system which may differ in individual cases."

6.5   Conclusion

AoA studies reveal significant evidence of deficits in L2A. This chapter has explored the possible causes for the deficits, including both non-biological reasons such as native language influence, instructional input and motivation, and biological factors relating to changes in the human brain during childhood and adolescence. Leather (2003, 29) notes that "the evidence for an irreversible neurobiological change that impedes post-primary language acquisition is inconclusive. There are some indications that primary and post-primary language activity are neurologically different, but this does not prove impaired potential." Whether and when there is a critical period for L2A remains controversial (Bialystok 1997, 2002b; Birdsong 1999a; DeKeyser 2000; Snow 2002), but the lack of conclusive evidence speaks against a strictly defined biologically based critical period. The selective impairment of different aspects of language at different chronological moments – phonology impairment precedes syntax impairment, for example – indicates that if there is a sensitive period, it is not the same time for all aspects of the grammar (Seliger 1978; Johnson and Newport 1989). Individual variation in L2 achievement (as compared to nearly uniform perfection in learning L1) is also problematic, since a critical period ability (or deficit) should apply across the board to all individuals as a function of age (Nikolov 2000; Jia et al. 2002; Jia and Aaronson 2003). Finally, it is unclear why any single factor would be the locus of purported sensitive period deterioration, rather than another factor or factors, ranging from physiological sensitivity to phonetic or semantic detail to process of acquisition. Age-related effects such as L2 phonetic inaccuracies might be caused either by physiological maturation or by depth of native language influence (Ellis and Lambon Ralph 2000).

Psycholinguistic evidence from behavioral studies, ERP investigations and neuroimaging show that monolingual language processing is qualitatively similar to bilingual processing of the L2. Early bilinguals who are proficient have nearly identical neural responses to those of monolinguals, but bilinguals who are adult learners and not very proficient may demonstrate rather divergent responses. Late bilinguals are generally slower in reaction time than early learners of an L2. ERP studies that examine reactions to semantic and morphosyntactic anomalies indicate that AoA is not relevant to semantic repair in processing, but that adult L2 learners gain morphosyntactic repair only with more advanced proficiency and partially as a function of the first language. The overall conclusion we can draw from this research is that, at initial stages, adult L2 learners may show quite nonnative-like neural responses, but with advanced proficiency they gain qualitatively similar processing mechanisms. Speed of processing is necessarily slower with an L2, as is timing and strength of ERP response to anomalies, but the differences are more quantitative than qualitative for proficient L2 speakers. Such differences suggest that processing strategies are established quite firmly at a very early age for native language, a fact that both facilitates and inhibits later language learning.

7   It's about time: evaluation of age sensitivity in language acquisition

7.0   Introduction

In the book of Genesis, just after Adam arrives in the Garden of Eden, he displays a command of vocabulary in naming all the animals. A little later he comments on his partner Eve: "This one at last is bone of my bones and flesh of my flesh. This one shall be called Woman, for from man was she taken" (*Tanakh*, 5). Adam improves substantially after his holophrastic period of animal naming to develop almost immediately a grammar using complete sentences with subordinate clauses, past tense and passive. A literal interpretation of Genesis – whatever literal might mean given the opacity of translations from the original Hebrew and the vagaries of individual exegesis – meets with as much success in describing the development of language as Shelley's account of Frankenstein's reanimation.

How the first humans came to have language is a question that relates both to ontogenetic development (the growth of individual language) and to phylogenetic (growth of the species' language). It is doubtful that we might learn how the first language developed, whether all at once by a mutated gene or in the gradual development of a symbolic system of communication, or by increases in brain size. "The amazing combinatorial productivity of human language [makes] it more than a set of arbitrary associative pairings of the kind that can be learned by most animals ... It may not be coincidental, then, that the phylogenesis of language coincided in evolutionary time with a ballooning in the size of the frontal lobe, such that human prefrontal cortex is more than twice the size predicted for a 'typical' primate brain" (Shapiro and Caramazza 2004, 812). If there is a critical period – if language acquisition is biologically restricted to a certain period of childhood – to what evolutionary cause might one attribute it? This chapter reviews the evidence presented in the previous six to elucidate the biological aspects of language acquisition and hazards in its conclusion some thoughts on the evolutionary implications.

Presupposing that there is a critical period for first and second language acquisition and that examining L2A provides an easy way to test the

212 Evaluation of age sensitivity in language acquisition

Critical Period Hypothesis for L1A as well, Bever (1981, 180) outlines three classes of theories that account for the "rapid loss of language learning ability with age: A precipitous loss of the neurological flexibility to learn a language (e.g. the permanent entrenchment of cerebral asymmetries in the brain); a 'filling up' of the language-learning capacity simply due to the experience with the first language; and the superposition of an intellectualized self-conscious way of learning everything." In fact, all three factors are at play in L2A, but only the first can be related to an age threshold that could be adduced as proof of a biological critical period. The first reason is the strictly maturational one of the most traditional definitions of a critical period, whereas the second reflects the experiential argument put forth by Kuhl and Flege, an argument that is in a sense the obverse of the maturational one; the third represents the "other" factors that impact language acquisition. These reasons are considered in the first section of this chapter, which recapitulates the themes and definitions raised in Chapter 1; the second section looks at neurological evidence as the most pertinent test of the strictly biological cause; the third and fourth sections examine child and adult acquisition in light of the biological evidence.

7.1 Evidence for a critical period

Before evaluating the evidence of the preceding chapters, let us return to the framework established initially, looking first at the definitions of a critical period and then at the causes proposed.

7.1.1 Definition of critical period

The original formulations of critical periods included the ideas that certain developmental processes are confined to a very limited time span and are totally irreversible (Lorenz 1978); that they involve rapid cell proliferation and developmental changes (Scott 1978); that such a period "implies a sharply defined phase of susceptibility preceded and followed by lack of susceptibility; if the relevant experience is provided before or after the period, no long-term effects are supposedly detectable" (Bateson 1987, 153). Bornstein's (1987b) five parameters repeat these characteristics:
- Onset
- Terminus
- Intrinsic maturation event
- Extrinsic trigger
- Organismic system affected

Oyama (1979) and Birdsong (2005a) adopt a broad definition that does not include irreversibility, but rather focuses on heightened sensitivity to environmental stimuli required to trigger development. For Oyama, the development may result in behavior that is replicable, such as learning another language subsequent to the first one.

Returning to Lenneberg's definition, we note that he views first language acquisition as subject to maturational constraints, the restriction of L1A to age two to twelve. In Bornstein's terms, for Lenneberg the organismic system is the human neuromuscular system exposed to human language, which triggers an onset of acquisition at two years of age, a duration of about ten years and then an offset decline for a few years, a terminus which marks an irreversible change after which input no longer has effect. Acquisition of first language appears at first glance to be subject to a critical period. It is usually irreversible – although the Korean adoptee study (Pallier et al. 2003) casts doubt on total irreversibility – it involves relatively rapid developmental changes in neuronal structure, and it represents a period of susceptibility followed by reduction of susceptibility. Lenneberg does not apply his maturational constraints to second language acquisition which he says "confuses the picture," but he does point out corollary effects of the terminus: post-puberty "automatic acquisition" is no longer possible from "mere exposure," and foreign accents are prevalent. His main point is that language is a species-specific biological phenomenon of which L1A is a critical developmental phase.

The core of Lenneberg's ideas on L1A constitute the essence of more recent critical period proposals, but the details need to be updated, taking into account advances in our knowledge of language and acquisition since 1967. The onset of L1A cannot be two years of age, but rather birth, while offset must begin after age five, the moment at which TD children exposed to language have most of the basic grammar of their language in place. On one interpretation, the offset decline begins around age five and lasts until twelve, but on another interpretation, the decline continues unabated into adulthood. On the first interpretation, our two benchmarks, five and twelve years of age, correspond to offset and terminus respectively; if age twelve is indeed a biological terminus, then no acquisition of L1 grammar should be possible after twelve and all learners deprived of input beyond age twelve should show comparable deficits (a "flattening out" where there should be no individual variation). The data available for L1 is as yet inadequate – Schaller's Ildefonso who learns ASL as an adult is only documented anecdotally, for example – to explore this last point, but the evidence we will look at for L2 sheds some light on the issue. It is not at all clear that there is a terminus after which input is ineffectual and developmental change is impossible for L1A. There is, however, substantial evidence of deficits in phonology and morphosyntax, certainly in the breadth of "perfection" in late L1A.

If most critical period factors seem relatively clear-cut for investigating L1A as a biological phenomenon, none is straightforward for L2A, because most of the five criteria are undefinable under the same terms of onset, duration and offset. Furthermore, there are so many additional factors that affect L2A that it is impractical to isolate the biological factors alone. Finally, there is the issue of when the critical threshold occurs and whether it is precipitous or gradual. In the literature reviewed in earlier chapters, just about every age between one and twenty has been proposed as the critical threshold for language acquisition, an *embarras de choix* that forces us to restrict our options. Biological maturation does not take place overnight, so one would not anticipate a punctual threshold. For example, maturational stages such as toddlerhood and puberty encompass a number of physiological changes relating to neuronal growth, cognitive knowledge, physical development, psycho-social evolution and hormonal modifications. Given all these considerations, we adopt the criteria used for L1A as an initial framework for examining L2A. We will assume that acquisition offset begins after age five and will test the terminus age twelve by examining endstate achievement of individuals with different AoA in Sections 7.3 and 7.4.

7.1.2   Causes of age effects in language acquisition

We can only test the notion of a critical period for language acquisition with biological evidence that links maturation to that process, with specific onset, duration, offset and terminus triggered by language input. For L1A there are three interrelated causes that have been distinguished, experience with the first language (Flege 1999; Kuhl 2000), neuromuscular achievements (Scovel 1988, 2000) and overall cerebral development, including synaptic expansion, neural reorganization and increasing lateralization (Bruer 1999; Calvin and Bickerton 2001; Neville 1995).

Flege, Kuhl and others have shown the importance of first language experience in cognitive development. They and others have argued that the establishment of prosodic dimensions of language forms the basis for later acquisition of lexicon and morphosyntax. The evidence from L1A by deaf children less than age six (of ASL and of English with cochlear implants) indicates that the infant's brain remains very receptive to language through the five-year-old threshold. Sharma et al. (2002b) note that children deprived of sound for three to four years gain normal capacities within six months after implantation of a cochlear device. They suggest that either auditory pathways develop normally in the absence of stimulation, even after periods of auditory deprivation up to four years, or deprived pathways may overcome deficits through plasticity. Recent work documenting neurogenesis supports the second option. Early learners are very native-like, but nevertheless may manifest slight deficits in phonology and morphosyntax. It appears that if the environmental input is not available at the very earliest period, the L1 learner may show subtle deficits with delayed AoA and much more severe deficits with late AoA. The experiential account is then a complementary theory that works with the cerebral development one. Cerebral development is a key biological factor for L1A in the first four to five years, and it tapers in importance in late childhood into adolescence.

Scovel's neuromuscular approach – based on the observation that phonology is "directly physical" whereas morphosyntax is only physically realized through phonology – restricts the biological basis of a critical period to mastery of L2 speech. "It is difficult to see how highly abstract concepts such as irregular moprhology or the subjacency principle would be directly linked to loss of nueromuscular plasticity" (Scovel 2000, 219). Other researchers indicate that phonology is not alone in depending on neuromuscular learning. Newport (1994) shows that "early" (age four to six) L1 learners of ASL do not perform as well on morphology as native learners, and Lillo-Martin and Berk (2003) find that a delay of a few years hinders acquisition of stylistic variation in syntax production. Emmorey (2002) likewise underscores the importance of early development not only of phonology, but also of morphosyntax and prosodic structuring.

Scovel's ideas on the importance of neurological development to critical linguistic development – "increased production of neurotransmitters, the process of myelinization, the proliferation of nerve pathways in the cerebral cortex, and the speeding up of synaptic transmission" (Scovel 1988, 62) – is central to the biological basis of the critical period, although his restriction of these developments to phonology alone is not justified. We see his proposal as part of the general cerebral development theory which includes early dendritic branching and neuronal exuberance, later pruning and network dedication. While the plasticity of the brain and its early specialization through circuit building is a crucial development of native language, Knudsen cautions against a simplistic notion of critical period. "Language depends on a wide range of specialized sensory, motor, and cognitive skills that involve many neural hierarchies distributed throughout much of the forebrain. For example, the analyses of phonetics, semantics, grammar, syntax, and prosody are likely to be accomplished by distinct hierarchies of neural circuits. The functional properties of each of these hierarchies are shaped by experience with language" (Knudsen 2004, 1421).

If cerebral development is key to L1A, it should also serve as the biological basis for an L2A critical period, although a number of other factors have been proposed (Singleton 1989; Singleton and Ryan 2004), including many which are not biological. Indeed, it is imperative to take into account a number of non-biological influences – sociocultural concerns, input, instruction, motivation, aptitude – in examining L2 endstate achievement in relation to age of onset of acquisition. In addition, the important impact of L1 experience, highlighted by Kuhl and Flege, must also be considered. When we examine the L2A evidence in 7.4, we will return to these mitigating pressures. In transferring the L1 paradigm to L2, we can hypothesize that L2A will be native-like up to age five, subject to offset decline from five to twelve, and then clearly nonnative-like in a steady manner. If acquisition abilities are not influenced by other factors as a purely biological perspective would require, then first language, education and numerous other factors should have no influence on L2A before or during the offset. If, on the other hand, acquisition possibilities and cerebral capacity change with increasing age (Kuhl's idea of how experience changes the very organism that takes it in), the respective roles of internal cerebral organization and external experiences will vary from individual to individual and at different stages of development (e.g. before or during the offset). As for the final terminus at age twelve, we have seen ample evidence in Chapters 5 and 6 that puberty is an arbitrary threshold that is not corroborated by numerous studies confirming AoA deficits.

A final reason invoked in generative literature for a critical period for language acquisition is the availability of Universal Grammar. On the UG = LAD approach, UG represents not only the universal properties of language, but also the blueprint for L1A, the program that directs the infant to acquire language (Herschensohn 2000). The heated debate of the early 1990s on access has mostly given way to acceptance of UG availability to L2 learners (Hawkins 2001; White 2003), but there remains a question concerning the ability of adult learners to gain L2 features of functional categories which differ in value from those of their native language. Investigations of Spanish and Greek DPs and clitics demonstrate critical period effects in incomplete acquisition of nominal features such as gender by post-critical period L2 learners, as compared to native speakers (Franceschina 2001; Hawkins and Franceschina 2004; Tsimpli and Mastropavlou 2004). The role of functional categories such as Determiner or Gender is crucial both to morphology and lexicon mastery and to syntactic parameter setting in L1A as well as L2A. The authors argue that while UG may be available to L2 learners, functional category values are fixed early during the critical period (by age eight according to Hawkins and Franceschina 2004), and cannot be modified to a new value once set. The theory is appealing in that it provides an explanation for the residual difficulties that L2 learners have with features such as gender, a topic that will be explored in greater detail below.

7.2   Age effects and the brain

Since language is mainly a cerebral operation, it is logical to look at the development and functioning of the neural areas and networks that permit linguistic procedures, especially because the maturing brain of the child is particularly adept at learning new things, both experience expectant milestones (e.g. theory of mind) and experience dependent skills such as playing a musical instrument. Development of the brain in the child is similar to bone growth – just as bones are flexible in early stages of growth, the human brain is plastic with respect to dedicated neural networks and synaptic connections. Even after adolescence, when the majority of brain dedication has been accomplished, individuals are still capable of reconfiguring networks or establishing new ones. This section recapitulates neural development and draws conclusions concerning age effects in language acquisition.

7.2.1   Brain development

The infant's brain is already developing in utero, during which time it grows most of the neurons it will need for life; yet at birth the brain weighs 335 grams, just a quarter of the adult's 1,300 grams. During the first three years of life the neurons make "exuberant" synaptic connections, the neural circuits that will later be modified. From age four to eighteen, the brain matures by creating new Hebbian patterns of synaptic linking and by pruning unnecessary synaptic connections, both of which render processing more efficient. It is clear that the patterns honed for the native language are well underway by age three and are highly dependent on the ambient input, as experience "warps" the developing organ (Kuhl 2000). As for language functions, different subcomponents such as phonology or syntax mature at different rates, as evidenced by variation in timing of myelination in different language regions: the left perisylvian area (responsible for phonological aspects of language) myelinates during the first year, whereas morphosyntactic Broca's area does so during the second (Pulvermüller and Schumann 1994). "Different areas begin postnatal maturation at different times and develop at different rates" (Paradis 2004, 119).

  While the brain is industriously creating circuits and specializing its hemispheres differentially, it is nevertheless plastic in its ability to create variations on the genetic theme. Depending on the modality of language in the environment, signed or spoken, the baby's brain adjusts its neural connections to be more or less attuned to visual cues, with signed language involving more right hemisphere involvement (Neville 1995; Petitto 2000; Sacks 1990). Such adjustments are rather minor compared to the major cerebral revisions that take place in young children with damaged or removed left hemispheres who are able to relocate language functions in the right hemisphere (Lenneberg 1967). The evidence for recuperation from severe left hemisphere damage is strongest for the very youngest children, a fact that is understandable given the importance of very early learning in, for example, vowel prototype (Kuhl 2000) or prosodic parsing (Cutler et al. 1992). Indeed, Dupoux and Peperkamp (2002) go so far as to say that adults are "phonologically deaf" to new language sounds, so attuned are they to their native phonology. Sharma et al. (2005) observe that deaf and blind subjects reorganize higher-order cortex function after long periods of sensory deprivation, but that plastic adaptation via inputs from cochlear implants diminishes around age seven, what they call "the end of the sensitive period."

The early establishment of dedicated native language neural circuits is not impervious to adjustment in later childhood. Pallier et al. (2003) report that adults with native Korean, who were adopted by French families (at three to eight years of age, average six) and subsequently learned French, show neither behavioral nor neuroimaging response to spoken Korean. The subjects, all fluent and native-like in French, report no conscious memory of Korean and respond to behavioral and neuroimaging measures as do French native controls. The authors argue that the evidence does not support a "crystallization" hypothesis holding that the brain experiences a permanent loss of plasticity related to the influence of the native language (because of either maturation or learning) and resulting in native "traces for life." They argue that the second language takes over the dedicated networks from the first language: "any child between three to eight years of age can succeed to a high degree and they do so by using the same brain areas as are recruited for first language acquisition" (ibid., 158). The only difference between the subjects and the controls is in the greater extent of activation indicated by the fMRI in the relevant neural areas of the French natives, a difference the authors suggest is a result of incomplete replacement of native Korean by L2 French.

The evidence from bilinguals generally corroborates Pallier et al.'s opinions in that neuroimaging confirms language functions to be located in the same areas of the brain for both languages, perhaps with the exception of late bilinguals' specialization of Broca's area. Grammatical integration related to production is centered in Broca's area for both languages in early bilinguals, although Kim et al. (1997) find that late bilinguals have non-overlapping sections dedicated to each language. Likewise, Wartenburger et al. (2003) find that late bilinguals of high proficiency – who are indistinguishable from early high bilinguals on behavioral and neuroimaging for semantic phenomena – show similar brain activity to late low-proficiency bilinguals on syntactic phenomena involving Broca's area. The late bilinguals show significantly more activity in Broca's area for the L2 than the L1, while early bilinguals are comparable in the two languages. The authors conclude that the importance of AoA for grammatical processing indicates maturation-sensitive development of areas involved in syntactic functions that are "early set."

In contrast to syntactic production, all bilinguals treat comprehension of both languages similarly in Wernicke's area (Kim et al. 1997; Perani et al. 1998), and vocabulary from both languages is distributed in patchwork patterns throughout the brain, with common accessing of the conceptual referents of the words. While early and late bilinguals show overlapping areas for the two languages in the specialized language areas that are established in early childhood, and are thus qualitatively comparable in terms of neural circuits and processing, monolinguals and bilinguals may differ in quantity of processing response, as for example, the French adoptees from Korea compared to the native French.

The development of the human brain from birth to age eighteen produces a progressively more elaborate cognitive organ, capable of adding knowledge and vocabulary throughout life. The establishment of language in the first five years of life is a major milestone for future cognitive development, a means to communicate with other members of the species, and a template for learning other languages. The refinement of linguistically dedicated areas mainly in the left hemisphere during the first and second years of life – particularly the modification of the phonological system that permits acquisition of lexicon and morphosyntax – is clearly experience expectant, a developmental phenomenon at the cellular level that meets the criteria of classical definitions of a critical period, that is rapid cell proliferation and rapid developmental changes (Scott 1978). The organismic system is genetically programmed to target certain environmental influences, which in turn transform the undifferentiated neurons through dendritic branching and eventual synapse pruning. From the perspective of the brain's development of language during infancy and the very constrained specializations for specific language functions, the inception of first language acquisition corresponds to the abrupt onset at birth and subsequent plateau of peak sensitivity of the beginning of a critical period.

7.2.2   Declarative and procedural knowledge

Of two rather obvious characteristics of adult L2A distinguishing it from L1A – lack of completeness and deliberation of learning (Herschensohn 2000) – the first has received perhaps disproportionate attention compared to the second in critical period research. Indeed, "lack of success" and "variability in success" in L2A "continue to be regarded as powerful arguments for cognitive differences between child and adult language acquisition and therefore for the CPH" (Klein and Martohardjono 1999b, 7). Nevertheless, the second characteristic has been dealt with in terms of learning theories of general cognition and psycholinguistics (Bialystok 2001; N. Ellis 1994; McLaughlin 1990) for several decades.

From an information processing perspective, learning can be distinguished as *explicit* or *implicit*, with or without conscious effort respectively (N. Ellis 1994; Paradis 2003, 2004), while the resultant knowledge can be described as *declarative* ("knowing what") or *procedural* ("knowing how"). Knowledge is accessed with respect to two parallel variables, *analysis* of representational structure and *control* of attention, where analysis refers to the "level of explicit structure and organization" (e.g. how facts are interrelated) and control refers to the "level of attention and inhibition recruited during cognitive processing" (Bialystok 2001, 14–15). Often L2 learners initially achieve explicit learning of, for example, a verb paradigm or vocabulary item, but they must *restructure* their new knowledge to integrate it with extant knowledge (e.g. understanding the new verb in terms of other familiar verbs) and to render it more accessible for automatic processing. McLaughlin (1990) suggests that explicit learning is transformed through restructuring to become more easily accessible or implicit, a procedure of *automaticity*. Paradis (2004) points out that it is a contradiction in terms to say that explicit knowledge (e.g. metalinguistic) *becomes* implicit, but rather that automaticity develops in parallel, with the explicit declarative knowledge always being available once the procedural knowledge has been established.

Two threads – adult/child differences in biology of language acquisition and learning/knowledge theories – have come together in the work of Ullman (2001a, b), who adopts the declarative/procedural distinction to put forth an account of L1/L2 differences relating AoA and extent of experience to neural representation. According to his model, conscious declarative memory contrasts significantly from unconscious procedural memory:

- Conscious declarative memory
  - is not encapsulated
  - accesses multiple response systems
  - encompasses "whats" such as facts and lexical items
  - is subserved by the medial temporal lobe.

In contrast,

- Unconscious procedural memory
  - is informationally encapsulated (Fodor 1983)
  - involves long-established motor and cognitive skills

- encompasses "hows" such as habits and grammatical processing
- is subserved by left frontal/basal ganglia (Paradis 2003)

In the native language, lexico-semantic information is stored in declarative memory (which the neural architecture studies we've seen show to be distributed in networks in both hemispheres), while morphosyntactic grammatical information is implemented particularly in the left frontal region and the subcortical basal ganglia. The basal ganglia are located next to the limbic system and are functionally important for motor control in initiating movements. For second languages, Ullman argues that with increasing AoA the learner shifts reliance from procedural to declarative memory (in all domains of learning), so the latter becomes the predominant mechanism for learning and storage in the adult second language for both lexical and grammatical information. Generally, first languages have two learning/memory systems for lexicon and grammar, whereas second languages have only one, although the procedural system is available in L2 if it is either acquired early enough or is sufficiently "practiced" (essentially corresponding to "proficiency level" or amount of "experience," other well-used terms).

Ullman employs evidence from bilingual aphasia, SLI, neuroimaging and ERPs to demonstrate that native language has separate cognitive systems for grammar versus lexicon, whereas L2 has weaker or no such distinctions; and that the two systems are localized in the aforementioned areas of the brain. The shift from procedural to declarative memory is seen in later AoA in the acquisition of L2 grammatical forms memorized as words and of grammatical rules learned explicitly in declarative memory (differing "radically" from implicit L1 grammar). For native speakers the dual mechanism model of morphology (Pinker 1999) holds that regular forms are rule governed (implicit, procedural) whereas irregular forms are declaratively stored as "words." Recent clinical studies of native language support the declarative/procedural distinction in that "two distinct cerebral pathways are used depending on the degree to whch a verbal task is controlled or automatic" (Paradis 2004, 12). Grammatically challenged SLI speakers, who have sequencing deficits and frontal/basal ganglia abnormalities, use declarative memory for regular as well as irregular forms, supporting Ullman's association of procedural with automatized grammatical and left frontal/basal ganglia localization. Similarly, bilingual aphasics with impairment to L1 grammar, such as the Veronese (L1)-Italian (L2) speaker who lost all ability in her first language but retained command of her L2 (Fabbro 2002), furnish evidence of damage to the same cerebral area that impacts L1 grammar. Neuroimaging and ERP studies show few L1/L2 differences for lexical processing, but more discrepancies for grammar processing. Fabbro (2002) confirms Ullman's proposal, noting that L1 and L2 lexicons are macroscopically represented in similar brain areas, while native morpho-syntax is left frontal specialized; in late bilinguals, however, morphosyntactic aspects rely more extensively on declarative memory and do not exploit the same frontal areas as the native tongue.

Given the wide acceptance of explicit/implicit learning, dual mechanism processing and AoA effects, what is new about Ullman's proposal is his linking of the declarative/procedural distinction to specific regions of the brain that change with age. The obvious difference in explicit learning between children and adults for language has often been recognized, as Klein (1996, 259) notes: "parts of linguistic knowledge which require 'higher cognitive abilities' are much less affected [in L2] than more peripheral properties such as accurate pronunciation, authentic prosody, correct morphological forms and the like," so Ullman's proposal furnishes a maturational reason for the change. Overall, his proposal fits well with the evidence that has been presented on L1/L2 differences, AoA effects and dissimilarity between lexical and grammatical phenomena in L1 and L2. The fact that late bilinguals not terribly proficient in an L2 demonstrate declarative memorization of words, grammatical chunks and explicit rules, using temporal areas that resemble lexical networks more than grammatical processing, is precisely what we would expect from years of research pointing to all those behavioral phenomena (Gass and Selinker 2001).

Far more interesting than L2 incompleteness is the fact that some learners do become very proficient with sufficiently rich input (Moyer 2004), and that they profile a typical procedural storage of L2 grammar. Ullman says "practice as well as age of exposure should affect both grammatical proficiency and the degree of dependence on procedural memory for grammmatical computations" (ibid., 110), but he does not give details on how that transition might be accomplished. His escape hatch to account for proficient late bilinguals who evidence procedural memory in L2 weakens his core proposal of maturational deterioration of procedural grammar processing abilities (AoA effects in grammar) and also fails to provide a solid account of how declarative knowledge becomes paralleled by procedural abilities. The advanced individuals must eventually automatize their grammatical knowledge. They are of particular interest to researchers because they may point the direction of how second languages might be learned to a more proficient level. Ullman's proposal furnishes the framework to do the follow-up work necessary to explore this question.

7.2.3   Bilingual processing

The processing studies discussed in Chapter 6 largely substantiate Ullman's proposal, but also elucidate the complexity and variability of the neural representation and implementation of language. In isolating certain factors one can clearly differentiate lexico-semantic from morpho-syntactic, as for example, in the differential ERP responses of monolin-guals to N400 semantic anomalies and to P600 syntactic anomalies. The difference is probably better described as a continuum of networks rather than as a dichotomy, since it is evident that a number of factors influence processing, and neural responses involve various regions, not a single one. Zatorre (2003) observes that the roles of classical functional models (pro-duction in Broca's area and comprehension in Wernicke's) are "reversed" and that syntactic processing shows a scattering of areas in neuroimaging studies (Friederici 2004; Kaan and Swaab 2002). Monolingual lexical processing is affected by frequency, length, uniqueness and neighborhood effects, as well as by morphosyntactic features such as gender, while morphosyntactic P600 may be influenced by semantic features of the verb. Finally, even monolinguals may manifest distinct reactions to the same linguistic phenomenon. Inoue (2005) shows that native Japanese speakers are not homogeneous in their processing of certain anomalies (illicit double case marking); for some the illicit structure evokes a semantic N400 response, while for others it evokes a morphosyntactic P600.

Given the benchmarks of monolingual patterns in behavioral, ERP and neuroimaging studies, studies of bilinguals provide insight into the struc-ture and functioning of the L2 lexicon and grammar. By and large, bilin-guals are qualitatively similar to monolinguals in their processing of L2 according to behavioral and cortical measures; the second language is not lodged in a totally distinct corner of the brain, but rather is distributed in similar areas to that of the L1, according to neuroimaging studies. While the big picture is that monolinguals and bilinguals (both early and late) treat language similarly, the more detailed view is that there are quantita-tive differences between monolinguals and late bilinguals with respect to RT, accuracy and morphosyntactic processing, taken up below.

As we have seen, bilinguals and monolinguals have cerebral differences that relate both to the second language and to the first (Cook 2003), and which also affect other aspects of behavior. There are well-established differences between balanced early bilinguals and monolinguals in both linguistic and cognitive terms (Bialystok 2001). Although bilingual chil-dren show an overall deficit in vocabulary in a given language compared to monolinguals, bilinguals display advantages in metalinguistic awareness. "Bilingual children perform better than their monolingual peers in tasks that demand high levels of control, but there is no consistent bilingual advantage in tasks for which the solution relies primarily on high levels of analysis of representational structures" (ibid., 149). Bilingual children thus have the advantage in doing tasks such as substituting one word consistently for another (e.g. "we" replaced by "spaghetti"), or doing gram-maticality judgement, whereas they have no advantage in doing grammati-cality correction which involves analysis more than control. The cognitive advantage that the bilinguals gain in increased control serves them in other domains as well, for example, in tasks involving counting. Bialystok and Codd (1997) assess cardinality acquisition with two tasks, one targeting analysis (counting) and the other targeting control (counting blocks with the misleading visual cue of two different sizes). The bilingual children, who are not misled in the high control demand task, outperform their mono-lingual peers, whereas both groups perform comparably in the analysis task. The evidence from linguistic and non-linguistic experiments indicates that their enhanced control abilities lead bilinguals to inhibit attention to mis-leading information to a greater degree than monolinguals.

Behavioral investigations of linguistic tasks by adult bilinguals, includ-ing ERP and neuroimaging which use behavioral experiments to test the process of interest, usually show that bilinguals have slower RT and lower accuracy than monolinguals, more so with increasing AoA (Birdsong 2005b; Dussias 2003; Frenck-Mestre 2002). The less efficient and less accurate responses of bilinguals have been attributed to increased memory load by the extra processing demands (Dewaele 2002; McDonald 2000), similar to extra demands on monolinguals in their decoding of more complex sentences (Hasegawa et al. 2002). Increased cognitive demand leads the brain to recruit additional cerebral resources to cope with the added difficulties of L2 processing, a load increase that early bilinguals establish automatized control to handle. Increased control comes through the interplay of explicit and implicit knowledge. Explicit knowledge requiring conscious effort clearly marshals a fair share of cognitive resour-ces for the necessary focused attention and analysis involved in initially acquiring it. With repeated use, the explicit knowledge is supplemented by integrated and automatized implicit knowledge. Once automatized, a procedure may be performed without conscious effort, such as depressing the brake in a car. It is difficult for individuals to solve more than one explicit problem at a time, but it is much easier for them to multi-task with automatized procedures. "Automatic memory processes are relatively unharmed by the need to solve a concurrent task," and are not impaired by aging, as intentional processes are (Bialystok 2001, 200).

Because faster processing frees up larger parts of working memory for other computations, the slower processing of late/non-proficient bilin-guals means that they are not just slower, they also have a much greater opportunity to make mistakes. Dewaele (2002) points out that the L2 speaker must "intervene" more often during production to address lacunae of implicit knowledge (both automatized grammar and "large chunks") using explicit knowledge. He presents evidence that the capacity and efficiency of working memory and short-term memory contribute to individual variation, giving advantage to those who can process more declarative knowledge simultaneously. He finally points to anxiety and perceived formality as variables that impact L2 processing. The reduced capacity for procedural memory and increased use of declarative memory by L2 learners means that they use distributed networks not only for vocabulary, but also for grammar, resulting in neuroimages that disclose greater activation in both hemispheres and greater variation among individuals compared to monolinguals (Paradis 2003). The bilateral activation indicative of engaged declarative memory reveals the extra intervention necessary in L2 and the transitional nature of the grammar processing mechanism.

ERP and neuroimaging studies confirm both the procedural-grammar/declarative-lexicon distinction and the localization of brain functions for monolinguals and early bilinguals. The research seems to indicate five years as a threshold of change. In ERP studies, bilinguals of all AoA show lexico-semantic responses (N400) qualitatively comparable to monolinguals, even after a mere fourteen hours of instruction (McLaughlin et al. 2004; Osterhout et al. 2004). Bilinguals differ on grammatical processing, for the P600 effect is often not observable or is reduced with increased latency in late bilinguals, except for those comparably proficient to monolinguals (Hahne 2001). Ongoing research by Foucart and Frenck-Mestre (2005) hints at the development of the P600 effect in late bilinguals. Their German learners of L2 French fall into a bimodal distribution in their reaction to French gender anomalies (one group shows P600 for all French anomalies, while the other shows P600 only for the French anomalies that are also anomalies in German). The evidence that P600 effects are indeed possible in an L2 implies that the second group is just not advanced enough to show the P600 for all L2 French gender errors, but should become so eventually.

In fMRI work, Wartenburger et al. (2003) investigate RT and accuracy in sentence acceptability judgements by subjects who determine grammatical or semantical accuracy. The three groups of German-Italian bilinguals of early high proficiency, late high proficiency and late low proficiency show comparable neural responses on the semantic judgement (broader activation in the low group), but the two high groups have equivalent RT and accuracy, higher than the low group. Unlike the semantic response, the grammatical judgement elicits a bilateral neural response in both late groups, who also have increased RT, while the early group shows more restricted neural activation, in keeping with other studies. Accuracy, however, is comparable for the high groups and greater than for the low group, indicating that the late high-proficiency learners have achieved a solid command of the grammar but still rely more on dispersed declarative than procedural memory.

The development of neural architecture dedicated to native language grammar, lexicon and processing is a clearly biological characteristic of typical human growth during the first few years of life that presents the onset and peak of sensitivity of a representative critical period. The left hemisphere neural circuits, especially those dedicated to grammatical processing in the frontal region, and phonology in the perisylvian region, launch implicit patterns of procedure that continue to be refined in the following years and that permit speakers to process phonology and morphosyntax instantaneously and unconsciously. As Shapiro and Caramazza (2004, 812) explain, human cognitive processes "all depend on a single remarkable skill: the ability to encode multiple bits of information quickly and efficiently in an abstract propositional format." It is clear why the period from birth to five years is indeed critical for first language acquisition, a period that sees dramatic changes in the organism as a function of the very experience of language (the brain at age five is far more dedicated than at age one). However, beyond that (somewhat arbitrary) threshold, the ability to gain language is not ended, but attenuated, and only in very rare and aberrant cases is acquisition of a modicum of language impossible. After age five lexical acquisition and semantic processing are relatively unaffected, but the establishment of new morphosyntactic processing networks becomes more difficult. The generalization that lexical acquisition and semantic processing are unaffected is not without qualification; later lexical learning is never as well-learned (AoA, experience effects), and later learned vocabulary may elicit slightly different neural responses. Furthermore, the evidence of adopted Koreans with native-like L2 French (Pallier et al. 2003) demonstrates that five years is not an absolute threshold, even for intransigent phonology. As the brain consolidates its functions through strengthening of active circuits and pruning of unnecessary ones, it loses plasticity; in cases of late L1A, the lost plasticity results in progressive deterioration of morphosyntactic ability with increasing AoA. Despite the crucial importance of L1 exposure from birth on, we do not have definitive evidence of a threshold of offset, a terminus or a post terminus plateau for L1A.

The same attenuation resulting from diminished brain plasticity for L1A is seen in L2A. Children below the age of five exposed to sufficient quantities of a second language acquire it with essentially native-like fluency and neural responses (although their fluency is never as rapid and crisp as monolinguals'). After age five, reaction time in L2 gradually increases as neural processing of morphosyntax relies less on procedural and more on declarative memory, a change that increases with increasing

AoA. The influence of native language on the L2 also increases with increasing AoA (which also represents increasing experience), but generally, deficits are associated with morphosyntax and phonology, not with lexico-semantics. The same decline in phonology and morphosyntax is seen in both L1A and L2A, related to AoA and corresponding to the period of neural specialization of later childhood. But L2A does not have the critical period profile of onset, offset or terminus; it may *happen to* coincide with the L1 peak of sensitivity, resulting in very solid acquisition of the L2 with appropriate neural responses etc., but that is fortuitous rather than biological. Since subsequent languages are parasitic on the neural architecture of the first, any purportedly maturational or learning effects/deficits associated with them could only be indirectly related to a critical period that might exist for the native language. An examination of child acquisition will help to clarify this issue.

7.3   Child acquisition

Children acquire first language unconsciously, systematically and in a relatively short time that is tightly sequenced. With adequate input, their acquisition of a second language resembles the L1A pathway more, the earlier the age of acquisition (that is, the closer L1A occurs to infancy); likewise, the endstate is closer to native completeness, the earlier the AoA. Deficits evident in late L1A are also apparent in L2A with increasing AoA, but what seems most salient about AoA deficits is the amount of variability among learners with increasingly later AoA; early learners are more homogeneous in achieving target-like grammar, whereas late learners demonstrate a range of final state competence. This section reviews the literature on child acquisition of first and second languages to determine what biological factors are at play that might determine critical period effects.

7.3.1   L1A

Fifty years of research on first language acquisition has furnished a rich resource of empirical data and theoretical conclusions on the what, how, when and why of the acquisition process. Typically developing children follow the same patterns cross-linguistically – an unsurprising attribute given the fact that the human genetic endowment is adaptable to all real and potential human languages – in first specializing in the native sound system (year one), then acquiring words and putting them together (year two), and finally perfecting morphosyntax (year three). Detailed studies of infants less than one year old have revealed that at birth a baby can discriminate all sounds of potential human languages (Eimas et al. 2004), but specializes in the native phonemes by ten months (Werker and Tees 1984), while perfecting the phonetic details in perception of native phonemes (Kuhl 1991a). During the second year the child begins production in earnest, after babbling and protowords are replaced by the first "real" words, at first alone but later combined, always with the correct native word order which is also evident in the child's comprehension, long before he can say very much. The development of morphology and syntax in the third year shows a clear linking of the two, with final mastery of the syntax (setting of the parameters determining word order, pronoun realization, question formation and other phenomena) tied to mastery of the regular morphology of the native tongue. Each child differs in the exact schedule, precise vocabulary, order of acquisition and external factors such as input, but the differences are far outweighed by the similarities, particularly striking in the case of parallel developments in languages that are unrelated.

So how do children accomplish this remarkable feat? Single cause explanations such as the behaviorist view of positive reinforcement by parents or the associationist idea of input alone do not account for the complex and multi-factored acquisition path. Furthermore, final state knowledge, a certain percentage of which is not taught or available in the input, and the rapid processing that is part of the native language mental package seem to require more complex explanation. Modular approaches emphasize the importance of the innate predisposition that leads children to select appropriate input from a sensorially overloaded environment, yet they do not focus on external factors such as enhancements of parentese, the role of frequency or the importance of saliency. The most convincing models take all factors into account, noting that the importance of different influences changes with increasing age, so that newborns pay close attention to prosody, while toddlers take a more interactive attitude with objects and their interlocuters.

Despite the clear role of a variety of influences in the acquisition process, what is perhaps most striking about the cross-linguistic similarities revealing the common genetic blueprint is the prosodic foundation of L1A. Infants become attuned to the rhythmic pattern of language in the first six months of life, establishing a procedure of parsing the incoming speech stream that matches native timing as stress, syllable or mora. The contribution of this processing mechanism permits babies to hone perception of phonemes and suprasegmentals that thereby allow recognition of words. Perceptual abilities are later turned to production, beginning with babbling and moving on to words. Prosodic segmentation aids in recognizing words, but also in distinguishing lexical and functional categories and syntactic boundaries that will be necessary at the next stages of development. The prosodic foundation of first language acquisition is not self-evident, and has only come to light through insightful experiments with infants and toddlers which have tested detailed hypotheses concerning the contributing causes.

L1A proceeds inexorably in TD monolingual children (both spoken and signed languages), in balanced bilinguals, and even in children developing creoles with limited input. Balanced bilingual children (2L1A) may show slower mastery than monolinguals, with differences stemming from cross-linguistic interference or slower development. For example, Hulk's (2004) Dutch-French bilingual subject Anouk takes eleven months to gain full DP competence compared to seven months for monolinguals. First language acquisition is indeed pre-programmed and unconscious, but it is not effortless. A child learning two languages has to devote neural resources to develop procedural proficiency and bilingual storage of vocabulary, grammar and phonology. The progression is not cost-free, as errors and processing lags demonstrate. Pater et al. (2004) find that fourteen-month-olds – who at a younger age can distinguish distinct phonemes such as /b/ and /d/ in minimal pairs [bɪn] / [dɪn] – do not respond to the minimal distinction at the later age. They conclude that children at this age focus more on lexical aspects of the environment as they are learning words. Toddlers reduce their attention in other domains because of the added processing load of attention to word shape and meaning.

Atypical L1A of Down Syndrome, Williams Syndrome, SLI, and other cognitively exceptional individuals, follows essentially the same path as for TD children, but is delayed. Rice and Wexler (1996) use a train metaphor to describe acquisition by SLI children, for the process starts late and takes longer than the TD process. Delay is also true of DS and WS, with cognitive deficits affecting subtler aspects of language perception and production. While they acquire most aspects of their native language, some of these exceptional learners retain residual deficits, lacunae that may also be present in unequal bilinguals who show deficiencies in the lesser language, particularly in its morphology (Schlyter 1993; Silva-Corvalan 1994). The exceptional cases also display processing difficulties, increased error rates and slower reaction time than that of TD children.

Late learners of first language are highly disadvantaged in the domains of phonology and morphology if they start after age 10–12, and after age 5 begin to show deficits in those areas that increase with increasing AoA. Genie, the abused and language-less child discovered at age 13, acquires a substantial vocabulary but is never able to use phonology or morphosyntax in any consistent manner (Curtiss 1977). She appears to be stuck at a VP stage that has been labeled Root Infinitive for L1 children, or Basic Variety for L2 adults, a level of syntactic achievement that enables sequencing of lexical items, but no use of functional categories (hence morphology) such as determiner, tense, agreement, or complementizers. While some scholars have dismissed Genie's case as irrelevant as evidence for a critical period because of her extreme deprivation (Snow 1987), what is perhaps more important to note is the clear disproportion between Genie's lexicon on the one hand and her grammar (phonology and morphosyntax) on the other. In the light of recent work using neuroimaging, the fact that Genie uses right hemisphere rather than left for her language corresponds to imaging reports that late bilinguals involve their right hemisphere more than native speakers and do not have the sharp left frontal processing of grammar that natives do.

Deaf children deprived of sign language input at an early age can gain fairly native-like grammar if they begin before age five, but after age five show AoA deficits related to processing and morphology especially. Emmorey (2002, 215) notes the crucial role of prosodic features, and the importance of gaining native prosody at an early age; she notes that early acquisition is critical both for effortless phonological processing and for establishment of "lexical, sentential and discourse structures." Although Emmorey is speaking of sign language, her comment captures the essence of TD acquisition path for all learners. Newport (1994) suggests that the reason young children are so much more adept at learning morphology is that they can (and must because of their limited processing abilities) pay attention to small details. L2 adults, on the other hand, see the global picture, learn the big items, and miss the small inflections, rendering them less accurate language learners in the long run. Children beyond the youngest ages show AoA deficits that increase with increasing age for L1A and also show a changed profile of acquisition. The deficits indicated after five years of age appear to represent an offset from a sensitivity for language acquisition, but there is no obvious terminus at puberty or any other stage.

7.3.2   Child L2A

The same patterns of increasing deficits and differing pathway of acquisition are true of children learning a second language, but these patterns are also affected by numerous other factors such as first language transfer, motivation, instruction and quality of input. Infants described as 2L1 learners acquire both languages as firsts, starting with a single lexical system that is later differentiated and then acquiring the discrete systems of morphosyntax (Bialystok 2001). These very early balanced bilinguals are not the equivalent of monolinguals in the amount of time required to achieve similar milestones (Hulk 2004), nor are their final state grammars the equivalent of monolinguals'. Grosjean (1989), who warns neurolinguists that a bilingual is not two monolinguals in one person, emphasizes that the bilingual mode of expression (including dual competence and code-switching as well as strict monolingual production in either language) is different enough to inhibit direct comparisons of monolinguals and bilinguals. Cook (1991, 1995, 2002, 2003) similarly sees multicompetence as an alternative language mode used by most of the world's speakers – it is monolingualism that is the exception – who may be equal or unequal bilinguals.

If infants perceiving and acquiring a first language follow a strict schedule, children and adults learning a second language follow timetables and pathways that seem less rigid. Younger children's L2A appears to resemble L1A in certain respects that older children's and adults' do not, in that children less than five are distinct in three ways:

- They are more capable of perceiving and later producing subtle phonetic fine points of the new language (Scovel 1988);
- They are adept at acquiring morphological details (Herschensohn et al. 2005);
- They are able to deploy verb morphology in accurate syntax by restricting non-finites to VP and only raising tensed verbs as in the L1A Optional Infinitive stage (Prévost and White 2000b).

These children nevertheless give indication of native language transfer, especially in the initial stages, even when they are as young as three years old (Belletti and Hamann 2004; Haznedar 2001, 2003). Even very early learners may show quite subtle shortcomings in all domains (Hyltenstam and Abrahamsson 2003). Although many studies which draw the line at five years seem to imply that children have the same potential for first and second language acquisition at any age within that period (a critical period plateau), it seems more likely that – given equal input and other factors – a child's potential for language acquisition changes as a function of the developing brain. A three-year-old has fewer dedicated circuits and has had less experience with the native language than a five-year-old, so we would expect that after an arbitrary period, say four years or twenty, that there might be differences between the two final state grammars (AoA three versus five). The extensive variation among individuals may make such a hypothesis untestable, but at least the principle should be taken into account to understand the decline in acquisition potential that occurs later.

With increasing AoA, children beyond age five show a gradual shift in acquisition pathway and final state grammar, resulting in less native-like achievement in phonology and morphosyntax, but with lexico-semantic learning basically unaffected. However, Hyltenstam (1992) does find nearly imperceptible lexico-semantic differences of early learners whose

L2 Swedish appears native-like, but this may result from the fact that they necessarily have less experience with the lexicon than do native speakers who have a five- to seven-year lead in knowing the vocabulary (best learned when longest learned for L1 and L2). In phonology, later learners are less capable of perceiving the prosodic dimensions of the new language, are inhibited by their ever growing experience in their native tongue (Kuhl 2000) and are restricted to their native segmentation system (Cutler 1994). In morphology, later learners of L2 adopt the adult-like holistic technique of discerning words and inflections, as, for example, the seven-year-old Spanish immersion learners whose mistakes indicate awareness of inflectional endings, but insufficient ability to gain control of them (Herschensohn et al. 2005). The morpheme order studies also show that older children follow an adult path of morpheme acquisition with L2A having a distinct order from L1A. Syntactic word order is an area that is relatively accessible to child and adult learners (Schwartz 2003), but word order is rather moot if the morphology is inaccurate. Children, infants and adults all seem to use similar strategies to learn and retain lexical items, and it is actually older children who mark the peak of vocabulary acquisition rate (Bloom 2002). Processing is another area of deficit, with slower reaction time and higher error rate being functions both of AoA and L1 interference, probably because of the additional "memory load imposed by decoding the surface form" (McDonald 2000, 417).

After age five learners' achievement is more evidently nonnative (hence age effects similar to those seen in late L1A), but deficits are subject to individual variability. As for L1, the deficits after five years of age might represent an offset from a sensitive period for language acquisition, but again there is no obvious terminus. The late L1 decline may be traceable to decreases in the brain's plasticity, a biological shift that marks a reduction of sensitivity to language input (prosody, phonology, lexicon, morphosyntax), particularly in the crucial language areas of the left hemisphere that become dedicated to extremely rapid processing. If the brain is less adept at language acquisition with increasing AoA – the brain does continue to change throughout one's life, declining in speed of operation – it would be expected that L2 as well as L1 would be susceptible to the decline. "If it is the case that the human brain is particularly adapted for language acquisition during an early period of life, but less so later in life, there should be manifestations of this adaptation in a second language context that are parallel to the manifestations in first language contexts" (Hyltenstam and Abrahamsson 2003, 544). It would also be expected that any influences on the brain such as experience with native language, nature of the L2 input, external factors and motivation would affect the learning process and product. Researchers have made all these observations concerning L2A by children after age five. Finally, while processing is often mentioned as an afterthought to nonnative accent or morphological deficits, it may be this much slower processing that distinguishes nonnative from native speakers.

7.4   Adult L2A

Even though the Fundamental Difference Hypothesis – as well as many strict critical period accounts of second language acquisition – maintains that the divide between L1 acquisition and adult L2 acquisition constitutes a nearly unbridgeable chasm, plentiful empirical evidence from a variety of sources indicates that the difference between the two is above all a quantitative one, not a qualitative one. If, for L2A, earlier is generally better, there is no guarantee of nativeness, or in contrast, no exclusion of near-nativeness for later acquisition. This section judges substantiation for or against a sensitive period of acquisition offered by L2 studies, first looking at the pathway and endstate product, then reconsidering the role of UG, and finally elucidating the interplay of processing and acquisition in L2.

7.4.1   L2 pathway and outcome

A major biological factor differentiating L1A and L2A is that the former is experience expectant and the latter (except in very young children) experience dependent, thus involving conscious effort on the part of the L2 learner. Nevertheless, L2 learning is not exclusively conscious, nor the attained knowledge exclusively declarative, for Doughty (2003) cites extensive research showing that implicit learning is more effective than explicit learning and that "declarative knowledge is a by-product of practice during implicit learning" (ibid., 295). Indeed, the influence of the native language, while often a negative interference, is in fact the foundation of the second language grammar, as Mayberry's (1993) contrast of L1A and L2A by twelve-year-olds demonstrates. Knowledge of native language primes speakers to a number of unconscious expectations such as distinctive features in phonology, functional categories in syntax, or constraints on coreference, that is, essentially the substantive and formal universals of language. In all domains the L2 acquisition process draws on L2 PLD, L1 influence, and UG, along with a coalition of numerous other factors, and in all domains L2A shares differences and similarities with L1A. The creation of dedicated neural networks for processing phonology, morphosyntax and lexicon leads to automaticity that frees up the brain to multitask on other cognitive problems. The sequence and endstate of native language development is on the one hand remarkable, and on the other the very means by which humans are able to build on their established cultural base.

L2 learners have all their native characteristics to start with, an advantage and disadvantage, but more the former than the latter since defective or non-existent L1 inhibits or prohibits L2A. Phonology is the area where L2 learners fare most poorly, perhaps because it is first learned in L1A, whereas in L2A it is nearly subsidiary to morphosyntax and lexicon. Perceptual acuity is necessary to L2 phonology as to L1, but often secondary learners misanalyze the new language in making it conform to the native one. Similarly in morphosyntax development, L2 learners may misanalyze a new structure to arrive at a superficially similar result that does not conform to the native grammar of that language. Another L1/L2 morphosyntactic difference is the uniform versus parallel development of morphology and syntax. Whereas in L1A morphological features of functional categories develop rapidly (often evident even before they are phonologically realizable), in tandem with setting of syntactic parameters, in L2A the syntax of word order and argument realization (e.g. null subjects) proceeds more quickly than the mastery of morphology. Thus, adult learners show a difference of procedure (separate development of syntax and morphology), and a difference of endstate, with morphological errors (missing or wrong inflection) even in very proficient L2 speakers.

The L1/L2 differences cited relate to the foundation provided by the native language and its influence on the acquisition of subsequent languages; once the L1 is learned, the speaker's brain is permanently altered, so acquisition of subsequent languages could never be comparable, even though it is not impossible. It is not therefore surprising that there are a number of similarities between L1A and L2A. Since native language provides a template and expectations about L2, the acquisitional tasks are the same, and procedures are often analogous.

Acquisition of both L1 and L2 is modular in that it operates independently of other cognitive attributes such as general intelligence, vision or hearing, following the same path to qualitatively the same endstate grammar as in typical development. Both employ a number of resources, although not the same ones or in the same order, with L1A focusing on a specific sequence, whereas L2A is less uniform. Primary linguistic data, input, is the most important factor for both phenomena, although L1A seems to compensate for a certain amount of input poverty while L2A requires extra priming. The roles of frequency and saliency (not to mention socio-cultural enhancements) have been demonstrated for L1 and L2 in strengthening input to facilitate acquisition. For both processes, learning strategies – such as the cognitive constraints on lexical learning that toddlers and adults share – are often similar, as are intermediate approximations (consonant cluster simplification, shortening of long words, telegraphic speech) and knowledge categorization (e.g. dual mechanism for regular and irregular morphology). Both L1 and L2 are UG constrained in phonology and morphosyntax although L2 is usually not totally native-like in its recognition of language specific instantiations of subtle UG characteristics such as grammaticality judgements. Monolingual adults have sharp intuitions about their native tongue that differ quantitatively (less sharp, less sure) from those of bilinguals, particularly late bilinguals; similarly, monolingual phonology employs subtle instantiations of UG that may elude bilinguals. UG is often cited as an essential player in age deficits, the topic of the next section.

7.4.2   UG and sensitive periods

Two perspectives on Universal Grammar – the genetic endowment leading humans to develop proficiency in languages whose structure and operation are universally constrained – lead to quite distinct roles for UG in L1 and L2 acquisition (Carroll 2001; Herschensohn 2000), perspectives called the *maturational* and *strong continuity* models by Flynn and Lust (2002). On the maturational view, age limits circumscribe acquisition, for UG is the acquisition device, creating the initial state that evolves into the mature grammar after which UG is "used up." On the strong continuity view, UG "remains distinct from the language specific grammar that is being acquired, and it remains constant over time" (ibid., 98). The maturational account echos the Fundamental Difference Hypothesis and the idea that UG is inaccessible in post-critical period acquisition, whereas strong continuity assumes uniform access to UG throughout life, thus permitting construction of new grammars at any age. In addition to the implausibility of a single use of UG for L1A given the abilities of bilingual children, the maturation account is unsubstantiated by the ample documentation of UG availability in L2. Nevertheless, strong continuity provides no biological dimension to explain observed changes in acquisition pathway, endstate and processing speed.

Given the detailed information examined, how should we conceive of UG and its role in L1 and L2 acquisition? The discussions of modularity show a clear function of a species-specific genetic predisposition that leads children to select and refine appropriate linguistic input from the environment to develop a mature grammar sharing the properties of all the other languages of the world in terms of phonology and morphosyntax, in brief, UG by any other name. The abstract properties that are subconsciously present, along with the native grammar, processing strategies, and numerous other influences are also brought to bear in L2A. Nevertheless, UG does not operate unfettered in L2A as in L1A, for there are AoA effects suggesting that aging, maturation and experience impact the efficacy of UG as an acquisition mechanism, with the notion of altered features being perhaps the best-framed argument. For example, Brown (2000) proposes that native instantiated phonological features can facilitate L2A of phonology, even if the segment inventory is different between the two languages. In the case she examines, L2A of English by Chinese, Korean and Japanese learners, Chinese speakers are better able than Korean or Japanese to gain the /r/l/ difference because both English and Mandarin use the feature [coronal], whereas the other languages don't exploit that feature. On this account, the native features are set for life and can transfer successfully in adult L2 learning. Likewise, in the realm of morphosyntax, several scholars have suggested that uninterpretable features of functional categories are set early for the native language during a critical period, and become inaccessible in adulthood (Franceschina 2001, 2002; Hawkins and Chan 1997; Hawkins and Franceschina 2004; Smith and Tsimpli 1995; Tsimpli and Roussou 1991).

Two recent volumes (Dewaele 2005; Prévost and Paradis 2004) shed light on the functional feature question through the exploration of the acquisition of French by different populations (L1A, 2L1A, L2A and SLI). Several of the articles confirm the observations in Chapters 2 and 4 emphasizing the early development of verbal tense/agreement and nominal gender/concord in L1 acquirers, as opposed to L2 learners. Hawkins and Franceschina (2004) propose that there is a critical period for parametrized uninterpretable features, so children acquire parametrized uninterpretable gender features of functional categories associated with determiners and adjectives (which agree with the interpretable [+/− fem] feature of the head noun). They argue that children initially have no uninterpretable feature, but gradually establish grammatical [gender] on D by age nine, while adults are able to acquire L2 [gender] only if their L1 has the parametrized feature. Adult L2 gender difficulties are clearly documented, while L1 studies show that children have essentially correct gender assignment from their earliest DPs, evidence that puts the age nine cutoff into doubt.

In contrast to Hawkins and Franceschina, Granfeldt (2005) argues that adults follow a slow acquisition of gender features and agreement, initially using default determiners and later modifying lexical entries for consistent gender. Children, on the other hand, have early access to uninterpretable gender, whose selection is triggered by both morphophonological and semantic properties. Granfeldt does not attribute L2 gender problems to a deficit, since his Swedish natives (with L1 gender) initially have difficulty with gendered L2 French and only acquire gender over a period of time. Indeed, L2 learners have more difficulty with adjective than determiner concord, and Prodeau (2005, 148) notes that, for L2 learners, "the information is not systematically available, more so when the constraints of the task imply too heavy a cognitive load," even when gender is known (ibid., 148).

While some evidence suggests that native-like acquisition of phonological and morphosyntactic features is restricted to young childhood at which time the human brain retains enough plasticity to establish new parametric values, not all functional categories hamper L2 learners in comparable ways. For anglophones learning L2 French, DP gender mistakes are not similar in all nominal domains, since adjectival concord is harder than determiner agreement, and parametrized functional features from different domains – nominal and verbal, for example – are not all acquired at a comparable rate or with analogous errors across different learning populations (Belletti and Hamann 2004; Hamann 2004; Hulk 2004; Paradis and Crago 2004; Granfeldt and Schlyter 2004). The cross-categorial inconsistencies remind us of Gregg's (1996, 2003) distinction between property and transition theories of L2A in that the properties of a given stage of interlanguage (say, when TP is accurately fixed, but DP isn't yet) must be considered in terms of the transitions that the L2 grammar has or will continue to undergo. The notion of transition again raises the question of how acquisition proceeds, leading us to return to processing, the key to incorporating input into the developing L2 grammar. The role of processing must be examined as carefully as that of UG in assessing contributions to L2A.

7.4.3 L2 input, learning and processing

The three most significant AoA effects that surface in all the literature are defective morphosyntax, nonnative phonology and slow processing, all of which are interrelated in that they depend on the neurological establishment of prosodic segmentation, phonetic perception and morphosyntactic parsing during the first two years of life. Morford and Mayberry (2000, 124) emphasize that the "true advantage of early exposure (during the first year) is the development of the phonological system prior to the development of the lexico-semantic and morpho-syntactic systems." These native language procedures, which facilitate further acquisition of L1 and may impede later learning of L2, can be seen as crucial to the designation of age effects, yet are peripheral to what is usually defined as Universal Grammar. As Scovel notes, it is phonology, not morphosyntax, that is most susceptible to AoA decline, yet the universal aspects of both phonology and morphosyntax persist in the L2, while phonetic detail and morphological crispness falter. It is clear that the devil is in the details and not in UG, and that the third area of AoA deficit, slow processing, is key to an understanding both of the pathway of L2A and the reasons for its incompleteness compared to the L1. Several recent theoretical models take these factors into account.

Klein and Martohardjono (1999b) outline a UG-based model of acquisition that incorporates UG principles and parameters as constraints on L2 hypothesis testing, while learnability and processing principles deal with input of various sorts. They (as Epstein et al. 1996 and Flynn and Lust 2002) suggest that both L1 and L2 learners are equipped with comparable acquisition principles, but that the two groups approach the input in different ways. "What is important to evaluate here, in other words, is not *that* FLA is different from SLA, but *in what ways* the conditions required for the mechanism of grammar construction to operate properly are not met in SLA, clearly a question concerning process, rather than property" (Klein and Martohardjono 1999b, 13). Towell (2000) and Doughty (2003) also call for the incorporation of processing into a model of L2A, taking into account UG as a morphosyntax template and functionalism as a learnability guide. While knowledge of language is modular and unaffected by other cognitive subsystems, processing is dependent on working and long-term memories, factors that L2A must acknowledge (Pienemann 1998; Skehan 1998; VanPatten 1996). Doughty (2003) proposes that training in processing can aid L2 learners to overcome native tendencies and can enhance implicit learning opportunities (to be favored over explicit or metalinguistic training). She does not reject a role for explicit training, however, noting "recent assessments by cognitive psychologists have produced a consensus that (i) implicit and explicit learning occur simultaneously (Stadler and Frensch 1998); and consequently, that (ii) implicit and explicit learning can never be disentangled empirically" (ibid., 293).

Carroll (2001) probably proposes the most comprehensive model of L2A to date, one that incorporates UG, processing, input and learning mechanisms. Carroll's framework links sequential property states through transitions, while explaining this restructuring as a function of induction (i-learning). Given that the "neurological system in which learning occurs is by adulthood stable and no longer growing," (ibid., 119) the Autonomous Induction Theory furnishes an initial L1 framework through which raw stimuli are parsed as evidence using L1 segmentation and categories; the input is taken in and later restructured to L2; and the interlanguage grammar is further modified through a range of feedback. In her substantial book (only touched on briefly here), Carroll fleshes out the cognitive basis for linguistic categories (primarily deriving from Jackendoff 1983, 1987, 1990) and for linguistic processing (primarily deriving from Holland et al. 1986), using instance-based learning, observational generalization and inferencing to induce the L2 grammar.

L2A involves "(i) creating lexical sound-meaning mappings, (ii) the development of novel parsing procedures for stimuli where transferred parsing procedures fail, (iii) the acquisition of any categories, relations or properties not instantiated in the L1, and (iv) the appropriate differentiation of categories insufficiently differentiated under (ii)" (ibid., 243). The differential input of L2 compared to L1 will eventually lead the learner to revised grammatical categories and new means of parsing; native influence is pervasive, and some L1 categories are never completely revised or suppressed.

Carroll's model accommodates the observations of L1, L2 and processing scholars examined in previous chapters. We have seen that the development of speech automaticity in monolinguals and early bilinguals plainly facilitates rapidity of processing, quick repair in morphosyntactic parsing, speed and accuracy of lexical access, and production capacity. Facilitation may be transferred from L1 to L2 if the two share characteristics, such as the gender feature that helps Portuguese learners of French, while its lack hinders anglophone learners. When automaticity is challenged by additional cognitive load – during L1A or L2A with unfamiliar material, in language regression, or simply in a cognitively challenging task – the L2 speaker is more prone to errors and slower processing. For monolinguals the built-in redundancy of linguistic knowledge and processing obscures their operation. For individuals whose language is less entrenched, more resources are necessary for production than comprehension and external factors such as frequency and recency of use are more significant (Hyltenstam and Stroud 1993). Finally, native influence interferes in inevitable and inconsistent ways, such as the difficulty of gender facility even for anglophones fluent in French (in contrast to their virtual mastery of tense). As Carroll (2001, 369) notes, "the relative difficulty of learning gender attribution in the face of large amounts of stimuli and correction, i.e. why gender should be harder to learn than word order" is not self-evident.

7.5   Conclusion

We have seen that first language acquisition is affected by age of acquisition in that it is incomplete if onset takes place after five years of age, with increasing incompleteness with increasing AoA. Late L1A is defective, even in a well-meaning social environment, not simply because of the lack of input, but also because the construction of language is a sociocultural process. An individual deprived of language in early childhood cannot have the requirements needed for normal human development, what Bruer (1999) calls the kinds of stimuli available in any child's environment. Second language acquisition is affected in a parallel manner to

L1A, especially with respect to processing speed, phonological nativeness and morphological crispness. But L1A – unlike the learning of birdsong or whale clicks – is *not* restricted to a tightly delimited period after which acquisition is totally impossible. One reason is the very nature of language in the human brain, its complexity and redundancy as evidenced by both structure and function. The dual articulation of language – the property of a finite set of meaningless units (phonemes) that combine into arbitrary signs (words) that concatenate to create meaningful propositions – creates a system whose superfluous subsystems compensate for each other in their overlap. The complexity is reflected at the cerebral level by tightly compact areas in the left hemisphere dedicated to procedural functions as well as ancillary neural resources distributed on both sides of the brain.

First language development is partially circumscribed by neural maturation, but it is also influenced by the very experiences that shape it, such as modality, as Sacks (1990, 117) notes: "This is precisely the situation of the deaf child: he is flung into a perceptual (and cognitive and linguistic) situation for which there is neither genetic precedent nor teaching to assist him; and yet, given half a chance, he will develop radically new forms of neural organization, neural mappings, which will allow him to master the language-world, and articulate it, in a quite novel way." The young child is driven to attain language even in the face of daunting circumstances and is able to create anew a creole, a signed language or the tongue of his parents. The ontogenetic path begins with the establishment of neurophysiological networks that automatize language processing at the earliest stages in order to free up the mind for other cognitive tasks that will need to be undertaken. It is the physiological aspects of language, rapidity of perception and production, acuity of phonology and detail of morphology that are initially entrenched, and deeply so, characteristics that are first acquired and last "rewired," in acquisition of subsequent languages. The corollary effect of the initial entrenchment of expertise in L1 is the adult disregard for nonnative distinctions and the consequent nonnative characteristics of second languages shown by both adult and child learners. Nonnative characteristics of L2 may not be pretty, but they cannot be interpreted as the main argument for a critical period for L2A.

Language is a human characteristic whose neural expression is established early in childhood, yet it is open to expansion throughout the lifetime in terms of native vocabulary or additional languages. Scholars' perception of maturational constraints on L1A and L2A has led to the theoretical question of why language evolved to be sensitive to age of acquisition. Scovel (1988) suggests that foreign accents emerge at adolescence to mark procreators as members of a given tribe. Pinker (1995) outlines the "use it and lose it" view of the language acquisition device in which it's lost when no longer needed. In addition, "the critical period for language acquisition may have evolved as part of a larger fact of life: the increasing feebleness and vulnerability with advancing age" (ibid., 295), a point relating to Hurford's (1991) idea of a selective advantage to acquisition sooner rather than later. Piaget, in his "debate" with Chomsky on language learning (Piattelli-Palmarini 1979, 97–98; Piaget and Chomsky 2004 [1979], 87), sees selection and mutation as too simplistic, refusing "to think that logico-mathematical structures [including language] would owe their origin to chance; there is nothing fortuitous about them. These structures could not be formed by survival selection but by an exact and detailed adaptation to reality." His view of adaptive phenotypes recalls Sacks' discussion of the adaptive brain, with the translation of ontogeny into phylogeny. Chomsky, for his part, has mostly remained agnostic on the evolutionary background of language, saying, for example, "phylogenesis seems a remote prospect at best" (Chomsky 2002, 84).

We are not in a position to know the origins of language, but the evolutionary question might better be posed the other way round: Why is human language *not* susceptible to a critical period as are communication systems of other species? What is remarkable in the evolution of this human characteristic is precisely its availability for reimplementation with only superficial shortcomings in the cases of expert L2A. The rich complexity of language allows it sufficient redundancy of systems for acquisition at any age. Under this interpretation, the observed deficits in L2A are due not to a biological critical period, but to the excellence of the neural architecture of the first language, the very architecture that permits second language acquisition.

Bibliography

Abel, Beate. 2003. English idioms in the first language and second language lexicon: A dual representation approach. *Second Language Research* 19: 329–358.

Abuhamdia, Zakaria A. 1987. Neurobiological foundations for foreign language. *International Review of Applied Linguistics* 25: 203–211.

Abutalebi, Jubin, Stefano F. Cappa and Daniela Perani. 2001. The bilingual brain as revealed by functional neuroimaging. *Bilingualism Language and Cognition* 4: 179–190.

Accardo, Pasquale J., Brian T. Rogers and Arnold J. Capute (eds.). 2002. *Disorders of Language Development*. Baltimore: York Press.

Allen, Mark and William Badecker. 2000. Morphology: The internal structure of words. In Kapp, 211–235.

Andersen, B. and V. Rutledge. 1996. Age and hemisphere effects on dendritic structure. *Brain* 119: 1983–1990.

Anderson-Hsieh, Janet, Ruth Johnson and Kenneth Koehler. 1992. The relationship between native speaker judgements of nonnative pronunciation and deviance in segmentals, prosody and syllable structure. *Language Learning* 42: 529–555.

Aoyama, Katsura. 2003. Perception of syllable-initial and syllable-final nasals in English by Korean and Japanese speakers. *Second Language Research* 19: 251–265.

Archibald, John. 1993. *Language Learnability and L2 Phonology: The acquisition of metrical parameters*. Dordrecht/Boston/London: Kluwer.

  1995 (ed.). *Phonological Acquisition and Phonological Theory*. Hillsdale, NJ: L. Erlbaum.

  1998. *Second Language Phonology*. Amsterdam/Philadelphia: John Benjamins.

  2000 (ed.). *Second Language Acquisition and Linguistic Theory*. Oxford/Malden, MA: Blackwell.

Archibald, John and Martha Young-Scholten. 2003. The second language segment revisited: Introduction to a special issue. *Second Language Research* 19 (3): 163–167.

Armen, Jean-Claude. 1971. *Gazelle-boy: A Child Brought up by Gazelles in the Sahara Desert*. London: The Bodley Head.

Aronoff, Mark, Irit Meir and Wendy Sandler. 2005. The paradox of sign language morphology. *Language* 81: 301–344.

Arteaga, Deborah and Julia Herschensohn. 1995. Using diachronic linguistics in the language classroom. *Modern Language Journal* 79: 212–222.

Asher, James and Ramiro García. 1982 [1969]. The optimal age to learn a foreign language. In Krashen et al., 3–12.

Atkinson, Martin. 1992. *Children's Syntax: An Introduction to Principles and Parameters Theory*. Oxford: Blackwell.

Avrutin, Sergei and Kenneth Wexler. 1992. Development of Principle B in Russian: Coindexation at LF and coreference. *Language Acquisition* 2: 259–306.

Avrutin, Sergei and Rosalind Thornton. 1994. Distributivity and binding in child grammar. *Linguistic Inquiry* 25: 165–170.

Bailey, Donald B., John T. Bruer, Frank J. Symons and Jeff W. Lichtman (eds.). 2001. *Critical Thinking about Critical Periods*. Baltimore/London: Paul H. Brookes.

Bailey, Nathalie, Carolyn Madden and Stephen D. Krashen. 1974. Is there a "natural sequence" in adult second language learning? *Language Learning* 24: 235–243.

Bakalar, Nicholas. 2005. Is it Dutch? Japanese? Why not ask the rat? *New York Times* January 11, D5.

Baker, C. L. and J. J. McCarthy (eds.). 1981. *The Logical Problem of Language Acquisition*. Cambridge, MA: MIT Press.

Baker, Marc C. 1988. *Incorporation: A Theory of Grammatical Function Changing*. Chicago: University of Chicago Press.

Banich, Marie and Molly Mack (eds.). 2003. *Mind, Brain and Language: Multidisciplinary Perspectives*. Mahwah, NJ: L. Erlbaum.

Barcroft, Joe. 2005. Effects of sentence writing in second language lexical acquisition. *Second Language Research* 20: 303–334.

Barlow, Michael and Suzanne Kemmer (eds.). 2000. *Usage Based Models of Language*. Stanford, CA: CSLI publications.

Bates, Elizabeth, Philip S. Dale and Donna Thal. 1995. Individual differences and their implications for theories of language development. In Fletcher and MacWhinney, 96–151.

Bates, Elizabeth, Antonella Devesconi, Arturo Hernandez and Luigi Pizzamiglio. 1996. Gender priming in Italian. *Perception and Psychophysics* 58: 992–1004.

Bates, Elizabeth and Brian MacWhinney. 1989. Functionalism and the competition model. In MacWhinney & Bates, 3–76.

Bateson, Patrick. 1987. Imprinting as a process of competitive exclusion. In Rauschecker and Marler, 151–168.

Beachley, Barbara, Amanda Brown and Frances Conlin (eds.). 2003. *Proceedings of the 27th Annual Boston University Conference on Language Development*. Somerville, MA: Cascadilla Press.

Beck, Maria-Luise. 1997. Regular verbs, past tense and frequency: Tracking down a potential source of native speaker/nonnative speaker competence differences. *Second Language Research* 13: 93–115.

  1998a (ed.). *Morphology and its Interfaces*. Amsterdam/Philadelphia: John Benjamins.

  1998b. L2 acquisition and obligatory head movement: English speaking learners of German and the Local Impairment Hypothesis. *Studies in Second Language Acquisition* 20: 311–348.

Belletti, Adriana and Cornelia Hamann. 2004. On the L2/bilingual acquisition of French by two young children with different source languages. In Prévost and Paradis, 147–174.

Bellugi, Ursula, Edward S. Klima and Paul P. Wang. 1996. Cognitive and neural development: Clues from genetically based syndromes. In Magnusson, 223–243.

Bellugi, Ursula, S. Marks, A. M. Bihrle and H. Salso. 1993. Dissociation between language and cognitive functions in Williams Syndrome. In Bishop and Mogford, 177–189.

Bellugi, Ursula, Liz Lichtenberger, Wendy Jones & Zona Lai. 2000. The neurocognitive profile of Williams Syndrome: A complex pattern of strengths and weaknesses. *Journal of Cognitive Neuroscience* 12 (supplement): 7–29.

Bellugi, Ursula and Marie St. George (eds.). 2001. *Journey from Cognition to Brain to Gene: Perspectives from Williams Syndrome.* Cambridge, MA: MIT Press.

Beretta, Alan, Robert Fiorentino and David Poeppel. 2005. The effects of homonymy and polysemy on lexical access: An MEG study. *Cognitive Brain Research* 24: 57–65.

Berger, James. 2005. Falling towers and postmodern wild children: Oliver Sacks, Don DeLillo, and turns against language. *PMLA* 120: 341–361.

Berko [Gleason], Jean. 2004 [1958]. The child's learning of English morphology. In Lust and Foley, 253–273.

Best, Catherine T. 1995. A direct realist view of cross-language speech perception. In Strange, 171–204.

Bever, Thomas G. 1981. Normal acquisition processes explain the critical period for language learning. In Diller, 176–198.

Bhatia, Tej K. and William C. Ritchie (eds.). 2004. *The Handbook of Bilingualism.* Oxford/Malden, MA: Blackwell.

Bialystok, Ellen. 1997. The structure of age: In search of barriers to second language acquisition. *Second Language Research* 13: 116–137.

2001. *Bilingualism in Development: Language, Literacy and Cognition.* Cambridge: Cambridge UP.

2002a. On the reliability of robustness: A reply to Dekeyser. *Studies in Second Language Acquisition* 24: 481–488.

2002b. Cognitive processes of L2 users. In Cook, 145–166.

Bialystok, Ellen and Judith Codd. 1997. Cardinal limits: Evidence from language awareness and bilingualism for developing concepts of number. *Cognitive Development* 12: 85–106.

Bialystok, Ellen and Kenji Hakuta. 1994. *In Other Words: The Science and Psychology of Second-language Acquisition.* New York: Basic Books.

Bialystok, Ellen and Kenji Hakuta. 1999. Confounded age: Linguistic and cognitive factors in age differences for second language acquisition. In Birdsong, 116–181.

Bialystok, Ellen and Barry Miller. 1999. The problem of age in second-language acquisition: Influences from language, structure, and task. *Bilingualism: Language and Cognition* 2: 127–145.

Bickerton, Derek. 1981. *Roots of Language.* Ann Arbor: Karoma.

1990. *Language and Species.* Chicago: University of Chicago Press.

1995. *Language and Human Behavior.* Seattle: University of Washington Press.

2004. Reconsidering Creole exceptionalism. *Language* 80: 828–833.

Birdsong, David. 1989. *Metalinguistic Performance and Interlinguistic Competence.* Berlin/New York: Springer-Verlag.

1992. Ultimate attainment in second language acquisition. *Language* 68, 706–755.

1999a. (ed.). *Second Language Acquisition and the Critical Period Hypothesis.* Mahwah, NJ: L. Erlbaum.

1999b. Introduction: Whys and why nots of the critical period hypothesis for second language acquisition. In Birdsong, 1–22.

2004. Second language acquisition and ultimate attainment. In Davies and Elder, 82–105.

2005a. Interpreting age effects in second language acquisition. In Kroll and De Groot, 109–127.

2005b. Nativelikeness and non-nativelikeness in L2A research. *International Review of Applied Linguistics* 43: 319–328.

2006a. Why not fossilization? In Han and Odlin, 173–188.

2006b. Dominance, proficiency and second language grammatical processing. *Applied Psycholinguistics* 27: 1–3.

2007. Nativelike pronunciation among late learners of French as a second language. In Bohn and Munro.

To appear. *Age and Second Language Acquisition.* Cambridge: Cambridge University Press.

Birdsong, David and James E. Flege. 2001. Regular-irregular dissociations in L2 acquisition of English morphology. *BUCLD* 25. Somerset, MA: Cascadilla Press, 123–132.

Birdsong, David and Michelle Molis. 2001. On the evidence for maturational constraints in second language acquisition. *Journal of Memory and Language* 44: 235–249.

Bishop, Dorothy and Kay Mogford (eds.). 1993. *Language Development in Exceptional Circumstances.* Hove: L. Erlbaum.

Bley-Vroman, Robert. 1983. The comparative fallacy in interlanguage studies: The case of systematicity. *Language Learning* 33: 1–17.

1989. What is the logical problem of foreign language learning? In Gass and Schachter, 41–68.

1990. The logical problem of foreign language learning. *Linguistic Analysis* 20: 3–49.

Bley-Vroman, Robert, W. F. Sascha and Georgette L. Ioup. 1988. The accessibility of Universal Grammar in adult language learning. *Second Language Research* 4: 1–32.

Bloom, Lois. 1970. *Language Development: Form and Function in Emerging Grammars.* Cambridge, MA: MIT Press.

Bloom, Paul (ed.). 1994. *Language Acquisition: Core readings.* Cambridge, MA: MIT Press.

2002. *How Children Learn the Meanings of Words.* Cambridge, MA: MIT Press.

Blumstein, Sheila. 1995. The neurobiology of the sound structure of language. In Gazzaniga, 915–929.

Bogaards, Paul. 2001. Lexical units and the learning of foreign language vocabulary. *Studies in Second Language Acquisition* 23: 321–343.

Bohn, O. S. and M. Munro (eds.). 2007. *Language Experience in Second Language Speech Learning: In Honour of James Emil Flege*. Amsterdam/Philadelphia: John Benjamins.

Bongaerts, Theo. 1999. Ultimate attainment in L2 pronunciation: The case of very advanced late L2 learners. In Birdsong, 133–159.

Bongaerts, Theo, Susan Mennen and Frans van der Slik. 2000. Authenticity of pronunciation in naturalistic second language acquisition: The case of very advanced late learners of Dutch as a second language. *Studia Linguistica* 54: 298–308.

Bongaerts, Theo, Brigitte Planken and Erik Schils. 1995. Can late learners attain a native accent in a foreign language? A test of the critical period hypothesis. In Singleton and Lengyel, 30–50.

Bongaerts, Theo, Chantal van Summeren, Brigitte Planken and Erik Schils. 1997. Age and ultimate attainment in the pronunciation of a foreign language. *Studies in Second Language Acquisition* 19: 447–465.

Borer, Hagit. 1996. Access to Universal Grammar: The real issues. *Behavioral and Brain Sciences* 19: 718.

Borer, Hagit and Bernhard Rohrbacher. 2002. Minding the absent: Arguments for the Full Competence Hypothesis. *Language Acquisition* 10: 123–175.

Bornstein, Marc H. (ed.). 1987a. *Sensitive Periods in Development: Interdisciplinary Perspectives*. Hillsdale, NJ/London: L. Erlbaum.

    1987b. Sensitive periods in development: Definition, existence, utility and meaning. In Bornstein, 3–18.

Bortfeld, Heather and Grover J. Whitehurst. 2001. Sensitive periods in first language acquisition. In Bailey et al., 173–192.

Boser, Katharina, Barbara Lust, Lynn Santelmann and John Whitman. 1992. The syntax of CP and V-2 in early child German: The strong continuity hypothesis. *Proceedings of the North East Linguistics Society* 22: 51–66.

Bottari, Piero, Paola Cipriani and Anna Maria Chilosi. 1993/94. Protosyntactic devices in the acquisition of Italian free morphemes. *Language Acquisition* 3: 327–369.

Bouillaud, Jean B. 1825. Recherches cliniques propres à démontrer que la perte de parole correspond à la lésion des lobules antérieures du cerveau et à confirmer l'opinion de M. Gall sur le siège de l'organe du langage articulé. *Archives Générales de Médecine* 8: 25–45.

Bowerman, Melissa. 1973. *Early Syntactic Development*. Cambridge: Cambridge University Press.

Boysson-Bardies, Bénédicte de. 1999. *How Language Comes to Children*. Cambridge, MA: MIT Press.

Boysson-Bardies, Bénédicte de, P. Hallé, L. Sagart and C. Durand. 1989. A cross-linguistic investigation of vowel formants in babbling. *Journal of Child Language* 16: 1–17.

Bradlow, Ann R., David B. Pisoni, Reiko AkahaneYamada and Yoh'ichi Tohkura. 1995. Training Japanese listeners to identify English /r/ and /l/. *Research on Spoken Language Processing Progress Report* 20. Bloomington, IN: Indiana University.

Braine, Martin D. S. 1971. On two types of models in the internalization of grammars. In Slobin, 153–188.

Brauth, Steven E., William S. Hall and Robert J. Dooling (eds.). 1991. *Plasticity of Development*. Cambridge MA: MIT Press.

Brenowitz, Eliot. 2004. Plasticity in the adult avian song control system. *Annals of the New York Academy of Sciences* 1016: 560–585.

Briones, Teresita L., Anna Y. Klintsova and William T. Greenough. 2004. Stability of synaptic plasticity in the adult rat visual cortex induced by complex environment exposure. *Brain Research* 1018: 130–135.

Broca, Pierre. 1861. Remarques sur le siège de la faculté du langage articulé, suivies d'une observation d'aphémie. *Bulletin de la Société Anatomique* 6: 330–357.

Broselow, Ellen and Daniel Finer. 1991. Parameter setting in second language phonology and syntax. *Second Language Research* 7: 35–59.

Broselow, Ellen and Hye-Bae Park. 1995. Mora conservation in second language prosody. In Archibald, 151–168.

Brown, Cynthia. 2000. The interrelation between speech perception and phonological acquisition from infant to adult. In Archibald, 4–63.

Brown, Roger. 1973. *A First Language: The Early Stages*. Cambridge, MA: Harvard University Press.

Bruer, John T. 1999. *The Myth of the First Three Years*. New York: The Free Press. 2001. A critical and sensitive period primer. In Bailey et al., 3–26.

Bruer, John T. and William T. Greenough. 2001. The subtle science of how experience affects the brain. In Bailey et al., 209–232.

Bruhn de Garavito, Joyce. 2003. The (dis)association between morphology and syntax: The case of L2 Spanish. In Montrul and Ordóñez, 398–417.

Bruhn de Garavito, Joyce. and Lydia White. 2002. L2 acquistion of Spanish DPs: The status of grammatical features. In Pérez-Leroux and Liceras, 153–178.

Burke, Sara N. and Carol A. Barnes. 2006. Neural plasticity in the ageing brain. *Nature Reviews Neuroscience* 7: 30–40.

Burzio, Luigi. 1986. *Italian Syntax: A Government-binding Approach*. Dordrecht: Reidel.

Byrnes, James P. 2001. *Minds, Brains, and Learning: Understanding the Psychological and Educational Relevance of Neuroscientific Research*. New York/London: Guilford Press.

Calvin, William H. and Derek Bickerton. 2001. *Lingua ex Machina: Reconciling Darwin and Chomsky with the Human Brain*. Cambridge, MA: MIT Press.

Calvin, William H. and George A. Ojemann. 1994. *Conversations with Neil's Brain: The Neural Nature of Thought and Language*. Reading, MA: Addison-Wesley.

Camps, Joaquim and Caroline R. Wiltshire (eds.). 2001. *Romance Syntax, Semantics and L2 Acquisition*. Amsterdam/Philadelphia: John Benjamins.

Capirci, Olga, Sandro Montanari and Virginia Volterra. 1998. Gestures, signs and words in early language development. In Iverson and Goldin-Meadow, 45–60.

Caplan, David, Nathaniel Alpert and Gloria Waters. 2002. Brain organization for syntactic processing. In Galaburda et al., 57–68.

Caplan, David and Rochel Gelman (eds.). *Epigenesis of Mind: Essays of Biology and Cognition*. Hillsdale, NJ: L. Erlbaum.

Carey, Susan. 1978. The child as word-learner. In Halle et al., 264–293.

Carpenter, Malinda, Katherine Nagell and Michael Tomasello. 1998. Social cognition, joint attention, and communicative competence from 9 to 15 months of age. *Monographs of the Society for Research in Child Development* 63, No. 4 (Serial No. 255).

Carreiras, Manuel and Charles Clifton, Jr. (eds.). 2004. *The On-line Study of Sentence Comprehension: Eyetracking, ERP, and beyond.* Psychology Press.

Carroll, Susanne E. 1999. Putting "input" in its proper place. *Second Language Research* 15: 337–388.

2001. *Input and Evidence: The Raw Material of Second Language Acquisition.* Amsterdam/Philadelphia: John Benjamins.

Cazzoli-Goeta, M., S. Pourcel and L. Van Espen (eds.). 2002. *Proceedings of the Fifth Durham Postgraduate Conference in Theoretical and Applied Linguistics.* Durham: School of Linguistics and Language, University of Durham.

Chadwick, Douglas H. 2005. Investigating a killer. *National Geographic April*: 86–105.

Chamberlain, Charlene, Jill P. Morford and Rachel I. Mayberry (eds.). 2000. *Language Acquisition by Eye.* Mahwah, NJ: L. Erlbaum.

Chapman, Robin S. 1995. Language development in children and adolescents with Down Syndrome. In Fletcher and MacWhinney, 641–663.

Chee, Michael W. L., Nicholas Hon, Hwee Ling Lee and Chun Siong Soon. 2001. Relative language proficiency modulates BOLD signal change when bilinguals perform semantic judgments. *Neuroimage* 6: 1155–1163.

Chee, Michael W. L., Chun Siong Soon, Hwee Ling Lee and Christophe Pallier. 2004. Left insula activation: A marker for language attainment in bilinguals. *Proceedings of the National Academy of Sciences* 101.

Chiarello, Christine. 2003. Parallel systems for processing language: Hemispheric complementarity in the normal brain. In Banich and Mack, 229–247.

Chien, Y.-C. and Kenneth Wexler. 1990. Children's knowledge of locality conditions in binding as evidence for the modularity of syntax and pragmatics. *Language Acquisition* 1: 225–295.

Chomsky, Noam. 1959. A review of B. F. Skinner's "Verbal Behavior." *Language* 35: 26–58.

1965. *Aspects of the Theory of Syntax.* Cambridge, MA: MIT Press.

1995. *The Minimalist Program.* Cambridge, MA: MIT Press.

2000. Minimalist inquiries: the framework. In Roger Martin, David Michaels and Juan Uriagereka (eds.). *Step by Step: Essays on Minimalist Syntax in Honor of Howard Lasnik.* Cambridge, MA: MIT Press [originally MITWPL 15].

2001a. Derivation by phase. In Michael Kenstowicz (ed.). *Ken Hale: A Life in Language.* Cambridge, MA: MIT Press [originally MITWPL 18].

2001b. Beyond explanatory adequacy. MITWPL 20.

2002. *On Nature and Language.* Ed. Adriana Belletti and Luigi Rizzi. Cambridge: Cambridge University Press.

Chomsky, Noam and Morris Halle. 1968. *The Sound Pattern of English.* New York: Harper and Row.

Clahsen, Harald. 1988. Parameterized grammatical theory and language acquisition: A study of the acquisition of verb placement and inflection by children and adults. In Flynn and O'Neil, 47–75.

1991. Constraints on parameter setting: A grammatical analysis of some acquisition stages in German child language. *Language Acquisition* 1: 361–391.

1996 (ed.). *Generative Perspectives on Language Acquisition.* Amsterdam/ Philadelphia: John Benjamins.

1997. German plurals in adult second language development: Evidence for a dual mechanism model of inflection. In Eubank et al., 123–138.

Clahsen, Harald, Fraibet Aveledo and Iggy Roca. 2002. The development of regular and irregular verb inflection in Spanish child language. *Journal of Child Language* 29: 591–622.

Clahsen, Harald, Sonja Eisenbeiss and Martina Penke. 1996. Lexical learning in early syntactic development. In Clahsen, 129–159.

Clahsen, Harald, Sonja Eisenbeiss and Anne Vainikka. 1994. The seeds of structure: A syntactic analysis of the acquisition of case marking. In Hoekstra and Schwartz, 85–118.

Clahsen, Harald, Martina Penke and Teresa Parodi. 1993/1994. Functional categories in early child German. *Language Acquisition* 3: 395–429.

Clahsen, Harald and Pieter Muysken. 1986. The availability of Universal Grammar to adult and child learners: A study of the acquisition of German word order. *Second Language Research* 2: 93–119.

1989. The UG paradox in L2 acquisition. *Second Language Research* 5: 1–29.

1996. How adult second language learning differs from child first language development. *Behavioral and Brain Sciences* 19: 721–723.

Clark, Eve. 1995. *The Lexicon in Acquisition.* Cambridge: Cambridge University Press.

Coady, James and Thomas Huckin (eds.).1997. *Second Language Vocabulary Acquisition: A Rationale for Pedagogy.* New York: Cambridge University Press.

Cochran, Barbara P., Janet L. McDonald and Susan J. Parault. 1999. Too smart for their own good: The disadvantage of a superior processing capacity for adult language learners. *Journal of Memory and Language* 41: 30–58.

Colé, Pascale and Juan Ségui. 1994. Grammatical incongruency and vocabulary types. *Memory and Cognition* 22: 387–394.

Condamine, Charles-Marie de la [Mme H . . . t.] 1761. *Histoire d'une jeune fille sauvage, trouvée dans les bois à l'age de dix ans.* Paris: Mme. H[ecquet].

Cook, Vivian. 1991. The poverty of the stimulus argument and multi-competence. *Second Language Research* 7: 103–117.

1993. *Linguistics and Second Language Acquisition.* New York: St. Martin's Press.

1995. Multicompetence and effects of age. In Singleton and Lengyel, 51–66.

2002 (ed.). *Portraits of the L2 User.* Clevedon: Multilingual Matters.

2003 (ed.). *Effects of the Second Language on the First.* Clevedon: Multilingual Matters.

Coppieters, René. 1987. Competence differences between native and nonnative speakers. *Language* 63: 544–573.

Corballis, Michael C. 1991. *The Lopsided Ape: Evolution of the generative mind.* Oxford: Oxford University Press.

2002. *From Hand to Mouth: The Origins of Language.* Princeton/Oxford: Princeton University Press.

Corder, S. Pit. 1967. The significance of learners' errors. *International Review of Applied Linguistics* 5: 161–170.

Costa, Albert. 2004. Speech production in bilinguals. In Bhatia and Ritchie, 201–223.

Crain, Stephen and Diane Lillo-Martin. 1999. *An Introduction to Linguistic Theory and Language Acquisition*. Oxford: Blackwell.

Crain, Stephen and Rosalind Thornton. 1998. *Investigations in Universal Grammar: A Guide to Experiments on the Acquisition of Syntax and Semantics*. Cambridge, MA: MIT Press.

Curtiss, Susan. 1977. *Genie: A Psycholinguistic Study of a Modern–day "Wild Child"*. New York: Academic Press.

   1988. Abnormal language acquisition and grammar: Evidence for the modularity of language. In Hyman and Li, 81–102.

Curtiss, Susan, Victoria Fromkin, Stephen Krashen, David Rigler and Marilyn Rigler. 2004 [1974]. The linguistic development of Genie. In Lust and Foley, 126–154.

Cutler, Anne. 1994. Segmentation problems, rhythmic solutions. In Gleitman and Landau, 81–104.

   1996. Prosody and the word boundary problem. In Morgan and Demuth, 87–99.

Cutler, Anne, Jacques Mehler, Dennis Norris and Juan Ségui. 1992. The monolingual nature of speech segmentation of bilinguals. *Cognitive Psychology* 24: 381–410.

Dale, Phillip. 1976. *Language Development: Structure and Function*. New York: Holt, Rinehart and Winston.

Damasio, Antonio R. and Hanna Damasio. 1988. Advances in the neuroanatomical correlates of aphasia and the understanding of the neural substrates of language. In Hyman and Li, 103–117.

   1992. Brain and language. *Scientific American* 267 (3): 88–95.

Damasio, Antonio R. et al. 1997. Neurology of naming. In Goodglass and Wingfield, 65–90.

Damasio, Hanna, Thomas J. Grabowski, Daniel Tranel, Laura L. B. Ponto, Richard D. Hichwa and Antonio R. Damasio. 2001. Neural correlates of naming actions and of naming spatial relations. *Neuroimage*: 1053–1064.

Davies, Alan, C. Criper, and A. P. R. Howatt (eds.). 1984. *Interlanguage*. Edinburgh: Edinburgh University Press.

Davies, Alan and C. Elder (eds.). 2004. *Handbook of Applied Linguistics*. Oxford: Blackwell.

Dax, Marc. 1865 [1836]. Lésion de la moitié gauche de l'encéphale coïncidant avec l'oubli des signes de la pensée. *Gazette Hebdomadaire de Médecine et de Chirurgie* 2e série 2: 259–260.

DeBot, Kees, Ralph B. Ginsberg and Claire Kramsch (eds.). 1991. *Foreign Language Research in Cross-cultural Perspective*. Amsterdam/Philadelphia: John Benjamins.

De Cat, Cécile. 2004. A fresh look at how young children encode new referents. *International Review of Applied Linguistics* 42: 111–127.

DeGraff, Michel. 1999. *Language Creation and Language Change*. Cambridge, MA: MIT Press.

   2003. Against Creole exceptionalism. *Language* 79: 391–410.

2004. Against Creole exceptionalism (redux). *Language* 80: 834–839.

De Groot, Annette M. B. and Judith F. Kroll (eds.). 1997. *Tutorials in Bilingualism: Psycholinguistic Perspectives*. Mahwah, NJ: L. Erlbaum.

Dehaene, Stanislas, Emmanuel Dupoux, Jacques Mehler, L. Cohen, Eraldo Paulesu, Daniela Perani, P. F. van de Mortele, S. Lehericy and D. Le Bihan. 1997. Anatomical variability in the cortical representation of first and second language. *NeuroReport* 8: 3809–3815.

DeKeyser, Robert. 2000. The robustness of critical period effects in second language acquisition. *Studies in Second Language Acquisition* 22: 499–533.

2003. Implicit and explicit learning. In Doughty and Long, 313–348.

Dekydtspotter, Laurent, Rex Sprouse and Bruce Anderson. 1997. The interpretive interface in L2 acquisition: The process-result distinction in English-French interlanguage grammars. *Language Acquisition* 6: 297–332.

De la Fuente, María José. 2002. Negotiation and oral acquisition of L2 vocabulary. *Studies in Second Language Acquisition* 24: 81–112.

Démonet, Jean-François and Guillaume Thierry. 2002. Spatial and temporal dynamics of phonological and semantic processes. In Galaburda et al., 69–79.

Demuth, Katherine. 1994. On the underspecification of functional categories in early grammars. In Lust et al., 119–134.

1996. The prosodic structure of early words. In Morgan and Demuth, 171–184.

Déprez, Viviane. 1994. Underspecification, functional projections, and parameter setting. In Lust et al. 249–271.

Déprez, Viviane and Amy Pierce. 1993. Negation and functional projections in early grammar. *Linguistic Inquiry* 24: 25–67.

1994. Crosslinguistic evidence for functional projections in early child grammar. In Hoekstra and Schwartz, 57–84.

de Villiers, Peter A. and Jill de Villiers. 1979. *Early Language*. Cambridge, MA: Harvard University Press.

Dewaele, Jean-Marc. 2002. Individual differences in L2 fluency: The effect of neurobiological correlates. In Cook, 219–249.

2004. The acquisition of sociolinguistic competence in French as a foreign language: An overview. *Journal of French Language Studies* 14: 301–320.

2005 (ed.). *Focus on French as a Foreign Language*. Clevedon, UK: Multilingual Matters.

Diller, Karl C. (ed.). 1981. *Individual Differences and Universals in Language Learning Aptitude*. Rowley, MA/London: Newbury House.

Doughty, Catherine. 2003. Instructed SLA: Constraints, compensation, and enhancement. In Doughty and Long, 256–310.

Doughty, Catherine and Michael H. Long. 2003. *The Handbook of Second Language Acquisition*. Oxford/Malden, MA: Blackwell.

Doughty, Catherine and J. Williams (eds.). 1998. *Focus on Form in Classroom Second Language Acquisition*. Cambridge: Cambridge University Press.

Doupe, Allison J. and Patricia K. Kuhl. 1997. Birdsong and human speech: Common themes and mechanisms. *Annual Review of Neuroscience* 22: 567–631.

Douthwaite, Julia V. 1994/95. Rewriting the savage: The extraordinary fictions of the wild girl of Champagne. *18th Century Studies* 28: 163–192.

2002. *The Wild Girl, Natural Man and the Monster.* Chicago: University of Chicago Press.

Draganski, Bogdan, Christian Gaser, Volker Busch, Gerhard Schuierer, Ulrich Bogdahn and Arne May. 2004. Changes in grey matter induced by training. *Nature* 427: 311–312.

Dulay, Heidi and Marina Burt. 1974a. Natural sequences in child second language acquisition. *Language Learning* 24: 37–53.

1974b. A new perspective on the creative construction process in child second language acquisition. *Language Learning* 24: 253–278.

Dulay, Heidi, Marina Burt and Stephen Krashen. 1982. *Language Two.* New York: Oxford University Press.

Du Plessis, Jean, Doreen Solin, Lisa Travis and Lydia White. 1987. UG or not UG, that is the question: A reply to Clahsen and Muysken. *Second Language Research* 3: 56–75.

Dupoux, Emmanuel (ed.). 2001. *Language, Brain, and Cognitive Development.* Cambridge, MA: MIT Press.

Dupoux, Emmanuel and Sharon Peperkamp. 2002. Fossil markers of language development: Phonological "deafness" in adult speech processing. In Durand and Laks, 168–190.

Durand, Jacques and Bernard Laks (eds.). 2002a. *Phonetics, Phonology, and Cognition.* Oxford: Oxford UP.

2002b. Phonology, phonetics and cognition. In Durand and Laks, 10–50.

Dussias, Paola E. 2003. Syntactic ambiguity resolution in L2 learners. *Studies in Second Language Acquisition* 25: 529–557.

2004. Parsing a first language like a second: the erosion of L1 parsing strategies in Spanish-English bilinguals. *International Journal of Bilingualism* 8: 355–371.

Eckman, Fred R. 1977. Markedness and the Contrastive Analysis Hypothesis. *Language Learning* 27: 195–216.

Eckman, Fred R., Abdullah Elreyes and Gregory K. Iverson. 2003. Some principles of second language phonology. *Second Language Research* 19: 169–208.

Eimas, Peter D., Einar R. Siqueland, Peter Jusczyk and James Vigorito. 2004 [1971]. Speech perception in infants. In Lust and Foley, 279–284.

Eling, Paul (ed.). 1994. *Reader in the History of Aphasia: From [Franz] Gall to [Norman] Geschwind.* Amsterdam/Philadelphia: John Benjamins.

Ellis, Andrew and Matthew Lambon Ralph. 2000. Age of acquisition effects in adult lexical processing reflect loss of plasticity in maturing systems: Insights from connectionist networks. *Journal of Experimental Psychology, Learning, Memory, Cognition* 26: 1103–1123.

Ellis, Nick C. 1993. Rules and instances in foreign language learning: Interactions of explicit and implicit knowledge. *European Journal of Cognitive Psychology* 5: 289–318.

1994 (ed.). *Implicit and Explicit Learning of Languages.* London: Academic Press/Harcourt Brace & Co.

1996. Sequencing in second language acquisition: Phonological memory, chunking and points of order. *Studies in Second Language Acquisition* 18: 91–216.

2003. Constructions, chunking and connectionism: The emergence of second language structure. In Doughty and Long, 63–103.

Ellis, Nick C. and Nadine Laporte. 1997. Contexts of acquisition: Effects of formal instruction and naturalistic exposure on second language acquisition. In De Groot & Kroll, 53–83.

Ellis, Nick C. and R. Schmidt. 1997. Morphology and longer distance dependencies: laboratory research illuminating the A in SLA. *Studies in Second Language Acquisition* 19: 145–171.

Ellis, Rod. 1990. *Instructed Second Language Acquisition: Learning in the classroom.* Oxford: Blackwell.

   1994. *The Study of Second Language Acquisition.* Oxford: Oxford University Press.

Ellis, Rod and Xien He. 1999. The roles of modified input and output in the incidental acquisition of word meanings. *Studies in Second Language Acquisition* 21: 285–301.

Elman, J.L., Elizabeth A. Bates, M.H. Johnson, Annette Karmiloff-Smith, D. Parisi and K. Plunkett. 1996. *Rethinking Innateness: A Connectionist Perspective on Development.* Cambridge, MA: MIT Press.

Emmorey, Karen. 2002. *Language, Cognition and the Brain: Insights from Sign Language Research.* Mahwah, NJ: L. Erlbaum.

Emonds, Joseph. 1978. The verbal complex V'-V in French. *Linguistic Inquiry* 9: 151–175.

Emsley, Jason G., Bartley D. Mitchell, Gerd Kempermann and Jeffrey D. Macklis. 2005. Adult neurogenesis and repair of the adult CNS with neural progenitors, precursors, and stem cells. *Progress in Neurobiology* 75: 321–341.

Epstein, S. David, Suzanne Flynn and Gita Martohardjono. 1996. Second language acquisition: Theoretical and experimental issues in contemporary research. *Behavioral and Brain Sciences* 19: 677–758.

Eubank, Lynn. 1991 (ed.). *Point Counterpoint: Universal Grammar in the Second Language.* Amsterdam/Philadelphia: J. Benjamins.

   1993/94. On the transfer of parametric values in L2 development. *Language Acquisition* 3: 183–208.

   1994. Optionality and the initial state in L2 development. In Hoekstra and Schwartz, 369–388.

   1996. Negation in early German–English interlanguage: More valueless features in the L2 initial state. *Second Language Research* 12: 73–106.

Eubank, Lynn and Sabine Grace. 1998. V–to–I and inflection in non-native grammars. In Beck, 69–88.

Eubank, Lynn and Kevin R. Gregg. 1995. "Et in amygdala ego"?: UG, (S)LA, and neurobiology. *Studies in Second Language Acquisition* 17: 35–57.

   1999. Critical periods and language acquisition: Divide et impera. In Birdsong, 65–199.

Eubank, Lynn, Larry Selinker and Michael Sharwood Smith (eds.). 1997. *The Current State of Interlanguage.* Amsterdam/Philadelphia: John Benjamins.

Eyer, Julia A. and Laurence B. Leonard. 1995. Functional categories and specific language impairment: A case study. *Language Acquisition* 4: 177–203.

Fabbro, Franco. 2002. The neurolinguistics of L2 users. In Cook, 199–218.

Feldman, Daniel E. and Michael Brecht. 2005. Map plasticity in somatosensory cortex. *Science* 310: 810–815.

Felix, Sascha. 1981. On the inapplicability of Piagetian thought to language learning. *Studies in Second Language Acquisition* 3: 201–220.

1985. More evidence on competing cognitive systems. *Second Language
Research* 1: 47–72.

1991. The accessibility of Universal Grammar in second language acquisition. In
Eubank, 89–103.

1997. Universal Grammar in L2 acquisition: Some thoughts on Schachter's
Incompleteness Hypothesis. In Eubank et al., 139–152.

Felser, Claudia. 2005. Experimental psycholinguistic approaches to second language acquisition. *Second Language Research* 21: 95–97.

Fennell, Chris and Janet Werker. 2003. Early word learners' ability to access
phonetic detail in well-known words. *Language and Speech* 46: 245–264.

Ferguson, Charles A. and Thom Huebner. 1991. Foreign language instruction
and second language acquisition research in the US. In DeBot et al., 3–19.

Fernández, Eva M. 1999. Processing strategies in second language acquisition:
Some preliminary results. In Klein and Martohardjono, 217–240.

2002. Relative clause attachment in bilinguals and monolinguals. In Heredia and
Altarriba, 187–216.

Fisher, Cynthia, D. Geoffrey Hall, Susan Rakowitz, and Lila Gleitman. 1994.
When it is better to receive than to give: Syntactic and conceptual constraints
on vocabulary growth. In Gleitman and Landau, 333–375.

Flege, James E. 1987a. The production of "new" and "similar" phones in a foreign
language: Evidence for the effect of equivalence classification. *Journal of
Phonetics* 15: 47–65.

1987b. A critical period for learning to pronounce foreign languages? *Applied
Linguistics* 8: 162–177.

1991. Perception and production: The relevance of phonetic input to L2 phonological learning. In Huebner and Ferguson, 249–290.

1995. Second language speech learning: Theory, findings and problems. In
Strange, 233–277.

1999. Age of learning and second language speech. In Birdsong, 101–131.

2002. Interactions between the native and second-language phonetic systems.
In P. Burmeister, T. Piske and A. Rohde (eds.). *An Integrated View of
Language Development*. Trier: Wissenschaftlicher Verlag Trier.

Flege, James E., E. M. Frieda, A. C. Walley and L. A. Randazza. 1998. Lexical
factors and segmental accuracy in second language speech production. *Studies
in Second Language Acquisition* 20: 155–187.

Flege, James E. and Serena Liu. 2001. The effect of experience on adults' acquisition
of a second language. *Studies in Second Language Acquisition* 23: 527–552.

Flege, James E. and Ian MacKay. 2004. Perceiving vowels in a second language.
Studies in Second Language Acquisition 26: 1–34.

Flege, James E., M. J. Munro and Ian MacKay. 1995. Factors affecting degree of
perceived foreign accent in a second language. *Journal of the Acoustical
Society of America* 97: 3125–3134.

Flege, James E., Grace H. Yeni-Komshian and Serena Liu. 1999. Age constraints
on second-language acquisition. *Journal of Memory and Language* 41:
78–104.

Fletcher, Paul and Richard Ingham. 1995. Grammatical impairment. In Fletcher and MacWhinney, 603–622.

Fletcher, Paul and Brian MacWhinney (eds.). 1995. *The Handbook of Child Language*. Oxford: Blackwell.

Flynn, Suzanne. 1987. *A Parameter Setting Model of L2 Acquisition*. Dordrecht: Reidel.

Flynn, Suzanne and Barbara Lust. 2002. A minimalist approach to L2 solves a dilemma of UG. In Cook, 95–120.

Flynn, Suzanne and Sharon Manuel. 1991. Age-dependent effects in language acquisition. An evaluation of "Critical Period" hypotheses. In Eubank, 117–146.

Flynn, Suzanne, Gita Martohardjono and Wayne O'Neil (eds.). 1998. *The Generative Study of Second Language Acquisition*. Mahwah, NJ: L. Erlbaum.

Flynn, Suzanne and William O'Neil (eds.). 1988. *Linguistic Theory in Second Language Acquisition*. Dordrecht: Kluwer.

Fodor, Jerry. 1983. *The Modularity of Mind*. Cambridge, MA: MIT Press.

2001. *The Mind Doesn't Work that Way*. Cambridge, MA: MIT Press.

Foucart, Alice and Cheryl Frenck-Mestre. 2005. ERP study of grammatical gender in second language. Unpublished MS, Centre National de Recherche Scientifique, Laboratoire Parole et Langage, Aix-en-Provence, France.

Franceschina, Florencia. 2001. Morphological or syntactic deficits in near-native speakers? An assessment of some current proposals. *Second Language Research* 17: 213–247.

2002. The Nature of Grammatical Representations in Mature L2 Grammars: The case of Spanish grammatical gender. Ph.D. dissertation, Department of Language and Linguistics, University of Essex.

2005. *Fossilized Second Language Grammars: The Acquisition of Grammatical Gender*. Amsterdam/Philadelphia: John Benjamins.

Freeman, Marc R. 2005. Glial control of synaptogenesis. *Cell* 120: 292–293.

Frenck-Mestre, Cheryl. 2002. An on-line look at sentence processing in the second language. In Heredia and Altarriba, 217–236.

2004. Ambiguities and anomalies: What can eye movements and event-related potentials reveal about second language sentence processing? In Kroll and De Groot.

2005. Eye-movement recording as a tool for studying syntactic processing in a second language: A review of methodologies and experimental findings. *Second Language Research* 21: 175–198.

Frenck-Mestre, Cheryl and S. Bueno. 1999. Semantic features and semantic categories: Differences in rapid activation of lexicon. *Brain and Language* 68: 100–204.

Frenck-Mestre, Cheryl and Joel Pynte. 1997. Syntactic ambiguity resolution while reading in second and native languages. *The Quarterly Journal of Experimental Psychology* 50A: 119–148.

Friedemann, Marc-Ariel and Luigi Rizzi (eds.). 2000. *The Acquisition of Syntax: Studies in Comparative Developmental Linguistics*. Harlow, England: Longman.

Friederici, Angela D. 2004. The neural basis of syntactic processes. In Gazzaniga, 789–801.

Friederici, Angela D., Merrill F. Garrett and Thomas Jacobsen. 1999. Editorial and introduction to Part I of the special issue Processing of grammatical gender. *Journal of Psycholinguistic Research* 28: 455–456.

Friederici, Angela D., Gregory Hickok and David Swinney (eds.). 2001. Brain imaging and language processing – A special issue. *Journal of Psycholinguistic Research* 30 (3): 221–224.

Friederici, Angela D., Karsten Steinhauer and Erdmut Pfeifer. 2002. Brain signatures of artificial language processing: Evidence challenging the critical period hypothesis. *Proceedings of the National Academy of Sciences* 99: 529–534.

Gaillard, William Davis, Ben Xu and Lyn Balsamo. 2002. Neuroimaging and disorders of communication. In Accardo et al., 125–148.

Galaburda, Albert, Stephen M. Kosslyn and Yves Christen (eds.). 2002. *The Languages of the Brain.* Cambridge, MA: Harvard University Press.

García Mayo, María del Pilar and María Luisa García Lecumberri (eds.). 2003. *Age and the Acquisition of English as a Foreign Language.* Clevedon: Multilingual Matters Ltd.

Gass, Susan M. 1999. Discussion: Incidental vocabulary learning. *Studies in Second Language Acquisition* 21: 319–333.

2003. Input and interaction. In Doughty and Long, 224–255.

Gass, Susan M. and C. Madden (eds.). 1985. *Input in Second Language Acquisition.* Rowley, MA: Newbury House.

Gass, Susan M., C. Madden, Dennis Preston and Larry Selinker (eds.). 1989. *Variation in Second Language Acquisition* (vol. I, *Discourse and Pragmatics*; vol. II, *Psycholinguistic Issues*). Clevedon: Multilingual Matters.

Gass, Susan M. and Jacqueline Schachter (eds.). 1989. *Linguistic Perspectives on Second Language Acquisition.* Cambridge: Cambridge University Press.

Gass, Susan M. and Larry Selinker. 2001. *Second Language Acquisition: An Introductory Course.* Mahwah, NJ: L. Erlbaum.

Gavruseva, Elena. 2004. Root infinitives in child second language English: An aspectual features account. *Second Language Research* 20: 335–371.

Gazzaniga, Michael S. (ed.). 1995. *The Cognitive Neurosciences* (first edition). Cambridge, MA: MIT Press.

1998. *The Mind's Past.* Berkeley/Los Angeles: University of California Press.

2000 (ed.). *The Cognitive Neurosciences* (second edition). Cambridge, MA: MIT Press.

2004 (ed.). *The Cognitive Neurosciences* (third edition). Cambridge, MA: MIT Press.

Geren, Joy, Jesse Snedeker and Laura Ax. 2005. Starting over: A preliminary study of early lexical and syntactic development in internationally adopted preschoolers. *Seminars in Speech and Language* 26: 44–53.

Gerken, Lou Ann. 1996. Prosodic structure in young children's language production. *Language* 72: 683–712.

Gerken, Lou Ann, B. Landau and R. E. Remez. 1990. Function morphemes in young children's speech perception and production. *Developmental Psychology* 27: 204–216.

Gesell, Arnold. 1941. *Wolf Child and Human Child.* London: The Scientific Book Club.

Gess, Randall and Julia Herschensohn. 2001. Shifting the DP Parameter: A study of anglophone French L2ers. In Camps and Wiltshire, 105–119.

Gleitman, Lila R. 1990. The structural sources of verb meanings. *Language Acquisition* 1: 3–55.

Gleitman, Lila R. and Barbara Landau (eds.). 1994. *The Acquisition of the Lexicon.* Cambridge, MA: MIT Press.

Gleitman, Lila R. and Mark Liberman (eds.). 1995. *An Invitation to Cognitive Science: Language* (vol. 1). Cambridge, MA: MIT Press.

Gleitman, Lila R. and Elissa L. Newport. 1995. The invention of language by children: Environmental and biological influences on the acquisition of language. In Gleitman and Liberman, 1–24.

Gleitman, Lila R. and E. Wanner. 1982. The state of the state of the art. In Wanner and Gleitman, 3–50.

Glennen, Sharon. 2005. New arrivals: Speech and language assessment for internationally adopted infants and toddlers within the first months home. *Seminars in Speech and Language* 26: 10–21.

Gohard-Radenkovic, Aline. 2000. *Communiquer en langue étrangère.*

Golato, Peter. 2002. Word parsing by late-learning French–English bilinguals. *Applied Psycholinguistics* 23: 417–446.

Goldin-Meadow, Susan. 1998. The development of gesture and speech as an integrated system. In Iverson and Goldin-Meadow, 29–44.

Goldin-Meadow, Susan and Carolyn Mylander. 1994 [1990]. Beyond the input given: The child's role in the acquisition of language. In Bloom, 507–542.

Goldschneider, Jennifer M. and Robert M. DeKeyser. 2001. Explaining the "natural order of L2 morpheme acquisition" in English: A meta-analysis of multiple determinants. *Language Learning* 51: 1–50.

Goodglass, Harold and Arthur Wingfield (eds.). 1997. *Anomia: Neuroanatomical and cognitive correlates.* San Diego: Academic Press.

Goodluck, Helen. 1991. *Language Acquisition: A Linguistic Introduction.* Oxford: Blackwell.

Gopnik, Myrna. 1990. Feature blindness: A case study. *Language Acquisition* 1: 139–164.

  1997 (ed.). *The Inheritance and Innateness of Grammars.* New York/Oxford: Oxford University Press.

Gopnik, Myrna, Jenny Dalakis, Suzy E. Fukuda and Shinji Fukuda. 1997. Familial language impairment. In Gopnik, 111–140.

Gould, James L. and Peter Marler. 2004 [1987]. Learning by instinct. In Lust and Foley, 190–207.

Granfeldt, Jonas. 2005. The development of gender attribution and gender concord in French: a comparison of bilingual first and second language learners. In Dewaele, 164–190.

Granfeldt, Jonas and Suzanne Schlyter. 2004. Cliticisation in the acquisition of French as L1 and L2. In Prévost and Paradis, 333–370.

Gray, P. H. 1978 [1958]. Theory and evidence of imprinting in human infants. In Scott, 95–106.

Gregg, Kevin R. 1996. The logical and developmental problems of second language acquisition. In Ritchie and Bhatia, 49–81.

2003. SLA theory: construction and assessment. In Doughty and Long, 831–865.

Grimshaw, Jane. 1994. Lexical reconciliation. In Gleitman and Landau, 411–430.

Grinstead, John. 2000. Case, inflection and subject licensing in child Catalan and Spanish. *Journal of Child Language* 27: 119–155.

2004. Subjects and interface delay in child Spanish and Catalan. *Language* 80: 40–72.

Grodzinsky, Yosef. 2000. The neurology of syntax: Language use without Broca's Area. *Behavioral and Brain Sciences* 23: 1–71.

Grondin, N. and Lydia White. 1996. Functional categories in child L2 acquisition of French. *Language Acquisition* 5: 1–34.

Grosjean, François. 1982. *Life with Two Languages: An Introduction to Bilingualism.* Cambridge, MA: Harvard University Press.

1989. Neurolinguists, beware! The bilingual is not two monolinguals in one person. *Brain and Language* 36: 3–15.

2004. Studying bilinguals: Methodological and conceptual issues. In Bhatia and Ritchie, 32–63.

Grosjean, François, Jean-Yves Pommergues, Etienne Cornu, Delphine Guillelmon and Carole Besson. 1994. Gender-marking effect in spoken word recognition. *Perception and Psychophysics* 56: 590–598.

Guasti, Maria Teresa. 1993/94. Verb syntax in Italian child grammar: Finite and non-finite verbs. *Language Acquisition* 3: 1–40.

2000. An excursion into interrogatives in early English and Italian. In Friedemann and Rizzi, 105–128.

2002. *Language Acquisition: The Growth of Grammar.* Cambridge, MA: MIT Press.

Guillelmon, Delphine and François Grosjean. 2001. The gender marking effect in spoken word recognition: The case of bilinguals. *Memory and Cognition* 29: 503–511.

Haegeman, Liliane. 2000. Adult null subjects in non-pro-drop languages. In Friedemann and Rizzi, 129–169.

Hahne, Anja. 2001. What's different in second language processing? Evidence from event related brain potentials. *Journal of Psycholinguistic Research* 30: 251–266.

Hahne, Anja and Angela D. Friederici. 2001. Processing a second language: Late learners' comprehension mechanisms as reavealed by event realated brain potentials. *Bilingualism: Language and Cognition* 4: 123–142.

Hakuta, Kenji. 2001. A critical period for second language acquisition? In Bailey et al., 193–205.

Hakuta, Kenji, Ellen Bialystok and Edward W. Wiley. 2003. Critical evidence: A test of the critical-period hypothesis for second language acquisition. *Psychological Science* 14: 31–38.

Hale, Kenneth and Samuel J. Keyser (eds.). 1993a. *The View from Building 20.* Cambridge, MA: MIT Press.

1993b. On argument structure and the lexical expression of syntactic relations. In Hale and Keyser, 53–110.

Halle, Morris, Joan Bresnan and G. A. Miller (eds.). *Linguistic Theory and Psychological Reality.* Cambridge, MA: MIT Press.

Hamann, Cornelia. 2000. The acquisition of constituent questions and the requirement of interpretation. In Friedemann and Rizzi, 170–201.

2002. *From Syntax to Discourse: Pronominal Clitics, Null Subjects and Infinitives in Child Language.* Dordrecht: Kluwer.

2004. Comparing the development of the nominal and verbal functional domain in French language impairment. In Prévost and Paradis, 109–144.

Han, Zhao-Hong. 2004. *Fossilization in Adult Second Language Acquisition.* Clevedon: Multilingual Matters.

Han, Zhao-Hong and Terence Odlin (eds.). 2005. *Studies of Fossilization in Second Language Acquisition.* Clevedon: Multilingual Matters.

Hannahs, S. J. and Martha Young-Scholten (eds.). 1997. *Focus on Phonological Acquisition.* Amsterdam/Philadelphia: John Benjamins.

Harley, Birgit. 1986. *Age in Second Language Acquisition.* San Diego: College-Hill Press.

1993 Instructional strategies and second language acquisition in early French immersion. *Studies in Second Language Acquisition* 15: 245–259.

Harley, Birgit and Doug Hart. 1997. Language aptitude and second language proficiency in classroom learners of different starting ages. *Studies in Second Language Acquisition* 19: 379–400.

2002. Age, aptitude and second language learning on a bilingual exchange. In Robinson, 301–330.

Harley, Birgit, J. Howard and Doug Hart. 1995. Second language processing at different ages: Do younger learners pay more attention to prosodic cues to sentence structure? *Language Learning* 45: 43–71.

Harley, Birgit and Wenxia Wang. 1997. The critical period hypothesis: Where are we now? In De Groot and Kroll, 19–51.

Harley, Heidi and Elizabeth Ritter. 2002. Structuring the bundle: A universal morphosyntactic feature geometry. In Simon and Wiese, 23–40.

Harris, R. J. (ed.). 1992. *Cognitive Processing in Bilinguals.* Amsterdam: North Holland.

Hasegawa, Mihoko, Patricia A. Carpenter and Marcel Adam Just. 2002. An fMRI study of bilingual sentence comprehension and workload. *Neuroimage* 15: 647–660.

Hawayek, Antoinette. 1995. Acquisition of functional categories and syntactic structure. *Probus* 7: 147–165.

Hawkins, Roger. 2001. *Second Language Syntax.* Oxford/Malden, MA: Blackwell.

Hawkins, Roger and CeciliaYuet–huang Chan. 1997. The partial availability of Universal Grammar in second language acquisition: The "failed functional features hypothesis." *Second Language Research* 13: 187–226.

Hawkins, Roger and Florencia Franceschina. 2004. Explaining the acquisition and non-acquisition of determiner-noun gender concord in French and Spanish. In Prévost and Paradis, 175–206.

Hawkins, Roger, Richard Towell and Nigel Bazergui. 1993. Universal Grammar and the acquisition of French verb movement by native speakers of English. *Second Language Research* 9: 189–233.

Haznedar, Belma. 1997. L2 acquisition by a Turkish-speaking child: Evidence for L1 influence. In Hughes et al., 245–256.

2001. The acquisition of the IP system in child L2 English. *Studies in Second Language Acquisition* 23: 1–39.

2003. The status of functional categories in child second language acquisition: Evidence from the acquisition of CP. *Second Language Research* 19: 1–41.

Haznedar, Belma and Bonnie D. Schwartz. 1997. Are there optional infinitives in child L2 acquisition? In Hughes et al., 257–268.

Head, Henry. 1926. *Aphasia and Kindred Disorders of Speech* (vols. I, II). New York: The Macmillan Company.

Hellige, Joseph B. 1993. *Hemispheric Asymmetry: What's Right and What's Left*. Cambridge, MA: Harvard University Press.

Henriksen, Birgit. 1999. Three dimensions of vocabulary development. *Studies in Second Language Acquisition* 21: 303–317.

Heredia, Roberto R. and Jeannette Altarriba (eds.). 2002. *Bilingual Sentence Processing*. Amsterdam/London: Elsevier.

Heredia, Roberto R. and Mark T. Stewart. 2002. On-line methods in bilingual spoken language research. In Heredia and Altarriba, 7–28.

Hernández, Arturo E., Mirella Dapretto, John Mazziotta and Susan Bookheimer. 2001. Language switching and language representation in Spanish–English bilinguals: An fMRI study. *Neuroimage*: 510–520.

Herodotus. 1954. *The Histories*. Translated and with an introduction by Aubrey de Sélincourt. Baltimore: Penguin Books.

Herschensohn, Julia. 1990. Toward a theoretical basis for current language pedagogy. *Modern Language Journal* 74: 451–458.

1993. Applying linguistics to teach morphology: Verb and adjective inflection in French. *International Review of Applied Linguistics* 30.1/2: 97–112.

1996. *Case Suspension and Binary Complement Structure in French*. Amsterdam/Philadelphia: John Benjamins.

2000. *The Second Time Around: Minimalism and L2 Acquisition*. Amsterdam/Philadelphia: John Benjamins.

2001. Missing inflection in L2 French: Accidental infinitives and other verbal deficits. *Second Language Research* 17: 273–305.

2003. Verbs and rules: Two profiles of French morphology acquisition. *Journal of French Language Studies* 13: 23–45.

2004. Functional categories and the acquisition of object clitics in L2 French. In Prévost and Paradis, 207–242.

2006. *Français langue seconde*: From functional categories to functionalist variation. *Second Language Research* 22.

Herschensohn, Julia, Enrique Mallén and Karen Zagona (eds.). 2001. *Features and Interfaces in Romance: Essays in Honor of Heles Contreras*. Amsterdam/Philadelphia: John Benjamins.

Herschensohn, Julia, Jeff Stevenson and Jeremy Waltmunson. 2005. Children's acquisition of L2 Spanish morphosyntax in an immersion setting. *International Review of Applied Linguistics* 43: 193–217.

Hilles, Sharon. 1986. Interlanguage and the pro-drop parameter. *Second Language Research* 2: 33–52.

1991. Access to Universal Grammar in second language acquisition. In Eubank, 305–338.

Hirsh, Katherine W., Catriona M. Morrison, Silvia Gaset and Eva Carnicer. 2003. Age of acquisition and speech production in L2. *Language and Cognition* 6: 117–128.

Hirsh-Pasek, Kathy and Roberta Michnick Golinkoff. 1996. *The Origins of Grammar: Evidence from Early Language Comprehension.* Cambridge, MA: MIT Press.

Hirsh-Pasek, Kathy, D. G. Kemler Nelson, P. W. Jusczyk, K. Wright, B. Druss and L. J. Kennedy. 1987. Clauses are perceptual units for young infants. *Cognition* 26: 269–286.

Hirsh-Pasek, Kathy, Michael Tucker and Roberta Michnick Golinkoff. 1996. Dynamic systems theory: Reinterpreting "prosodic bootstrapping" and its role in language acquisition. In Morgan and Demuth, 449–466.

Hoekstra, Teun and Bonnie D. Schwartz. 1994. *Language Acquisition Studies in Generative Grammar.* Amsterdam/Philadelphia: John Benjamins.

Holland, John H., Keith J. Holyoak, Richard E. Nisbett and Paul R. Thagard. 1986. *Induction: Processes of Inference, Learning and Discovery.* Cambridge, MA: MIT Press.

Hollich, George J., Kathy Hirsh-Pasek and Roberta Michnick Golinkoff. 2000. Breaking the language barrier: An emergentist coalition model for the origins of word learning. *Monographs of the Society for Research in Child Development* 65, No. 3 (Serial No. 262).

Hubel, D. H. and T. N. Wiesel. 1962. Receptive fields, binocular interaction and functional architecture in the cat's visual cortex. *Journal of Physiology* 160: 106–154.

   1965. Binocular interaction in the striate cortex of kittens reared with artificial squint. *Journal of Neurophysiology* 21: 1041–1059.

Huckin, Thomas and James Coady. 1999. Incidental vocabulary acquisition in a second language: A review. *Studies in Second Language Acquisition* 21: 181–193.

Huebner, Thom and Charles A. Ferguson (eds.). 1991. *Crosscurrents in Second Language Acquisition and Linguistic Theories.* Amsterdam/Philadelphia: John Benjamins.

Hughes, Elizabeth, Mary Hughes and Annabel Greenhill (eds.). 1997. *Proceedings of the 21st Annual Boston University Conference on Language Development.* Someville, MA: Cascadilla Press.

Hulk, Aafke. 1991. Parameter setting and the acquisition of word order in L2 French. *Second Language Research* 7: 1–34.

   2004. The acquisition of French DP in a bilingual context. In Prévost and Paradis, 243–274.

Hurford, James R. 1991. The evolution of the critical period for language acquisition. *Cognition* 40: 159–201.

Hyams, Nina. 1986. *Language Acquisition and the Theory of Parameters.* Dordrecht: Reidel.

   1996. The underspecification of functional categories in early grammar. In Clahsen, 91–128.

Hyams, Nina and Kenneth Wexler. 1993. On the grammatical basis of null subjects in child language. *Linguistic Inquiry* 24: 421–459.

Hyltenstam, Kenneth. 1992. Non-native features of near-native speakers: On the ultimate attainment of childhood L2 learners. In Harris, 351–368.

Hyltenstam, Kenneth and Niclas Abrahamsson. 2000. Who can become native-like in a second language? All, some or none? On the maturational constraints controversy in SLA. *Studia Linguistica* 54: 150–166.

2001. Comments on Stefka H. Marinova-Todd, D. Bradford Marshall, and Catherine E. Snow's "Three misconceptions about age and L2 learning"; Age and L2 learning: The Hazards of matching practical "implications" with theoretical "facts." *TESOL Quarterly* 35: 151–170.

2003. Maturational constraints in SLA. In Doughty and Long, 539–588.

Hyltenstam, Kenneth and Loraine K. Obler (eds.). 1989. *Bilingualism across the Lifespan: Aspects of Acquisition, Maturity and Loss.* Cambridge: Cambridge University Press.

Hyltenstam, Kenneth and Christopher Stroud. 1993. Second language regression in Alzheimer's dementia. In Hyltenstam and Viberg, 222–242.

Hyltenstam, Kenneth and Åke Viberg (eds.). 1993. *Progression and Regression in Language: Sociocultural, Neuropsychological, and Linguistic Perspectives.* Cambridge: Cambridge University Press.

Hyman, Larry M. and Charles N. Li (eds.). 1988. *Language, Speech and Mind: Studies in Honour of Victoria A. Fromkin.* London/New York: Routledge.

Illes, Judy, Wendy S. Francis, John E. Desmond, John D. E. Gabrieli, Gary H. Glover, Russell Poldrack, Christine J. Lee and Anthony D. Wagner. 1999. Convergent cortical representation of semantic processing in bilinguals. *Brain and Language* 70: 347–363.

Imai, Satomi, Amanda C. Walley and James E. Flege. 2005. Lexical frequency and neighborhood density effects on the recognition of native and Spanish-accented words by native English and Spanish listeners. *Journal of the Acoustical Society of America* 117: 896–907.

Inagaki, S. 2001. Motion verbs with goal PPs, in the L2 acquisition of English and Japanese. *Studies in Second Language Acquisition* 23: 153–70.

Indefrey, Peter and Anne Cutler. 2004. Prelexical and lexical processing in listening. In Gazzaniga, 759–774.

Ingham, Richard. 1998. Tense without agreement in early clause structure. *Language Acquisition* 7: 51–81.

Ingram, David. 1989. *First Language Acquisition.* Cambridge: Cambridge University Press.

Ingram, David and William Thompson. 1996. Early syntactic acquisition in German: Evidence for the modal hypothesis. *Language* 72: 97–120.

Inoue, Kayo. 2004. MRI/fMRI and EEG/ERP techniques. Unpublished Ph.D. Generals Paper, Psychology Department, University of Washington.

2005. Cross-linguistic Studies of Syntactic and Semantic Processing: Electrophysiological investigations. Ph.D. dissertation Psychology Department, University of Washington.

Ionin, Tania and Kenneth Wexler. 2002. Why is "is" easier than "-s"?: Acquisition of tense/agreement morphology by child second language learners of English. *Second Language Research* 18: 95–136.

Ioup, Georgette. 1984. Is there a structural foreign accent?: A comparison of syntactic and phonological errors in second language acquisition. *Language Learning* 34: 1–17.

  1989. Immigrant children who have failed to acquire English. In Gass et al., 160–175.

  1995. Evaluating the need for input enhancement in post-critical period language acquisition. In Singleton and Lengyel, 95–123.

Ioup, Georgette, Boustagui, E., El Tigi, M. and Moselle, M. 1994. Reexamining the Critical Period Hypothesis: A case study of successful adult second language acquisition in a naturalistic environment. *Studies in Second Language Acquisition* 16: 73–98.

Ioup, Georgette and Steven Weinberger (eds.). 1987. *Interlanguage Phonology: The Acquisition of a Second Language Sound System.* New York: Newbury House/ Harper & Row.

Isurin, Ludmila. 2000. Deserted island or a child's first language forgetting. *Bilingualism: Language and Cognition* 3: 151–166.

Itard, Jean-Marc-Gaspard. 1801. *De l'éducation d'un homme sauvage ou des premiers développements physiques et moraux du jeune sauvage de l'Aveyron.* Paris: Gouyon.

Iverson, Jana M. 1998. Gesture when there is no visual model. In Iverson and Goldin-Meadow, 89–100.

Iverson, Jana M. and Susan Goldin-Meadow (eds.). 1998. *The Nature and Functions of Gesture in Children's Communication.* San Francisco: Jossey-Bass. [*New Directions for Child Development* 79].

Jackendoff, Ray. 1983. *Semantics and Cognition.* Cambridge, MA: MIT Press.

  1987. *Consciousness and the Computational Mind.* Cambridge, MA: MIT Press.

  1990. *Semantic Structures.* Cambridge, MA: MIT Press.

Jaeger, Jeri J., Alan H. Lockwood, David L. Kemmerer, Robert D. Van Valin, Brian W. Murphy and Hanif G. Khalak. 1996. A positron emission tomographic study of regular and irregular verb morphology in English. *Language* 72: 451–497.

Jakobson, Roman. 1968 [1941]. *Child Language, Aphasia and Phonological Universals.* The Hague: Mouton.

  1980. [with the assistance of Kathry Santilli]. *Brain and Language: Cerebral Hemispheres and Linguistic Structure in Mutual Light.* Columbus, OH: Slavica Publishers.

  1990 [1971]. The sound laws of child language and their place in general phonology. In Waugh and Monville-Burston, 294–304.

  1990. Two aspects of language and two types of aphasic disturbances. In Waugh and Monville-Burston, 115–133.

James, Allan and Jonathan Leather (eds.). 1987. *Sound Patterns in Second Language Acquisition.* Dordrecht: Foris.

Jia, Gisela, Doris Aaronson, and Yanhong Wu. 2002. Long-term attainment of bilingual immigrants: Predictive variables and language group differences. *Applied Psycholinguistics* 23, 599–621.

Jia, Gisela and Doris Aaronson. 2003. A longitudinal study of Chinese children and adolescents learning English in the United States. *Applied Psycholinguistics* 24: 131–161.

Jiang, Nan. 2002. Form-meaning mapping in vocabulary acquisition in a second language. *Studies in Second Language Acquisition* 24: 617–637.

Joe, Angela. 1995. Text-based tasks and incidental vocabulary learning. *Second Language Research* 11: 149–158.

Johnson, Jacqueline. 1992. Critical period effects in second language acquisition: The effect of written vs. auditory materials on the assessment of grammatical competence. *Language Learning* 42: 217–248.

Johnson, Jacqueline and Elissa Newport. 1989. Critical Period effects in second language learning: The influence of maturational state on the acquisition of English as a second language. *Cognitive Psychology* 21: 60–99.

1991. Critical period effects on universal properties of language: The status of subjacency in the acquisition of a second language. *Cognition* 39: 215–58.

Johnson, Jacqueline, Kenneth Shenkman, Elissa Newport and Douglas Medin. 1996. Indeterminacy in the grammar of adult language learners. *Journal of Memory and Language* 35: 335–352.

Jones, Francis B. 1995. Learning an alien lexicon: A teach-yourself case study. *Second Language Research* 11: 95–111.

Jordaan, Heila, Gill Shaw-Ridley, Jean Serfontein, Kerry Orelowitz and Nicole Monaghan. 2001. Cognitive and linguistic profiles of Specific Language Impairment and Semantic-Pragmatic Disorder in bilinguals. *Folia Phoniatrica et Logopaedica* 53: 153–165.

Jueptner, M. and C. Weiller. 1995. Review: Does Measurement of Regional Cerebral Blood Flow Reflect Synaptic Activity? – Implications for PET and fMRI. *Neuroimage* 2: 148–156.

Juffs, Alan. 2000. An overview of the second language acquisition of links between verb semantics and morpho-syntax. In Archibald, 187–227.

Jusczyk, Peter W. 1997. *The Discovery of Spoken Language*. Cambridge, MA: MIT Press.

Kaan, Edith and Tamara Y. Swaab. 2002. The brain circuitry of syntactic comprehension. *Trends in Cognitive Sciences*: 350–356.

Kanno, Kazue. 1997. The acquisition of null and overt pronominals in Japanese by English speakers. *Second Language Research* 13: 265–287.

Kaplan, Alice. 1993. *French Lessons: A Memoir*. Chicago/London: University of Chicago Press.

Kapp, Brenda (ed.). 2000. *The Handbook of Cognitive Neuropsychology: What Deficits Reveal About the Human Mind*. Psychology Press.

Karmiloff-Smith, Annette. 1979. *A Functional Approach to Child Language: A Study of Determiners and Reference*. Cambridge: Cambridge University Press.

Karmiloff-Smith, Annette, Julia Grant, Ioana Berthoud, Mark Davies, Patricia Howlin and Orlee Udwin. 1997. Language and Williams syndrome: How intact is "intact"? *Child Development* 68: 246–262.

Kegl, Judy, Ann Senghas, and Marie Coppola. 1999. Creation through contact: Sign language emergence and sign language change in Nicaragua. In DeGraff, 179–237.

Kehoe, Margaret and Carol Stoel-Gammon. 1997. The acquisition of prosodic structure: An investigation of current accounts of children's prosodic development. *Language* 73: 113–144.

Keller, Helen. 1954 [1902]. *The Story of my Life*. Garden City, NY: Doubleday & Co.

Kellerman, Eric. 1995. Age before beauty: Johnson and Newport revisited. In Eubank et al., 219–231.

Kessler, Carolyn and Imelda Idar. 1979. Acquisition of English by a Vietnamese mother and child. *Working Papers on Bilingualism* 18: 66–79.

Kim, Eun Joo. 1997. The sensitive periods for the acquisition of L2 lexico-semantic and syntactic systems. In Hughes et al., 354–365.

Kim, Karl H. S., Norman R. Relkin, Kyoung-Min Lee and Joy Hirsch. 1997. Distinct cortical areas associated with native and second languages. *Nature* 388: 171–174.

Klein, Elaine C. 1999. Just parsing through: Notes on the state of L2 processing research today. In Klein and Martohardjono, 197–216.

Klein, Elaine C. and Gita Martohardjono (eds.). 1999a. *The Development of Second Language Grammars: A Generative Approach*. Amsterdam/Philadelphia: John Benjamins.

Klein, Elaine C. and Gita Martohardjono. 1999b. Investigating second language grammars: Some conceptual and methodological issues in generative SLA research. In Klein and Martohardjono, 3–34.

Klein, Wolfgang. 1986. *Second Language Acquisition*. Cambridge: Cambridge University Press.

1996. Language acquisition at different ages. In Magnusson, 244–264.

Klein, Wolfgang and Clive Perdue. 1992. *Utterance Structure: (Developing Grammars Again)*. Amsterdam/Philadelphia: John Benjamins.

1997. The Basic Variety (or: Couldn't natural languages be much simpler?). *Second Language Research* 13: 301–347.

Klima, Edward S. and Ursula Bellugi-Klima. 2004 [1966]. Syntactic regularities in the speech of children. In Lust and Foley, 344–366.

Knudsen, Erik I. 2004. Sensitive periods in the development of the brain and behavior. *Journal of Cognitive Neuroscience* 16: 1412–1425.

Krakow, Rena, Shannon Tao and Jenny Roberts. 2005. Adoption age effects on English language acquisition: Infants and toddlers from China. *Seminars in Speech and Language* 26: 33–43.

Krashen, S. 1973. Lateralization, language learning and the critical period: Some new evidence. *Language Learning* 23: 63–74.

1975. The critical period for language acquisition and its possible bases. *Annals of the New York Academy of Sciences* 263: 211–224.

1985. *The Input Hypothesis: Issues and Implications*. London: Longman.

Krashen, S., N. Houck, P. Giunchi, S. Bode, R. Birnbaum and G. Strei. 1977. Difficulty order for grammatical morphemes for adult second language performers using free speech. *TESOL Quarterly* 11: 338–441.

Krashen, S., Robin Scarcella and Michael Long (eds.). 1982. *Child-Adult Differences in Second Language Acquisition*. Rowley, MA: Newbury House.

Kroll, Judith F. and Annette M. B. De Groot (eds.). 2005. *Handbook of Bilingualism: Psycholinguistic Perspectives*. Cambridge: Cambridge University Press.

Kroll, Judith F. and Paola E. Dussias. 2004. The comprehension of words and sentences in two languages. In Bhatia and Ritchie, 169–200.

Kroll, Judith F., Michael Tokowicz and Robert Dufour. 2002. Development of lexical fluency in a second language. *Second Language Research* 18: 137–171.

Kuhl, Patricia. 1991a. Human adults and human infants show a "perceptual magnet effect" for the prototypes of speech categories, monkeys do not. *Perception and Psychophysics* 50: 93–107.

1991b. Perception, cognition and the ontogenetic and phylogenetic emergence of human speech. In Brauth et al., 73–106.

2000. Language mind, brain: Experience alters perception. In Gazzaniga.

2004. Early language acquisition: Cracking the speech code. *Nature Reviews Neuroscience* 5: 831–843.

Kuhl, Patricia and P. Iverson. 1995. Linguistic experience and the "Perceptual Magnet Effect." In Strange, 121–154.

Kuhl, Patricia and Andrew Meltzoff. 1984. The intermodal representation of speech in infants. *Infant Behavior and Development* 7: 361–381.

Kuhl, Patricia, Karen A. Williams, Francisco Lacerda, Kenneth N. Stevens and Bjorn Lindblom. 1992. Lingustic experiences alter phonetic perception in infants by 6 months of age. *Science* 255: 606–608.

Kutas, Marta and S. A. Hillyard. 1980. Event related brain potentials to semantically inappropriate and surprisingly large words. *Biological Psychology* 11: 99–116.

Kutas, Marta and Bernadette M. Schmitt. 2003. Language in microvolts. In Banich and Mack, 171–209.

Lado, Robert. 1957. *Linguistics across Cultures: Applied Linguistics for Language Teachers*. Ann Arbor: University of Michigan Press.

Lakshmanan, U. 1994. *Universal Grammar in Child Second Language Acquisition: Null Subjects and Morphological Uniformity*. Amsterdam/Philadelphia: John Benjamins.

1995. Child second language acquisition of syntax. *Studies in Second Language Acquisition* 17: 301–329.

1998. Functional categories and related mechanisms in child second language acquisition. In Flynn et al., 3–16.

Landau, Barbara and Lila R. Gleitman. 1985. *Language and Experience: Evidence from the Blind Child*. Cambridge, MA: MIT Press.

Lane, Harlan. 1976. *The Wild Boy of Aveyron*. Cambridge, MA: Harvard University Press.

Lardiere, Donna. 1995. L2 acquisition of English synthetic compunding is not constrained by level ordering (and neither, probably, is L1). *Second Language Research* 11: 20–56.

1998a. Case and Tense in the "fossilized" steady state. *Second Language Research* 14: 1–26.

1998b. Dissociating syntax from morphology. *Second Language Research* 14: 359–375.

2000. Mapping features to forms in second language acquisition. In John Archibald (ed.), *Second Language Acquisition and Linguistic Theory*. Oxford/Malden, MA: Blackwell, 102–129.

Lardiere, Donna and Bonnie D. Schwartz. 1995. On the L2 acquisition of deverbal compounds: Evidence for agreement. In MacLaughlin and McEwen, 335–347.

Leather, Jonathan (ed.). 1999. Second language speech research: An introduction. Special Issue *Language Learning* 49: Supplement 1: 1–56.

2003. Phonological acquisition in multilingualism. In García Mayo and García Lecumberri, 23–58.

Leather, Jonathan and Allan James. 1999. Second language speech. In Ritchie and Bhatia, 269–316.

Lee, Chang-rae. 1995. *Native Speaker*. New York: Riverhead Books.

Lee, James & Albert Valdman (eds.). 2000. *Form and Meaning: Multiple Perspectives*. Boston: Heinle.

Legendre, Géraldine, Paul Hagstrom, Anne Vainikka and Marina Todorova. 2002. Partial constraint ordering in child French syntax. *Language Acquisition* 10: 189–227.

Lenhoff, Howard M., Paul P. Wang, Frank Greenberg and Ursula Bellugi. 1997. Williams Syndrome and the brain. *Scientific American* 277: 68–73.

Lenneberg, Eric H. 1967. *Biological Foundations of Language*. New York: Wiley.

Lenneberg, Eric H. and Elizabeth Lenneberg (eds.). 1975. *Foundations of Language Development: A Multidisciplinary Approach* (vol. I). New York: Academic Press.

Leow, Ronald P. 1998. The effects of amount and type of exposure on adult learners' L2 development in second language acquisition. *Modern Language Journal* 82: 49–68.

Levy, Yonata and Jeannette Schaeffer (eds.). 2003. *Language Competence across Populations: Toward a Definition of Specific Language Impairment*. Mahwah, NJ: L. Erlbaum.

Lewis, Michael B., Simon Gerhand and Hadyn D. Ellis. 2001. Reevaluating age of acquisition effects: Are they simply cumulative frequency effects? *Cognition* 78: 189–205.

Léwy, Nicolas, François Grosjean, Lysiane Grosjean, Isabelle Racine and Carole Yersin. 2005. Un modèle psycholinguistique informatique de la reconnais-sance des mots dans la chaîne parlée du français. *Journal of French Language Studies* 15: 25–48.

Liceras, Juana. 1986. *Linguistic Theory and Second Language Acquisition: The Spanish nonnative grammar of English speakers*. Tübingen: Gunter Narr Verlag.

1989. On some properties of the "pro-drop" parameter. Looking for missing subjects in nonnative Spanish. In Gass and Schachter, 109–133.

Liceras, Juana, E. Valenzuela and Lourdes Díaz. 1999: L1/L2 Spanish grammars and the pragmatic deficit hypothesis. *Second Language Research* 15: 161–190.

Lichtman, Jeff W. 2001. Developmental neurobiology overview: Synapses, circuits and plasticity. In Bailey et al., 27–42.

Lightfoot, David and Norbert Hornstein (eds.). 1994. *Verb Movement*. Cambridge: Cambridge University Press.

Lillo-Martin, Diane and Stephanie Berk. 2003. Acquisition of constituent order under delayed language exposure. In Beachley et al., 485–507.

Lin, Jo-Fu Lotus. 2003. Training American 14-year-olds to Perceive Mandarin Chinese Lexical Tones: A behavioral and fMRI study. M.Sc. dissertation, Department of Speech and Hearing Sciences, University of Washington.

Lleó, Conxita. 2001. Determining the acquisition of determiners: On the innateness of functional categories. In Herschensohn et al., 189–202.

Lleó, Conxita and Michael Prinz. 1997. Syllable structure parameters and the acquisition of affricates. In Hannahs and Young-Scholten, 143–163.

Long, Michael. 1990. Maturational constraints on language development. *Studies in Second Language Acquisition* 12: 251–285.

1991. Focus on form: A design feature in language teaching methodology. In DeBot et al., 39–52.

1993. Second language acquisition as a function of age: Research findings and methodological issues. In Hyltenstam and Viberg, 196–221.

1996. The role of linguistic environment in second language acquisition. In Ritchie and Bhatia, 413–468.

2003. Stabilization and fossilization in interlanguage development. In Doughty and Long, 487–535.

Lopez-Ornat, S. 1997. What lies in between a pre-grammatical and a grammatical representation? In Pérez-Leroux and Glass, 3–20.

Lorenz, Konrad Z. 1978 [1937]. The companion in the bird's world. In Scott, 85–94.

Losh, Molly, Ursula Bellugi, Judy Reilly and Diane Andersen. 2000. Narrative as a social engagement tool: The excessive use of evaluation in narratives from children with Williams Syndrome. *Narrative Inquiry* 10: 265–290.

Lust, Barbara and Claire Foley (eds.). 2004. *First Language Acquisition: The Essential Readings*. Oxford/Malden, MA: Blackwell.

Lust, Barbara, Margarita Suñer and John Whitman (eds.). 1994. *Heads, Projections, and Learnability* (vol. I, *Syntactic Theory and First Language Acquisition: Cross-linguistic Perspectives*). Hillsdale, NJ: L. Erlbaum.

MacIntyre, Peter D. 2002. Motivation, anxiety and emotion in second language acquisition. In Robinson, 45–68.

MacKay, Ian R. A. and James E. Flege. 2004. Effects of the age of second language learning on the duration of first and second language sentences: The role of suppression. *Applied Psycholinguistics* 25: 373–396.

MacLaughlin, Dawn and Susan McEwen (eds.). 1995. *Proceedings of the Nineteenth Annual Boston University Conference on Language Development*. Somerville, MA: Cascadilla Press.

Maclean, Charles. 1977. *The Wolf Children*. London: Allen Lane.

MacLeod, Andrea. 2006. Production and perception of VOT and high vowels by bilingual and monolingual speakers of Canadian English and Canadian French. Ph.D. dissertation, Department of Speech and Hearing Sciences, University of Washington.

MacWhinney, Brian. 1997. Second language acquisition and the competition model. In De Groot and Kroll, 113–142.

1999 (ed.). *The Emergence of Language*. Mahwah, NJ: L. Erlbaum.

2000. Connectionism and language learning. In Barlow and Kemmer, 121–149.

MacWhinney, Brian and Elizabeth Bates (eds.). 1989. *The Crosslinguistic Study of Sentence Processing*. Cambridge: Cambridge University Press.

Magen, Harriet S. 1998. The perception of foreign-accented speech. *Journal of Phonetics* 26: 381–400.

Magnusson, David (ed.). 1996. *The Lifespan Development of Individuals: Behavioral, Neurobiological and Psychosocial Perspectives*. Cambridge: Cambridge University Press.

Maguire, Eleanor A., David G. Gadian, Ingrid S. Johnsrude, Catriona D. Good, John Ashburner, Richard S. J. Frackowiak and Christopher D. Frith. 2000. Navigation-related structural change in the hippocampi of taxi drivers. *Proceedings of the National Academy of Science* 97: 4398–4403.

Major, Roy C. 1987. A model for interlanguage phonology. In Ioup and Weinberger, 101–125.

1992. Losing English as a first language. *Modern Language Journal* 76: 190–208.

2001. *Foreign Accent: The Ontogeny and Phylogeny of Second Language Phonology*. Mahwah, NJ/London: L. Erlbaum.

Major, Roy C. and Eunyi Kim. 1999. The Similarity Differential Rate Hypothesis. In Leather, 151–183.

Marcus, Gary. 2001. *The Algebraic Mind: Integrating Connectionism and Cognitive Science*. Cambridge, MA: MIT Press.

Marian, Viorica, Michael Spivey and Joy Hirsch. 2003. Shared and separate systems in bilingual language processing: Converging evidence from eyetracking and brain imaging. *Brain and Language* 86: 70–82.

Marinis, Theodore. 2003. Psycholinguistic techniques in second language acquisition research. *Second Language Research* 19: 144–161.

Marinova-Todd, Stefka H. 2003. Know your grammar: What the knowledge of syntax and morphology in an L2 reveals about the critical period for second/foreign language acquisition. In García Mayo and García Lecumberri, 59–73.

Marinova-Todd, Stefka H., D. Bradford Marshall and Catherine E. Snow. 2000. Three misconceptions about age and L2 learning. *TESOL Quarterly* 34: 9–34.

Markman, Ellen M. 1994. Constraints children place on word meanings. In Bloom, 154–173.

Markson, L. and Paul Bloom. 1997. Evidence against a dedicated system for word learning in children. *Nature* 385: 813–815.

Marler, Peter. 1987. Sensitive periods and the roles of specific and general sensory stimulation in birdsong learning. In Rauschecker and Marler, 99–135.

Martohardjono, Gita and Suzanne Flynn. 1995. Is there an age factor in Universal Grammar? In Singleton and Lengyel, 135–153.

Mayberry, Rachel I. 1993. First-language acquisition after childhood differs from second-language acquisition: The case of American Sign Language. *Journal of Speech and Hearing Research* 36: 1258–1270.

Mazuka, Reiko. 1996. Can a grammatical parameter be set before the first word? Prosodic contributions to early setting of a grammatical parameter. In Morgan and Demuth, 313–330.

McDonald, Janet L. 2000. Grammaticality judgments in a second language: Influences of age of acquisition and native language. *Applied Psycholinguistics* 21: 395–423.

McKee, Cecile. 1992. A comparison of pronouns and anaphors in Italian and English acquisition. *Language Acquisition* 1: 21–55.

McLaughlin, Barry. 1990. Restructuring. *Applied Linguistics* 11: 113–128.

McLaughlin, Judith. 1999. Event related potentials reflect the early stages of second language lexical acquisition. Ph.D. dissertation, Psychology Department, University of Washington.

McLaughlin, Judith, Lee Osterhout and Albert Kim. 2004. Neural correlates of second-language word learning: Minimal instruction produces rapid change. *Nature Neuroscience* 7: 703–704.

McManus, Chris. 2003. *Right Hand, Left Hand*. London: Phoenix.

Meara, Paul. 1983. *Vocabulary in a Second Language*. London: CILT.

1984. The study of lexis in interlanguage. In Davies et al.

1995 (ed.). Single subject studies of lexical acquisition. Special issue. *Second Language Research* 11 (2).

Meara, Paul and Clarissa Wilks. 2002. Untangling word webs: Graph theory and the notion of density in second language word association networks. *Second Language Research* 18: 303–324.

Mechelli, Andrea, Jenny T. Crinion, Uta Noppeney, John O'Doherty, John Ashburner, Richard S. Frackowiak and Cathy J. Price. 2004. Structural plasticity in the bilingual brain. *Nature* 431: 757.

Mehler, Jacques, E. Dupoux, T. Nazzi and G. Dehaene-Lambertz. 1996. Coping with linguistic diversity: The infant's viewpoint. In Morgan and Demuth, 101–116.

Mehler, Jacques, Peter Jusczyk, G. Lambertz, N. Halsted, J. Bertoncini and C. Amiel-Tison. 1988. A precursor of language acquisition in young infants. *Cognition* 29: 144–178.

Meisel, Jürgen M., 1991. Principles of Universal Grammar and strategies of language learning: Some similarities and differences between first and second language acquisition. In Eubank, 231–276.

1994 (ed.). *Bilingual First Language Acquisition: French and German Grammatical Development*. Amsterdam/Philadelphia: John Benjamins.

1997a. The acquisition of the syntax of negation in French and German: contrasting first and second language acquisition. *Second Language Research* 13: 227–263.

1997b. The Basic Variety as an I-language. *Second Language Research* 13: 374–385.

Menn, Lise and Carol Stoel-Gammon. 1995. Phonological development. In Fletcher and MacWhinney, 335–359.

Menyuk, Paula, Jacqueline W. Liebregott and Martin C. Schultz. 1995. *Early Language Development in Full Term and Premature Infants*. Hillsdale, NJ: L. Erlbaum.

Mitchell, Rosamond and Florence Myles. 1998. *Second Language Learning Theories*. London: Arnold.

Mogford, Kay. 1993. Oral language acquisition in the prelinguistically deaf. In Bishop and Mogford, 110–131.

Mogford, Kay and Dorothy Bishop. 1993. Five questions about language acquisition considered in the light of exceptional circumstances. In Bishop and Mogford, 239–260.

Mondria, Jan-Arjen. 2003. The effects of inferring, verifying and memorizing on the retention of L2 word meanings: An experimental comparison of the meaning-inferred method and meaning-given method. *Studies in Second Language Acquisition* 25: 473–499.

Montaigne, Michel de. 1962 [1580]. *Œuvres complètes*. Paris: Gallimard.

Montesquieu. 1949 [1777]. *Œuvres complètes: Mes pensées*. Paris: Gallimard (vol. I).

Montrul, Silvina (ed.). 2001a. Acquisition of argument structure. Special issue. *Studies in Second Language Acquisition* 23 (2).

2001b. Agentive verbs of manner of motion in Spanish and English as second languages. *Studies in Second Language Acquisition* 23: 171–206.

Montrul, Silvina and Francisco Ordóñez (eds.). 2003. *Linguistic Theory and Language Development in Hispanic Languages*. Somerville, MA: Cascadilla Press.

Moreno, Eva M., Kara D. Federmeier and Marta Kuta. 2002. Switching languages, switching *palabras* (words): An electrophysiological study of code switching. *Brain and Language* 80: 188–207.

Morford, Jill P. and Rachel I. Mayberry. 2000. A reexamination of "early exposure" and its implications for language acquisition by eye. In Chamberlain et al., 111–127.

Morgan, J. L. and Katherine Demuth (eds.). 1996. *Signal to Syntax: Bootstrapping from Speech to Grammar in Early Acquisition*. Mahwah, NJ: L. Erlbaum.

Moyer, Alene. 1999. Ultimate attainment in L2 phonology: The critical factors of age, motivation and instruction. *Studies in Second Language Acquisition* 21: 81–108.

2004. *Age, Accent and Experience in Second Language Acquisition: An Integrated Approach to Critical Period Inquiry*. Clevedon: Multilingual Matters Ltd.

Mueller, Jutta L. 2005. Electrophysiological correlates of second language processing. *Second Language Research* 21: 152–174.

Mueller Gathercole, Virginia, Eugenia Sebastian and Pilar Soto. 1999. The early acquisition of Spanish verbal morphology: Across the board or piecemeal knowledge? *International Journal of Bilingualism* 2/3: 133–182.

Myers-Scotton, Carol. 1993. *Duelling Languages: Grammatical Structure in Code Switching*. Oxford: Clarendon Press.

Myles, Florence. 2005. The emergence of morphosyntactic structure in French L2. In Dewaele, 88–113.

Myles, Florence, Janet Hooper and Rosamond Mitchell. 1998. Rote or rule? Exploring the role of formulaic language in classroom foreign language learning. *Language Learning* 48: 323–363.

Myles, Florence, Rosamond Mitchell and Janet Hooper. 1999. Interrogative chunks in French L2: A basis for creative construction? *Studies in Second Language Acquisition* 21: 49–80.

Nation, I. S. P. 2001. *Learning Vocabulary in Another Language*. Cambridge: Cambridge University Press.

Nation, Robert and Barry McLaughlin. 1986. Novices and experts: An information processing approach to the "good language learner" problem. *Applied Psycholinguistics* 7: 41–56.

Neufeld, Gerald. G. 1979. Toward a theory of language learning ability. *Language Learning* 29: 227–241.

1980. On the adult's ability to acquire phonology. *TESOL Quarterly* 14: 285–298.

Neville, Helen J. 1995. Developmental specificity in neurocognitive development in humans. In Gazzaniga, 219–231.

Neville, Helen J. and John T. Bruer. 2001. Language processing: How experience affects brain organization. In Bailey et al., 173–192.

Neville, Helen J., Sharon A. Coffey, Donald S. Lawson, Andrew Fischer, Karen Emmorey and Ursula Bellugi. 1997. Neural Systems Mediating American Sign Language: Effects of Sensory Experience and Age of Acquisition. *Brain and Language* 57: 285–308.

Newmeyer, Frederick. 1983. *Grammatical Theory: Its Limits and Its Possibilities.* Chicago: University of Chicago Press.

1997. Genetic dysphasia and linguistic theory. *Journal of Neurolinguistics* 10: 47–73.

1998. *Language Form and Language Function.* Cambridge, MA: MIT Press.

2003. Grammar is grammar and usage is usage. *Language* 79: 682–707.

Newport, Elissa. 1991. Contrasting conceptions of the critical period for language. In Carey and Gelman, 111–130.

1994 [1990]. Maturational constraints on language learning. In Bloom, 543–560.

1999. Reduced input in the acquisition of signed languages: Contributions to the study of creolization. In DeGraff, 161–178.

Newport, Elissa J., Daphne Bavelier and Helen J. Neville. 2001. Critical thinking about critical periods: Perspectives on a critical period for language acquisition. In Dupoux, 481–502.

Nichols, Sharon, Wendy Jones, Mary J. Roman, Beverly Wulfeck, Dean C. Delis, Judy Reilly and Ursula Bellugi. 2004. Mechanisms of verbal memory impairment in four neurodevelopmental disorders. *Brain and Language* 88: 180–189.

Nikolov, Marianne. 2000. The Critical Period Hypothesis reconsidered: Successful adult learners of Hungarian and English. *International Review of Applied Linguistics* 38: 109–124.

Nottebohm, F. 1978 [1969]. The "Critical Period" for song learning. In Scott, 239–241.

Novoa, Loriana, Deborah Fein and Loraine K. Obler. 1988. Talent in foreign languages: A case study. In Obler and Fein, 294–302.

Obler, Loraine K. 1989. Exceptional second language learners. In Gass et al., 141–159.

1993. Neurolinguistic aspects of language development and attrition. In Hyltenstam and Viberg, 178–195.

Obler, Loraine K. and Deborah Fein (eds.). 1988. *The Exceptional Brain: Neuropsychology of Special Talents and Abilities.* New York: Guilford Press.

Obler, Loraine K. and Kris Gjerlow. 1999. *Language and the Brain.* Cambridge: Cambridge University Press.

Obler, Loraine K. and Sharon Hannigan. 1996. Neurolinguistics of second language acquisition and use. In Ritchie and Bhatia, 509–523.

Oetting, Janna B. and Mabel L. Rice. 1993. Plural acquisition in children with Specific Language Impairment. *Journal of Speech and Hearing Research* 36: 1236–1248.

Ohta, Amy Snyder. 2001. *Second Language Acquisition Processes in the Classroom: Learning Japanese.* Mahwah, NJ: L. Erlbaum.

Ojima, Shiro, Hiroki Nakata, and Ryusuke Kakigi. 2005. An ERP study of second language learning after childhood: Effects of proficiency. *Journal of Cognitive Neuroscience* 17: 1212–1228.

Orsolini, Margherita, Rachele Fanari and Hugo Bowles 1998. Acquiring regular and irregular inflection in a language with verb classes. *Language and Cognitive Processes* 13: 425–464.

Osterhout, Lee, Mark Allen and Judith McLaughlin. 2002. Words in the brain: Lexical determinants of word-induced brain activity. *Journal of Neurolinguistics* 15: 171–187.

Osterhout, Lee and Phillip J. Holcomb. 1992. Event related brain potentials elicited by syntactic anomaly. *Journal of Memory and Language* 31: 785–806.

   1993. Event-related potentials and syntactic anomaly: Evidence of anomaly detection during the perception of continuous speech. *Language and Cognitive Processes* 8: 413–437.

Osterhout, Lee, Judith McLaughlin, Mark Allen and Kayo Inoue. 2002. Brain potentials elicited by prose-embedded linguistic anomalies. *Memory and Cognition* 30: 1304–1312.

Osterhout, Lee, Judith McLaughlin and Michael Bersick. 1997. Event-related brain potentials and human language. *Trends in Cognitive Sciences* 1: 203–209.

Osterhout, Lee, Judith McLaughlin, Albert Kim and Kayo Inoue. 2004. Sentences in the brain: Event-related potentials as real-time reflections of sentence comprehension and language learning. In Carreiras and Clifton.

Osterhout, Lee, Judith McLaughlin, Ilona Pitkänen, Cheryl Frenck-Mestre and Nicola Molinaro. 2006. Novice learners, longitudinal designs and event-related potentials: A paradigm for exploring the neurocognition of second-language processing. *Language Learning*.

Ostrin, Ruth K. and Lorraine K. Tyler. 1995. Dissociations of lexical function: Semantics, syntax and morphology. *Cognitive Neuropsychology* 12: 345–389.

Oyama, Susan C. 1978. The sensitive period and comprehension of speech. *Working Papers on Bilingualism* 16: 1–17.

   1979. The concept of the sensitive period in developmental studies. *Merrill-Palmer Quarterly* 25: 83–103.

   1982. The sensitive period and comprehension of speech. In Krashen et al., 39–51.

Padden, Carol. 1988. *Interaction of Morphology and Syntax in American Sign Language*. New York: Garland Press.

Padden, Carol, Irit Meir, Wendy Sandler and Mark Aronoff. 2006. Against all expectations: Encoding subjects and objects in a new language.

Pallier, Christophe, Laura Bosch and Núria Sebastián-Gallés. 1997. A limit on behavioral plasticity in speech perception. *Cognition* 64: B9–B17.

Pallier, Christophe, Stanislas Dehaene, J-B. Poline, D. LeBihan, A. M. Argenti, Emmanuel Dupoux and Jacques Mehler. 2003. Brain imaging of language plasticity in adopted adults: Can a second language replace the first? *Cerebral Cortex* 13: 155–161.

Papadopoulou, Despina and Harald Clahsen. 2003. Parsing strategies in L1 and L2 sentence processing. *Studies in Second Language Acquisition* 25: 501–528.

Paradis, Johanne and Martha Crago. 2001. The morphosyntax of Specific Language Impairment in French: An extended optional default account. *Language Acquisition* 9: 269–300.

   2004. Comparing L2 and SLI grammars in child French. In Prévost and Paradis, 89–107.

Paradis, Johanne, Martha Crago and Fred Genesee. 2003. Object clitics as a clinical marker of SLI in French: Evidence from French-English bilingual children. In Beachley et al., 638–649.

Paradis, Johanne and Fred Genesee. 1996. Syntactic acquisition in bilingual children. *Studies in Second Language Acquisition* 18: 1–25.

1997. On continuity and the emergence of functional categories in bilingual first language acquisition. *Language Acquisition* 6: 91–124.

Paradis, Johanne, Heather Golberg and Martha Crago. 2005. Distinguishing between typically-developing L2 children and L2 children with SLI: Verb diversity and tense morphology over time. Poster presentation at the *International Symposium on Bilingualism*, Barcelona, Spain.

Paradis, Johanne, Mathieu LeCorre and Fred Genesee. 1998. The emergence of tense and agreement in child L2 French. *Second Language Research* 14: 227–256.

Paradis, Michel. 1994. Neurolinguistic aspects of implicit and explicit memory: Implications for bilingualism and second language acquisition. In Ellis, 393–419.

1997. The cognitive neuropsychology of bilingualism. In De Groot and Kroll, 331–354.

2003. Differential use of cerebral mechanisms in bilinguals. In Banich and Mack, 351–370.

2004. *A Neurolinguistic Theory of Bilingualism.* Amsterdam/Philadelphia: John Benjamins.

Parodi, Teresa. 2000. Finiteness and verb placement in second language acquisition. *Second Language Research* 16: 355–381.

Parodi, Teresa, Bonnie D. Schwartz and Harald Clahsen. 1997. On the L2 acquisition of the morpho-syntax of German nominals. *Essex Research Reports in Linguistics* 15: 1–43.

Pater, Joe. 1997. Metrical parameter missetting in second language acquisition. In Young-Scholten and Hannahs, 235–261.

2003. The perceptual acquisition of Thai phonology by English speakers: Task and stimulus effects. *Second Language Research* 19: 209–223.

Pater, Joe, Christine Stager and Janet Werker. 2004. The perceptual acquisition of phonological contrasts. *Language* 80: 384–402.

Patkowski, Mark. 1982. The sensitive peiod for the acquisition of syntax in a second language. In Krashen et al., 52–63.

1990. Age and accent in a second language: A reply to James Emil Flege. *Applied Linguistics* 11, 73–89.

Pearlmutter, Neal J., Susan M. Garnsey and Kathryn Bock. 1999. Agreement processes in sentence comprehension. *Journal of Memory and Language* 41: 427–456.

Penfield, Wilder and Lamar Roberts. 1959. *Speech and Brain-Mechanisms.* Princeton: Princeton University Press.

Penner, Zvi. 1994. Asking questions without CP? On the acquisition of root wh-questions in Bernese Swiss German and Standard German. In Hoekstra and Schwartz, 177–214.

Perani, Daniela, Eraldo Paulesu, Núria Sebastián-Gallés, Emmanuel Dupoux, Stanislas Dehaene, Valentino Bettinardi, Stefano F. Cappa, Ferrucio Fazio

and Jacques Mehler. 1998. The bilingual brain: Proficiency and age of acquisition of the second language. *Brain* 121: 1841–1852.

Pérez-Leroux, Ana-Teresa and Juana Liceras (eds.). 2002. *The Acquisition of
Spanish Morphosyntax: The L1/L2 connection*. Dordrecht: Kluwer.

Pérez-Leroux, Ana-Teresa and William R. Glass (eds.). 1997. *Contemporary
Perspectives on the Acquisition of Spanish*. Somerville, MA: Cascadilla Press.

Pérez-Pereira, Miguel. 1991. The acquisition of gender: What Spanish children tell
us. *Journal of Child Language* 18: 571–590.

Petitto, Laura A. 2000. The acquisition of natural signed languages: Lessons in the
nature of human language and its biological foundations. In Chamberlain
et al., 41–50.

Petitto, Laura A. and Paula F. Marentette. 1991. Babbling in the manual mode:
Evidence for the ontogeny of language. *Science* 251: 1493–1496.

Phinney, Marianne. 1987. The pro-drop parameter in second language acquisition.
In Roeper and Williams, 221–238.

Piaget, Jean. 1971 [1954]. *The Construction of Reality in the Child*. New York:
Ballantine.

1959. *The Language and Thought of the Child*. London: Routledge & Kegan Paul Ltd.

Piaget, Jean and Noam Chomsky. 2004 [1979]. Language and learning: The debate
between Jean Piaget and Noam Chomsky. In Lust and Foley, 64–97.

Piattelli-Palmarini, Massimo (ed.). 1979. *Théories du langage, théories de l'appren-
tissage: Le débat entre Jean Piaget et Noam Chomsky*. Paris: Editions du
Seuil.

Pienemann, Manfred. 1998. *Language Processing and Second Language
Development*. Amsterdam/Philadelphia: John Benjamins.

Pierce, Amy. 1992. *Language Acquisition and Syntactic Theory: A Comparative
Analysis of French and English Child Grammars*. London/Dordrecht/Boston:
Kluwer.

Pinker, Steven. 1984. *Language Learnability and Language Development*.
Cambridge, MA: MIT Press.

1989. *Learnability and Cognition: The Acquisition of Argument Structure*.
Cambridge, MA: MIT Press.

1994a. How could a child use verb syntax to learn verb semantics? In Gleitman
and Landau, 377–410.

1994b. Rules of grammar. In Bloom, 472–484.

1995. *The Language Instinct*. New York: Harper Perennial.

1999. *Words and Rules: The Ingredients of Language*. New York: Basic Books.

Pinker, Steven and Alan Prince. 1988. On language and connectionism: Analysis of
a Parallel Distributed Processing model of language acquisition. *Cognition* 28:
73–193.

Piske, Thorsten, Ian R. A. MacKay and James E. Flege. 2001. Factors affecting
degree of foreign accent in an L2. *Journal of Phonetics* 29: 191–215.

Pizzuto, Elena and Maria Cristina Caselli. 1992. The acquisition of Italian morphology: Implications for models of language development. *Journal of Child
Language* 19: 491–557.

Plaut, David C. 2003. Connectionist modeling of language: Examples and implications. In Banich and Mack, 143–167.

Plunkett, Kim. 1997. Theories of early language acquisition. *Trends in Cognitive Sciences* 1: 146–153.

Poeppel, David and Kenneth Wexler. 1993. The Full Competency Hypothesis of clause structure in early German. *Language* 69: 1–33.

Poizner, Howard, Edward S. Klima and Ursula Bellugi. 1987. *What the Hands Reveal about the Brain.* Cambridge, MA: MIT Press.

Pollock, Jean-Yves. 1989. Verb movement, universal grammar and the structure of IP. *Linguistic Inquiry* 20: 365–424.

Pollock, Karen E. 2005. Early language growth in children adopted from China: Preliminary normative data. *Seminars in Speech and Language* 26: 22–32.

Pollock, Karen and J. Price. 2005. Phonological skills in children adopted from China: Implications for assessment. *Seminars in Speech and Language* 26: 54–63.

Prévost, Philippe. 2003. Truncation and missing inflection in initial child L2 German. *Studies in Second Language Acquisition* 25: 65–97.

2004. The semantic and aspectual properties of child L2 root infinitives. In Prévost and Paradis, 305–331.

2006. Knowledge of morphology and syntax in early adult L2 French: Evidence for the missing surface inflection hypothesis. In H. Goodluck, J. M. Liceras et H. Zobl (eds.), *The Role of Formal Features in Second Language Acquisition.* Mahwah, NJ: Lawrence Erlbaum.

Prévost, Philippe and Johanne Paradis (eds.). 2004. *The Acquisition of French in Different Contexts.* Amsterdam/Philadelphia: John Benjamins.

Prévost, Philippe and Lydia White. 2000a. Missing surface inflection or impairment in second language acquisition? Evidence from tense and agreement. *Second Language Research* 16: 103–134.

2000b. Accounting for morphological variation in second language acquisition: truncation or missing inflection? In Friedemann and Rizzi, 202–235.

Prinz, Philip M. (ed.). 1998. ASL proficiency and English literacy acquisition: New perspectives. *Topics in Language Disorders* 18: v–viii.

Prinz, Philip M. and Michael Strong. 1998. ASL proficiency and English literacy within a billingual deaf education model of instruction. *Topics in Language Disorders.* 18: 47–61.

Prodeau, Mireille. 2005. Gender and number in French L2: Can we find out more about the constraints on production in L2? In Dewaele, 114–134.

Pulvermüller, Friedemann and John H. Schumann. 1994. Neurobiological mechanisms of language acquisition. *Language Learning* 44: 681–734.

Pynte, Joel and Saveria Colonna. 2001. Competition between primary and non-primary relations during sentence comprehension. *Journal of Psycholinguistic Research* 30: 569–599.

Racine, Louis. 1808 [1747]. *Œuvres: Epitre II sur l'homme* (vol. II). Paris: Le Normant.

Radford, Andrew. 1990. *Syntactic Theory and the Acquisition of English Syntax: The Nature of Early Child Grammars of English.* Oxford: Blackwell.

Rasetti, Lucienne. 2000. Null subjects and root infinitives in the child grammar of French. In Friedemann and Rizzi, 236–268.

Rauschecker, Josef P. and Peter Marler (eds.). 1987. *Imprinting and Cortical Plasticity.* New York: John Wiley & Sons.

Reilly, Judy, Molly Losh, Ursula Bellugi and Beverly Wulfeck. 2004. "Frog, where are you?" Narratives in children with specific language impairment, early focal brain injury and Williams Syndrome. *Brain and Language* 88: 229–247.

Rice, Mabel (ed.). 1996. *Towards a Genetics of Language.* Mahwah, NJ: L. Erlbaum.

Rice, Mabel and Kenneth Wexler. 1996. A phenotype of specific language impairment: Extended optional infinitives. In Rice, 215–237.

Riney, Thomas J. and James E. Flege. 1998. Changes over time in global foreign accent and liquid identifiability and accuracy. *Studies in Second Language Acquisition* 20: 213–243.

Ritchie, William C. (ed.). 1978. *Second Language Acquisition Resarch: Issues and Implications.* New York: Academic Press.

Ritchie, William C. and Tej K. Bhatia (eds.). 1996. *Handbook of Second Language Acquisition.* San Diego: Academic Press.

1999. *Handbook of Child Language Acquisition.* San Diego: Academic Press.

Rizzi, Luigi. 1986. Null objects in Italian and the theory of pro. *Linguistic Inquiry* 17: 501–557.

1993/94. Some notes on linguistic theory and language development: The case of root infinitives. *Language Acquisition* 3: 371–393.

1994. Early null subjects and root null subjects. In Hoekstra and Schwartz, 151–176.

2000. Remarks on early null subjects. In Friedemann and Rizzi, 269–292.

Robinson, Peter (ed.). 2002. *Individual Differences and Instructed Language Learning.* Amsterdam/Philadelphia: John Benjamins.

Rochet, B. 1995. Perception and production of L2 speech sounds by adults. In Strange, 379–410.

Roeper, Thomas and Edwin Williams. 1987. *Parameter Setting.* Dordrecht: Reidel.

Rohde, Andreas and Christine Tiefenthal. 2000. Aspects of lexical acquisition: Fast mapping in early L2 lexical acquisition. *Studia Linguistica* 54: 167–174.

Rondal, Jean A. 1993. Down's syndrome. In Bishop and Mogford, 165–177.

Ross, Steven, Naoko Yoshinaga and Miyuki Sasaki. 2002. Aptitude-exposure interaction effects on Wh-movement violation detection by pre- and post-critical period Japanese bilinguals. In Robinson 267–300.

Rumelhart, D. E. and J. L. McClelland. 1994. [1986]. On learning the past tenses of English verbs. In Bloom, 423–471.

Rumelhart, D. E. and the PDP Research Group. 1986. *Parallel Distributed Processing: Explorations in the Microstructure of Cognition.* Vol. I: *Foundations.* Cambridge, MA: MIT Press.

Rymer, Russ. 1993. *Genie: A Scientific Tragedy.* New York: Harper Perennial.

Sacks, Oliver. 1990. *Seeing Voices: A Journey into the World of the Deaf.* New York: Harper Collins.

Saffran, Eleanor M. 2003. Evidence from language breakdown: Implications for the neural and functional organization of language. In Banich and Mack, 251–281.

Sandler, Wendy and Diane Lillo-Martin. 2006. *Sign Language and Linguistic Universals.* Cambridge: Cambridge University Press.

Sandler, Wendy, Irit Meir, Carol Padden and Mark Aronoff. 2005. The emergence of grammar: Systematic structure in a new language. *Proceedings of the National Academy of Sciences* 102(7): 2661–2665.

Saville-Troike, Muriel. 2006. *Introducing Second Language Acquisition*. Cambridge: Cambridge University Press.

Schachter, Jacqueline. 1990. On the issue of completeness in second language acquisition. *Second Language Research* 6: 93–124.

1996. Maturation and the issue of UG in second language acquisition. In Ritchie and Bhatia, 159–193.

Schachter, Jacqueline and Susan Gass. (eds.). 1996. *Second Language Classroom Research: Issues and Opportunities*. Mahwah NJ: L. Erlbaum.

Schaller, Susan. 1995. *A Man Without Words*. Berkeley: University of California Press.

Schiff-Myers, N. 1993. Hearing children of deaf parents. In Bishop and Mogford, 47–61.

Schlaggar, Bradley L., Timothy T. Brown, Heather M. Lugar, Kristina M. Visscher, Frances M. Miezin and Steven E. Peterson. 2002. Functional neuroanatomical differences between adults and school-age children in the processing of single words. *Science* 296: 1476–1479.

Schlyter, Suzanne. 1993. The weaker language in bilingual Swedish-French children. In Hyltenstam and Viberg, 289–308.

Schmid, Monika S. 2002. *First Language Attrition, Use and Maintenance: The Case of German Jews in Anglophone Countries*. Amsterdam/Philadelphia: John Benjamins.

Schmidt, Richard. 1990. The role of consciousness in second language learning. *Applied Linguistics* 11: 129–158.

1992. Psychological mechanisms underlying second languge fluency. *Studies in Second Language Acquisition* 14: 357–385.

Schneiderman, Eta I. and Chantal Desmarais. 1988. A neuropsychological substrate for talent in second language acquisition. In Obler and Fein, 103–126.

Schriefers, Herbert and J. D. Jescheniak. 1999. Representation and processing of grammatical gender in language production: A review. *Journal of Psycholinguistic Research* 28: 575–600.

Schumann, John. 1978. *The Pidginization Process: A Model for Second Language Acquisition*. Rowley, MA: Newbury House.

1997. *The Neurobiology of Affect*. Oxford/Malden, MA: Blackwell.

Schwartz, Bonnie D. 1992. Testing between UG-based and problem-solving models of L2A: Developmental sequence data. *Language Acquisition* 2: 1–19.

1993. On explicit and negative data effecting and affecting competence and linguistic behavior. *Studies in Second Language Acquisition* 15: 147–163.

1997. On the basis of the Basic Variety. *Second Language Research* 13: 386–402.

2000. When syntactic theories evolve: Consequences for L2 acquisition research. In Archibald, 156–186.

2003. Child L2 acquisition: Paving the way. In Beachley et al., 26–50.

Schwartz, Bonnie D. and Lynn Eubank (eds.). 1996. What is the "L2 initial state"? Special issue. *Second Language Research* 12 (1).

Schwartz, Bonnie D. and Magda Gubala-Ryzak. 1992. Learnability and grammatical reorganization in L2A: Against negative evidence causing the unlearning of verb movement. *Second Language Research* 8: 1–38.

Schwartz, Bonnie D. and Rex Sprouse. 1996. L2 cognitive states and the full transfer/full access model. *Second Language Research* 12: 40–72.

Scott, John Paul (ed.). 1978. *Critical Periods*. Stroudsburg, PA: Dowden, Hutchinson & Ross.

Scovel, Thomas 1988. *A Time to Speak: A Psycholinguistic Inquiry into the Critical Period for Human Speech*. Cambridge, MA: Newbury House.

1995. Differentiation, recognition, and identification in the discrimination of foreign accents. In Archibald, 169–181.

2000. A critical review of the critical period research. *Annual Review of Applied Linguistics* 20: 213–223.

Sedaris, David. 2000. *Me Talk Pretty One Day*. Boston: Little Brown and Company.

Ségui, Juan and Ludovic Ferrand. 2002. The role of the syllable in speech perception and production. In Durand and Laks, 151–167.

Seliger, Herbert. 1978. Implications of a multiple critical periods hypothesis for second language learning. In Ritchie, 11–20.

1989. Deterioration and creativity in chldhood bilingualism. In Hyltenstam and Obler, 173–184.

Selinker, Larry. 1972. Interlanguage. *International Review of Applied Linguistics* 10: 209–231.

Selkirk, Elizabeth. 1996. The prosodic structure of function words. In Morgan and Demuth, 187–214.

Shapiro, Kevin and Alfonso Caramazza. 2004. The organization of lexical knowledge in the brain: The grammatical dimension. In Gazzaniga, 803–814.

Sharma, Anu C., Michael F. Dorman and Andrej Kral. 2005. The influence of a sensitive period on central auditory development in children with unilateral and bilateral cochlear implants. *Hearing Research* 203: 134–143.

Sharma, Anu C., Michael Dorman and Anthony J. Spahr. 2002a. Rapid development of cortical auditory evoked potentials after early cochlear implantation. *Neuroreport*. 13(10): 1365–1368.

2002b. A sensitive period for the development of the central auditory system in children with cochlear implants: Implications for age of implantation. *Ear and Hearing* 23(6): 532–539.

Sharwood Smith, Michael. 1994. *Second Language Learning: Theoretical Foundations*. London: Longman.

Shattuck, Roger. 1980. *The Forbidden Experiment: The Story of the Wild Boy of Aveyron*. New York: Farrar Straus Giroux.

Shelley, Mary. 1989 [1818]. *Frankenstein: The Modern Prometheus*. New York: Peter Bedrick.

Silva-Corvalán, Carmen. 1994. *Language Contact and Change: Spanish in Los Angeles*. Oxford: Clarendon.

Silverberg, Stu and Arthur G. Samuel. 2004. The effect of age of second language acquisition on the representation and processing of second language words. *Journal of Memory and Language* 51: 381–398.

Simms, Paul. 2005. Talking chimp gives his first press conference. *The New Yorker* (June 6, 2005): 44–45.

Simon, Horst J. and Heike Wiese (eds.). 2002. *Pronouns – Grammar and Representation*. Amsterdam/Philadelphia: John Benjamins.

Singh, J. A. L. and Robert M. Zingg. 1966. *Wolf-children and Feral Man*. Archon Books.

Singleton, David. 1989. *Language Acquisition: The Age Factor*. Clevedon: Multilingual Matters.

1999. *Exploring the Second Language Mental Lexicon*. Cambridge: Cambridge University Press.

2000. *Language and the Lexicon: An Introduction*. London: Arnold.

2001. Age and second language acquisition. *Annual Review of Applied Linguistics* 21: 77–89.

2003. Critical period or general age factor(s)? In García Mayo and García Lecumberri, 3–22.

2005. The Critical Period Hypothesis: A coat of many colours. *International Review of Applied Linguistics* 43: 269–285.

Singleton, David and Z. Lengyel (eds.). 1995. *The Age Factor in Second Language Acquisition*. Clevedon: Multilingual Matters.

Singleton, David and Lisa Ryan. 2004. *Language Acquisition: The Age Factor* (2nd edition). Clevedon: Multilingual Matters.

Singleton, Jenny L. and Elissa L. Newport. 2004. When learners surpass their models: The acquisition of American Sign Language from inconsistent input. *Cognitive Psychology* 49: 370–407.

Skehan, Peter. 1998. *A Cognitive Approach to Language Learning*. Oxford: Oxford University Press.

2002. Theorizing and updating aptitude. In Robinson, 69–94.

Skinner, B. F. 1957. *Verbal Behavior*. New York: Appleton-Century-Crofts.

Skuse, David H. 1993. Extreme deprivation in early childhood. In Bishop and Mogford, 29–46.

Slabakova, Roumyana. 2001. *Telicity in Second Language*. Amsterdam/Philadelphia: Benjamins.

Slavoff, Georgina R. and Jacqueline S. Johnson. 1995. The effects of age on the rate of learning a second language. *Studies in Second Language Acquisition* 17, 1–16.

Slobin, Dan (ed.). 1971. *The Ontogenesis of Grammar*. New York: Academic Press.

1985 (ed.). *The Crosslinguistic Study of Language Acquisition* (vol. I, *The Data*; vol. II, *Theoretical Issues*). Hillsdale, NJ: L. Erlbaum.

Smith, Linda B. 1999. Children's noun learning: How general learning processes make specialized learning mechanisms. In MacWhinney, 277–303.

Smith, Neil and Maria-Ianthi Tsimpli. 1995. *The Mind of a Savant: Language Learning and Modularity*. Oxford: Blackwell.

Snow, Catherine. 1987. Relevance of a Critical Period to language acquisition. In Bornstein, 183–210.

2002. Second language learners and understanding the brain. In Galaburda and Christen, 151–165.

Snow, Catherine and Marian Hoefnagel-Hoehle. 1978. The critical age for SLA: Evidence from second language learning. *Child Development* 49: 1114–1128.

1982a. Age differences in the pronunciation of foreign sounds. In Krashen et al., 84–92.

1982b. The critical period for language acquisition: Evidence from second language learning. In Krashen et al., 93–111.

Snow, Catherine and Michael Tomasello. 1989. Data on language input: Incomprehensible omission indeed! *Behaviorial and Brain Sciences* 12: 357–358.

Snyder, William, Ann Senghas and Kelly Inman. 2001. Agreement morphology and the acquisition of noun-drop in Spanish. *Language Acquisition* 9: 157–173.

Sorace, Antonella. 1993. Incomplete vs. divergent representations of unaccusativity in nonnative grammars of Italian. *Second Language Research* 9: 22–47.

　1996. The use of acceptability judgements in second language acquisition research. In Ritchie and Bhatia, 375–409.

　1997. Acquiring linking rules and argument structures in a second language: The unaccusative/unergative distinction. In Eubank et al., 153–175.

　2003. Near-nativeness. In Doughty and Long, 130–151.

Sorace, Antonella and Yoko Shomura. 2001. Lexical constraints on the acquisition of split intransitivity. *Studies in Second Language Acquisition* 23: 247–278.

Sperber, Dan. 2001. In defense of massive modularity. In Dupoux, 47–57.

Spinney, Laura. 2005. Optical topography and the color of blood. *The Scientist* 19: 25–34.

Sprouse, Rex A. 1998: Some notes on the relationship between inflectional morphology and parameter setting in first and second language acquisition. In Beck, 41–68.

Stadler, Michael A. and Peter A. Frensch (eds.). 1998. *Handbook of Implicit Learning*. Thousand Oaks, CA: Sage.

Stager, Christine and Janet Werker. 1997. Infants listen for more phonetic detail in speech perception than in word-learning tasks. *Nature* 388: 381–382.

Steedman, Mark. 1999. Grammar-based connectionist approaches to language. *Cognitive Science* 23: 615–634.

Sternberg, Robert J. 2002. The theory of successful intelligence and its implications for language aptitude testing. In Robinson, 13–44.

Stevens, Gillian. 1999. Age at immigration and second language proficiency among foreign born adults. *Language in Society* 28: 555–578.

　2004. Using census data to test the critical-period hypothesis for second-language acquisition. *Psychological Science* 15: 215–216.

Stevenson, Jeff. 2006. On the contribution of ERP studies to the Critical Period Hypothesis debate. Unpublished Ph.D. Generals paper, Linguistics Department, University of Washington.

Stockard, C. R. 1978 [1921]. Developmental rate and structural expression: An experimental study of twins, "double monsters" and single deformities, and the interaction among embryonic organs during their origin and development. In Scott, 14–31.

Stoel-Gammon, Carol and K. Otomo. 1986. Babbling development of hearing-impaired and normally hearing subjects. *Journal of Speech and Hearing Disorders* 51: 33–41.

Strange, Winifred (ed.). 1995. *Speech Perception and Linguistic Experience: Issues in Cross-language Research*. Baltimore: York Press.

Strong, Michael and Philip Prinz. 2000. Is American Sign Language skill related to English literacy? In Chamberlain et al., 131–142.

Strozer, J. 1994. *Language Acquisition after Puberty*. Washington, D.C.: Georgetown University Press.

Swain, Merrill. 1985. Communicative competence: Some roles of comprehensible input and comprehensible output in its development. In Gass and Madden, 235–252.

Tanakh, The Holy Scriptures. 1988. Philadelphia/New York/Jerusalem: The Jewish Publication Society.

Tanner, Darren S. 2005. A generative approach to the second language acquisition of German and the verb second parameter. M.A. Thesis, Linguistics Department, University of Washington.

Thomas, Margaret. 1993. *Knowledge of Reflexives in a Second Language.* Amsterdam/Philadelphia: John Benjamins.

Thornton, Rosalind and Stephen Crain. 1994. Succesful cyclic movement. In Hoekstra and Schwartz, 215–264.

Timney, Brian. 1987. Dark rearing and the sensitive period for monocular deprivation. In Rauschecker and Marler, 321–345.

Tinland, Franck. 1971. *Histoire d'une jeune fille sauvage.* Bordeaux: Ducros.

Tomaselli, Alessandra and Bonnie D. Schwartz. 1990. Analyzing the acquisition stages of negation in L2 German: Support for UG in adult second language acquisition. *Second Language Research* 6: 1–38.

Tomasello, Michael and N. Akhtar. 1995. Two-year-olds use pragmatic cues to differentiate reference to objects and actions. *Cognitive Development* 10: 201–224.

Towell, Richard. 2000. Second language acquisition: Holes in the parts and parts of a whole. *Studia Linguistica* 54: 109–122.

Towell, Richard and Roger Hawkins. 1994. *Approaches to Second Language Acquisition.* Clevedon: Multilingual Matters.

Towell, Richard, Roger Hawkins and Nigel Bazergui. 1996. The development of fluency in advanced learners of French. *Applied Linguistics* 17: 84–119.

Trahey, M. and Lydia White. 1993. Positive evidence and preemption in the second language classroom. *Studies in Second Language Acquisition* 15: 181–204.

Tranel, Daniel, Ralph Adolphs, Hanna Damasio and Antonio R. Damasio. 2001. A neural basis for the retrieval of words for actions. *Cognitive Neuropsychology* 18: 655–674.

Tranel, Daniel, Hanna Damasio and Antonio R. Damasio. 1997. On the neurology of naming. In Goodglass and Wingfield, 65–90.

Tromblin, J. Bruce. 1996. Genetic and environmental contributions to the risk for specific language impairment. In Rice, 191–210.

1997. Epidemiology of specific language impairment. In Gopnik, 91–110.

Tsimpli, Maria-Ianthi and Maria Mastropavlou. 2004. Feature-Interpretability in child and adult L2 acquisition, and SLI. Unpublished paper, Aristotle University of Thessaloniki.

Tsimpli, Maria-Ianthi and Anna Roussou. 1991. Parameter resetting in L2? *UCL Working Papers in Linguistics* 3: 149–169.

Ullman, Michael T. 2001a. The declarative/procedural model of lexicon and grammar. *Journal of Psycholinguistic Research* 30: 37–69.

2001b. The neural basis of lexicon and grammar in first and second language: The declarative/procedural model. *Bilingualism: Language and Cognition* 4: 105–122.

Unsworth, Sharon. 2002. Young (and older) L2 learners and Dutch scrambling. In Cazzoli-Goeta et al., 205–214.

2005. *Child L2, Adult L2, Child L1: Differences and Similarities: A Study on the Acquisition of Direct Object Scrambling in Dutch*. Utrecht: Netherlands Graduate School of Linguistics.

Vainikka, Anne and Martha Young-Scholten. 1994. Direct access to X' theory: Evidence from Korean and Turkish adults learning German. In Hoekstra and Schwartz, 265–316.

1996. Gradual development of L2 phrase structure. *Second Language Research* 12: 7–39.

1998. Morphosyntactic triggers in adult SLA. In Beck, 89–114.

2005. Organic Grammar. In T. Parodi, A. Sorace, S. Unsworth and M. Young-Scholten (eds.). *Paths of Development*. Amsterdam/Philadelphia: Benjamins.

Valian, Virginia. 1991. Syntactic subjects in the early speech of American and Italian children. *Cognition* 40: 21–81.

Van der Lely, Heather and Kenneth Wexler. 1998. Introduction to the Special Issue on Specific Language Impairment in Children. *Language Acquisition* 7: 83–85.

VanPatten, Bill. 1996. *Input Processing and Grammar Instruction in Second Language Acquisition*. Norwood, NJ: Ablex.

VanPatten, Bill and T. Cadierno. 1993. Explicit instruction and input processing. *Studies in Second Language Acquisition* 15: 225–243.

Vargha-Khadem, Faraneh, Lucinda J. Carr, Elizabeth Isaacs, Edward Brett, Christopher Adams and Mortimer Mishkin. 1997. Onset of speech after left hemispherectomy in a nine-year-old boy. *Brain* 120: 159–182.

Véronique, Daniel. 2004. The development of referential activities and clause-combining as aspects of the acquisition of discourse in French as L2. *Journal of French Language Studies* 14: 257–280.

2005. Syntactic and semantic issues in the acquisition of negation in French. In Dewaele, 114–134.

Vigneau, M., V. Beaucousin, P. Y. Hervé, H. Duffau, F. Crivello, O. Houdé, B. Mazoyer and N. Tzourio-Mazoyer. 2005. Meta-analyzing left hemisphere language areas: Phonology, semantics, and sentence processing. *Neuroimage*.

Vihman, Marilyn May. 1996. *Phonological Development: The Origins of Language in the Child*. Oxford/Cambridge, MA: Blackwell.

Wade, Nicholas. 2005. A new language arises, and scientists watch it evolve. *New York Times* February 1, D3.

Walsh, Terence and Karl C. Diller. 1981. Neurolinguistic considerations on the optimum age for second language learning. In Diller, 3–21.

Wang, Yue, Dawn M. Behne, Allard Jongman and Joan A. Sereno. 2004. The role of linguistic experience in the hemispheric processing of lexical tone. *Applied Psycholinguistics* 25: 449–466.

Wanner, E. and Lila Gleitman (eds.). 1982. *Language Acquisition: The State of the Art*. Cambridge: Cambridge University Press.

Wartenburger, Isabell, Hauke R. Heekeren, Jubin Abutalebi, Stefano F. Cappa, Arno Villringer and Daniela Perani. 2003. Early setting of grammatical processing in the bilingual brain. *Neuron* 37: 159–170.

Waugh, Linda and Monique Monville-Burston (eds.). 1990. *On Language* (by R. Jakobson). Cambridge, MA: Harvard University Press.

Weber-Fox, Christine and Helen J. Neville. 1996. Maturational constraints on functional specializations for language processing: ERP and behavioral evidence in bilingual speakers. *Journal of Cognitive Neuroscience* 8: 231–256.

    1999. Functional neural subsystems are differentially affected by delays in second language immersion: ERP and behavioral evidence in bilinguals. In Birdsong, 23–38.

Weerman, F. 2002. *Dynamiek in Taal en de Explosie van de Neerlandistiek* [Dynamics in Language and the Explosion of Dutch]. Amsterdam: University of Amsterdam.

Weinreich, Uriel. 1953. *Languages in Contact*. The Hague: Mouton.

Weismer, Susan E. and Elin T. Thordardottir. 2002. Cognition and language. In Accardo et al., 21–37.

Weissenborn, Jürgen. 1994. Constraining the child's grammar: Local well-formedness in the development of verb movement in German and French. In Lust et al., 215–247.

Werker, Janet and Richard C. Tees. 1984. Cross-language speech perception: Evidence for perceptual reorganization during the first year of life. *Infant Behavior and Development* 7: 49–63.

    1999. Influences on infant speech processing: Toward a new synthesis. *Annual Review of Psychology* 50: 509–535.

Wernicke, Carl. 1874. *Der aphasische Symtomencomplex*. Breslau.

Wesche, Marjorie and T. Sima Paribakht (eds.). 1999. Incidental L2 vocabulary acquisition: Theory, current research and instructional implications. Special issue. *Studies in Second Language Acquisition* 21 (2).

Wexler, Kenneth. 1994. Optional infinitives, head movement and the economy of derivations. In Lightfoot and Hornstein, 305–350.

    1996. The development of inflection in a biologically based theory of language acquisition. In Rice, 113–144.

    2003. Lenneberg's dream: Learning, normal language development, and Specific Language Impairment. In Levy and Schaeffer, 11–62.

Wexler, Kenneth and Peter Culicover. 1980. *Formal Principles of Language Acquisition*. Cambridge, MA: MIT Press.

Wexler, Kenneth and Tony Harris. 1996. The Optional Infinitive stage in child English. In Clahsen, 1–42.

White, Lydia. 1985. The pro-drop parameter in adult second language acquisition. *Language Learning* 35: 47–62.

    1989. *Universal Grammar and Second Language Acquisition*. Amsterdam: John Benjamins.

    1990/91. The verb movement parameter in second language acquisition. *Language Acquisition* 1: 337–360.

    1991a. Argument structure in second language acquisition. *French Language Studies* 1: 189–207.

    1991b. Adverb placement in second language acquisition: Some effects of positive and negative evidence in the classroom. *Second Language Research* 7: 133–161.

    1992. Long and short verb movement in second language acquisition. *Canadian Journal of Linguistics* 37: 273–286.

2003. *Second Language Acquisition and Universal Grammar*. Cambridge: Cambridge University Press.

White, Lydia and Fred Genesee. 1996. How native is near–native? The issue of ultimate attainment in adult second language acquisition. *Second Language Research* 12: 233–265.

White, Lydia, Elena Valenzuela, Martyna Kozlowska-Macgregor and Yan-Kit Ingrid Leung. 2004. Gender and number agreement in nonnative Spanish. *Applied Psycholinguistics* 25: 105–133.

Whitman, John. 1994. In defense of the strong continuity account of the acquisition of verb-second. In Lust et al., 273–287.

Wiley, Edward W., Ellen Bialystok and Kenji Hakuta. 2005. New approaches to using census data to test the Critical-Period Hypothesis for second language acquisition. *Psychological Science* 16: 341–343.

Witelson, Sandra F. 1987. Neurobiological aspects of language in children. *Child Development* 58: 653–688.

Whong-Barr, Melinda and Bonnie D. Schwartz. 2002. Morphological and syntactic transfer in child L2 acquisition of the English dative alternation. *Second Language Research* 24: 579–616.

Wode, H. 1994. Nature, nurture and age in language acquisition. *Studies in Second Language Acquisition* 16: 325–345.

Woll, Bencie and Ros Herman. 2003. Using a standardized test of sign language development to examine the effects of input in the acquisition of British Sign Language. In Beachley et al., 51–62.

Yamada, Jeni E. 1990. *Laura: A Case for the Modularity of Language*. Cambridge, MA: MIT Press.

Yamada, Reiko A. 1995. Age and acquisition of second language speech sounds: Perception of American English /r/ and /l/ by native speakers of Japanese. In Strange, 305–320.

Yoshinaga-Itano, Christine. 2002. Sensitive periods in the development of language of children who are deaf or hard of hearing. In Accardo et al., 57–82.

Young-Scholten, Martha and S. J. Hannahs (eds.). 1997. *Focus on Phonological Acquisition*. Amsterdam/Philadelphia: John Benjamins.

Yuan, Boping. 2001. The status of thematic verbs in the second language acquisition of Chinese. *Second Language Research* 17: 248–272.

Zatorre, Robert J. 2003. Functional and structural imaging in the study of auditory language processes. In Banich and Mack, 211–227.

Zobl, Helmut. 1998. Representational changes: From listed representations to independent representations of verbal affixes. In Beck, 339–371.

Zobl, Helmut and Juana Liceras. 1994. Functional categories and acquisition orders. *Language Learning* 44: 159–180.

Zurif, Edgar. 2002. The neurological organization of some language-processing constituents. In Galaburda et al., 43–56.

Index